Qualitative Research Methods

Edited by

Darin Weinberg

BLACKWELL
Publishers

Copyright © Blackwell Publishers Ltd 2002; editorial introductions and arrangement copyright © Darin Weinberg 2002

First published 2002

2 4 6 8 10 9 7 5 3 1

Blackwell Publishers Inc.
350 Main Street
Malden, Massachusetts 02148
USA

Blackwell Publishers Ltd
108 Cowley Road
Oxford OX4 1JF
UK

Library of Congress Cataloging-in-Publication Data

Qualitative research methods / edited by Darin Weinberg.
    p. cm.—(Blackwell readers in sociology)
A collection of 17 articles previously published by scholars in books and journals between 1960–1997.
Includes bibliographical references and index.
ISBN 0–631–21761–4 (alk. paper)—ISBN 0–631–21762–2 (pb.: alk. paper)
  1. Social sciences—Research. 2. Qualitative research. I. Weinberg, Darin. II. Series.

H62.Q3545 2001
001.4'2—dc21

2001018433

British Library Cataloguing in Publication Data
A CIP catalogue record for this book is available from the British Library.

Typeset in 10/12 Sabon
by Kolam Information Services Pvt. Ltd, Pondicherry, India
Printed in Great Britain by TJ International, Padstow, Cornwall

This book is printed on acid-free paper.

Contents

Acknowledgments   vii

Qualitative Research Methods: An Overview
Darin Weinberg   1

Part I   The Legacy of Qualitative Research Methods   23

      Introduction to Part I   25
1 The Stranger
    Georg Simmel   30
2 Paradigmatic Traditions in the History of Anthropology
    George W. Stocking, Jr.   35
3 Everett C. Hughes and the Development of Fieldwork
    in Sociology
    Jean-Michel Chapoulie   49

**Part II   Qualitative Interviewing, Life History,
and Narrative Analysis**   73

      Introduction to Part II   75
4 The Life History and the Scientific Mosaic
    Howard S. Becker   79
5 Talking and Listening from Women's Standpoint:
    Feminist Strategies for Interviewing and Analysis
    Marjorie L. DeVault   88
6 Active Interviewing
    James A. Holstein and Jaber F. Gubrium   112
7 Narrative Authenticity
    Elinor Ochs and Lisa Capps   127

Part III   Observational Fieldwork   133

      Introduction to Part III   135
8 The Place of Field Work in Social Science
    Everett C. Hughes   139
9 On Fieldwork
    Erving Goffman   148
10 Difference and Dialogue: Members' Readings
    of Ethnographic Texts
    Robert M. Emerson and Melvin Pollner   154
11 In Search of Horatio Alger: Culture and
    Ideology in the Crack Economy
    Phillipe Bourgois   171

Part IV   Conversation and Discourse Analysis   187

        Introduction to Part IV   189
12   Activity Types and Language
      Stephen C. Levinson   193
13   Reflections on Talk and Social Structure
      Emanuel A. Schegloff   221
14   Refusing Invited Applause: Preliminary Observations
      from a Case Study of Charismatic Oratory
      J. Maxwell Atkinson   244

Part V   Research Using Artifacts as Primary Sources   261

        Introduction to Part V   263
15   The Interpretation of Documents and Material Culture
      Ian Hodder   266
16   Professional Vision
      Charles Goodwin   281
17   Artwork: Collection and Contemporary Culture
      Chandra Mukerji   313

Index   329

Acknowledgments

My tastes in, and thoughts on, qualitative research methods have been guided by too many lights to be recounted here. However, I would like to acknowledge a few friends and colleagues in particular. First, I would like to thank Jay Gubrium, without whose help this book would not have come to be. Thanks to Bob Emerson, Mel Pollner, Jack Katz, John Heritage, and Harold Garfinkel for teaching me the vast majority of what I know about qualitative research. Thanks also to Byron Burkhalter, Spencer Cahill, Jim Holstein, Doni Loseke, Gale Miller, and Geoff Raymond for your ideas, inspiration, and encouragement at various stages of the book's development.

The authors and publishers gratefully acknowledge the following for permission to reproduce copyright material:

Atkinson, J. Maxwell, "Refusing Invited Applause: Preliminary Observations from a Case Study of Charismatic Oratory" from Teun A. Van Dijk (ed.), *Handbook of Discourse Analysis*, vol. 3, pp. 161–81 (London: Academic Press, 1985); reprinted by permission of the publisher;

Becker, Howard S., "The Life History and the Scientific Mosaic" from *Sociological Work: Method and Substance*, pp. 63–73 (Chicago: Aldine Publishing Company, 1970);

Bourgois, Phillipe, "In Search of Horatio Alger: Culture and Ideology in the Crack Economy" from Craig Reinarman and Harry G. Levine (eds.), *Crack in America: Demon Drugs and Social Justice* (Berkeley: University of California Press, 1997), pp. 57–76; reprinted by permission of Elsevier Science;

Chapoulie, Jean-Michel, "Everett C. Hughes and the Development of Fieldwork in Sociology" from *Urban Life and Culture* 15(nos. 3 and 4) (January 1987), pp. 259–98; reprinted by permission of Sage Publications Inc.;

DeVault, Marjorie L., "Talking and Listening from Women's Standpoint: Feminist Strategies for Interviewing and Analysis," copyright © 1990 by The Society for the Study of Social Problems, reprinted by permission from *Social Problems* 37, no. 1 (February 1990), pp. 96–116;

Emerson, Robert M. and Melvin Pollner, "Difference and Dialogue: Members' Readings of Ethnographic Texts" from James A. Holstein and Gale Miller (eds.), *Perspectives on Social Problems*, vol. 3 (Greenwich, CT: JAI, 1991); reprinted by permission of Elsevier Science;

Goffman, Erving, "On Fieldwork" from *Journal of Contemporary Ethnography* 18 (1989), pp. 123–32;

Goodwin, Charles, "Professional Vision" from *American Anthropologist* 96, no. 3 (1994). Photographs copyright © George Holliday;

Hodder, Ian, "The Interpretation of Documents and Material Culture" from Norman K. Denzin and Yvonna S. Lincoln (eds.), *Handbook of Qualitative Research* (Thousand Oaks, CA: Sage Publications, 1994), pp. 393–402. Reprinted by permission of Sage Publications, Inc.;

Holstein, James A. and Jaber F. Gubrium, "Active Interviewing" from David Silverman (ed.), *Qualitative Research: Theory, Method and Practice* (Thousand Oaks, CA: Sage Publications, 1997), pp. 123–32; reprinted by permission of Sage Publications Ltd, London;

Hughes, Everett C., "The Place of Field Work in Social Science" from Buford H. Junker (ed.), *Field Work: An Introduction to the Social Sciences* (Chicago: University of Chicago Press, 1960), pp. v–xv;

Levinson, Stephen C., "Activity Types and Language" from *Linguistics* 17 (1979), reprinted by permission of the author and Mouton de Gruyter, Berlin;

Mukerji, Chandra, "Artwork: Collection and Contemporary Culture" from *American Journal of Sociology* 84, no. 2 (1978), pp. 348–65; reprinted by permission of University of Chicago Press, Chicago;

Ochs, Elinor, and Lisa Capps, "Narrative Authenticity" from *Journal of Narrative and Life History* 7 (1997), pp. 83–9; reprinted by permission of Lawrence Erlbaum Associates;

Schegloff, Emanuel A., "Reflections on Talk and Social Structure" from Deirdre Boden and Don H. Zimmerman (eds.), *Talk & Social Structure: Studies in Ethnomethodology and Conversation Analysis* (Berkeley: University of California Press, 1991), pp 44–70; copyright © 1991 Polity Press;

Simmel, Georg, "The Stranger" [1908] from Donald N. Levine (ed.), *On Individuality and Social Forms: Selected Writings* (Chicago: University of Chicago Press, 1971);

Stocking, George W. Jr., "Paradigmatic Traditions in the History of Anthropology" from R. C. Olby et al. (eds.), *Companion to the History of Modern Science* (London: Routledge, 1990).

The publishers apologize for any errors or omissions in the above list and would be grateful to be notified of any corrections that should be incorporated in the next edition or reprint of this book.

To
Diana, Ethan, and Tristan,
for the meanings we share.

Qualitative Research Methods: An Overview

Darin Weinberg

> there are an infinite number of facts about the motorcycle, and the right ones don't just dance up and introduce themselves. The right facts, the ones we really need, are not only passive, they're damned elusive, and we're not going to just sit back and "observe" them. We're going to have to be in there looking for them...The difference between a good mechanic and a bad one, like the difference between a good mathematician and a bad one, is precisely this ability to select the good facts from the bad ones on the basis of quality. He has to care! This is an ability about which formal traditional scientific method has nothing to say. It's long past time to take a closer look at this qualitative preselection of facts which has seemed so scrupulously ignored by those who make so much of these facts after they are "observed." I think that it will be found that a formal acknowledgement of the role of Quality in the scientific process doesn't destroy the empirical vision at all. It expands it, strengthens it and brings it far closer to actual scientific practice.
>
> **Robert M. Pirsig, *Zen and the Art of Motorcycle Maintenance***

In the above passage, novelist Robert Pirsig puts his finger on a point that qualitative social scientists have taken very seriously for quite some time. That point is this. Whether they are mechanics, mathematicians, farmers, physicists, basketball players, bird watchers, drug smugglers, police officers, social scientists, or college students, people notice and appreciate some facts rather than others according to whether they deem those facts relevant, useful, valuable, important, or interesting in light of their own particular practical concerns. Indeed whether or not something is even considered a "fact" in the first place depends on qualities that people actively find in it rather than some sort of timeless property the thing displays for all to see. If this were not so, there would be no sense in distinguishing good fact finding from bad fact finding, revolutionary discoveries from trivial ones. Of course, it is certainly true that some qualities are easier to discover than others. For instance, it is a lot easier to discover that boiling water burns our skin than that it is comprised of molecules which are themselves comprised of two hydrogen atoms and one oxygen atom. But the comparative ease of discovery does not obviate the need for discovery. Whether we regard the truth as "right in front of us," "down deep," "out there," or elsewhere, it is in any case something that requires an act of discovery. In its broadest sense, the study of research methods is simply the study of what we are really doing, or should be doing, when we discover.

If we accept that discovery entails learning something we did not already know, it becomes clear that acts of discovery inevitably occur against horizons composed of "the already known." Hence, it follows that depending on what different people already do and do not know, they will regard different sorts of things as discoveries. Something we may personally regard as a breathtaking discovery may very well appear to others as the dullest of platitudes. Worse yet, the insight we thought was a breathtaking discovery might appear to others as just downright mistaken. In this case, our presumed discovery might be dismissed, not simply as old hat, but as completely illusory! In science, no less than any other type of practice, determinations as to both the importance and the veracity of a discovery are inevitably made with recourse to an extant set of presuppositions regarding the already known (cf. Kuhn 1970). And in science, no less than any other type of practice, there is almost always some level of disagreement about what is and is not already known. These kinds of disagreements then provide bases for disagreements over what is and is not an important or veracious scientific discovery. Some prominent students of science have indeed gone so far as to argue that competitive participation in such disagreements is the very *sine qua non* of scientific work (cf. Bourdieu 1975, 1991).

Though this image of science-as-competition requires qualification, it nonetheless captures a very important point for those of us interested in scientific methodology. Too often we are inclined to think of scientific methodologies as settled principles of inquiry and/or principles of proof that have been agreed upon and ratified by a given scientific community and fail to sufficiently consider the intrinsically contestable (and, indeed, contested) status of their legitimacy. This oversight has been encouraged by a long procession of philosophers of science who have argued that the essential character of "the scientific method" can be fully specified in terms of its basic formal logic (cf. Carnap 1928; Hempel 1965; Popper 1963). Once persuaded that the proper conduct of scientific inquiry can be decided abstractly on the basis of formal logic alone, scientists have often prejudicially dismissed any methodology that departed from their own favored orthodoxy. Thankfully, however, the formal logical approach to scientific method has lost a good deal of its former luster (Harre 1990; Putnam 1990). Critics both within and outside the philosophy of science have shown that this approach fatally fails to appreciate that controversies over scientific method unfold under particular socio-historical conditions and that the direction of their development cannot be properly understood outside the context of those conditions (cf. Feyerabend 1975; Haraway 1991; Knorr-Cetina 1999; Lynch 1993; Shapin 1994). The formal logical approach also dulls our sensitivities to the concrete realities and evolution of the scientific enterprise. This kind of intellectual inertia has slowed the progress of science generally but has been especially damaging to the scientific fortunes of qualitative research. Too often, knowledge gained through qualitative methodologies has been disdainfully and prejudicially dismissed by adherents to the groundless belief that there is (and/or should be) a scholarly consensus regarding the formal character of truly *scientific* research.

In this introduction, I want to offer a few observations of my own regarding scientific methodology, happily acknowledging from the outset that they are certainly contestable. Furthermore, I want to argue that this fact does not diminish their scientific legitimacy in the slightest. The view that by using scientific methods one might come to possess ideas that are absolutely uncontestable, though perhaps consistent with some popular images of science, is in fact completely absurd (Putnam 1990). In place of this view, I will defend here a thoroughly sociological understanding of scientific methods, one that locates their utility and validity within the specific social contexts of their actual use. My basic argument, then, is that the scientific validity and importance of qualitative research methods can only be sensibly decided within the contexts of specific *dispute domains*.[1] These dispute domains are always embodied by specific contributors and take shape in response to identifiable socio-historical and social situational contingencies. It is only by identifying these contributors and contingencies that we may begin to understand and evaluate the distinctive logic according to which particular dispute domains endure and by which the particular methodological and theoretical practices that comprise them are judged. In this effort, it is especially important to understand the specific types of *reactions* to their ideas that people can reasonably anticipate given the particular dispute domains into which they have intervened. The upshot of this approach to scientific method is this: it is only by explicitly granting that our ideas are *always* contestable, and endeavoring to discover, anticipate, and respond effectively to the precise ways in which they are contestable, that we might give our ideas whatever scientific legitimacy they may come to possess. This argument flies in the face of some very long-standing assumptions regarding scientific methodology. Therefore, in the interest of making my position as clearly and as strongly as possible, I will begin with a brief sketch of the general debates concerning scientific methodology.

A Review of the General Debates Concerning Scientific Methodology

Whether or not we agree as to the tenability of such a project, most of us think the work of science entails trying to grasp the true nature of our surroundings and ourselves. Implicit in this project are at least two fundamental presuppositions: (1) that grasping the true nature of our surroundings and ourselves does in fact require work (we must accept that we are all sometimes prone to misunderstanding), and (2) that through due diligence we may overcome our false consciousness and begin to see the world as it really is. Discussions of scientific method arise when we begin to consider how best to go about accomplishing this ambitious project. Though such discussions can be traced back to Antiquity, it was not until the Enlightenment (circa eighteenth century) that our modern sensibilities regarding scientific methodology began to take form. It was at this time that the pioneering work of such legendary figures as Galileo Galilei and Sir Isaac Newton began to inspire widespread fascination with, and a growing reliance upon, the *experimental method* in science. This entailed adopting the slightly ironic view that in Francis Bacon's words "the nature of things betrays itself more readily under the vexations of art than in its natural freedom" (Weinberger 1989, p. 28). By these lights, the "nature of things" is not self-evident but may be grasped only through carefully securing and manipulating the specific conditions under which those things are observed to occur. The earliest systematic discussions of scientific method were overwhelmingly focused on the exigencies of experimentation.

Thus, for example, would be scientists were enjoined to collect a large number of cases, systematically altering the conditions under which they examined the phenomenon in which they were interested. This method was held to ensure the most thorough grasp of the phenomenon in all its manifold dimensions. There was the common insistence that scientists actively seek out negative cases – that is, cases of a phenomenon that appeared contrary to accepted generalizations regarding its essential nature. By this method, it was argued, one might systematically strengthen and extend one's theoretical generalizations. Care was to be taken in arranging experiments so as to prevent any unknown variable from exerting its effects. It is in this sense that scientists have insisted that the topical field of experimental activity must be a "closed system," a system within which every prospective cause is known and anticipated in the procedures of the experiment. It is only if experimental conditions were completely controlled that the true causes of experimentally observed events could be positively identified. Methods debates were as yet focused only on the *technical*[2] challenges of producing theoretical generalizations that mapped accurately onto the natural universe. The possibility of perfect correspondence between theory and nature was not yet seriously doubted.

In its earliest incarnations, this type of advice regarding scientific methodology reflected an optimistic faith in what Pollner (1987, p. 29) calls "a determinate, non-contradictory, self-identical, and coherent world" that exists independently of anyone's particular conceptions of it. It was just this faith that lent credence to early experimenters' efforts to coax nature herself into decisive endorsements of some theories and/or decisive rejections of others. As many have noted, this faith in the uniformity and constancy of nature, or what Putnam (1987) calls "seventeenth century objectivism," entailed acceptance of the doctrine that nature was ultimately amenable to only one comprehensively true theory and that all scientific work must seek to converge upon this one theory. Methodologically, faith in the unity and constancy of nature tended to foster a reductionist impulse toward physicalism that still snaps at the heels of the social sciences – most notably in the form of sociobiology. This doctrine continues to exercise a powerful influence on the minds of scientists and non-scientists alike (cf. Wilson 1998). But despite its enduring popularity, it has by no means been without able and incisive critics.

Let us begin with what is arguably the scientific methodologist's greatest torment – the doctrine of Skepticism. Skepticism regarding the very possibility of ever fully grasping the "nature of things" (and/or that indeed there is a "nature of things" to begin with) has for centuries fueled circumspection, and a healthy modesty, regarding the achievements and potential of the so-called "scientific method." In a somewhat smaller way, it has also helped foster an intellectual openness, pluralism, and tolerance both in specifically scientific inquiry and throughout Western culture more generally (Levine 1999). But while the Skeptic's judicious tolerance toward different ways of thinking does sound tempting, as an epistemological doctrine it turns out rather less appealing than it first appears. Understood as a wholesale rejection of the very notion of truth, the doctrine of Skepticism requires that we treat no one belief as any more truthful than another. As it happens, then, consistently conducting oneself in accordance with this doctrine is plainly impossible. Though we might nod courteously as Chicken Little informs us that the sky is falling, we will not likely race for cover. I would contend that our personal regard for the truth of Chicken Little's warning is a good deal more evident in our failure to take heed than in our courteous abstention from critique. Since, in practice, we cannot for long dispense with comparative evaluations of the truth of different ideas about the world, we might as well think seriously about how best to go about making them (Rabinow 1983).

More fruitful than an all-encompassing radical skepticism regarding the very possibility of grasping the true nature of things, is to consider what we really mean when we talk about grasping the true nature of things. As I noted above, early scientific methodologists meant by this the production of theoretical generalizations that *correspond* with a unified and constant natural universe. This view has been criticized on several grounds. First and foremost, one must point to the critique of inductive inference. Inductive inference has very often been held up as the methodological foundation of scientific reasoning. It is based on the presumption that through careful observation one may detect general patterns that might then be verified through empirical tests. Once verified these general patterns may be stated as universal laws of nature. The difficulty with induction is its requirement of a jump from empirically observed patterns to universal law. Seeing a thousand dogs and observing that all of them chase cats does not support the inference of a universal law that "*all* dogs chase cats." Unless one empirically observes the *total* population of dogs, past, present, and future, one can never be certain that unobserved dogs don't disprove the universality of one's law. This critique of induction is often held to show that absolute certainty regarding the nature of things is impossible and that all knowledge, including scientific knowledge, is necessarily fallible (cf. Chalmers 1982). Moreover, by proclaiming the fallibility of scientific knowledge, the critique of induction also suggests the faith in a uniform and constant nature of things may be groundless. Without embracing the doctrine of skepticism, we must still ask: what evidence is there to support belief in a unified and constant natural universe? If we find that there is none (and that, indeed, there is good evidence we should reject this belief) then we must reformulate what we mean when we talk about grasping the true nature of things. And, of course, we must reformulate what we mean when we talk about *our efforts* to grasp the true nature of things – that is, when we talk about scientific method.

Acknowledgment of the fallibility of inductive inference has generally led those concerned to preserve the epistemological privilege accorded "the scientific method" and scientific knowledge in one of two conceptual directions: (1) probability theory, and (2) falsificationism. Each of these methodological programs has spawned immense literatures, generated lively methodological disputes, and given rise to numerous hybrid variations on their themes. But, though they have informed a great deal of undeniably important scientific research, this does not mean they provide any kind of support (logical, empirical, or otherwise) for the inference of a unified and constant natural universe. Nor does it mean they are defensible as accounts of a unified and constant scientific method that may be decisively distinguished from non-scientific methods of fact-finding and belief legitimation. As I will show, probability theory and falsificationism are both very seriously limited as either empirically adequate descriptions of, or defensible normative prescriptions for, a singular "scientific method" uniquely entitled to unrivaled epistemological privilege. Let us begin with probability theory.

Many scientists and philosophers of science have accepted that inductive inference cannot produce *absolutely certain* knowledge of the world but have still sought to argue that ideas produced scientifically are nonetheless *probably* truer than ideas produced otherwise. I refer to these types of efforts as probability theories. The theories I have in mind are only a small subset of those that rely on probabilistic calculations. The theories I have in mind are those which specifically seek to defend science as a whole, as a categorically distinct "way of knowing," by invoking the notion that scientific methods are uniquely capable of establishing the objective probability of a given idea's truth (cf. Hempel 1965). The most important question to keep in mind when considering these types of theories is: *what* exactly are these theories suggesting is probable? If one remains focused on this question, it becomes clear that though probability theories may suppose the existence of a unified and constant "nature of things," they offer no reason whatsoever for adopting this supposition.[3] In other words, they simply assume that which is in need of demonstration.

The classic statements of objective probability concern calculations regarding causation and reflect efforts to ease the insurmountable scientific burden of empirically proving that one event (or set of events) caused another (Hempel 1965). The methodological problem that probability theorists are seeking to overcome is basically this. It turns out to be extremely difficult, if not altogether impossible, to empirically distinguish cases wherein one event always follows another event but is not actually caused by that event, from cases wherein the later event actually is caused by the former event. One example will illustrate the problem. I begin most mornings with a cup of coffee, which I prepare by first boiling a pot of water. There are a large number of events that usually figure in this ritual and which precede the water's boiling. To name just a handful: I turn on the tap at my kitchen sink, I wash the coffeepot, I select a certain volume of water, I turn the back left oven coil on high, and place the pot on this particular coil. After about five minutes the water comes to a boil. Were each of these events essential to the eventual outcome? Certainly not. But which were essential and which were not? How might we identify which events figured as genuine causes of the water's boiling and which figured only incidentally? Probability theorists suggest that while we can offer no absolute answer to this question we can establish with certainty the objective probability that particular events are causally significant and that other events are not.

Their recipe for doing so goes something like this. Establish the specific set of elements you consider to be candidate causes of the phenomenon in which you are interested – for the sake of simplicity, let's stick with the example of my morning coffee-making ritual. In this case, then, we are interested in the events that preceded the water in my coffeepot coming to a boil (turning on the tap, washing the pot, turning on the stove, etc.). Collect a large number of cases of the ritual, making certain to determine in each case whether or not each of our candidate causes appeared. If we are lucky, this procedure will yield different rates of occurrence for each of our candidate causes. In other words, some of our candidate causes will have occurred more often than other candidate causes. With this information we can calculate the probability that a given candidate cause will occur prior to the water's boiling. This probability is then held to provide evidence to support the inference that the candidate cause was indeed an actual cause of the water's boiling. As the reader may well have detected already, there are some difficulties with this recipe. It appears we have inferred a relationship of genuine *causation* from evidence that indicates only the probability of *correlation*. For example, if we discover that my washing of the coffeepot occurred prior to the water's coming to a boil in every one of our cases we will then possess data that these events were correlated 100 percent of the time. Does that support the hypothesis that water boils only in clean coffeepots? No, it does not.

Probability theorists go to admirable lengths to detect and weed out such spurious conclusions, but their efforts in this regard are inevitably based on a foundation of assumptions that are not themselves put in question *or even assigned specific probabilities of their own*. These assumptions are presumed, for the sake of the project at hand, to be absolutely true (Coulter 1996). Objective probability theorists would have us believe that these background assumptions derive from proven theories and/or laws of nature but in that case we are back to the problem of induction. What reason do we have to suppose these assumed theories and/or laws not only reflect the received wisdom of a particular scientific community but actually correspond with a uniform and constant natural universe that is in itself wholly independent of the received wisdom of any particular scientific community? The answer is that we have no reason to do so whatsoever. We see, then, that in the case of scientific methods grounded in probabilistic calculations, the foundational reference points of any particular piece of research are not to be found in "nature," nor in formal logic alone, but in the substantive assumptions currently presumed reasonable within a particular scientific field (Putnam 1990). Hence, far from giving us good reasons to suppose the existence of a formally invariant "scientific method," or a unified and constant natural universe to which this method uniquely provides access, probability theorists exemplify my own claim that the utility and validity of particular scientific methods are inevitably contestable and derive their sense and value only within the contexts of particular *dispute domains*.

What about the falsificationists? Like the probability theorists, falsificationists also acknowledge the critique of induction as a valid one (Popper 1963). That is, they accept the claim that one can never know for certain that a given theory corresponds with the nature of things in themselves. However, instead of arguing that we can obtain certain knowledge of the objective probability of a theory's truth, falsificationists argue that we can only obtain certain knowledge of a theory's falsity. Therefore the formal characteristics of scientific method can, and should, be founded not on efforts to confirm the truth of theories but on efforts to falsify them. Their argument runs as follows. The critique of induction is based on a logical problem that can be demonstrated in the form of a syllogism. Let us return to the case of cat chasing dogs. Our inductive inference in this case can be stated:

Premise 1:   Many dogs chase cats.
Premise 2:   This animal is a dog.
Conclusion: This animal chases cats.

This inference is problematic because one can imagine a case wherein the premises of the inference are both true but the conclusion is false. In other words, there is no logical necessity to the inference. Falsificationists argue that though this critique of inductive inference is valid, it is not a problem for scientific method because the logic of properly scientific inferences are not inductive but deductive. Instead of thinking of science as building from the ground of empirical observation up to the level of general theory, falsificationists insist that we begin with speculative theoretical hypotheses. These hypotheses are generated as prospective answers to problems about which a community of scientists is currently concerned. They are then rigorously tested through efforts to generate empirical evidence not of their truth but of their falsity. According to falsificationists, these types of tests rely on inferences that do not suffer from the same logical indeterminacy as do inductive inferences. This can be demonstrated through a syllogism that recasts our inquiry regarding dogs and cats into falsificationist terms. Here we start not with many observations but with a general theoretical proposition that all dogs chase cats. If and when we discover a dog that does not chase cats we may then formulate a syllogism that does indeed proceed by logical necessity:

Premise: On this day in this place a dog that does not chase cats was discovered.
Conclusion: Not all dogs chase cats.

Based on this point of logic, falsificationists insist that genuinely scientific statements about the world must be stated in falsifiable terms. That is, they must clearly posit the empirical nonexistence of certain logically possible phenomena – in the above case, that logically possible phenomenon was a dog that does not chase cats. If such a logically possible phenomenon is shown to actually exist in the empirical world, then the theory is said to have been decisively refuted. According to this approach, major scientific breakthroughs should be viewed less in terms of finding new things in nature than as conclusive refutations of widely accepted theories. Furthermore, in the expectation that they will be immediately bombarded with unyielding critical scrutiny, scientists should strive to formulate their theoretical generalizations in the most sweeping and counterintuitive fashion possible. Why? Because if efforts to refute them fail, such rash generalizations will be transformed from outlandish conjectures into revolutionary scientific triumphs. Of course, the difficulty with sweeping and counterintuitive generalizations is that they tend to be rather easy to refute. Therefore scientists must always navigate between the Scylla of producing trivial truths and the Charybdis of producing grandiose falsehoods.

Falsificationism was intended as a universal statement of the formal structure of "the scientific method." It was intended to simultaneously dodge the critique of induction and to indicate how decisive boundaries must be drawn between genuinely scientific rationality and that motley collection of superstition and dogma that otherwise cluttered our cultures and our minds. But falsificationism's intellectual destiny fell far short of its proponents' ambitions. Just as the critique of induction demonstrated the impossibility of certain knowledge of a theory's truth, critiques of falsificationism demonstrated the impossibility of certain knowledge of a theory's falsity. Inevitably, when experiments are devised to refute or confirm a theory, these experiments are based on a foundation of theoretical assumptions that are not themselves subject to test. This can be shown by returning to our example of dogs that chase cats. Remember that the falsificationist argued the universal law that all dogs chase cats was conclusively refuted by the finding of a single dog that did not. The falsificationists' difficulty lies in the unrealistic simplicity with which this example was laid out.

For this proof to stand, a number of conditions must have been met to the satisfaction of all concerned. By what methods, for example, was it determined that the animal in question was in fact a dog (and not a wolf) and the animal it did not chase was in fact a cat (and not a sorcerer in disguise)? The answer is that these methods could not have been drawn from anything other than the contemporary wisdom regarding dogs, wolves, cats, and sorcerers. Can we be certain that the contemporary wisdom will always remain exactly as it was at the time of this experiment? Of course not. And because we can never rule out the possibility that the initial premises upon which our test is based may one day be shown faulty, we can never rule out the possible fallibility of the test's results. This is no less true for tests designed to conclusively *falsify* a theory than it is for tests designed to conclusively *confirm* a theory. We see, then, that in the case of scientific methods grounded in the doctrine of falsificationism, the foundational reference points of any particular piece of research are not to be found in "nature," nor in formal logic alone, but in the substantive assumptions currently presumed reasonable within a particular scientific field. Hence, once again, far from giving us good reasons to suppose the existence of a formally invariant "scientific method," or a unified and constant natural universe to which this method uniquely provides access, falsificationists also exemplify my own claim that the utility and validity of particular scientific methods are inevitably contestable and derive their sense and value only within the contexts of particular *dispute domains.*

Perhaps most damaging of all to the traditional faith in either a formally invariant "scientific method" or a unified and constant natural universe was the discovery that empirical observation can never be free of conceptual presuppositions. As we have seen, according to Putnam's (1987) "seventeenth century objectivism," methodological choices are properly concerned with forging valid links between one's conceptual generalizations, on the one hand, and the natural universe, on the other hand. By this view, data, or evidence, absolutely must consist in conceptually neutral information about nature. It is only if data can be freed from prejudicial *preconceptions* that it might be held up as any kind of valid proxy for a unified and constant natural universe that is independent of anyone's conceptions of it. Only if our data can be gathered and discussed atheoretically, or entirely free of conceptual taint, can it be held capable of genuinely confirming or refuting the correspondence of our concepts and theories with anything that exists entirely apart from them. But as it has turned out, all efforts to formulate the nature of data in some type of conceptually neutral "observation language" have been soundly discredited (Gibson 1979; Hanson 1958).

Hence, for example, collecting data using attitude-scales must prejudicially presume the existence of things in the world that warrant use of the concept "attitude" (Blumer 1955; Deutscher, Pestello, and Pestello 1993). Though such data may help us decide between theories presuming different *types* of attitudes in a given group, it will be of little use in deciding between these theories and theories that *altogether reject* the independent existence of *anything* warranting the use of the concept "attitude" in that group. One must believe there are such things as attitudes in the first place for this sort of data to be meaningful. This same point holds generally because *all* data must always be *about* a given subject matter before it can confirm or refute specific theories concerning that subject matter. Scientific research is, then, always based on a foundation of provisional assumptions regarding the basic characteristics of one's subject matter. And by necessity, it will always provisionally presume, rather than prove, the existence of certain basic facts about the world. These presumptions profoundly affect how scientific researchers select, defend, and critique particular methods of data collection and analysis.

My hope is that this brief treatment of the general debates concerning scientific methodology will have put to rest some of the old philosophical ghosts that have long vexed discussions of qualitative research methods. Debates about the nature of objectivity, Skepticism, the validity of inductive inference, probability, falsification, and the theory-ladenness of observation all indicate the following conclusion. Evaluations of the validity and importance of particular research methods, be they qualitative or quantitative, must inevitably be made in light of the substantive assumptions current in particular scientific communities. At least in some respects, the authority of these substantive assumptions is always contested. Hence, good scientific research must do more than blithely conform to a fixed set of cannonical assumptions regarding method or anything else. Good scientific researchers must explicitly address the critics of their assumptions. And, of course, questions regarding the methodological *means* of scientific research cannot be divorced from questions regarding its theoretical goals. Answers to methodological questions cannot, then, be settled "once and for all," but must be sought in light of detailed consideration of the unique constellation of challenges that confront any particular research project. In my view, considerations of this kind are best viewed as efforts to both understand and constructively contribute to empirically identifiable *dispute domains*.

Some General Remarks on Dispute Domains

With few exceptions, texts concerning scientific methods omit consideration of the *organizational* contexts within which these methods are authorized and employed. No doubt, one will occasionally find discussions of the *intellectual* history of a methodological tradition. Having dutifully read Kuhn (1970), some authors may even acknowledge their remarks are intended for scientists, or would-be scientists, working within a particular "paradigm." But the meaning of such acknowledgements or, more importantly, their specific import for understanding the use of scientific methods, are seldom, if ever, really explored. Though the tendency to ignore the social forces that shape scientific production can be found in qualitative methods texts as well as texts concerned with quantitative methods, this inattention has been a good deal less pervasive among qualitative social scientists (Emerson 1981; Van Maanen 1995). At least since the 1960s, qualitative social scientists have grown increasingly dissatisfied with the haughty tradition of scientific disregard for the social organization of scientific work.

Analytic attention has been turned upon the social organization of science in at least two distinct sorts of ways. On the one hand, a growing body of qualitative research trains the sociological gaze on the actual work of natural scientists (cf. Knorr-Cetina and Mulkay 1983; Pickering 1992; Star 1995). To the extent social scientists have historically sought to model their own scientific methods on research in the natural sciences, empirical investigations of natural scientists actually doing their research are profoundly instructive. Indeed, social studies of science have revolutionized debate concerning the relationship of science and society. Among the most important of their many achievements has been a thorough demolition of the analytic partitions that once isolated discussions of the social, material, and cognitive dimensions of scientific work (Lynch 1993; Shapin 1995). Time and again, the cognitive logic and material contents of the natural sciences have been shown to literally *consist* in the inescapably social procedures through which they are elicited and manipulated (cf. Garfinkel, Lynch, and Livingston 1981). Lynch and Bogen (1997, p. 483) develop this point as follows:

> the claim that the contents of science are "social" means that the form and the material contents of laboratory discourses, actions, instruments, and findings are bound up with specific historical and cultural ways of life... Consequently, the traditional focus on the intellectual feats of the great men of science has been replaced by an attention to the mundane details of practice, the role of technicians in experimentation, and the intra- and interorganizational relations that contribute to scientific and technological innovation. Considered in this way, the social context of scientific practice is not an external "factor" impinging on the laboratory, nor is it a surrounding set of institutions; it is a matrix for producing facts and artifacts.

I use the expression *dispute domain* in just this sense to indicate the comparatively bounded social context of scientific debate, considered not as "an 'external' factor impinging on the laboratory, nor... a surrounding set of institutions; [but] a matrix for producing facts and artifacts." Like other varieties of social organization, dispute domains in science are by no means hermetically sealed environments. They overlap with one another as well as with dispute domains that are not credited as scientific. While, ideally, they should follow a basically discursive logic, inevitably they consist of elements that cannot always be reduced to strictly symbolic exchange. Various practical operations, material artifacts, research instruments, intra- and interorganizational arrangements, not to mention economic, political, and cultural relations may both reflect and preserve the character of particular scientific dispute domains. Moreover, scientific dispute domains are marked by what Clifford (1983), following the Russian literary theorist Mikhail Bakhtin, calls "heteroglossia."[4] Hence, discerning the boundaries, the genealogies, and the practical operations through which scientific dispute domains are realized can be an ambiguous task. But this mustn't count against the effort for as Levine (1985, p. 17) writes, "the toleration of ambiguity can be productive if it is taken not as a warrant for sloppy thinking but as an invitation to deal responsibly with issues of great complexity." If we are to resist both blind orthodoxy and the fatuous exaltation of uncertainty one finds among some postmodernists, we must begin by acknowledging and investigating the complex social worlds in and for which our research is conducted (Halliday and Janowitz 1992; Miller 1995; Platt 1996; Rabinow 1986; Turner and Turner 1990). It is only in doing so that we will come to discover the specific possibilities for establishing the rigor and unique value of our ideas about the world.

The second way that the analytic attentions of qualitative researchers have been turned upon the social organization of science is more self-conscious. In addition to studies of the natural sciences, one may observe over the last three decades a steadily growing interest in how qualitative social science is itself socially organized. Some of the earliest and most influential work in this regard called attention to the colonialistic context within which the modern discipline of anthropology was forged (cf. Asad 1973). This research fiercely criticizes some of anthropology's foundational concepts (e.g. *culture, other*) for the colonialistic habits of mind they appear to reflect. The penchant for self-criticism was further developed in studies that addressed the various ways in which ethnographers had failed to live up to their own scientific pretensions. Anthropology's scientific authority historically rested in a two part methodological procedure: (1) provide evidence of having "been there" as an eye-witness, or virtual eye-witness, to the phenomena described, and (2) somehow deny or suppress the idea that eye-witness accounts cannot be objective because they can only ever be accounts from a particular *subjective* point of view. As criticisms of this claim to scientific authority mounted, a number of qualitative researchers began to explore and experiment with the rhetorical performances through which the authority of qualitative research is sustained (cf. Atkinson 1990; Clifford and Marcus 1986; Pollner 1992; Van Maanen 1988; Woolgar 1988).

In addition to studies that address the rhetoric of scientific *authority*, epistemologically self-conscious studies of the mundane practice of qualitative *data collection* and *analysis* are also appearing increasingly frequently (cf. Bourdieu 1996; DeVault 1999; Emerson, Fretz, and Shaw 1995; Gubrium and Holstein 1997; Harding 1991; Holstein and Gubrium 1995; Pollner and Emerson 1988; Smith 1989). These works demonstrate the value in turning methodological attention toward the specific social contexts, or organizational embeddedness (Gubrium 1988), of qualitative research projects. But there is a growing need for more work of this kind. If we are to more effectively ground our methodological choices we must become still more discerning and more explicit in our regard for the warrants of our research (Katz 1997). The best social scientists know perfectly well it is no longer defensible to piously invoke the formal logic of our methods nor to insist upon an invariant natural universe that will decisively confirm or refute the validity of our ideas (Harre 1990). But polemics against method (Feyerabend 1975), and postmodern reductions of all thought to poetics and politics may be counterproductive as well. To quote Chalmers (1982, p. 170), we must seek,

> to undermine illegitimate uses of conceptions of science and scientific method, [but] also ... do something to counter the extreme individualist or relativist reactions against the ideology of science. It is not the case that any view is as good as any other. If a situation is to be changed in a controlled way, whether the situation involves the state of development of some branch of knowledge or the state of development of some aspect of society, this will best be achieved by way of a grasp of the situation and a mastery of the means available for changing it ... The policy of "anything goes", interpreted in a more general sense than Feyerabend probably intended, is to be resisted because of its impotence ... *anything goes* ... means that in practice, *everything stays.*

If we are to foster progress at either the methodological or the substantive levels of our research we must transcend the stale opposition of "rationalist" and "realist" adherents to a singular and invariant picture of scientific method and scientific knowledge and "relativist" adherents to the view that no method or form of knowledge is better than any other. In my view, the most effective way to carry this project forward is to learn as much as we possibly can regarding the characteristics and the genealogies of the dispute domains into which we seek to intervene (Dean 1994). Sometimes these genealogies will be comparatively brief, sometimes they might trace back over centuries, or more. Whether our project is "applied," or aimed exclusively to develop a scientific corpus, the logic of our inquiry will remain the same. The warrant for our research and for our choice of research methods will be discovered through thorough acquaintance with the unique aims, procedures, prides, prejudices, and anomolies of the dispute domains into which we seek to intervene. Though I do insist that the assessment of methodological adequacy cannot be extricated from the horizons that mark actually existing dispute domains, this must not be mistaken for relativism as it is generally construed (Hollis and Lukes 1982). I am not exalting dogmatism, irrationality, nor the underdetermination of theory choice by evidence (see Quine 1963). My position is more akin to Putnam's (1990) "internal realism." Though we must forego the chimera of a fixed gold standard for truth, we need not therefore distrust that on any actual occasion of dispute there will be resources at hand, sufficient for all practical purposes, to determine the most adequate among competing accounts. Reliance, then, is placed not in an invariant scientific method, nor an invariant natural universe, but in the ongoing, and indispensably communal, *process* of investigation and contestation itself.[5]

The Sciences of Meaning and Human Practice

Qualitative social science is overwhelmingly predicated on the presumption that meaning and human practice merit scientific interest as genuine and significant phenomena in their own right. Though this presumption hails from a variety of discrete sources, its best known source in the annals of social science methodology can be traced to Germany during the late nineteenth century. Though the nuances of the original dispute have long since been forgotten, the *Methodenstreit*, or "dispute over method" as it was to become known, embroiled some of Germany's finest social thinkers in debate regarding the particular *nature* of social life and its amenability to the methods of analysis found in the natural sciences. Thinkers like Wilhelm Dilthey, Hans-Georg Gadamer, Georg Simmel, and Max Weber became figureheads for an intellectual movement that sought to decisively distinguish the social sciences from the natural sciences on the grounds that their methods and/or subject matters were irreducibly unique. Scholars argued that whereas natural scientists study inanimate objects and "lower" forms of life, social scientists study people. Unlike the behavior of inanimate objects or lower life forms, the behavior of human beings is not caused by *uniform laws* but by sentient, creative *subjects* imbued with an understanding of the worlds in which they live and act (Outhwaite 1976). Hence, the effort to grasp the nature of social life must begin with an appreciation of one's research subjects' own understandings of their circumstances.

These ideas were appropriated by the pioneers of qualitative research methods in the social sciences (cf. Bunzl 1996; Chapoulie 1987). However, unlike some of the more romantically inclined among the nineteenth-century German theorists, the pioneers of qualitative methodology generally insisted that we combine an appreciation of human creativity with an equally serious commitment to scientific rigor (Rabinow 1983). The two best known pioneers of ethnographic fieldwork in anthropology, Franz Boas and Bronislaw Malinowski, are archetypal in this respect. Both promoted efforts to grasp indigenous peoples' meaningful understandings of their worlds as a decidedly *scientific* corrective to the unsystematic collection of cultural artifacts and specimens that they felt characterized pre-scientific anthropological research (Urry 1984). Analytic attention was as yet projected exclusively outward onto the lives of people researchers regarded fundamentally different from, and socially distant to, themselves (Chapoulie 1987; Stocking 1990). But the social scientific project was cast expansively as a project of grasping the complex relationships that link variations in human biology, psychology, geography, culture, and history, on the one hand, and peoples' subjective experiences and activities on the other.

The earliest excursions into systematic empirical field research were predicated on a holistic, if somewhat diffuse, sense of social groups as relatively situated, relatively distinctive, and relatively homogeneous both in terms of the objective conditions under which members of the group were compelled to live and in the customary mental attitudes and practical responses to those conditions they developed. Empirical research was designed to illuminate these dimensions of a particular group's existence and to facilitate efforts to link them to one another theoretically. At first these efforts were fairly unself-conscious, opportunistic and eclectic (Bulmer 1984; Platt 1983; Urry 1984). Data were drawn from a variety of sources and theorizing was often both miscellaneous and more implicit than explicit (cf. Park 1915). Eventually, though, a variety of historical events converged to constrain this original eclecticism. Beginning with Boas' vigorous campaign to combat the overt racism prevalent in nineteenth-century anthropology, physically based theories of human thought and action were pushed to the margins of American social science (Stocking 1990). In Britain, Malinowski's eclecticism came in for serious abuse from the followers of A. R. Radcliffe-Brown (some of whom were Malinowski's own former students) who advocated a more formal, systematic, and exclusively sociological approach to anthropological research (Dahrendorf 1995; Firth 1957).

Though some social scientists have turned to Freudian and other psychodynamic theories, the more general trend has been opposed to presumptions of innate psychic processes (Chodorow 1999). Similarly, many social scientists in the first half of the twentieth century grew disenchanted with behavioral psychologists' refusal to acknowledge the role of meaning and creativity in human action and experience (cf. Camic 1986). As physically and psychologically deterministic understandings of human action and experience were repudiated, social scientists increasingly viewed their subject matter as a domain unto itself, fundamentally irreducible to forces that were not themselves also social (Blumer 1969; Geertz 1973; Parsons 1937). Concurrent with these theoretical developments, universities were expanding and the academic universe was being divided into a larger number of distinct scientific disciplines and subdisciplines. As a result, new generations of *social* scientists felt ever less compelled to defend their analyses against the competing claims of scientists who focused on our physical or psychic inheritances (Porter 1990). At a very general level, their own dispute domain was gradually disjoined from these others, and scientific dialogue was increasingly confined to colleagues who sought to illuminate human action and experience from within and with respect to the *social world* sui generis (Kuklick 1980). Data collection was thus delimited to *social* phenomena and analysis to *social* causes and processes.

To be sure, the isolation of disputes regarding the social dimensions of human life from those regarding our physical and psychic inheritance was never total. And, indeed, this isolation was always less pervasive in anthropology where the collegial co-mingling of social and natural scientists was widely institutionalized through their sharing of a single academic department. But even when their research efforts were collaborative, cultural and physical anthropologists have always stood in uneasy analytic relation to one another. Though both strove to illuminate the causes and characteristics of the human condition, their theories and methods have often seemed to defy rigorous comparison with one another (cf. Freese and Powell 1999). Hence, the more popularly traveled disputes on both sides of this antinomy have been those that did not seek to disturb the culture/nature divide. If ethnographers have spoken to the "natural" dimensions of the human condition they have overwhelmingly focused only on the symbolic meaning and cultural function of natural objects rather than the details of their characteristic effects on human action. Devising research methods capable of *empirically* recuperating the corporeal and intrapsychic dimensions of human subjectivity within a culturally sensitive framework is only beginning to receive the attention it deserves (Chodorow 1999; Csordas 1994; Goodwin 1994; Katz 1999; Knorr-Cetina 1992; Turner 1984). More generally, insofar as qualitative methods became all but definitive of their craft, cultural anthropologists have not often thought to seriously question their scientific legitimacy. While disputes have raged over competing theories, qualitative methods have themselves remained largely beyond scientific reproach.

Things have been rather different in sociology. Since at least the turn of the twentieth century, American sociologists have struggled to distance themselves from their roots in social reform movements (Lengermann and Niebrugge-Brantley 1998; Turner 1994). Early on, this entailed little more than a movement away from pontification and toward empirically grounded commentary on social events. However, as the discipline grew larger, more diverse, and more thoroughly ensconced in academia, disputes arose as to the kinds of investigations that were to qualify as genuinely *scientific* studies of social life. These disputes often focused on the comparative strengths and weaknesses of qualitative and quantitative research methods. In the 1930s and 1940s, the largely qualitative "case study" tradition associated with the University of Chicago came under serious attack from a coterie of researchers fiercely committed to fashioning sociology in the image of the natural sciences (Bannister 1987). A confluence of several complex changes within the Chicago department itself, in the discipline of sociology, in academia, and in American society generally, eventually tipped the balance of power between practitioners of qualitative and quantitative techniques toward the latter (Bulmer 1984; Lengermann 1979; Platt 1996). This was evident as early as the late thirties, when proponents of qualitative methods began to defend their scientific legitimacy with explicit reference to criteria enforced by their quantitative colleagues (cf. Blumer 1939; Lindesmith 1938). Whether they opposed them, endorsed them, or strove for some other manner of conciliation, qualitative sociologists have felt powerful pressures to attend to the methodological arguments of quantitative sociologists (Wax 1971). This has had a dramatic effect on the history of qualitative research methods.

The survey researchers who rose to power in the 1940s and 1950s pressed to measure the value of qualitative research by the lights of their own positivistic philosophy of science. By suppressing or ignoring issues of meaning and what Garfinkel (1967) called the intrinsic "artfulness" of social life, positivist sociologists ascribed a second class status to qualitative research. Though the doctrines that sustained the positivist ascendancy have long since been discredited among philosophers of science themselves, news of their demise has traveled slowly through the social sciences. Regrettably, qualitative research continues to be commonly disparaged for its putative nonconformity to an antiquated and hopelessly flawed conception of scientific work. But, on the bright side, it is widely evident that the situation is improving. Virtually every major social theorist in the last thirty years has come down in opposition to the positivism that alienated qualitative research from the mainstream of the social sciences (cf. Alexander 1982; Bourdieu 1990; Calhoun 1995; Collins 1991; Collins 1994; Foucault 1980; Gergen 1994; Giddens 1984; Habermas 1984; Harding 1991; Harre 1990; Smith 1989; Turner 1984). And at an institutional level, qualitative researchers have successfully carved out niches for themselves throughout the academic world. Beyond anthropology and sociology, one can now find growing qualitative contingents in such fields as business administration, communications, education, folklore, linguistics, nursing, political science, and public health. And, indeed, there is growing interest in qualitative research beyond the confines of the academy (Suchman 1987). The future looks a good deal brighter than the past. But there remains important work to be done.

If we are to effectively promote their improvement, we must not forget that the scientific legitimacy of qualitative research methods is to be achieved in no small part through direct dialogue with the specific critiques that have been arrayed against them. In the foregoing pages I have argued that critiques based on faith in the view that science does or should possess an invariant formal logic are fatally flawed. Equally flawed are those critiques based in Putnam's "seventeenth century objectivism," – or the position that nature will herself rise up unaided to arbitrate the validity of competing accounts. But beyond such admittedly generic efforts, the merits of qualitative research methods must be articulated with conscientious attention to the specific characteristics of more particular dispute domains. One major dispute domain that is on the rise concerns how best to empirically re-appropriate the corporeal and intrapsychic dimensions of human subjectivity within a culturally sensitive framework (cf. Turner, 1984). Another concerns how best to relate empirical considerations of "global" and "local" processes (Burawoy et al. 1991; Drew and Heritage 1992; Schegloff 1991). Yet another concerns how best to address the relationship of naturalist and constructionist approaches to the understanding of social life (Gubrium and Holstein 1997; Hazelrigg 1986). And, of course, there are countless others ranging over dozens of substantive fields. Qualitative studies have become renowned classics in the substantive fields of criminology, deviance, emotions, gender, gerontology, health and illness, occupations, race, science, technology, urban sociology, and youth not by their conformity to generic methodological cannons, but by creatively marshaling richly detailed empirical materials to effectively address questions central to these fields. This point can be generalized. Great qualitative research inevitably entails combining vigilant sensitivity to the worlds we seek to understand with an equally vigilant sensitivity to the worlds *for which* we seek to understand.

The Plan of the Book

This collection of readings is intended to acquaint the reader not only with the full range of contemporary qualitative research methods, but to locate these methods in the wider scientific legacies in which they emerged and to point to new directions in qualitative research. Though they are written in prose that is well within the grasp of an untrained reader, the articles included in this collection represent some of the finest classic and contemporary scholarship in the field. Rather than endeavoring to advance the vanguard of any particular approach, I have sought to provide a holistic overview of extant achievements within the confines of a text that might remain conceptually accessible and reasonably concise.

The book includes five parts, each of which includes three or four essays respectively. Part I is comprised of essays that speak to the historical emergence and development of qualitative research methods in sociology and anthropology. This section is intended to provide a background for understanding the more recent proliferation of distinctive genres of qualitative research and the genealogical relationship these genres bear to one another. An acquaintance with this historical background should help the reader to grasp what is distinctive about current styles of research and more effectively assess their comparative merits. Parts II–V cover: qualitative interviewing, life histories, and narrative analysis; observational fieldwork; conversation analysis and discourse analysis; and research using artifacts as primary sources. In each part, I have sought to concentrate primarily on pieces that articulate major perspectives on the method, its distinctive challenges and opportunities, and at least one exemplary instantiation of the methodological approach as applied in a substantive empirical analysis.

Notes

1   The expression *dispute domain* is borrowed from Miller and Holstein (1993, 1995) who define it as follows:

> A dispute domain consists of the fundamental assumptions, vocabularies, orientations, concerns, and constraints that circumscribe conflictual interactions within particular organizational circumstances... dispute domains provide the local *conditions of possibility* for disputing – the parameters for what disputes might become and the resources and orientations for their articulation. (Miller and Holstein 1995, p. 38)

My use of their concept should not be held to suggest they necessarily endorse the manner in which I have appropriated it. I am not certain they would want to cast *scientific* work in these terms. But see Miller (1995) and Gubrium and Holstein (1997) for views on scientific method very similar to the one presented here.

2   The expression "technical" is here used to indicate that methodological problems were thought to be confined to the *means* of scientific work and unrelated to its ultimate theoretical goals – which were considered unproblematic and settled (i.e. grasping nature's eternal truths). Contemporary scholarship tends to be a bit more philosophically cautious, casting scientific goals more specifically in terms of producing valid answers to particular scientific questions. From this vantage, analytically isolating the methodological *means* from the theoretical *goals* of science begins to appear untenable because evaluations of the soundness and/or importance of specific theoretical goals and the soundness and/or importance of particular methodological means of achieving those goals are always mutually implicative (cf. Calhoun 1998; Gubrium and Holstein 1997). Scientific goals always take shape through decidedly methodological choices regarding the selection and

framing of research questions. Conversely, methods of data collection and analysis are best chosen with respect to the specific question[s] one seeks to answer.

3   Interest is growing among philosophers and scientists in a type of probability theory that does not necessarily need to assume a unified and constant natural universe. This theory is known as Bayesian, or subjective, probability theory. Unlike objective probability theorists, Baysians are not concerned to calculate the probability of an idea's correspondence with a unified and constant natural universe. Instead, Baysians attend to the relative degree to which people are rationally entitled to believe in an idea given their own subjective exposure to a body of evidence (see Howson and Urbach 1989). This approach to probability need not assume that the "nature of things" is amenable to only one comprehensively true theory or that scientists possess a uniquely superior set of methods for fact finding and belief legitimation.

4   Clifford (1983, pp. 142–3) quotes Bakhtin and comments as follows,
"Heteroglossia" assumes that "languages do not *exclude* each other, but rather intersect with each other in many different ways (the Ukranian language, the language of the epic poem, of early Symbolism, of the student, of a particular generation of children, of the run-of-the-mill intellectual, of the Nietzschean and so on). It might even seem that the very word 'language' loses all meaning in this process – for apparently there is no single plane on which all these 'languages' might be juxtaposed to one another." What is said of languages applies equally to "cultures" and "subcultures."

5   This should not be mistaken for an endorsement of scientific discourse construed in the image of the "ideal speech situation" envisaged by Habermas (1984). I think we must expect that a good deal more than mutual understanding will be sought in even the most "disinterested" of intellectual disputes.

References

Alexander, Jeffrey C. 1982. *Theoretical Logic in Sociology: Positivism, Presuppositions, and Current Controversies, vol. 1.* Berkeley: University of California Press.

Asad, Talal, ed. 1973. *Anthropology & the Colonial Encounter.* New York: Humanities Press.

Atkinson, Paul. 1990. *The Ethnographic Imagination: Textual constructions of reality.* London: Routledge.

Bannister, Robert C. 1987. *Sociology and Scientism: The American Quest for Objectivity, 1880–1940.* Chapel Hill, NC: University of North Carolina Press.

Blumer, Herbert. 1939. *An Appraisal of Thomas and Znaniecki's "The Polish Peasant in Europe and America,"* New York: Social Science Research Council.

—— 1955. "Attitudes and the Social Act." *Social Problems* 3(2): 59–65.

—— 1969. *Symbolic Interactionism: Perspective and Method.* Berkeley: University of California Press.

Bourdieu, Pierre. 1975. "The Specificity of the Scientific Field and the Social Conditions for the Progress of Reason." *Social Science Information* 14(5): 119–47.

—— 1990. *The Logic of Practice,* trans. Richard Nice. Stanford: Stanford University Press.

—— 1991. "The Peculiar History of Scientific Reason." *Sociological Forum* 6(1): 3–26.

—— 1996. "Understanding." *Theory, Culture and Society* 13(2): 17–37.

Bulmer, Martin. 1984. *The Chicago School of Sociology: Institutionalization, Diversity, and the Rise of Sociological Research.* Chicago: University of Chicago Press.

Bunzl, Matti. 1996. "Franz Boas and the Humboldtian Tradition: From Volkgeist and Nationalcharakter to an Anthropological Concept of Culture." In *Volkgeist as Method and Ethic: Essays on Boasian Ethnography and the German Anthropological Tradition.* Edited by George W. Stocking, Jr. Madison, WI: University of Wisconsin Press.

Burawoy, Michael, Alice Burton, Ann Arnett Ferguson, Kathryn J. Fox, Joshua Gamson, Nadine Gartrell, Leslie Hurst, Charles Kurzman, Leslie Salzinger, Josepha Shiffman, and Shiori Ui. 1991. *Ethnography Unbound: Power and Resistance in the Modern Metropolis.* Berkeley: University of California Press.

Calhoun, Craig. 1995. *Critical Social Theory: Culture, History, and the Challenge of Difference.* Oxford: Blackwell.

—— 1998. "Explanation in Historical Sociology: Narrative, General Theory, and Historically Specific Theory." *American Journal of Sociology* 104(3): 846–71.

Camic, Charles. 1986. "The Matter of Habit." *American Journal of Sociology* 91(5): 1039–87.

Carnap, Rudolf. 1928 [1967]. *The Logical Structure of the World and Pseudo-problems in Philosophy.* Trans. Rolf A. George. Berkeley: University of California Press.

Chalmers, A. F. 1982. *What is this Thing Called Science?: An assessment of the nature and status of science and its methods.* Milton Keynes: Open University Press.

Chapoulie, Jean-Michel. 1987. "Everett C. Hughes and the Development of Fieldwork in Sociology." *Urban Life* 15: 259–98.

Chodorow, Nancy J. 1999. *The Power of Feelings: Personal Meaning in Psychoanalysis, Gender, and Culture.* New Haven: Yale University Press.

Clifford, James. 1983. "On Ethnographic Authority." *Representations* 1:2 (Spring): 118–46.

Clifford, James, and George E. Marcus, eds. 1986. *Writing Culture: The Poetics and Politics of Ethnography.* Berkeley: University of California Press.

Collins, Patricia Hill. 1991. *Black Feminist Thought: Knowledge, consciousness, and the politics of empowerment.* New York: Routledge.

Collins, Randall. 1994. *Four Sociological Traditions.* New York: Oxford University Press.

Coulter, Jeff. 1996. "Chance, cause, and conduct: probability theory and the explanation of human action." In *Philosophy of Science, Logic, and Mathematics in the Twentieth Century.* Edited by Stuart G. Shanker. London: Routledge.

Csordas, Thomas J., ed. 1994. *Embodiment and Experience: The existential ground of culture and self.* Cambridge: Cambridge University Press.

Dahrendorf, Ralf. 1995. *LSE: a history of the London School of Economics and Political Science, 1895–1995.* Oxford: Oxford University Press.

Dean, Mitchell. 1994. *Critical and Effective Histories: Foucault's Methods and Historical Sociology.* London: Routledge.

Deutscher, Irwin, Fred P. Pestello, and H. Francis Pestello. 1993. *Sentiments and Acts.* New York: Aldine de Gruyter.

DeVault, Marjorie L. 1999. *Liberating Method: Feminism and Social Research.* Philadelphia: Temple University Press.

Drew, Paul and John Heritage, eds. 1992. *Talk at Work: Interaction in Institutional Settings.* Cambridge: Cambridge University Press.

Emerson, Robert M. 1981. "Observational Field Work." *Annual Review of Sociology* 7: 351–78.

Emerson, Robert M., Rachel I. Fretz, and Linda L. Shaw. 1995. *Writing Ethnographic Fieldnotes.* Chicago: University of Chicago Press.

Feyerabend, Paul K. 1975. *Against Method: Outline of an anarchistic theory of knowledge.* London: NLB.

Firth, Raymond William, ed. 1957. *Man and Culture: an evaluation of the work of Bronislaw Malinowski.* London: Routledge & Kegan Paul.

Foucault, Michel. 1980. *Power/Knowledge.* Edited by Colin Gordon. New York Pantheon.

Freese, Jeremy and Brian Powell. 1999. "Sociobiology, Status, and Parental Investment in Sons and Daughters: Testing the Trivers–Willard Hypothesis." *American Journal of Sociology* 104(6): 1704–43.

Garfinkel, Harold. 1967. *Studies in Ethnomethodology.* Englewood Cliffs, NY: Prentice-Hall.

Garfinkel, Harold, Michael Lynch, and Eric Livingston. 1981. "The Work of a Discovering Science Construed with Materials from the Optically Discovered Pulsar." *Philosophy of the Social Sciences* 11: 131–58.

Geertz, Clifford. 1973. *The Interpretation of Cultures*. New York: Basic Books.

Gergen, Kenneth J. 1994. *Realities and Relationships: Soundings in Social Construction*. Cambridge, MA: Harvard University Press.

Gibson, James J. 1979. *The Ecological Approach to Visual Perception*. Boston: Houghton Mifflin.

Giddens, Anthony. 1984. *The Constitution of Society: Outline of the Theory of Structuration*. Berkeley: University of California Press.

Goodwin, Charles. 1994. "Professional Vision." *American Anthropologist* 96(3): 606–33.

Gubrium, Jaber F. 1988. *Analyzing Field Reality*. Newbury Park, CA: Sage.

Gubrium, Jaber F. and James A. Holstein. 1997. *The New Language of Qualitative Method*. New York: Oxford University Press.

Habermas, Jürgen. 1984. *The Theory of Communicative Action, vol. 1: Reason and the Rationalization of Society*. Boston: Beacon Press.

Halliday, Terence C. and Morris Janowitz, eds. 1992. *Sociology and its Publics: The Forms and Fates of Disciplinary Organization*. Chicago: University of Chicago Press.

Hanson, Norwood R. 1958. *Patterns of Discovery; an inquiry into the conceptual foundations of science*. Cambridge: Cambridge University Press.

Haraway, Donna J. 1991. *Simians, Cyborgs, and Women: The Reinvention of Nature*. London: Routledge.

Harding, Sandra. 1991. *Whose Science? Whose Knowledge?: Thinking from Women's Lives*. Ithaca, NY: Cornell University Press.

Harre, Rom. 1990. "Exploring the Human Umwelt." In *Harre and his Critics: Essays in honor of Rom Harre with his commentary on them*. Edited by Roy Bhaskar. Oxford: Basil Blackwell.

Hazelrigg. Lawrence E. 1986. "Is There a Choice Between 'Constructionism' and 'Objectivism'?" *Social Problems* 33(6): s1–s13.

Hempel, Carl G. 1965. *Aspects of Scientific Explanation*. New York: Free Press.

Hollis, Martin and Steven Lukes, eds. 1982. *Rationality and Relativism*. Oxford: Basil Blackwell.

Holstein, James A. and Jaber F. Gubrium. 1995. *The Active Interview*. Thousand Oaks, CA: Sage.

Howson, Colin and Peter Urbach. 1989. *Scientific Reasoning: The Bayesian Approach*. La Salle, IL: Open Court.

Katz, Jack. 1997. "Ethnography's Warrants." *Sociological Methods & Research* 25(4): 391–423.

—— 1999. *How Emotions Work*. Chicago: University of Chicago Press.

Knorr-Centina, Karin. 1992. "The Couch, the Cathedral, and the Laboratory: On the Relationship between Experiment and Laboratory in Science." In *Science as Practice and Culture*. Edited by Andrew Pickering. Chicago: University of Chicago Press.

—— 1999. *Epistemic Cultures: How the Sciences Make Knowledge*. Cambridge, MA: Harvard University Press.

Knorr-Cetina, Karin and Michael Mulkay, eds. 1983. *Science Observed: Perspectives on the Social Study of Science*. London: Sage.

Kuhn, Thomas S. 1970. *The Structure of Scientific Revolutions, second edition, enlarged*. Chicago: University of Chicago Press.

Kuklick, Henrika. 1980. "Boundary Maintenance in American Sociology: Limitations to Academic 'Professionalization'." *Journal of the History of the Behavioral Sciences* 16: 201–19.

Lengermann, Patricia Madoo. 1979. "The Founding of the *American Sociological Review*: The Anatomy of a Rebellion." *American Sociological Review* 44(2): 185–98.

Lengermann, Patricia Madoo and Jill Niebrugge-Brantley. 1998. *The Women Founders: Sociology and Social Theory, 1830–1930*. Boston: McGraw-Hill.

Levine, Alan, ed. 1999. *Early Modern Skepticism and the Origins of Toleration*. Oxford: Lexington Books.

Levine, Donald N. 1985. *The Flight from Ambiguity: Essays in Social and Cultural Theory*. Chicago: University of Chicago Press.

Lindesmith, Alfred R. 1938. "A Sociological Theory of Drug Addiction." *American Journal of Sociology* 43(4): 593–613.

Lynch, Michael. 1993. *Scientific Practice and Ordinary Action: Ethnomethodology and the social studies of science*. Cambridge: Cambridge University Press.

Lynch, Michael, and David Bogen. 1997. "Sociology's Asociological 'Core': An Examination of Textbook Sociology in Light of the Sociology of Scientific Knowledge." *American Sociological Review* 62(3): 4811–93.

Miller, Gale and James A. Holstein. 1993. "Disputing in Organizations: Dispute Domains and Interactional Process." *Mid-American Review of Sociology* 17(2): 1–18.

—— 1995. "Dispute Domains: Organizational Contexts and Dispute Processing." *The Sociological Quarterly* 36(1): 37–59.

Miller, Gale. 1995. "Reflections on Ethnographic Knowledge and Constituencies." *Studies in Symbolic Interaction* 17: 73–88.

Outhwaite, William. 1976. *Understanding Social Life: The Method Called Verstehen*. New York: Holmes & Meier.

Park, Robert E. 1915. "The City: Suggestions for the Investigation of Human Behavior in the Urban Environment." *American Journal of Sociology* 20(5): 577–612.

Parsons, Talcott. 1937. *The Structure of Social Action; a study in social theory with special reference to a group of recent European writers*. New York: McGraw-Hill.

Pickering, Andrew, ed. 1992. *Science as Practice and Culture*. Chicago: University of Chicago Press.

Platt, Jennifer. 1983. "The Development of the 'Participant Observation' Method in Sociology: Origin Myth and History." *Journal of the History of the Behavioral Sciences* 19(4): 379–93.

—— 1996. *A History of Sociological Research Methods in America, 1920–1960*. Cambridge: Cambridge University Press.

Pollner, Melvin. 1987. *Mundane Reason: Reality in everyday and sociological discourse*. Cambridge: Cambridge University Press.

—— 1992. "Left of Ethnomethodology: The Rise and Decline of Radical Reflexivity." *American Sociological Review* 56(3): 370–80.

Pollner, Melvin and Robert M. Emerson. 1988. "The Dynamics of Inclusion and Distance in Fieldwork Relations." In *Contemporary Field Research: A collection of readings*. Edited by Robert M. Emerson. Prospect Heights, IL: Waveland Press, Inc.

Popper, Karl R. 1963. *Conjectures and Refutations: The Growth of Scientific Knowledge*. London: Routledge and Kegan Paul.

Porter, Theodore M. 1990. "Natural science and social theory." In *Companion to the History of Modern Science*. Edited by R. C. Olby, G. N. Cantor, J. R. R. Christie, and M. J. S. Hodge. London: Routledge.

Putnam, Hilary. 1987. *The Many Faces of Realism*. La Salle, IL: Open Court.

—— 1990. *Realism with a Human Face*. Edited by James Conant. Cambridge, MA: Harvard University Press.

Quine, W.V.O. 1963. "Two Dogmas of Empiricism." In *From a Logical Point of View, second edition*. New York: Harper & Row.

Rabinow, Paul. 1983. "Humanism as Nihilism: The Bracketing of Truth and Seriousness in American Cultural Anthropology." In *Social Science as Moral Inquiry*. Edited by Norma Haan, Robert N. Bellah, Paul Rabinow, and William M. Sullivan. New York: Columbia University Press.

—— 1986. "Representations are Social Facts: Modernity and Postmodernity in Anthropology." In *Writing Culture: The Poetics and Politics of Ethnography*. Edited by James Clifford and George E. Marcus. Berkeley: University of California Press.

Schegloff, Emanuel. 1991. "Reflections on Talk and Social Structure." In *Talk & Social Structure: Studies in Ethnomethodology and Conversation Analysis*. Edited by Deidre Boden and Don H. Zimmerman. Berkeley: University of California press.

Shapin, Steven. 1994. *A Social History of Truth: Civility and Science in Seventeenth Century England*. Chicago: University of Chicago Press.

—— 1995. "Here and Everywhere: Sociology of Scientific Knowledge." *Annual Review of Sociology* 21: 289–321.

Smith, Dorothy E. 1989. *The Everyday World as Problematic: A Feminist Sociology*. Boston: Northeastern University Press.

Star, Susan Leigh, ed. 1995. *Ecologies of Knowledge: Work and Politics in Science and Technology*. Albany, NY: SUNY Press.

Stocking, George W., Jr. 1990. "Paradigmatic Traditions in the History of Anthropology." In *Companion to the History of Modern Science*. Edited by R. C. Olby, G. N. Cantor, J. R. R. Christie, and M. J. S. Hodge. London: Routledge.

Suchman, Lucille A. 1987. *Plans and Situated Actions: The Problem of Human–Machine Communication*. Cambridge: Cambridge University Press.

Turner, Bryan S. 1984. *The Body and Society: Explorations in Social Theory*. Oxford: Basil Blackwell.

Turner, Stephen P. 1994. "The Origins of 'Mainstream Sociology' and Other Issues in the History of American Sociology." *Social Epistemology* 8(1): 41–67.

Turner, Stephen P. and Jonathan H. Turner. 1990. *The Impossible Science: An Institutional Analysis of American Sociology*. Newbury Park, CA: Sage.

Urry, James. 1984. "A History of Field Methods." In *Ethnographic Research: A guide to general conduct*. Edited by R. F. Ellen. London: Academic Press.

Van Maanen, John. 1988. *Tales of the Field: On Writing Ethnography*. Chicago: University of Chicago Press.

Van Maanen, John, ed. 1995. *Representation in Ethnography*. Thousand Oaks: CA: Sage.

Wax, Rosalie. 1971. *Doing Fieldwork: Warnings and advice*. Chicago: University of Chicago Press.

Weinberger, Jerry, ed. 1989. *New Atlantis and The Great Instauration, revised edition*. By Francis Bacon. Arlington Heights, IL: Harlan Davidson, Inc.

Wilson, Edward O. 1998. *Consilience: The Unity of Knowledge*. New York: Knopf.

Woolgar, Steve, ed. 1988. *Knowledge and Reflexivity: New Frontiers in the Sociology of Knowledge*. London: Sage.

Part I

The Legacy of Qualitative Research Methods

INTRODUCTION TO PART I

The readings that comprise this section have been selected with a mind to acquaint the reader with the legacy of qualitative research methods in anthropology and sociology, and to provide some background for understanding the genealogical relationship contemporary genres of qualitative research bear to one another. My remarks here will be confined to flagging some of the key issues raised by these readings and which I think warrant particular attention.

The first point that deserves mention in this respect is the general historical development of qualitative social science from original concerns to understand the worlds of peoples that researchers considered alien and inferior to themselves toward investigations of practices and institutions researchers considered closer to home. As Chapoulie (1987, p. 260) observes, "the first attempts at empirical research in social science dealt with subjects . . . distant from the researcher in time or in social space." Chapoulie traces a historical movement of social scientific interest from "primitive" peoples and the working classes and peasants of industrializing nations, through to the middle classes and middle-class institutions, to "everyday behavior," and only most recently, to the work of social and natural scientists themselves. In light of the field's inaugural interests in alien "others," Simmel's meditation on *the stranger* provides a fitting place to begin our examination of the legacy of qualitative research methods. This essay is of historical interest insofar as it did in fact serve as a favored model of the social researcher's role among some of the earliest qualitative sociologists at the University of Chicago (Chapoulie 1987). However, beyond its historical interest, it is also of substantive relevance to our topic. Simmel's essay speaks incisively to some of the basic issues that arise when we enter the worlds of others with no intention to assimilate to those worlds but only to more fully understand them.

Simmel does not write of the social scientist specifically. Instead, he writes generally of the role of one who has come to live with a social group that is not his or her own. This is important to keep in mind. Why? Because it suggests the insights available to people who assume this role may at times arise apart from (and perhaps indeed despite) any theoretical expectations engendered by their scientific training. Simmel's remarks imply that the insights available to the stranger are not quite the same as those that arise from efforts to confirm, falsify, extend, or reformulate received scientific wisdom. They arise more naturally from ongoing and direct contact with the group. At the same time, the stranger's insights are not identical with the local knowledge of local affairs possessed by group members themselves. The stranger is defined by the fact that s/he is not bound by the local economy of rights and obligations that ordinarily binds group members to each other. Thus, whereas the judgments of group members are generally informed by their specific positions within the group and the patterned associations, entitlements, and obligations that define those positions, the stranger's judgments flow from a position proximal to this network of relations but distinctly apart from it.

This position of detachment affords the stranger a type of objectivity, a freedom from the partisan interests and obligations that normally orient group members in their relations with one another. It also allows the stranger a level of *mobility* within the group that is generally denied to group members themselves. The stranger is less obliged to observe the boundaries that sometimes segregate group members or to conform to the class and status hierarchies that may fetter interaction between those of different stations within the group. The stranger may be privy to information that group members conceal from those with whom they are more closely affiliated. Precisely because s/he is an outsider, the stranger may be seen as someone with whom one might confide without threat of repercussions. Simmel also notes that "the stranger makes his appearance everywhere as a trader" (p. 144). Though this remark is a literal one regarding economic history, I like to think of it a bit more broadly. Applied to the practice of qualitative research, the image of the trader serves well to remind us that as fieldworkers we simultaneously inhabit at least two distinguishable worlds – the worlds with which we trade and the ones from which we trade. The image of the trader serves further to remind us of two facts central to qualitative research: (1) that as traders we most certainly owe a debt of exchange to those who allow us into their lives and worlds, and (2) that though we will very likely find a great deal that is interesting and unusual in the course of our travels, these discoveries will inevitably be viewed as variously "tradeworthy" by our friends and colleagues back home!

Finally, Simmel observes that, though essentially different, the stranger can never be *completely* alien to the group with whom s/he lives. Indeed, to be at all intelligible to one another the stranger and the native must strive to forge at least some degree of identity between themselves. Hence, this relation compels its participants to transcend the "custom, piety, and precedent" (p. 146) that binds them separately to their respective tribes and to seek out that which unites them as a more generally encompassing humanity. Stocking (1990, p. 713) makes a similar point to characterize the history of anthropology itself:

> to study the history of anthropology is to study the attempt to describe and to interpret or explain the "otherness" of populations encountered in the course of European overseas expansion. Although thus fundamentally (and oppositionally) diversitarian in impulse, such study has usually implied a reflexivity which re-encompassed European self and alien "other" within a unitary humankind.

In his essay, Stocking traces the paradigmatic frames that anthropologists have historically implemented in this effort. He argues that in the years prior to 1900, anthropological thought was largely divided into two dominant camps – one which invoked a Biblical frame to interpret and explain the diversity of the world's peoples and one which drew upon Graeco-Roman intellectual traditions. The former camp tended to explain the differentiation of humanity in degenerative terms – as indicative of the fall from God's grace that was suffered by the descendents of Adam and Eve. In opposition to this view, the later camp tended to explain human difference in more utilitarian terms. By their lights, otherness did not reflect the loss of divine guidance but the acquisition of new traits and new knowledge in efforts to satisfy basic needs in the face of diverse environmental conditions. Alongside these dominant traditions, rose a third which held the various human "races" stemmed from entirely distinct origins. These models eventually gave way to what was to become ethnology (the study of human cultural variation) and physical anthropology (the study of human physical variations) respectively.

Though early physical anthropologists received it coolly, Darwinian thought inspired a veritable revolution among ethnologists. European "armchair ethnologists" speculated of general evolutionary stages of human cultural development that cast non-European others as living incarnations of Europe's own prehistoric evolutionary past. An evolutionary continuum was drawn which linked the primitive mentality of non-European "savages" at one end with the rational mentality possessed by "civilized" Europeans at the other end. It was not long before this paradigm came to be articulated in overtly racist directions. Beginning in the late nineteenth century, Franz Boas attacked the idea of a "primitive mentality," arguing that variations in human thought processes were culturally conditioned and did not implicate our evolutionary inheritances as a species. At the same time, he and others began to promote a more systematic approach to data collection that gave rise to the modern tradition of ethnographic fieldwork. Eventually, thanks largely to the rise of Radcliffe-Brown's synchronic (read ahistorical) functionalist approach to research, social and cultural anthropologists grew increasingly uninterested in linking their ethnographic investigations of the present to either the sociohistorical, or the evolutionary, pasts of the societies they studied. By the mid-twentieth century, the archetypal approach to cultural anthropological research entailed a relatively ahistorical analyses of ethnographic data one had personally collected during a stint of fieldwork conducted among some fairly small population. It was this model of ethnographic research that was appropriated by Everett Hughes and other sociologists at the University of Chicago.

Chapoulie's essay traces the legacy of fieldwork in American sociology. He notes that while figures like Robert Park and W. I. Thomas were the first to introduce non-quantitative research methods to American sociology, it was Everett Hughes and Herbert Blumer who figured most prominently in affecting how later sociologists came to understand these methods. It was only after they were challenged by quantitative researchers that an explicit discourse on the specific strengths and proper implementation of qualitative methods began to flourish. The scientific value of qualitative methods was always fundamentally predicated on the paired claims that (1) social scientists must grasp the meanings that social actors themselves give to their activities, and (2) quantitative research methods do not adequately capture these meanings. Though many studies based on these claims have sought only to faithfully describe the "native's point of view," Chapoulie observes that efforts to produce only "pure" descriptions of people's experiences may be misguided. Qualitative researchers need not be bound by the theoretical assumptions of their profession, but this does not mean they are just passive receptacles of local meanings. Whether or not they reflect their scientific training, researchers inevitably confer their own meanings upon the events they observe. Because the study of members' meanings is itself an interpretive enterprise, we must resist construing it as "pure" description.

Between the analytic poles of "pure" description and "pure" hypothesis testing, one may locate the activity of creative social research. Apropos to this activity, Chapoulie finds in Hughes' work a worthy precedent for what he calls the "comparative method" of social research. The comparative method begins with a provisional reliance on categories drawn variously from one's professional milieu, one's research subjects themselves, or elsewhere. These categories are then articulated, refined, and reformulated by comparing their suitability to different research subjects, settings, and temporal periods. By continuously using them to facilitate comparison of empirical cases, our categories inevitably become "terms of art," increasingly implicative of the dispute domains in and for which they are used as opposed to any other discursive environment. In this sense such categories grow increasingly *analytic*. However, analytic categories so derived do not necessarily amount to formal theories. They are better understood as providing orienting frameworks for investigation "capable of guiding empirical work without reducing it to the simple verification [or falsification] of previously formulated hypotheses" (p. 279).

References

Chapoulie, Jean-Michel. 1987. "Everett C. Hughes and the Development of Fieldwork in Sociology." *Urban Life* 15: 259–98.

Simmel, Georg. [1908] 1971. "The Stranger." In *On Individuality and Social Forms: Selected Writings*. Edited by Donald N. Levine. Chicago: University of Chicago Press.

Stocking, George W., Jr. 1990. "Paradigmatic Traditions in the History of Anthropology." In *Companion to the History of Modern Science*. Edited by R. C. Olby, G. N. Cantor, J. R. R. Christie, and M. J. S. Hodge. London: Routledge.

Further Reading on the History of Anthropology and Sociology

Anthropology

Asad, Talal, ed. 1973. *Anthropology & the Colonial Encounter*. New York: Humanities Press.

Hodgen, Margaret T. 1964. *Early Anthropology in the Sixteenth and Seventeenth Centuries*. Philadelphia: University of Pennsylvania Press.

Kucklick, Henrika. 1991. *The Savage Within: The Social History of British Anthropology, 1885–1945*. Cambridge: Cambridge University Press.

Marcus, George E. and Michael M. J. Fischer. 1986. *Anthropology as Cultural Critique: An Experimental Moment in the Human Sciences*. Chicago: University of Chicago Press.

McGrane, Bernard. 1989. *Beyond Anthropology: Society and the Other*. New York: New York University Press.

Pagden, Anthony. 1982. *The Fall of Natural Man: The American Indian and the Origins of Comparative Ethnology*. Cambridge: Cambridge University Press.

Stocking, George W. 1987. *Victorian Anthropology*. New York: Free Press.

Sociology

Bulmer, Martin. 1984. *The Chicago School of Sociology: Institutionalization, Diversity and the Rise of Sociological Research*. Chicago: University of Chicago Press.

Fine, Gary Alan, ed. 1995. *A Second Chicago School?: The Development of a Postwar American Sociology*. Chicago: University of Chicago Press.

Hammersley, Martyn. 1989. *The Dilemma of Qualitative Method: Herbert Blumer and the Chicago Tradition*. London: Routledge.

Heritage, John. 1984. *Garfinkel and Ethnomethodology*. Cambridge: Polity Press.

Platt, Jennifer. 1983. "The Development of the 'Participant Observation' Method in Sociology: Origin myth and history." *Journal of the History of the Behavioral Sciences* 19: 379–93.

—— 1996. *A History of Sociological Research Methods in America, 1920–1960*. Cambridge: Cambridge University Press.

Viditch, Arthur J. and Sanford M. Lyman. 1994. "Qualitative Methods: Their History in Sociology and Anthropology." In *Handbook of Qualitative Research*. Edited by Norman K. Denzin and Yvonne S. Lincoln. Thousand Oaks, CA: Sage

Schegloff, Emanuel A. 1992. "Introduction." In *Lectures on Conversation, vol. 1*. By Harvey Sacks, edited by Gail Jefferson. Oxford: Blackwell.

1 The Stranger

Georg Simmel

If wandering, considered as a state of detachment from every given point in space, is the conceptual opposite of attachment to any point, then the sociological form of "the stranger" presents the synthesis, as it were, of both of these properties. (This is another indication that spatial relations not only are determining conditions of relationships among men, but are also symbolic of those relationships.) The stranger will thus not be considered here in the usual sense of the term, as the wanderer who comes today and goes tomorrow, but rather as the man who comes today and stays tomorrow – the potential wanderer, so to speak, who, although he has gone no further, has not quite got over the freedom of coming and going. He is fixed within a certain spatial circle – or within a group whose boundaries are analogous to spatial boundaries – but his position within it is fundamentally affected by the fact that he does not belong in it initially and that he brings qualities into it that are not, and cannot be, indigenous to it.

In the case of the stranger, the union of closeness and remoteness involved in every human relationship is patterned in a way that may be succinctly formulated as follows: the distance within this relation indicates that one who is close by is remote, but his strangeness indicates that one who is remote is near. The state of being a stranger is of course a completely positive relation; it is a specific form of interaction. The inhabitants of Sirius are not exactly strangers to us, at least not in the socio-logical sense of the word as we are considering it. In that sense they do not exist for us at all; they are beyond being far and near. The stranger is an element of the group itself, not unlike the poor and sundry "inner enemies" – an element whose member-ship within the group involves both being outside it and confronting it.

The following statements about the stranger are intended to suggest how factors of repulsion and distance work to create a form of being together, a form of union based on interaction.

In the whole history of economic activity the stranger makes his appearance everywhere as a trader, and the trader makes his as a stranger. As long as production for one's own needs is the general rule, or products are exchanged within a relatively small circle, there is no need for a middleman within the group. A trader is required only for goods produced outside the group. Unless there are people who wander out into foreign lands to buy these necessities, in which case they are themselves "strange" merchants in this other region, the trader *must* be a stranger; there is no opportunity for anyone else to make a living at it.

This position of the stranger stands out more sharply if, instead of leaving the place of his activity, he settles down there. In innumerable cases even this is possible only if he can live by trade as a middleman. Any closed economic group where land and handicrafts have been apportioned in a way that satisfies local demands will still support a livelihood for the trader. For trade alone makes possible unlimited combinations, and through it intelligence is constantly extended and applied in new areas, something that is much harder for the primary producer with his more limited mobility and his dependence on a circle of customers that can be expanded only very slowly. Trade can always absorb more men than can primary production. It is therefore the most suitable activity for the stranger, who intrudes as a super-numerary, so to speak, into a group in which all the economic positions are already occupied. The classic example of this is the history of European Jews. The stranger is by his very nature no owner of land – land not only in the physical sense but also metaphorically as a vital substance which is fixed, if not in space, then at least in an ideal position within the social environment.

Although in the sphere of intimate personal relations the stranger may be attract-ive and meaningful in many ways, so long as he is regarded as a stranger he is no "landowner" in the eyes of the other. Restriction to intermediary trade and often (as though sublimated from it) to pure finance gives the stranger the specific character of *mobility*. The appearance of this mobility within a bounded group occasions that synthesis of nearness and remoteness which constitutes the formal position of the stranger. The purely mobile person comes incidentally into contact with *every* single element but is not bound up organically, through established ties of kinship, locality, or occupation, with any single one.

Another expression of this constellation is to be found in the objectivity of the stranger. Because he is not bound by roots to the particular constituents and partisan dispositions of the group, he confronts all of these with a distinctly "objective" attitude, an attitude that does not signify mere detachment and nonparticipation, but is a distinct structure composed of remoteness and nearness, indifference and involvement. I refer to my analysis of the dominating positions gained by aliens, in the discussion of superordination and subordination,[1] typified by the practice in certain Italian cities of recruiting their judges from outside, because no native was free from entanglement in family interests and factionalism.

Connected with the characteristic of objectivity is a phenomenon that is found chiefly, though not exclusively, in the stranger who moves on. This is that he often receives the most surprising revelations and confidences, at times reminiscent of a confessional, about matters which are kept carefully hidden from everybody with whom one is close. Objectivity is by no means nonparticipation, a condition that is altogether outside the distinction between subjective and objective orientations. It is rather a positive and definite kind of participation, in the same way that the objectivity of a theoretical observation clearly does not mean that the mind is a passive tabula rasa on which things inscribe their qualities, but rather signifies the full activity of a mind working according to its own laws, under conditions that exclude accidental distortions and emphases whose individual and subjective differ-ences would produce quite different pictures of the same object.

Objectivity can also be defined as freedom. The objective man is not bound by ties which could prejudice his perception, his understanding, and his assessment of data. This freedom, which permits the stranger to experience and treat even his close relationships as though from a bird's-eye view, contains many dangerous possibilities.

From earliest times, in uprisings of all sorts the attacked party has claimed that there has been incitement from the outside, by foreign emissaries and agitators. Insofar as this has happened, it represents an exaggeration of the specific role of the stranger: he is the freer man, practically and theoretically; he examines conditions with less prejudice; he assesses them against standards that are more general and more objective; and his actions are not confined by custom, piety, or precedent.[2]

Finally, the proportion of nearness and remoteness which gives the stranger the character of objectivity also finds practical expression in the more *abstract* nature of the relation to him. That is, with the stranger one has only certain *more general* qualities in common, whereas the relation with organically connected persons is based on the similarity of just those specific traits which differentiate them from the merely universal. In fact, all personal relations whatsoever can be analyzed in terms of this scheme. They are not determined only by the existence of certain common characteristics which the individuals share in addition to their individual differences, which either influence the relationship or remain outside of it. Rather, the kind of effect which that commonality has on the relation essentially depends on whether it exists only among the participants themselves, and thus, although general within the relation, is specific and incomparable with respect to all those on the outside, or whether the participants feel that what they have in common is so only because it is common to a group, a type, or mankind in general. In the latter case, the effect of the common features becomes attenuated in proportion to the size of the group bearing the same characteristics. The commonality provides a basis for unifying the members, to be sure; but it does not specifically direct *these* particular persons to one another. A similarity so widely shared could just as easily unite each person with every possible other. This, too, is evidently a way in which a relationship includes both nearness and remoteness simultaneously. To the extent to which the similarities assume a universal nature, the warmth of the connection based on them will acquire an element of coolness, a sense of the contingent nature of precisely *this* relation – the connecting forces have lost their specific, centripetal character.

In relation to the stranger, it seems to me, this constellation assumes an extraordinary preponderance in principle over the individual elements peculiar to the relation in question. The stranger is close to us insofar as we feel between him and ourselves similarities of nationality or social position, of occupation or of general human nature. He is far from us insofar as these similarities extend beyond him and us, and connect us only because they connect a great many people.

A trace of strangeness in this sense easily enters even the most intimate relationships. In the stage of first passion, erotic relations strongly reject any thought of generalization. A love such as this has never existed before; there is nothing to compare either with the person one loves or with our feelings for that person. An estrangement is wont to set in (whether as cause or effect is hard to decide) at the moment when this feeling of uniqueness disappears from the relationship. A skepticism regarding the intrinsic value of the relationship and its value for us adheres to the very thought that in this relation, after all, one is only fulfilling a general human destiny, that one has had an experience that has occurred a thousand times before, and that, if one had not accidentally met this precise person, someone else would have acquired the same meaning for us.

Something of this feeling is probably not absent in any relation, be it ever so close, because that which is common to two is perhaps never common *only* to them but belongs to a general conception which includes much else besides, many *possibilities* of similarities. No matter how few of these possibilities are realized and how often we may forget about them, here and there, nevertheless, they crowd in like shadows between men, like a mist eluding every designation, which must congeal into solid corporeality for it to be called jealousy. Perhaps this is in many cases a more general, at least more insurmountable, strangeness than that due to differences and obscurities. It is strangeness caused by the fact that similarity, harmony, and closeness are accompanied by the feeling that they are actually not the exclusive property of this particular relation, but stem from a more general one – a relation that potentially includes us and an indeterminate number of others, and therefore prevents that relation which alone was experienced from having an inner and exclusive necessity.

On the other hand, there is a sort of "strangeness" in which this very connection on the basis of a general quality embracing the parties is precluded. The relation of the Greeks to the barbarians is a typical example; so are all the cases in which the general characteristics one takes as peculiarly and merely human are disallowed to the other. But here the expression "the stranger" no longer has any positive meaning. The relation with him is a non-relation; he is not what we have been discussing here: the stranger as a member of the group itself.

As such, the stranger is near and far *at the same time*, as in any relationship based on merely universal human similarities. Between these two factors of nearness and distance, however, a peculiar tension arises, since the consciousness of having only the absolutely general in common has exactly the effect of putting a special emphasis on that which is not common. For a stranger to the country, the city, the race, and so on, what is stressed is again nothing individual, but alien origin, a quality which he has, or could have, in common with many other strangers. For this reason strangers are not really perceived as individuals, but as strangers of a certain type. Their remoteness is no less general than their nearness.

This form appears, for example, in so special a case as the tax levied on Jews in Frankfurt and elsewhere during the Middle Ages. Whereas the tax paid by Christian citizens varied according to their wealth at any given time, for every single Jew the tax was fixed once and for all. This amount was fixed because the Jew had his social position as a *Jew*, not as the bearer of certain objective contents. With respect to taxes every other citizen was regarded as possessor of a certain amount of wealth, and his tax could follow the fluctuations of his fortune. But the Jew as taxpayer was first of all a Jew, and thus his fiscal position contained an invariable element. This appears most forcefully, of course, once the differing circumstances of individual Jews are no longer considered, limited though this consideration is by fixed assessments, and all strangers pay exactly the same head tax.

Despite his being inorganically appended to it, the stranger is still an organic member of the group. Its unified life includes the specific conditioning of this element. Only we do not know how to designate the characteristic unity of this position otherwise than by saying that it is put together of certain amounts of nearness and of remoteness. Although both these qualities are found to some extent in all relationships, a special proportion and reciprocal tension between them produce the specific form of the relation to the "stranger."

Notes

1 Simmel refers here to a passage which may be found in *The Sociology of Georg Simmel*, pp. 216–21.
2 Where the attacked parties make such an assertion falsely, they do so because those in higher positions tend to exculpate inferiors who previously have been in a close, solidary relationship with them. By introducing the fiction that the rebels were not really guilty, but only instigated, so they did not actually start the rebellion, they exonerate themselves by denying that there were any real grounds for the uprising.

2 Paradigmatic Traditions in the History of Anthropology

George W. Stocking, Jr.

I Defining the Domain of Anthropology

In 1904 Franz Boas defined the domain of anthropological knowledge as "the biological history of mankind in all its varieties; linguistics applied to people without written languages; the ethnology of people without historic records; and prehistoric archeology". More than any other "anthropologist", Boas (1858–1942) may be said to exemplify the putative unity of this domain, since (virtually alone among his confrères) he made significant contributions to each of these four inquiries in the course of his long career. But despite the fact that he was perhaps the most important single figure in the institutionalisation of an academic discipline called "anthropology" in university departments in the United States, Boas already felt in 1904 that there were "indications of its breaking up". The "biological, linguistic and ethno-logic-archeological methods are so distinct", he believed, that the time was "rapidly drawing near" when the two former branches of anthropology would be taken over by specialists in those disciplines, and "anthropology pure and simple will deal with the customs and beliefs of the less civilized peoples only...."[1]

Given the weight of institutional inertia and of residual commitment to the norm of disciplinary unity, it remains arguable today whether Boas' prediction is yet likely to be achieved. Nevertheless, the fact that its leading practical exemplar regarded the unity of anthropology as historically contingent rather than epistemologically determined suggests that no general historical account of that "science" may take its unity for granted. In spite of the all-embracing etymological singularity of the term anthropology (Greek *anthropos*: man; *logos*: discourse), the diverse discourses that may be historically subsumed by it have only in certain moments and places been fused into anything approximating a unified science of humankind. In continental Europe in Boas' time, "anthropology" referred (and often does today) to what in the Anglo-American tradition has been called "physical anthropology". As such, it was distinguishable from and historically opposed to "ethnology" – a discourse that, etymologically, was somewhat more diversitarian (Greek *ethnos*: nation).

In this context, the historical development of anthropology may be contrasted to two ideal typical views of disciplinary development. The first is a Comtean hier-archical model in which the impulse of positive knowledge is successively extended into more complex domains of natural phenomena. The second is a genealogical model in which, within each domain, disciplines may be visualised as growing from a single undifferentiated "ur" discourse (with the biological sciences developing out of natural history, the humanities out of philology and the social sciences out of moral philosophy). As against these two fission models, "anthropology" in its inclusive Anglo-American sense is better viewed as an imperfect fusion of modes of inquiry that were quite distinct in origin and in character – deriving in fact from all three of these undifferentiated "ur"-discourses.

In so far as a common denominator may be extracted from Boas' contingent descriptive definition of anthropology, it would seem to imply an opposition between Europeans, who have written languages and historical records, and "others", who have not. Indeed, it may be argued that the greatest retrospective unity of the discourses subsumed within the rubric "anthropology" is to be found in this substantive concern with the peoples who were long stigmatised as "savages", and who, in the nineteenth century, tended to be excluded from other human scientific disciplines by the very process of their substantive-cum-methodological definition (the economist's concern with the money economy; the historian's concern with written documents, etc.). From this point of view, to study the history of anthropology is to study the attempt to describe and to interpret or explain the "otherness" of populations encountered in the course of European overseas expansion. Although thus fundamentally (and oppositionally) diversitarian in impulse, such study has usually implied a reflexivity which re-encompassed European self and alien "other" within a unitary humankind. This history of anthropology may thus be viewed as a continuing (and complex) dialectic between the universalism of "anthropos" and the diversitarianism of "ethnos" or, from the perspective of particular historical moments, between the Enlightenment and the Romantic impulse. Anthropology's "recurrent dilemma" has been how to square both generic human rationality and the biological unity of mankind with "the great natural variation of cultural forms".[2]

2   The Biblical, Developmental and Polygenetic Traditions

A second unifying tendency within Boas' definition is historical, or more generally, diachronic, since history in the narrow sense seemed precluded by the lack of documents. For Boas, the "otherness" which is the subject-matter of anthropology was to be explained as the product of change of time. Although Boas in fact wrote on the verge of a revolutionary shift towards a more synchronic anthropology, the history of anthropology up until his time may be schematised in terms of the interplay of two major diachronic traditions that were, in a broad sense, paradigmatic, both of them counterpointed by a more synchronic tradition which, because of its heterodoxy, only very briefly achieved paradigmatic status. In the discussion that follows, these traditions will be designated as the "biblical" (or "ethnological"), the "developmental" (or "evolutionist"), and the "polygenetic" (or "physical anthropological").

The ultimate roots of anthropological thought are more often traced to the Greek than to the biblical tradition. However, it may be argued that during the period of European expansion the underlying paradigmatic framework for the explanation of "otherness" derived from the first ten chapters of Genesis. Many intellectual currents contributed to anthropological speculation, among them environmentalist and humoralist assumptions from the Hippocratic and Galenic traditions, hierarchical notions from the "Great Chain of Being", mediaeval conceptions of the monstrous, etc. But the dominant paradigmatic tradition (paradigmatic in the sense of providing a more or less coherent *a priori* framework of assumption defining both relevant problems and the data and methods for their solution) was that iconically embodied in the second of John Speed's "Genealogies of Holy Scriptures" in the King James Bible. There, growing from the roof of the Ark resting on the top of Mt. Ararat in Armenia, was a genealogical tree with three major branches: the descendants of Japhet in Europe, of Sem in Asia and of Ham in Africa, traced on out to their various representatives in the ancient world ("Phrigians", "Bactrians", "Babylonians", etc.).[3] In this context, the fundamental anthropological problem was to establish putative historical links between every present human group and one of the branches of a biblical ethnic tree that linked all of humankind to a single descendant of Adam and Eve. Since what had diversified humankind in the first instance was the confusion of tongues at Babel, the privileged data for re-establishing connections were similarities of language, augmented by such similarities of culture as survived the degenerative processes which were a con-comitant of migration towards the earth's imagined corners. Since all humans were offspring of a single family, and ultimately of a single pair, the physical differences among them were secondary phenomena, characteristically attributable to the influence of the environments through which they had migrated during the six millennia allowed by the biblical chronology, if not to the direct intervention of God (as in "the curse of Ham").

The biblical anthropological tradition, which saw the (characteristically degenerative) differentiation of humankind in terms of movement through space within a limited and event-specific historical time, may be contrasted with a Graeco-Roman paradigmatic tradition deriving from the speculations of Ionian materialists. Perhaps most influentially embodied in Lucretius's *De Rerum Natura*, this tradition saw time as an enabling rather than a limiting factor, and conceived diachronic change in progressive processual rather than degenerative historical terms. Rather than losing divinely given knowledge as they moved through space in time, human groups acquired knowledge gradually, responding to organic needs and environmental stimuli in an adaptive utilitarian manner, as they groped their way forwards step by step from a state near the brutes to that of the most advanced civil society. Although human differentiation was construed in terms of status on a generalised developmental scale rather as the product of a specific sequence of historical events, the Graeco-Roman paradigm was still in a broad sense diachronic.

While the biblical and the developmental traditions represent the dominant paradigmatic alternatives in Western anthropological thought before 1900, it is useful to distinguish a third major paradigmatic tradition: the polygenetic. Foreshadowed in tribal and classical notions of autochthonous origin, it became a matter of more serious speculation in the aftermath of the discovery of the New World, the peopling of which posed a major problem for the orthodox monogenetic tradition. A few writers, most notoriously Isaac de la Peyrère in 1655, went so far as to suggest that the peoples of the New World did not descend from Adam. However, it was nearly a century before Linnaeus (1707–78) included mankind (American/choleric; European/sanguine; Asiatic/melancholic; African/phlegmatic) in the *System of Nature* (1735), and still a generation later before systematic comparative human anatomical data began to be collected. Even then, most of the early physical anthropologists remained, like Johann Blumenbach (1752–1840), staunchly monogenist. But given the growth of comparative data within the framework of a static pre-evolutionary view of biological species, a "polygenetic" approach to human differentiation became in the nineteenth century an alternative to be considered seriously. From this point of view, human "races" (often distinguished by the forms of their crania) were, like animal species, aboriginally distinct. Unaffected by the forces of environment, they had remained constant throughout the relatively short span of human historical time – as the images on the 4,000 year-old monuments discovered by Napoleon's expedition to Egypt confirmed.

3   The Darwinian Revolution and the Differentiation of National Anthropological Traditions

Although Rousseau (1712–78) had envisioned in 1755 a unified science of man carried on by philosopher-voyagers who, shaking off "the yoke of national prejudices", would "learn to know men by their likenesses and their differences",[4] it was more than a century before his dream began to be realised. For most of that time, the vast bulk of anthropological data was collected incidentally by travellers, missionaries, colonisers and naturalists. In so far as the activity was tied to a knowledge-tradition, it was much more likely to be that of natural history than social theory. Furthermore, the forms of "anthropology" institutionalised in the major European nations differed strikingly in their relation to the three paradigmatic traditions just described.

During the pre-Darwinian nineteenth century, the focal anthropological issue was posed by the explosion of the data of human diversity that was produced by European expansion, in the context of advances in the regnant sciences in the human and biological domains – comparative linguistics and comparative anatomy. From a classificatory and/or genetic point of view, the central question was "is mankind one or many?". Until mid-century, comparative Indo-European (i.e. Japhetic) linguistics provided a model of inquiry which promised to provide a classification of humankind in terms of its most distinctive feature, but which would also link all human groups to a single source. Exemplified in the works of the staunchly monogenist James Cowles Prichard (1786–1848), this goal was institutionalised in several of the "ethnological" societies founded around 1840.

By the 1850s, however, a distinctly physical anthropological current, modelling itself on comparative anatomy and often polygenist in tendency, had begun to separate itself from the ethnological (formerly biblical) paradigm. Foreshadowed in the works of certain French investigators, and in the "American School" of Samuel G. Morton (1799–1851), this trend was realised institutionally in the "anthropological" societies founded by Paul Broca (1824–80) in Paris in 1859 and by James Hunt (1833–69) in London in 1863. Although the term "anthropological" had in fact been previously employed as a theological/philosophical category, it was now used to affirm the need for a naturalistic study of humankind as one or more physical species in the animal world.

This newly asserted physical anthropological tendency in fact proved resistant to Darwinism, which seemed to the polygenetically-inclined simply a new and speculative form of monogenism. However, the Darwinian revolution was to have a major impact on speculation in the older ethnological tradition. On the one hand, the greatly extended "antiquity of man", confirmed by the discoveries at Brixham

Cave in 1858, made the gradual formation of contemporary races by modification of a single ape-like progenitor seem more plausible. On the other, the revolution in time made extremely unlikely the ethnological task of establishing plausible historical connections over the whole span of human existence. Furthermore, Darwinism posed a problem for which the new "pre-historic" archeology offered extremely inadequate evidence: providing a convincing evolutionary account of the cultural development that might link modern man with an ape-like ancestor. In this context, the developmental paradigm came again to the forefront of anthropological attention in the last third of the nineteenth century, especially in the Anglo-American tradition.

During this period, socio-cultural evolutionists attempted to synthesise the data of contemporary "savagery" collected by travellers and naturalists (including that now obtained by correspondence or in response to more formal questionnaires such as the *Notes and Queries in Anthropology* prepared by a committee of the British Association for the Advancement of Science in 1874). By arranging such present synchronic data on a diachronic scale, it was possible for "armchair" anthropologists to construct generalised stage-sequences of development in each area of human culture. In Britain, E. B. Tylor (1832–1917) traced the evolution of religion from primitive "animism" through polytheism to monotheism, while John McLennan (1827–81) followed the evolution of marriage from primitive promiscuity through polyandry to monogamy. In the United States, Lewis Henry Morgan (1818–81) traced a more general development from "lower savagery" through three phases of "barbarism" up to "civilisation".

These sequences depended on a generalised assumption of human "psychic unity", which enabled anthropologists to reason backwards from an irrational "survival" in a higher stage to the rational utilitarian practice underlying it. However, the sequences thus reconstructed by the "comparative method" in fact assumed a polar opposition between "primitive" and "civilised" mentality. And in the mixed Darwinian/Lamarckian context of late nineteenth-century biological thought these cultural evolutionary sequences took on a racialist character. The human brain was seen as having been gradually enlarged by the accumulative experience of the civilising process, and the races of the world were ranked on a double scale of colour and culture (as when Tylor suggested that the Australian, Tahitian, Aztec, Chinese and Italian "races" formed a single ascending cultural sequence). While much of day-to-day anthropological inquiry reflected a continuing interest in the ethnological affinities of different groups, what is sometimes called "classical evolutionism" was both the theoretical cynosure and the dominant ideological influence in anthropology in the later nineteenth century.

In general, anthropological thought in the late nineteenth century attempted to subsume the study of human phenomena within positivistic natural science. However, "anthropology" itself was by no means a trans-national scientific category. In England, the post-Darwinian intellectual synthesis of ethnological and polygenist tendencies in "classical evolutionism" was reflected institutionally in 1871 by the unification of the Ethnological and Anthropological Societies in the Anthropological Institute. In the United States, a similarly inclusive viewpoint was evident in J. W. Powell's governmental Bureau of Ethnology (1879), which, despite its title, had as its avowed mission the organisation of "anthropologic" research among American

Indians. In principle if not always in practice, "anthropology" in the Anglo-American tradition attempted to unify the four fields later specified by Franz Boas. By contrast, on the continent where Darwinism did not exert such a strongly unifying influence, "anthropology" continued to refer primarily to physical anthropology. Although Broca's École d'Anthropologie included chairs in sociology and ethnology, those studies had for the most part a quite separate development, largely under the aegis of Emile Durkheim (1858–1917) and his students. And although by 1900 the fossil gap between existing primate forms and the anomalously large-brained Neanderthals had been narrowed by the discovery of "Java Man", physical anthropology continued to be heavily influenced by a static, typological approach to the classification of human "races", primarily on the basis of measurements of the human cranium, using the "cephalic index" developed by Anders Retzius (1796–1860) in the 1840s.

4   The Critique of Evolutionism in American Cultural Anthropology

In this context, the critique of evolutionary assumption elaborated by Franz Boas between 1890 and 1910 contributed to a revolutionary re-orientation in the history of anthropology. Born of a liberal and assimilated German-Jewish family, and trained in both physics and geography, Boas began his career from a position of cultural marginality and scientific intermediacy, somewhere between the dominant positivistic naturalism on the one hand, and the romantic and *Geisteswissenschaft* traditions, on the other (an opposition classically delineated in his 1885 essay on "The Study of Geography").

After a year of ethnogeographic fieldwork among the Baffin Island Eskimo, Boas settled in the United States, carrying on general anthropological fieldwork among the Indians of the Pacific northwest, where he worked under the auspices both of Powell's Bureau of Ethnology and a committee of the British Association for the Advancement of Science chaired by Tylor. By 1896, Boas had developed a neo-ethnological critique of "the comparative method" of classical evolutionism. Arguing on the basis of a study of the borrowing and diffusion of cultural elements among Northwest Coast Indians, he insisted that the detailed historical investigations of specific culture histories must precede the attempt to derive laws of cultural development. Parallel to this, Boas criticised the evolutionary idea of "primitive mentality", arguing that human thought generally was conditioned by culturally varying bodies of traditional assumption – a viewpoint sustained also by his analyses of American-Indian grammatical categories. Similarly, his physical anthropological researches – including a study of the modification of headform in the children of European immigrants – called into question racialist arguments based on cranial typology.

Boas' anthropology was characteristically critical rather than constructive. Nevertheless, his work laid the basis for the modern anthropological conception of culture as pluralistic, relativistic and largely freed from biological determinism. His student, A. L. Kroeber (1876–1960), a major articulator of the cultural viewpoint, initially invoked the autonomy of the cultural in 1917, simply as a heuristic device, and since then, there has been a recurrent anthropological interest in the culture/biology interface. But the general thrust of Boasian anthropology was to mark off a domain from which biological determinism was excluded. Initially, that delimitation depended on an insistence on the essentially historical character of cultural phenomena, as exemplified in Edward Sapir's *Time Perspective in Aboriginal American Culture: A Study of Method* (1916). But if the first generation Boasians occasionally spoke of themselves as the "American historical school", the major thrust of Boasian anthropology after 1920 was in fact away from historical reconstruction. On the one hand, the emergence of a more time-specific archeology (with the development of stratigraphic approaches after 1910, augmented after the Second World War by carbon 14 dating) tended to devalue historical reconstructions based on the distribution of "culture elements" over "cultural areas". On the other, the Boasian interest in the cultural basis of human psychological differences led towards a synchronic study of the integration of cultures and of the relation of "culture and personality" – tendencies archetypified in Ruth Benedict's widely-influential *Patterns of Culture* (1934).

Although the "culture and personality" movement and the study of "acculturation" were being superseded by the 1950s by more sociologically oriented approaches, "culture" remained the predominant focus of anthropological inquiry in the United States. As graduate training began its explosive spread beyond the four centres founded before the First World War (Harvard, Columbia, Berkeley and Pennsylvania) and the half dozen additions of the inter-war period, it usually continued to include at least introductory training in each of the "four fields". Most practitioners, however, had long since specialised in no more than one of them; and physical anthropologists, linguists and archeologists had, during the inter-war period, founded their own professional organisations. While the American Anthropological Association (founded in 1902) continued to include specialists in all four fields, it was dominated by those who specialised in what Boas and the first generation of his students still called "ethnology" – which by the 1930s was in the process of being rechristened "cultural anthropology".

5   Fieldwork, Functionalism and British Social Anthropology

In Great Britain, the early twentieth-century "revolution in anthropology" took a somewhat different course. As in the United States, where the Boasians carried on and elaborated the "fieldwork" tradition pioneered by the Bureau of Ethnology, a key factor was the development of a corps of academically-trained ethnographic fieldworkers. However, what was to become the archetypical field situation for British anthropologists differed considerably from that of their early Boasian counterparts. In the United States, where transcontinental railways facilitated relatively short visits to Indian reservations, ethnographers studied the "memory culture" of elder informants, often by collecting "texts" (which Boas thought might provide for a non-literate culture the equivalent of the documentary heritage that was the basis of humanistic study in the Western tradition). By contrast, British ethnographers, travelling weeks by sea to the darker reaches of the world's largest empire, became the archetypical practitioners of extended "participant observation" of the current behaviour of still-functioning social groups. Foreshadowed in the work of Baldwin Spencer (1860–1929) and Frank Gillen (1855–1912) among the Australian Arunta in 1896, implemented among the graduates of A. C. Haddon's Torres Straits

Expedition (1898) and by younger members of the "Cambridge School" in the first decade of the century, the "lone-ethnographer" model of inquiry was in fact formalised by W. H. R. Rivers (1864–1922) in his description of the "concrete method" for the 1912 revision of *Notes and Queries*. The person most closely associated with this development, however, was Bronislaw Malinowski (1883–1942), who came from Poland in 1910 to study under Edward Westermarck (1862–1939) and Charles Seligman (1873–1940) at the London School of Economics. During the First World War, Malinowski spent almost two years among the Trobriand Islanders off the Northeast Coast of New Guinea, and in 1922 he gave the new methodology its mythic charter in the opening chapter of *Argonauts of the Western Pacific*.

During the 1920s, Malinowski moved briefly toward Freudian psychoanalysis by offering the matrifocal Trobriand family to suggest a modification of the universal Oedipus Complex. However, there was no British analogue to the American culture and personality movement. The latter may be regarded as offering an explanatory alternative to nineteenth-century evolutionary assertions of racial mental differences. In Britain, however, the critique of evolutionism focused not on its biological implications, but rather on its tendency, archetypified in the *Golden Bough* of James G. Frazer (1854–1941), to explain human behaviour in intellectualist utilitarian terms. By 1900, attacks had already begun on Tylor's doctrine of animism, which had explained human religious belief as a premature and failed science (with the experience of dreams and death suggesting the hypothesis of a soul distinct from the human body). Echoing William James, R. R. Marett (1866–1943) suggested a "pre-animistic" basis of religious belief in the much more effect-laden Melanesian concept of *mana* (an awe-inspiring supernatural power manifesting itself in the natural world). During the following decade, theoretical discussion centred on the mixed socio-religious phenomenon of totemism, which McLennan had defined in 1869 in terms of the linkage of animistic belief and exogamous matrilineal social organisation. To this, William Robertson Smith (1846–1894) had added the idea of the occasional communal consumption of the totem animal – an armchair conception which to Frazer seemed confirmed ethnographically by Spencer and Gillen's research among the Arunta. In the decade before the First World War, social anthropological debate swirled about the problem of totemism, with special reference to the Arunta and other Australian data, which were assumed by evolutionists to provide evidence of the most primitive human state.

It was in this context that British anthropology, which in its Tylorian and Frazerian phase gave priority to the problem of religious belief, shifted towards the study of religious ritual, and more generally, toward the study of kinship and social organisation, which had been a special concern of the American evolutionist Lewis Henry Morgan during his pre-evolutionary "ethnological" phase. Building on his own pioneering ethnographic study of the Iroquois in the 1840s, Morgan had attempted to solve the problem of the peopling of America by using an ethnographic questionnaire to collect world-wide data on *Systems of Consanguinity and Affinity* (1869). Recast in developmental terms, his distinction between the "classificatory" and "descriptive" systems of kinship provided a conceptual framework for the ethnographic work of his Australian correspondents Lorimer Fison (1832–1907) and A. W. Howitt (1830–1908). Augmented by the "genealogical method" developed by Rivers in the Torres Straits in 1898, Morgan's approach was eventually to provide the conceptual groundwork for modern British social anthropology, although not, however, until it had been detached from its diachronic evolutionary framework.

That process took place in two phases in the work of Rivers and his student A. R. Radcliffe-Brown (1881–1955). Rivers himself underwent a "conversion" from evolutionism to a diffusionary "ethnological analysis of culture" in 1911. However, his attempt to reconstruct *The History of Melanesian Society* (1916) was still heavily dependent on the evolutionary concept of "survival" which assumed that certain existing social customs or kinship terms need not be explained in terms of their present function, but rather in terms of their correspondence with prior social organisational forms. In contrast, Radcliffe-Brown moved away from evolutionism via the more functionalist sociology of Emile Durkheim. His break with Rivers focused specifically on the utility of "survivals" in sociological analysis, and involved a general rejection of any "conjectural" approach to diachronic problems in "social anthropology", which in 1923 he took some pains to differentiate from "ethnology".

At that time British anthropology was excited by the confrontation between the "heliolithic" diffusionism of Rivers's disciples Grafton Elliot Smith (1871–1937) and William Perry (1889–1940) at University College London and the psycho-biological functionalism of Malinowski at the London School of Economics. Sustained by grants from the Rockefeller Foundation, Malinowskian functionalism had, by 1930, become the dominant British current. But during the next few years some of Malinowski's more important students shifted their theoretical allegiance to Radcliffe-Brown, who after two decades of academic wanderings (from Cape Town to Sydney to Chicago), finally succeeded in 1937 to the chair at Oxford. Although the Association of Social Anthropologists formed at Oxford in 1946 included representatives of several different view-points, it was Radcliffe-Brown's synchronic natural scientific study of "social systems" – overlaid upon the Malinowskian fieldwork tradition – that gave British social anthropology its distinctive character.

6   The Synchronic Revolution, the "Classical Period" and the Emergence of International Anthropology

Despite these differences of phase and focus, there were many common features in the development of British social and American cultural anthropology in the first half of the twentieth century. In both countries, anthropology in the pre-academic museum period had been oriented largely towards the collection of material objects (whether artefacts or bones) carried into the present from the past; in both cases there was a dramatic turn towards the observational study of behaviour in the present. Although an interest in evolutionary or historical questions never disappeared entirely from either national tradition, anthropological inquiry was no longer primarily conceived in diachronic terms. And while Radcliffe-Brown insisted, during his Chicago period, on the differences between his viewpoint and the more dilute "functionalism" of some American cultural anthropologists, there is a looser sense in which one may speak of synchronic functionalism as a paradigm in the Anglo-American tradition. This was even more the case after the Second World War, when American anthropologists went overseas in large numbers for fieldwork, and began at home to feel the influence of functionalist theory in American sociology.

In both countries, one may speak of anthropology as having become "ethnographicised". Although the goal of cross-cultural comparison and scientific generalisation continued to be acknowledged, the most distinctive common feature of Anglo-American anthropology in what may be called its "classical" period (c. 1925–c. 1965) was the central role of ethnographic fieldwork. Rather than providing items of information for armchair anthropological theorists, fieldwork became the certifying criterion of membership in the anthropological community and the underpinning of its central methodological values; i.e. participant observation in small-scale communities, conceived holistically and relativistically, and given a privileged role in the constitution of theory. In both countries, this ethnographically-oriented study of social and cultural behaviour tended to separate from and to dominate the other anthropological subdisciplines, although in the more pluralistic structure of American academic life, the ideal of a "general anthropology" uniting the traditional "four fields" continued to have a certain potency.

Elsewhere, however, the course of sub-disciplinary development was rather different. On the European continent, where the inclusive "four field" tradition had never taken root, physical anthropology continued to have a largely separate development on into the twentieth century, and to be relatively unaffected by the Boasian critique – especially in Germany, where during the Nazi period, the discipline was redefined as *Rassenkunde*. In Germany and in central Europe, the ethnological tradition continued to be strongly diffusionist and historical up until the mid-twentieth century, although some ethnographic fieldwork was carried on. In France a modern ethnographic tradition did not develop until after the founding in the 1920s of the Institut d'Ethnologie, in which Durkheim's nephew Marcel Mauss played a leading role. It was not until 1982 that the French equivalents of cultural anthropologists were to take the lead in founding the Société d'Anthropologie française after the American model. This development reflected not only the intellectual interchange that had occurred between the French and the Anglo-American traditions after 1960 under the influence of the "structuralism" of Claude Lévi-Strauss (b. 1909) but also the influence of a tendency that can be called "international anthropology", or the internationalisation of the Anglo-American tradition.

Although international congresses of "anthropologists" or "prehistorians" or "Americanists" had been held periodically since the 1860s, it is only since the Second World War that International Congresses of Anthropological and Ethnological Sciences have been held on a regular basis over a long period (in Philadelphia, Moscow, Tokyo, Chicago, Vancouver, Delhi and Zagreb). Reinforced after 1960 by the international journal *Current Anthropology*, edited by Sol Tax (b. 1907), these congresses have been at the same time forums for diversity and media for the diffusion of a certain homogenising tendency, in which socio-cultural anthropology in the emergent Anglo-Franco-American mode has predominated, but the other major sub-disciplines have continued to be represented. However, the embracive "four field" conception associated with the American tradition has still had a certain inertial influence, reinforced by the overwhelming numerical predominance of American anthropologists within the world anthropological community.

7   The "Crisis" and "Reinvention" of Anthropology

In the very period in which an "international anthropology" began to be realised, however, there were dramatic changes in the world historical relationship of the peoples who had traditionally provided the scholars and the subject-matter of anthropological inquiry. For more than a century, the anticipated disappearance of "savage" (or "primitive" or "tribal" or "pre-literate") peoples under the impact of European expansion had been a major impetus to ethnographic research, which was carried on under an umbrella of colonial power. By the 1930s, these categories had already become problematic, and field research was beginning to be undertaken in "complex" societies. But despite the postwar interest in peasant communities and the processes of "modernisation", anthropology retained its archetypically asymmetrical character, as a study of dark-skinned "others" by light-skinned Euro-Americans. With the end of colonial empires, however, the peoples anthropologists had traditionally studied were now part of "new nations" oriented towards rapid socio-cultural change and their leaders were often unreceptive to an inquiry which, even after the critique of evolutionary racial assumption, continued to be premised on socio-cultural asymmetry. Indeed, many Third World intellectuals now began to regard as ideologically retrograde (and even as racist) the characteristic modern anthropological attitude of relativistic tolerance of cultural differences. What had served in the 1930s to defend "others" against racialism seemed now to justify the perpetuation of a backwardness founded on exploitation. In the politically-charged context of major episodes of post-colonial warfare, there had developed by the late 1960s what some were inclined to call the "crisis of anthropology".

The sense of malaise – which was widespread in the human sciences – manifested itself in a number of ways: substantively, ideologically, methodologically, epistemologically, theoretically, demographically and institutionally. In the face of rapid social change and restrictions on access to field sites, it was no longer realistic, even normatively, to regard the recovery of pure, uncontaminated non-European "otherness" as the privileged substantive focus of anthropological inquiry. Nor was it possible to regard such inquiry as ethically neutral, or innocent of political consequences. A new consciousness of the inherently problematic reflexivity of participant observation called into question both the methodological and epistemological assumptions of traditional ethnographic fieldwork. In the context of a general questioning of positivist assumption in the human sciences, there were signs of a shift from homeostatic theoretical orientations to more dynamic ones. And even the very growth of the field was now a problem, as the government funding of the 1950s and 1960s began to be restricted, and PhDs began to overflow their accustomed academic niches, beyond which anthropology had yet to establish a viable claim to significant domestic social utility. In the face of predictions of the "end of anthropology", there were, by the early 1970s, radical calls for its "reinvention".

The majority of anthropologists, however – reflecting either a residue of prelapsarian confidence or a sense of the weight of institutional inertia – seem to have taken for granted that the discipline would carry on indefinitely. And indeed, it seemed clear that by the mid-1980s, the crisis had been domesticated. A decade after the call for the discipline's "reinvention", the major academic anthropology departments continued to carry on a kind of "business as usual", despite the difficulties of funding research and the still-constricted job market for the students they were training. Nevertheless, it seems clear that the "classical" period of modern anthropology had come to an end sometime after 1960, and the usual business of post-classical anthropology differed in significant respects from what had gone before.

8   Reflexivity, Fission and the Dualism of the Anthropological Tradition

At the demographic centre of the discipline in the United States, the centrifugal forces observed by Boas in 1904 had multiplied. It was no longer a question simply of the coherence of the four major subdisciplines, but of a multiplication of "adjectival anthropologies" (applied, cognitive, dental, economic, educational, feminist, historical, humanistic, medical, nutritional, philosophical, political, psychological, symbolic, urban, etc.) – many of them organised into their own national societies. And while it was possible to interpret this proliferation as a sign of the continued adaptive vigour (or the successful reinvention) of the disciplinary impulse, there was inevitably concern about how, in the last decade of the twentieth century, that impulse might be defined.

Once the reflexivity implied in the original anthropological impulse had been raised permanently to disciplinary consciousness, and the forces of sociocultural change had removed many of the more obvious distinctions on which an asymmetrical anthropology had been premised, it was clear that "anthropology pure and simple" would *not* "deal with the customs and beliefs of the less civilised peoples only". But it was less clear how a more anthropologically-embracive study would be carried on. In many situations, both in the developing countries and the traditional centres of the discipline, the line between anthropology and applied sociology was no longer clear. At the same time, the traditional concern with exotic "otherness" persisted, although now once again historically and textually oriented, in the context of rapid cultural change and the reaction against positivistic natural scientific models. Not only were particular cultural groups beginning to be studied in more historical terms, but the distinctive features of "otherness" itself – including now the notion of the "tribe" – were beginning to be seen as contingent products of the historical interaction of European and non-European peoples in the context of world historical processes. As the manifestly observable differences between peoples diminished, culture was pursued into the crevices of encroaching homogeneity. In this context, there was an increasing sense of the problematic character of the central concept in terms of which "otherness" had long been interpreted by anthropologists.

For more than a century, the idea of culture had been the single most powerful cohesive force in anthropological inquiry. Although that concept was relativised and given an autonomous determinism by the Boasian critique of evolutionary racial assumption, biological and evolutionary concerns were not eliminated from anthropology. And while a systematic evolutionary viewpoint was slow to inform physical anthropology and archeology, the period after the Second World War saw important developments in the field of "paleoanthropology", as well as the resurgence of a submerged neo-evolutionary tendency within American cultural anthropology. During the same years, in the context of a closer association with Parsonian sociology, cultural anthropologists began to think more seriously about just what "culture" was. By the end of the 1960s, a conceptual polarisation was beginning to be evident. On the one hand, there was a tendency – most strikingly evident in what came to be called symbolic anthropology – to treat cultures in humanistic idealist terms as "systems of symbols and meanings", with relatively little concern for the adaptive, utilitarian aspect of cultural behaviour. On the other hand, there was a materialist countercurrent which insisted that culture must be understood scientifically in adaptive evolutionary terms, whether in the form of "techno-environmental determinism", or in the even more controversial form of "socio-biology", which seemed to many to threaten a resurgence of racialist thought in the human sciences.

Although the vast majority of American anthropologists came to the defence of Margaret Mead (1901–76) when a critique of her Samoan fieldwork was generalised as an attack on the notion of cultural determinism, it is by no means clear that the ambiguities of the culture concept have been resolved. Indeed, it might be argued that beneath the recent polarisation lies the paradigmatic opposition that characterised thinking about human differences prior to the early twentieth-century "revolution in anthropology". In the case of Graeco-Roman developmentalism, the continuity with neo-evolutionism is manifest; in the case of the biblical/ethnological paradigm, it is less clear cut. But the fact that the emergence of symbolic and "interpretive" anthropology is spoken of as the "hermeneutic" turn, and also the fact of preoccupation with linguistic phenomena, suggest a level at which it may exist. Be that as it may, the historically constituted epistemic dualism underlying modern anthropology is real enough, and seems likely to endure. From this point of view, Boas – who in other writings insisted on the independent legitimacy of both the *natur*-and the *geisteswis-senschaftliche* approaches to the study of human phenomena – may perhaps serve as a guide to the future as well as to the past of the discipline.

Notes

1 F. Boas, "The history of anthropology", as reprinted in G. Stocking, (ed.), *The Shaping of American anthropology, 1883–1911: a Franz Boas reader* (New York, 1974), p. 35.
2 C. Geertz, *The interpretation of cultures* (New York, 1973), p. 22.
3 J. Speed, "The genealogies of holy scriptures", in *The Holy Bible: a facsimile in a reduced size of the authorised version published in the year 1611* (Oxford, 1911), no. 2.
4 J. Rousseau, *Discourse on the origin and foundations of inequality*, in R. D. Masters, (ed.), *The first and second discourses* (New York, 1964), p. 211.

Further Reading

P. J. Bowler, *Theories of human evolution. A century of debate, 1844–1944* (Baltimore, 1986; Oxford, 1987).
C. Hinsley, *Savages and scientists: the Smithsonian Institution and the development of American anthropology, 1846–1910* (Washington, DC, 1981).
M. Hodgen, *Early anthropology in the sixteenth and seventeenth centuries* (Philadelphia, 1964).
R. Kemper and J. Phinney, (eds.), *The history of anthropology: a research bibliography* (New York, 1977).
B. Rupp-Eisenreich, (ed.), *Histoires de l'anthropologie (xvie–xixe siècles)* (Paris, 1984).

J. S. Slotkin, (ed.), *Readings in early anthropology* (Chicago, 1965).

W. Stanton, *The leopard's spots: scientific attitudes toward race in America, 1815–1859* (Chicago, 1960).

G. Stocking, Jr., *Race, culture and evolution: essays in the history of anthropology* (New York, 1968).

—— (ed.), *The shaping of American anthropology, 1883–1911: a Franz Boas Reader* (New York, 1974).

—— (ed.), *Observers observed: essays on ethnographic fieldwork* [History of Anthropology, vol. 1] (Madison, Wis., 1983).

—— (ed.), *Functionalism historicized: essays on British social anthropology* [History of Anthropology, vol. 2] (Madison, Wis., 1984).

—— (ed.), *Objects and others: essays on museums and material culture* [History of Anthropology, vol. 3] (Madison, Wis., 1985).

—— (ed.), *Malinowski, Rivers, Benedict and others: essays on culture and personality* [History of Anthropology, vol. 4] (Madison, Wis., 1986).

—— *Victorian anthropology* (New York, 1987).

—— (ed.), *Bones, bodies, behavior: essays on biological anthropology* [History of Anthropology vol. 5] (Madison, Wis., 1988).

3 Everett C. Hughes and the Development of Fieldwork in Sociology

Jean-Michel Chapoulie

Translated by Michal M. McCall

To make progress in our job, we need to give full and comparative attention to the not-yets, the didn't-quite-make-its, the not quite respectable, the unremarked, and the openly "anti" goings-on in our society. *(E. C. Hughes 1971: 53)*

The method of observation has a sure procedure: it gathers facts to compare them, and compares them to know them better. The natural sciences are in a way no more than a series of comparisons. As each particular phenomenon is ordinarily the result of the combined action of several causes, it would be only a mystery for us if we considered it on its own; but if it is compared with analogous phenomena, they throw light on each other. The particular action of each cause we see as distinct and independent, and general laws are the result. Good observation requires analysis; now, one carries out analysis in philosophy by comparisons, as in chemistry by the play of chemical affinities.

(J.-M. De Gerando, 1800, 1969)

The history of the social sciences is not just one of "theories" or successive "paradigms"; it is also a history in which new areas of empirical research are opened up and new methods of data gathering are worked out simultaneously. In general, the first attempts at empirical research in social science dealt with subjects that were distant from the researcher in time or in social space: either with "primitive" populations or with the working class and peasants in countries undergoing industrialization. Empirical researchers did not discover the middle class and its institutions for many years, until after 1940 in the United States. It took another twenty years, and Goffman's work, before they included everyday behavior among the

Author's Note: This article is an adaptation in English of an article published in 1984 in *Revue Française de Sociologie* (25, 4: 582–608). I wish to thank the many English and American sociologists who gave me access to unpublished articles or articles unavailable in France, and in particular, Lester R. Kurtz, Ruth S. Cavan, Robert S. Weiss, and Jennifer Platt, who also made useful comments on the first draft of the French version. Jean Peneff allowed me to consult several documents – among others, an interview with Everett Hughes in October 1982 – and also gave me critical comments. This work has also benefited from numerous discussions with Jean-Pierre Briand and Henri Péretz. The English version has benefited from many talks with Howard Becker, Arlene Daniels, Anselm Strauss, and Paule Verdet. For the English version, I did some additional research in the papers of Everett C. Hughes at the Joseph Regenstein Library at the University of Chicago, where I checked some hypotheses put forward in the French version. I have also removed some analysis and some references that seemed to me less useful for English readers, and added some material (indicated by smaller type) that seemed more relevant to them. I am very grateful to Michal M. McCall, of Macalester College, who translated the French version and helped me give shape to the English one.

subjects of research (before that, it was a domain reserved for etiquette books), and ten years more for them to include the work activities of researchers in the natural and social sciences.

Social scientists' prolonged avoidance of subjects closely related to them shows how difficult they found it to be objective about the social reality around them; we see the same phenomenon in their choice of methods, since they had similar problems integrating the simplest method of all – observation *in situ* by the researcher – into the panoply of ordinary social science methods. It took ethnographers, for example, more than a century to put into practice the recommendations formulated by De Gerando at the beginning of the nineteenth century, substituting direct and prolonged observation for the collection of uncertain testimony in unknown conditions.[1] Even Malinowski (who was both the initiator and propagandist of this method) did not actually use it, although he described it in the *Argonauts*.[2]

In studies of their own societies, the first researchers to use empirical methods favored the use of official statistics or, sometimes, legal texts, even if those trained as physicians or naturalists – such as Villermé, Parent-Duchâtelet, or LePlay in France – did not look down on the collection of evidence by direct observation.[3] Those who used these methods worked outside the academic framework, while the first university sociologists either failed in their attempts at empirical research (Weber, for example)[4] or, like Durkheim, developed epistemological arguments that dissuaded people from collecting data by direct observation. Such data, suspected of depending on the subjectivity of researchers were not considered useful for scientific purposes. As a result, they were left to people who used them routinely, like journalists and administrators on inspection visits, or to the moving spirits of various social movements, like LePlay's disciples, who became observers of the working class.[5]

The Department of Sociology at the University of Chicago was the first academic group to develop an empirical research enterprise making much use of observation *in situ*, along with other sources of data. At first, researchers – most of them from rural middle-class Protestant families in the Midwest – used this method primarily to study populations socially very distant from them. They used Simmel's description of "the stranger" as an analogy when they tried to explain the role of the observer. (See, for instance, Paul G. Cressey, 1983).

Beginning in the 1940s in the United States, studies of the middle class (or at least, of subjects involving it) showed how inadequate this analogy was, when sociologists found themselves in the role of "native" rather than "stranger." The first research on subjects connected to the middle class was done, in midcareer, by sociologists born around the turn of the century: Parsons, Lazarsfeld, Merton, and Hughes. Among them, Everett C. Hughes and, in another way, Herbert Blumer, became the principal proponents of observation *in situ* as a method of data gathering, through both their publications and their teaching at the University of Chicago, widely considered "influential," although it is not always clear just how that influence was exercised.[6] In this article I will analyze, from a historical point of view, the context in which the use of observation *in situ* and, more generally, fieldwork, developed in sociology. I take as my central point of reference the research style Hughes represented and as my principal example of that style in action the research in the sociology of work he sponsored at the University of Chicago.[7]

The vocabulary used to designate research based, at least in part, on observation is confusing – like the English language itself – because the terms are used in so many different ways and, even more, because there are so many different perspectives in social science on the use of observation as a method of data gathering. I have used a terminology derived from Hughes's own; he used "observation *in situ*" or "direct observation" to designate the activities of researchers who observe personally and for an extended time some situation or behavior that interests them and who are not therefore reduced to understanding these situations or behaviors only through the categories used by participants. I have used the term "fieldwork" to designate the research design that includes observation *in situ*, plus collecting interviews and the use of archives. I have, on the other hand, avoided the term "participant observation" because its meaning is ambiguous: sometimes it simply means fieldwork (see, for example, McCall and Simmons, 1969), and sometimes *only* cases where researchers become members, in fact or in name only, of the social groups they study (see, for example, Wax, 1968).

Hughes and the "Chicago Tradition"

Although Hughes has been called a typical representative of the "Chicago School of sociology," that claim is as ambiguous as the idea of "schools" in social science generally.[8] The concept of a Chicago School of sociology is among the most ambiguous, and to link Hughes with the Chicago School, we must stipulate precisely what we mean by that expression, which has been used in so many different ways. Although he was Park's student and the editor of his works, Hughes was not really connected with the theory of urban development we associate with Park, Burgess, and MacKenzie. Nor was he connected with the theory of social disorganization actively supported by Park, Burgess, and Wirth.[9] Likewise, Hughes's references to the familiar ideas of George Herbert Mead are rare and cursory, and one of his principal empirical studies is based on the analysis of biographies à la Thomas and Znaniecki. Nevertheless, Hughes's affiliation with the Chicago School is clear if we use the expression to refer to the multiform enterprise of empirical research that developed in the Department of Sociology at the University of Chicago under the impetus of Thomas and later Park, and produced a series of monographs, including some of the "minor classics" in the discipline.[10]

Sociologists who are the more or less distant heirs of the Chicago tradition often use the term "Chicago tradition" or "Chicago style," instead of Chicago School, which appeared only after 1940. (See, for example, Fisher and Strauss, 1978, or the remarks by Hughes and Blumer in Lofland, 1980.) Since the early 1960s and the publication of Rose's (1962) edited volume, the term "interactionism" (or "symbolic interactionism"), coined by Blumer before 1940, has frequently been used to identify research belonging to that tradition: the work of sociologists known as students or associates of Hughes and Blumer (although the same terms are applied to the more "positivist" followers of the social psychologist Manfred Kuhn). More recently, since the founding of the Society for the Study of Symbolic Interaction, these same labels have been applied to a much wider range of research, including work by sociologists who adopt a "phenomenological" point of view (usually that of Alfred Schutz).

I have used the terms "Chicago tradition" or "interactionism" to refer to what is common in the approaches to social reality of several successive generations of researchers. We can refer, for examples, to the work of Park and Ellsworth Faris in the first generation, Hughes and Blumer in the second generation, and Strauss, Becker, Freidson, and, for his early work, Goffman in the third generation. Of course, we cannot expect the body of research defined by these terms to have the same homogeneity and coherence as each one has, taken in isolation.

Like Park, whose most direct follower he seems to be in this regard, Hughes was primarily interested in the study of contemporary social reality and eclectic in his choice of research methods. His monograph on the effects of industrialization on a French Canadian town (Hughes, 1943), for example, relied on the same kinds of evidence as the monographs of Wirth (1928) or Thrasher (1927): a combination of official statistics, archives and journals, interviews he gathered himself, and, finally, on more or less systematic observations of the ordinary life of the community.

Nevertheless, like Park – or perhaps this is better seen as an echo of the pragmatism Ellsworth Faris introduced into the Chicago department – Hughes always preferred to observe the phenomena he studied *in situ*. This technique has an affinity with a sociology that puts at the center of its program of study, not "facts" constituted in the manner of Durkheim, but collective actions and social processes that can be understood, in part, through direct interaction, and whose meaning for those involved is neither given nor negligible.

> Here, I must insist, against the most frequent interpretation, that the term "interaction" was used neither by Park, nor later in the Chicago tradition, to mean only face-to-face interactions among individuals. According to the terminology in the Park and Burgess textbook, it first referred to relations of competition among groups that did not imply actual contact. (On the other hand, Park and Burgess used "conflict" to mean antagonisms manifested in direct contacts.) The emphasis on direct interaction in many interactionist studies results primarily from an almost exclusive use of observation *in situ* and interviews as data, and not from an a priori refusal to analyze what other traditions call "objective facts." For instance, in critical remarks about studies of industrial sociology during the 1940s, Blumer insisted on the importance of chronic conflict between management and trade unions and on the nature of these two types of organization; he observed that local "relations between management and workers tend to lose their autonomous character" and to be determined by the "policies ... projects, and strategies of central organizations," that is, national unions and industrial federations. (Blumer, 1947: 273)

Hughes also retained, from the Chicago tradition of the 1930s, an attachment to the unity of the social sciences – or, one might say, an indifference to academic boundaries – that was relatively rare in that period, when each discipline was concerned with establishing itself and defending its specialty. His frequent references to anthropological research served as antidotes to the ethnocentrism of American sociology and as a source of examples furnishing points of comparison for the construction of analytic categories. Furthermore, Hughes insisted over and over (for example, apropos the division of labor) that empirical research must use a long temporal perspective, like the one historians develop during their training (Hughes, 1971: 292–4).

Finally, even more than Park, Hughes's familiarity with German social science from around the turn of the century – with the work of Weber but even more than that of Simmel – convinced him that the analysis of social reality should be based on the construction of abstract and general categories.

If the continuity between Hughes's and Park's conceptions of social science is always evident,[11] notable differences nevertheless exist in the research styles each helped to promote in the different sociopolitical, university, and intellectual contexts in which they operated.

With Hughes, sociology first diverged from social work, which, as is well known, was very much present when the Department of Sociology at Chicago was first organized (Diner, 1975; Carey, 1975). In Park's time, the boundary between these two activities had already developed, but Burgess remained in contact with charitable institutions, and numerous studies between 1920 and 1940 reflected the maintenance of privileged ties between sociology and social work: for example, those of Shaw and McKay, Thrasher, and Wirth, who had been a part-time social worker.[12] At the opposite extreme, Hughes's use of the comparative method to construct his analytic categories reveals a religious, moral, and social relativism far removed from the reformism (and the ethnocentrism) latent in most of the research done between 1930 and 1950. This relativism, as we shall see, led him to apply analytic categories that had proved pertinent in studies of professionally marginal groups of lesser status to studies of the medical profession.

The growing distance between sociology and social work coincided with a broadening of research topics in sociology, itself correlated with the diversification of topics for which one could obtain financing for research. Hughes thus participated in a study of the socialization of medical doctors[13] at about the same time as that of Merton at Columbia,[14] and in another study of the profession of nursing (Hughes et al., 1958), two types of projects without equivalence in the 1930s.[15]

Finally, Hughes's insistence on observation *in situ* was not derived, as Park's was, from journalistic experience (or a knowledge of journalists' working methods), but from a great familiarity with the studies, the problems, and the methods of anthropology in the post-Malinowski era. Except that his field experience was relatively closer to home, with respect to his relation to the population studied, his study of a French Canadian town resembles studies done at the same time by anthropologists like Redfield.

As Jennifer Platt remarked in her study of the history of participant observation, sociologists of the 1930s interpreted their research methods in terms of an opposition between case studies and statistical studies.[16] "Case studies" included the collection of biographical accounts produced at the request of the researcher (see, for example, Shaw, 1930); descriptions of a milieu or an activity, collected from people involved in them (for example, *The Professional Thief* by Sutherland and Conwell, 1937); the collection of talk in a situation; and observations carried out by the researcher himself or herself.[17] The distinctions were not always clearly recognized. It was not until the end of the 1930s that the outlines of fieldwork, with its insistence on direct observation, were a little more defined. After 25 years that design was already familiar to Anglo-Saxon ethnographers, of course, but they had hardly developed any analysis of it – nor, it seems, any specific instruction in it – and, in any case, its transfer to the study of researchers' own societies encountered other obstacles. The University of Chicago provided an intellectual and institutional setting favorable to the rapproachement of anthropology and sociology: the two disciplines were only separated administratively after 1928, and even then they remained interdependent as far as teaching was concerned. But above all there were anthropologists close to sociology at the University of Chicago – like Park's son-in-law, Robert Redfield; Conrad Arensberg, who was then working on his study of a rural community in Ireland; or Lloyd Warner, who was then studying in Newburyport (Yankee City), as well as sociologists close to anthropology, like Hughes,[18] and those who developed a perspective in affinity with the anthropologists' perspective, like Blumer. If the latter did not himself do fieldwork, he nevertheless made a large contribution to this type of research: His essays and his teaching furnished a framework and epistemological justifications for "naturalistic" studies where the subjects of research are studied in their natural environment. Blumer's contribution was fundamental all through the period in which fieldwork research had not yet gained an assured scientific status.

Collaboration between sociologists and anthropologists was primarily carried on by interdisciplinary research committees. The Committee on Human Relations in Industry, for example, led by Warner and Hughes among others, provided an institutional framework for the occupational research that Hughes and his associates carried on.

The recognition of fieldwork as a legitimate research design in sociology did not depend only on the example of ethnography. It was also a product of the Chicago School's reaction to research based on the collection and statistical analysis of questionnaires, developed after 1940 by Stouffer, Lazarsfeld, and Merton.

In comparison with the questionnaire method, the Chicago research of the 1930s – a combination of not very systematic direct observations, analyses of official statistics, and collections of biographical documents – seemed to belong to the past. In 1948 Edward Shils – a former student of Park's, and Wirth's research assistant – published an influential book on the state of sociology. Laid out like a balance sheet, it crystallized negative judgments of the research conducted at Chicago during Park's time. Shils stressed the absence of systematic (that is, statistical) verification of explicitly formulated propositions in the Chicago monographs of the 1930s, implicitly taking as his model of the scientific method the one sociologists then attributed to the physical sciences, which questionnaire research seemed to resemble most closely. This very general critique was accompanied by a relative devaluation of direct observation as a method of data gathering: It was judged less rigorous because it seemed to depend on the individual characteristics of researchers and because it was harder to conduct according to the principles of systematic sampling. Observational data, considered suggestive at best, were relegated to the initial stages of research, when one prepares to gather the kind of data susceptible to statistical treatment. This use of observation was stressed in the well-known article by Barton and Lazarsfeld (1955), for example.

> Throughout the 1950s, sociologists in the Chicago tradition had very little public debate with the detractors of observation *in situ* as a primary method of data gathering. Their most influential spokesman, Blumer, spent less time defending fieldwork than pointing out the weaknesses in research based on questionnaires and standardized interviews. Behind Blumer's criticisms – which rested on the illusory character of standardization, on the arbitrariness of the categories used as variables, and on the uncertain relationship between behavior in real situations and responses gathered

in interview situations – it is easy to glimpse a defense of fieldwork. But he did not provide an argument justifying fieldwork until much later (in the introduction to his 1969 volume). As Richard LaPiere's retrospective testimony suggests, arguments by the detractors of questionnaire research carried less weight in the 1940s and 1950s than arguments by the adversaries of observation.[19] Looking back, it is possible to see that the controversy in fact concerned the criteria according to which one measures the rigor of a method, criteria that determine the weight accorded to this or that argument.[20]

If one relies on Chicago monographs of the 1930s and 1940s, some of the criticisms formulated against data gathering by observation are, based on the evidence, partially founded. At first, the conditions of data gathering and especially the dealings researchers had with the people they studied, were shadowy, confirming the impression that they did not try to exercise systematic control over the "facts" they reported and that interpretations of those facts were therefore dependent, insofar as it is possible to estimate, on the subjectivity of the researchers and on the conditions in which they worked.[21] Besides, even if some "model" monographs (Thrasher's on adolescent gangs and especially Cressey's on dance halls) reproduced numerous extracts from observation notes, these consisted of imprecise descriptions (especially Thrasher's) interspersed with miscellaneous value judgments. Furthermore, these extracts were used exactly as extracts from interviews and documents were used: for the information they explicitly contained and not for the elaboration of analytic categories.[22]

On these different points, the studies based on fieldwork after 1940 are much less criticizable, probably due to the indirect influence of questionnaire research.[23] Beginning early in the 1950s, fieldwork researchers published detailed accounts of the conditions in which they carried out their research and of the practical problems they encountered in getting access to their subjects and gathering their data. These provided their readers with some rudimentary estimates of the validity of their analyses: the appendix W. F. Whyte added to the 1955 edition of *Street Corner Society* is one of the best and most often cited. Starting with the 1960s, almost every monograph based on fieldwork contains such an account.[24] At the same time, various articles examined three groups of problems that confront fieldworkers: first, the appropriate mode of relations with the population studied, at the beginning, during, or at the end of research; second, the problems posed by the construction of analytic categories; and finally, problems of the validity of the data gathered.[25]

Accounts of research based on fieldwork also became more precise. Instead of briefly summarizing fieldnotes and remarks gathered by interviewing, or even simply referring to these data, many of these accounts cited them word for word, which forced researchers to construct finer categories of analysis and to explain their interpretations of remarks and behavior in more detail. For the most part, the occupational studies carried on under Hughes's patronage are examples.[26] This change in the direction of greater rigor and precision, in the norms of composition and in the collection of observations, seems to have been encouraged by the previously mentioned critiques by partisans of questionnaire research. One can measure the extent of the change by comparing Hughes's study of a city in Quebec with the one he did 20 years later on the socialization of medical students.

Although one finds very few published debates among sociological fieldworkers, except the one concerning the moral problems posed by clandestine observation, the mass of studies based on field research between 1945 and the middle 1960s does not constitute a unified whole with regard to conceptions of the fieldwork design. Certainly, all the studies list, among their objectives, understanding the meaning people give to their activities. In this, they are conspicuously different from all those forms of research that consider such meanings to be obvious, quasi-obvious, or, most frequently, negligible and superficial aspects of social reality.[27] However, that is the end of fieldworkers' agreement about objectives. One can compare at least two contrasting conceptions of fieldwork, clearly recognizable in programmatic essays, although accounts of actual research are ranged along a continuum between them.[28]

The first conception of fieldwork attributes to it an essentially descriptive purpose. Advocates of this conception expect researchers to describe the "culture" of the population studied, from the point of view of those who have experienced it. Among them there is often an emphatic insistence on "participation" by the researcher as the unavoidable means of gathering data.

This insistence is principally found in the work of researchers who belong to the tradition of cultural anthropology – for example, Spradley (1980) or Wax (1968) – and also in certain essays by Blumer, in which he argues against positivist research in social science. In an article first published in 1962 and often cited, Blumer asserts, for example:

> To catch the process [of interpretation], the student must take the role of the acting unit whose behavior he is studying. Since the interpretation is being made by the acting unit in terms of the objects designated and appraised, meanings acquired, and decisions made, the process has to be seen from the standpoint of the acting unit.... To try to catch the interpretive process by remaining aloof as a so-called "objective" observer and refusing to take the role of the acting unit is to risk the worst kind of subjectivism – the objective observer is likely to fill in the process of interpretation with his own surmises in place of catching the process as it occurs in the experience of the acting unit which uses it. (Blumer, 1969: 86)

In fact, outside of programmatic essays, the term "participation" often seems to mean that the researcher has to undergo a kind of socialization in the milieu studied and not that the researcher must have done the activities he or she gives an account of, which would often be absurd anyway, given the subjects studied.

The accounts that illustrate this first conception of fieldwork always include, in a mixture of social science language and the language of everyday life, descriptions of the group studied (its locale, the circumstances its members act in, and so on), and explanations of members' "definition of their situation," which constitute a kind of translation of these accounts into the experience of supposed readers, the educated public. These accounts do not use elaborate analytic ideas and are limited in general to making behavior appear coherent and relating the categories explicitly used by actors and the tacit categories underlying their behavior.[29]

A second group of researchers consider participant observation research to be a means of gathering evidence for the objectification of the activities and lived experiences of some actors. For these researchers, description of the actors' subjectivity ceases to be an end in itself, whenever it does not appear as a contradiction in terms,[30] and knowledge of the categories of language and action used by the "subjects" studied is merely the basic material from which sociologists construct analytic categories. It is not considered a necessity or even an advantage in every case to participate as closely as possible in the life of the people studied; in principle, the degree of participation is determined by the characteristics of the subject being studied and of the researcher (his or her individual characteristics, mode of access into the milieu, and so on).

The best, and most convincing, illustration of this second conception of fieldwork is made up of the occupational studies carried out by Hughes and some of his students and associates.[31] Hughes's methodological essays, published toward the end of his career, and the ideas he developed throughout his publications, provide an overview of that research enterprise, an enterprise that combined empirical work and the construction of a system of analytic categories not reducible to the categories used by the actors themselves.

According to his own testimony (see, for example, his interview with Weiss, 1981), Hughes's thoughts on fieldwork were based in large part on his teaching at the University of Chicago. The belated publication of his methodological essays partially explains why recent analyses (see Douglas, 1976) contend that Hughes used fieldwork in a nonreflexive manner, just as the authors of Chicago monographs in the 1930s did. In his 1969 book on interactionism, which in fact focuses on studies of the 1960s, Rock attributes to Hughes and to all sociologists of his time an analogous conception of fieldwork, although he regards as a merit what Douglas considers a failing. In my judgment, Rock exaggerates the importance of direct knowledge and has not examined the fieldwork practiced by Hughes and his associates closely (or critically) enough. On the contrary, Hughes's originality and, for example, Anselm Strauss's in the second generation, lie in the care they took to explain the different stages of fieldwork and to maintain a reflexive attitude with regard to these stages, instead of praising the observer's direct subjective experience as do many field researchers, particularly ethnographers.

Studies in the Sociology of Work from 1940–1960 and the Maturing of Fieldwork Research

After 1945, studies in the sociology of work were an appreciable part of fieldwork research at the University of Chicago. These studies are distinguishable from the research done there twenty years earlier, not only, as we have seen, because the data gathering is more systematic and the research accounts more explicit, but also because their focus is more restricted. The published articles generally center on a theme that is narrow enough to allow for examination of a circumscribed social situation: for example, the way workers control their work situations, the institution of norms of production, or the types of relations between a category of workers and those who use their services.[32] In addition, these articles use almost the same set of ideas as Hughes presented and discussed in several articles he published in the same period of time.[33] But the relationship between these empirical studies and Hughes's more general essays is not simply that of a theory to its "applications" or "illustrations"; it is rather a process of elaboration in which empirical studies and more abstract analyses are conducted abreast.[34]

Some of these empirical studies – maybe the majority, if one believes certain suggestions by Hughes – were done by researchers already familiar, by virtue of their own biographies and even before beginning their research, with the occupations or institutions they studied. For example, Roy worked on an assembly line before undertaking his study of restriction of production, Becker was a jazz pianist before he did the study republished in *Outsiders*, Dalton was employed as a manager in a business concern, Davis drove a taxi to pay for his education, and so on.[35]

Their familiarity with the milieu or institution studied, acquired by acting in another role than that of "disinterested" observer, put these researchers in a radically different position vis-à-vis their subject than ethnographers or, with very rare exceptions, the Chicago sociologists who published monographs during the 1930s.[36] For those earlier researchers, access to the subject of study was often a critical problem and, having resolved it, they had to find a way of behaving that did not block the collection of data. In the 1930s, for example, when sociologists from the rural middle classes studied the behavior of members of the urban working classes, they had to bracket the moral judgments these behaviors aroused in them and also participate according to established norms in the domain of relations between middle and working classes. In contrast, researchers who study populations or situations with which they are familiar have to substitute, for the attitude of immediate participation they had before they started doing research, the point of view of the "disinterested" observer, unconstrained by the norms and judgments that accompany the position they occupied.[37] This connection with the subject studied, "a subtle equilibrium between detachment and participation" (Hughes, 1971: 420), cannot be established by a simple decision in principle, but proceeds through a prolonged process that Hughes called, in various descriptions he gave of it, "emancipation."[38] This process varies with the sociohistorical context and with the social, cultural, and religious characteristics of the researcher. Therefore, according to Hughes, it was in part due to certain peculiarities in their social trajectories that some of the young sociologists participating in research on the sociology of work at the University of Chicago after 1945 could adopt an attitude of objectivity vis-à-vis their subjects.[39]

Within the limits of their own sociohistorical context, field researchers must depend upon two kinds of resources to establish adequate rapport with the subjects they study: first, knowledge of other researchers' experiences and a reflexive attitude vis-à-vis their own research acts; and, second, the use of a comparative method in a much larger framework than the one ordinarily used by sociologists.

Hughes's methodological essays furnish examples of a reflexive attitude toward research activities without equivalence at that time. He applied to observation and interviewing the analytic schemes unearthed in studies of other types of interaction[40] or, to take another point of view, analytic categories borrowed from the sociology of work[41] (since, after all, the work of sociologists is only one kind of work among many). Hughes also questioned the relations among the three languages sociologists must use: that of the people whom they study, that of their colleagues, and that of the public that reads their published accounts (Hughes, 1962).

These thoughts on sociology as an activity obviously did not emerge from a body of rules to be followed in all circumstances when gathering data by observation or interviewing, like the rules one finds in methods texts. Unlike those who put the accent on researchers' participation in the social life they study, Hughes insisted that the roles from which researchers can observe a social activity can only be controlled within narrow limits. We learn from the experience of past research what the basic elements are from which one can evaluate what this or that position of observation implies. Hence, Hughes made it his project, which Junker's (1960) work realized in part, to gather and compare various accounts of research experiences, particularly accounts by students at the University of Chicago.

But the comparative method not only permits field researchers to take an objective point of view toward their own activities and thus exercise a certain control over them, it also allows them to avoid established representations of the subjects they study, especially those associated with their own familiar, everyday points of view. Thus, the originality of Hughes's analysis of the division of labor is derived from his unconventional and irreverent (in the context of sociology and American society at that time) use of the comparative method.

Since the middle of the 1930s, social science studies of middle-class occupations in the United States had inevitably encountered the ideas of "profession" and "professionalism" as elaborated by members of occupations ambitious to reach the status and privileges of medicine, the model of a profession in the Anglo-Saxon meaning of that term.[42] After 1940 Hughes was convinced of the sterility of the approach – used by his colleagues and, earlier, by Parsons, Merton, and their students – which took its problematic from the profession being studied and depended upon comparisons between concrete examples of occupations and an "ideal type" abstracted from the supposed characteristics of medicine (Hughes, 1951b; 1970b; 1971: 339–40). Almost alone at that time, he was interested in the concrete processes through which the division of labor is established and in the appropriation by some workers of the tasks of other categories of workers. Thus Hughes broke with the idea, unanimously but tacitly accepted, that professional groups are categories naturally defined by the technical division of labor.[43] Furthermore, starting with the common-place idea "that all sorts of occupations belong in the same series, regardless of their place in hierarchies of prestige or of moral value" (Hughes, 1951a; 1971: 316), he concluded that one could expect to find many characteristics of professional work in "humble" occupations: among plumbers and prostitutes as well as doctors and psychiatrists.

From the first studies of marginal professions and lower-status occupations, Hughes concluded that these constitute a privileged field of observation, because their members are less capable than high-status professions of maintaining a facade and opposing their own value symbols ("professional ethics" or "scientific knowledge") to those that researchers by virtue of their own social position, are inclined to adhere (Hughes, 1951b; 1971: 342). Therefore, Hughes and his associates sought, through research that was the inverse of that done by students of Parsons and Merton, to study professions of high standing with reference to conclusions they unearthed in studying occupations of lower standing. Then, by enlarging the range of professions and work situations they compared, they progressively elaborated a framework of questions that proved fruitful for studying the processes by which the division of labor is established and transformed, the way groups of workers try to exercise control over their own activities, and the unfolding of professional careers.

Hughes thus used the comparative method, not for demonstrating proofs, but to construct analytic categories free from value judgments and from the categories used by workers themselves (or by their employers) for practical purposes. This is why the comparisons Hughes made were rarely of a global character and, as a general rule, only dealt with particular aspects of situations and work behaviors – those related to his favorite notions of *dirty work, routine and emergency, restriction of production* or *career line.*

Although the studies that used these ideas in the 1940s and 1950s focused on relations among workers or between workers and others with whom they interacted directly, Hughes did not overlook the importance of relationships between occupations and the surrounding society: several of his essays elaborate analytic categories (license, mandate, and so forth) capable of accounting for complex transactions between professional groups, which always develop their own conceptions of their activities, and groups that, in title or otherwise, use the products of professionals' work.[44] In this sense, one finds in Hughes's work the point of departure for Freidson's later analyses of physicians' control of their medical practices and the relations between the culture of patients and the culture of practitioners (Freidson, 1971).

The occupational studies of Hughes and his associates did not emerge from a definite theory (in the sense of a body of propositions claiming to establish and account for a series of "facts"), but from a framework of investigation capable of guiding empirical work without reducing it to the simple verification of previously formulated hypotheses. Moreover, these studies are consistent with the interactionist conception of sociology: that the final product of research is a set of ideas – what Blumer called sensitizing concepts – and a list of questions, not a catalogue of definitive assertions about the relations between this or that aspect of social reality. According to their perspective, these relations are affected by social actors' uninterrupted interpretations. Thus, as Daniels noted (1972), the remark Hughes made about the "classic" authors of sociology applies perfectly to his own essays: "What you get from... [Durkheim, Park, Weber, and Simmel]... is a statement of general problems, a set of concepts and sometimes some fruitful ideas and hypotheses with which to enrich your own thinking and to suggest methods for solving the problems with which you are concerned" (Hughes, 1961; 1971: 565).

Conclusion: Fieldwork Studies in the United States after 1960

The continuing process of explanation, and therefore control, of fieldwork research was not completed by the beginning of the 1960s, although Hughes's career at the University of Chicago ended and so did the collective research enterprise in the sociology of work, which he had begun.[45] Thereafter, the interactionist tradition was enriched by numerous studies of either deviance or organizations (hospitals, for example), and by Glaser and Strauss's (1967) attempt to define a way of using the comparative method to construct analytic categories, a stage of research that had seemed, in Hughes's formulation, to depend on the individual imagination or the individual virtuosity of researchers.

During the 1960s there was a renewed interest in fieldwork, as shown by the publication of textbooks and the creation of doctoral programs. By the end of that decade, however, sociologists had created a new division of work, which led to the establishment of two separate domains, each with publications specific to it: "quantitative studies" (that is, studies using statistical instruments) and "qualitative studies" (those that rely on field research, autobiographies, and so on). In this new context, research in the interactionist tradition was labeled "qualitative" research, along with two other kinds of field research. One is made up of monographs written by anthropologists who were converted, by necessity, to the study of their own society; most often these studies are direct intellectual heirs of the cultural anthropology of the 1950s, and do not show any noteworthy innovation in the collection or interpretation of data.[46] The second is the product of the conjunction of ideas borrowed from Schutz, Garfinkel, and phenomenology more generally, with the point of view of fieldwork in the interactionist style.

In the matter of fieldwork research, the relationship between the interactionist tradition and phenomenology seems complex, and cannot be understood completely without explicitly describing the network of relationships among sociologists in the 1960s and 1970s.[47] But, without anticipating the results of this analysis, one may suggest that some of the young sociologists in the 1960s who were most interested in phenomenology were also closely connected with sociologists in the interactionist tradition; and notice that the differences in research practice were certainly far less radical than the differences in vocabulary. On the other hand, no clues of a direct contact with phenomenology can be found in the published work of interactionists before 1965. One never finds references to philosophical works in Hughes's essays and Blumer's are almost always presented as refinements in the philosophy of G. H. Mead, the only author Blumer cites. Nevertheless, several articles by Schutz were published in the *American Journal of Sociology* during the time Blumer was its editor, and there is also evidence (see Bruyn, 1967) of similarities between the methods of field research as practiced by interactionists and the method of phenomenology. However, it was not until the middle of the 1960s – and principally through the intermediary of Garfinkel – that the thematic of phenomenology found a rather large audience among sociologists who did empirical research. Several remarks suggest that, at least in the beginning, phenomenology chiefly furnished a language that allowed some young sociologists (for example, Manning, 1973, and Douglas, 1976) to express their misgivings about the structural-functionalist perspective and research based on the use of questionnaires, and some sociologists of earlier generations (for example, Deutscher, 1973, and Davis 1973) to reformulate their familiar themes.

One contribution the researchers who called themselves phenomenologists made to the explanation of fieldwork lies in the attention they paid to the social construction, in concrete interactions, of what sociologists ordinarily treat as data: that is, categorizations of behavior and persons in social life, the statistics that follow from these categorizations, and even interviews about them, produced at the initiative of a researcher (Cicourel, 1968, 1974; Sudnow, 1967). Many fieldwork studies influenced by phenomenology also analyzed the effective use of formal rules in organizations (see Bittner, 1967; Cicourel, 1968; Emerson, 1969), whereas this subject of investigation was only peripheral in interactionist studies. Methodologically, some of these studies focused on the relation between the observer and his or her subject, abandoning the "absolutist" conception of description – that is, the idea that descriptions are independent of the researcher's point of view (Douglas, 1976;

Manning, 1973). From there, they went on to analyze the implicit models around which researchers organize their accounts and researchers' methods of composition.

I will not develop this examination of changes in the conception of fieldwork in American sociology after 1960 any further here. These brief remarks are only intended to show the originality of Hughes's work – and the originality of the Chicago tradition – in the context of the whole, and his contribution to the rational use of data produced by field research.

By drawing attention to details of the circumstances in which observation *in situ* was first used systematically as a source of data for sociological analyses, I intended to accomplish two other more immediate objectives. First, I have tried to show that one can find, in essays by the first generation of academic sociologists to conduct empirical research, most of the themes around which later field researchers' thoughts on their activities were arranged, so that the originality of most recent publications on the subject consists almost entirely of formulations the first generation proposed. Thus, knowledge of the history of sociology gives the discipline, on one hand, access to a certain cumulative knowledge (or at least, knowledge about) and, on the other hand, discourages the periodic treatment of reports of recurrent research problems as if they were original discoveries. Also, when referring intellectual works to their conditions of production, historical studies of sociology favored a more detached appraisal of research enterprises, refraining from interpreting these works as if they were holy texts free of worldly entrenchment (exactly the misfortune of the founding fathers of sociology like Marx, Durkheim, and the rest).

More implicitly, I have also tried to show the mutual relationships among three aspects of the development of social science, usually considered separately: the elaboration and transformation of methods of gathering and using data; the conditions of researchers' work and their position in the social structure; and the intellectual influences that are always blurred, only partially and with difficulty perceptible, when one does not limit oneself to the examination of systems of general ideas in which researchers formulate their programs of study a priori or a posteriori and in which they tend always to accentuate their affiliations with some and their differences with others.

Notes

1   The story of De Gerando's report seems typical. It was written for the *Société des Observateurs de l'Homme*, whose members were preparing an expedition to Australia with, among other things, scientific aims. De Gerando's report did not have any influence on the expedition, for evident reasons. Though republished in 1883, the report remained almost unknown among French anthropologists and sociologists. It was rediscovered by English historians of anthropology in the 1960s, and in 1969, translated and republished in English by F. C. T. Moore, with a preface by E. E. Evans-Pritchard. The report was later published in French in Jean Copans et al. (1978). A young philosopher when the wrote the report, De Gerando became a high official in the empire and, for the rest of his life, was involved in various philanthropic enterprises, most notably in the diffusion of elementary education. He died in 1842.

2   The recent publication of Malinowski's *Journal* made the slight differences between his method and the account he gave of it in the Introduction to the *Argonauts* (1922) more

apparent. In particular, he relied more on informants than on his own observation, without doubt because of the social position he occupied in the village he studied: on this point, see M. Wax (1972). One will find in concise form some elements of a history of observation in the social sciences in R. Wax (1971).

3   Despite his arguments in favor of observation, in his first book of family monographs (1855), LePlay himself relied principally on interviews with interested parties as a means of displaying the budgets that he attributed to families; indeed, he seems to have occasionally taken some pains to distinguish between what he could verify himself and the "facts" reported by interviewees. Among other early users of observation are the researchers associated with Charles Booth's investigations in a working class area of London and, so it would seem, with other investigations of the working class being done at the same time in England and the United States. In Germany, one of the first and foremost users of observation was Paul Gohre, a student of theology who published in 1891 a study of the workers in an industrial enterprise (see Obershall, 1965).

4   Obershall's study (1965) contains a precise description of these unsuccessful attempts, particularly the research on agricultural workers that Weber attempted in association with Gohre.

5   The distrust that the first university specialists of social science maintained to the end of the nineteenth century with regard to any method based on a researcher's own collection of data was in part a result of the situation they found themselves in. Because their place in the university was poorly defined – somewhere between the classic humanities and the physical and natural sciences – they deemed it necessary (judging from the rhetoric they used) to justify their activities as conforming to what they considered the "scientific model" or, at least, to insist on the rigorous, critical examination of documents as was done by the French historians Langlois and Seignobos in their book on the historical critique (1897); in fact, this book was used as a methods textbook by certain departments of sociology in American universities at the beginning of the twentieth century.

6   Everett C. Hughes (1897–1983), born in Ohio, was the son of a minister (which those familiar with his essays could not overlook), and was a student at the University of Chicago in the same doctoral class as Louis Wirth, Robert Redfield, and Herbert Blumer. He taught at McGill University in Montreal (1927–38), then at the University of Chicago (1938–61), afterwards ending his career at Brandeis, followed by Boston College. He was editor of the *American Journal of Sociology* from 1952 to 1960.

Herbert Blumer (born in 1901) remained at the University of Chicago as a professor after obtaining his doctorate in 1928. He was the representative of George Herbert Mead's teaching after Mead's death. He was editor of the *American Journal of Sociology* from 1941 to 1952, when he left for a position at Berkeley. Blumer's principal essays on methodological problems were republished in his 1969 collection.

One can find a first appraisal of their influence in two collections of papers: one in honor of Hughes (Becker, Geer, Riesman and Weiss, 1968) and one in honor of Blumer (Shibutani, 1970).

7   Hughes's principal articles on the sociology of work have been republished in his 1958 and 1971 collections of articles. The second collection also contains his principal essays on methodological problems, with the exception of one article published in 1974, and essays on institutions and race relations.

Recall, too, that Hughes's *oeuvre* also includes numerous publications on cultural contacts, the central theme of his doubtless most finished work (Hughes and Hughes, 1952), and a monograph on a little town in French Canada.

8   These ambiguities result, in part, from the fact that the history of sociology is done mainly by sociologists with a normative point of view and an interest in the current state of the discipline. They search for intellectual unity where there are only enterprises in

universities and research institutions; they use equivocal folk concepts without any critical analysis (see, for example, the frequent use of the concept "student" to describe relations between sociologists of two generations). I will develop these points in a paper to be published about the recent history of the Chicago School of sociology.

9   On Hughes's distance from the theory of social disorganization, see the testimony of Whyte (1981/1943: 354–8). Wirth seems to have been a more constant defender of these theories, which one finds in certain of Park's essays, than Hughes and as a result he is frequently seen as the more direct follower of Park.

10   Since the book by Ellsworth Faris's son, Robert Faris, was published (1962), there have been many analyses of different aspects of the Chicago School of sociology: Carey (1975); Bulmer (1984); Raushenbush (1979), a biography of Park largely inspired by Hughes; and, in my opinion the best, Matthews (1977). See also the recent special issue of *Urban Life* (January 1982) and many testimonies: Anderson (1961, 1982, 1983), Cavan (1983), Hughes (1981), Hughes (1980–81), Lofland (1980), and Shils (1981).

The most continuously cited monographs are probably Anderson (1923) on hoboes, Thrasher (1927) on juvenile gangs, Wirth (1928) on the Jewish ghetto in Chicago, Zorbaugh (1929) on "natural areas" of Chicago, and Cressey (1932) on taxi dance halls; to this list one should also add life histories like the one Shaw (1930) gathered from a young delinquent. In fact, the enterprise was much broader, with other monographs published later – for example, Hayner (1936), and various research reports, such as *The Negro in Chicago* (Chicago Commission on Race Relations, 1922) and Landesco (1929). Hughes himself wrote a monograph on real estate agents in Chicago, but it was not typical of the Chicago School monographs of the 1930s and was not published until 1979.

11   Faught (1980) presents evidence of the similarities between Park's approach and Hughes's, drawn from their most general and programmatic texts. Such an exercise is patently misleading because it rests on statements of principle and not on finished products, that is, published accounts of research. One doubts that the examination of these accounts would lead to the same conclusions.

12   About Shaw and McKay, see Snodgrass (1976). On the role of Burgess as intermediary between sociology and social work, see Hughes's testimony in Raushenbusch (1979). The closeness of Wirth's point of view to that of social work, always evident to outside observers, has been noted by Hughes (1981).

13   See Becker et al. (1961) for the final published account of the first part of that research, begun in 1956; see Becker, Geer, and Hughes (1968) for the second part. (In both cases, the principal authors of the empirical work and of the published accounts of it were Becker and Geer.)

14   See Merton et al. (1957) for a first report of this research, undertaken in 1952, which has until now only been published in scattered reports.

15   Recall, however, Parson's attempt to study medicine at the end of the 1930s, using observation and interviews, which never produced a final published report. (On this point, see the testimony of the author in Parsons, 1970).

16   See Platt (1983). The two foremost examples of use of the expression "participant observation" with the meaning common at the present time are a rather obscure article by Lohman (1937), a student of Park's who taught at the University of Chicago after 1939, and a still often-cited article by anthropologist Kluckhohn (1940), based on her research experience in a Hispanic village in New Mexico.

17   In fact, this distinction between testimony and direct observation has been acquired only with difficulty (if at all) by the rest of the social sciences, as is suggested by the examples given from LePlay and Malinowski. To neglect it obviously leads to ignoring the problem of the construction of categories by the researcher or those he or she interviews.

18   At the level of teaching, Hughes began (when he arrived in Chicago in 1938) a beginning course in fieldwork (see Hughes, 1960, 1981), which according to many people played a large part in orienting many members of the next generation to the use of this method: see Becker and Debro (1970), Polsky (1969), and Becker, Geer, Riesman, and Weiss (1968). One can get a precise idea of the influence on Hughes of the ethnographic tradition (or, perhaps better, of how he relied equally and without discriminating on both sociological and anthropological researches) by comparing the book by Junker (1960) to the similar manual used by Park's students (Palmer, 1928) in which references to anthropology are absent.

19   The first of these is located in Deutscher (1966); the second is located in LaPiere (1969).

20   On the other hand, this intellectual disdain for ethnographic methods did not prevent several sociologists trained in other methods (for example, at Harvard or Columbia) from using it: see, for example, Whyte (a little before 1940) and Gouldner in the 1950s.

21   Several authors of classic Chicago School monographs have since written analyses of their methods of research: see, for example, Anderson (1961, 1982, 1983) or the recently discovered article by Cressey (1983). Anthropologists began publishing concrete descriptions of their field research earlier, maybe because they had to insist on the differences that separated their analyses from those of other travelers – missionaries, colonial administrators, and even traders – with whom they had ambivalent relationships. The foremost example is the Introduction to *Argonauts of the Western Pacific*, published in 1922.

22   Indeed, Thrasher's writing is much more typical of Chicago monographs of the 1930s than Cressey's who, with his numerous and doubtless literal citations from interviews and his effort to construct analytic schemes, anticipated the style of reporting research that was later adopted. However, this originality seems not to have been perceived at the time.

23   My interpretation on this point is a rejoinder to one by Wax (1971: 40).

24   One of the best examples in sociology of a detailed description of the conditions of data gathering in a fieldwork study is, to my knowledge, the one Stein wrote for Gouldner's book (1954). The methodological appendix by Dalton (1959), a more developed version of which was published in 1964, helped to establish the convention of publishing an account of the research process. After 1970, paradoxically, several descriptions of research projects were published without analyses of their results, interest in the research method having replaced interest in substantive results.

25   Among the best examples of this kind of article are Miller (1952), Vidich and Bensman (1954), Vidich (1955), Gusfield (1955), Schwartz and Schwartz (1955), Becker and Geer (1957), Becker (1958), and Gold (1958). To these one may add several contributions and research notes published in *Human Organization* and, in some cases, reprinted in Adams and Preiss (1960).

26   For examples, see the articles on jazz musicians published in Becker (1963). Of course, one also finds research accounts, written by sociologists in the Chicago tradition, that do not give explicit documentation (for example, Goffman's).

27   It follows from this interest in actors' lived meanings that fieldwork studies cannot be described as verifications of precise propositions formulated in advance; instead, their themes are almost always established in the course of collecting data. See, for example, Schatzman and Strauss (1973: 7) and Becker (1958: 653). Thus, the accusation of "empiricism," often made against these studies, is a complete misunderstanding of fieldwork research.

28   In making this distinction, analogous to the one Emerson (1981) applies to some recent studies, I only intend to make clear where Hughes's research style fits in the realm of fieldwork studies. Other equally pertinent distinctions exist and cannot be reduced to this one.

29   For a good example of these monographs, see Liebow (1967).
30   See, for example, Bittner's incisive remarks (1973).
31   Another illustration of these ideas about fieldwork, inspired more by phenomenology than by interactionism, is an article by Manning (1979).
32   Some of these articles originated as doctoral dissertations or even master's theses. Among the best known are several that have become the kind of classic republished in numerous collections: Becker's on jazz musicians (reprinted in Becker, 1963), Roy's on assembly line work (1952, 1954), Dalton's on managers (reprinted in his 1959 volume), and Gold's on janitors (1952). To these one can add Davis's on taxicab drivers (1959) and Westley's on the police (1953), although they are not so closely related to Hughes's analyses; studies that rely less on observation than on a series of interviews like Hall's on physicians (1949) and Becker's on school teachers (reprinted in Becker, 1970); and various studies that deal more with the functioning of an institution than with the problems of a category of workers, like that of Roth (1963).
33   Hughes's 1958 volume was based on these articles, although it lacks his suggestive analysis of the division of labor based on studies of the occupation of nursing. All the principal themes in Hughes's essays on the sociology of work are presented in an excellent article by Daniels (1972).
34   Explicit references to these concrete studies by his students are rather infrequent in Hughes's essays, which abound instead with allusions to published articles. As a remark of Platt's suggested to me, some of the studies Hughes frequently referred to belong to the body of industrial research sponsored by Warner. Treating the studies Hughes frequently cited as a relatively coherent whole must not, therefore, be interpreted to mean that Hughes influenced all of them, exclusively or preponderantly. Indeed, it is clearly impossible to isolate the influences of Hughes, Blumer, Warner, or Wirth on each generation of sociologists. Or to say it better, the idea of influence (like that of "student") is profoundly ambiguous since it is merely a convention researchers use to recognize or deny this or that form of originality in their own work and the work of others. This article is centered on Hughes because his essays contain the most inclusive and the most lucid discussions of fieldwork research in the Chicago tradition.
35   See Becker and Debro (1970), Dalton (1964), and the suggestive description later written by Davis (1974). Examination of a much larger range of monographs based on fieldwork suggests that their previous familiarity with their research settings was not unusual: see, for example, Roth (1963 and 1974b), Liebow (1967), Polsky (1969), and Humphreys (1970).
36   The only one of these well-known monographs of the 1930s done by a researcher who was not a "stranger" seems to be Anderson's, and even he spent a period of time tracking down the existence of hoboes before undertaking the principal study. Wirth seems to have been less familiar with his subject even though he came from a little town in Rhenamie and had lived in rural areas of the United States from 1911 until his arrival in Chicago. In some cases the authors of monographs written at Chicago in the 1930s discovered their research subjects through their social work activities, but this was not an advantage because of the difficulty they had in abandoning that point of view.
37   Dubin's article (1983), which examines the reports of research on dance halls carried out in 1920 by four students (among them, Saul Alinsky and Paul G. Cressey), illustrates the variety of problems fieldworkers encountered, depending upon their relationships to the subjects they studied. The poorest accounts are those whose authors locate themselves at the two extremes of intense participation and moral condemnation of dance hall activities.
38   Hughes developed the theme of emancipation – as opposed to alienation – in discussions of the sociology of work (1940–60), the sociology of religion (1955), the several generations of students whom he taught (1970a), and even his own biography (1981).

39   Among them were members of several minority ethnic groups and former GIs returning to their studies on scholarships, who were emancipated from their ethnic, working-class, or provincial origins.

40   See, for example, Hughes (1952), where one finds certain of the themes later developed by Goffman, who studied with Hughes (among others) at Chicago.

41   This point of view has since been developed by Roth (1956, 1966), another "student" of Hughes's.

42   On this point, often discussed in studies of the professions after 1970, see Roth (1974a) or Chapoulie (1973).

43   See Hughes (1959 and 1971: 292–4). Several years later, some sociological studies of deviance – those done by Becker, by Goffman, and even, in one case, by Cicourel – adopted a perspective like the one Hughes adopted vis-à- vis the division of labor.

44   See, for example, chapter 6 of *Men and Their Work* (Hughes, 1958). This chapter is the only previously unpublished one in that work.

45   The beginning of the 1960s was without doubt the period when American sociologists were least interested in fieldwork and interactionism was most discredited, but it was also the period when the field research for several studies that became famous at the end of the 1960s was carried out (studies by Becker, Goffman, Strauss, and others). During the same period one also discerns a relative lack of interest in the sociology of work and a fortiori in the essays of Hughes. These found a much larger audience at the end of the 1960s, as suggested by numerous replications and references to them in research reports.

46   Although ethnographers have carried out studies in their own societies almost continuously since 1945 – primarily studies of communities – only a few of them (to whom I have not referred here) have shown any familiarity with interactionist works. Since the beginning of the 1960s these studies have been more numerous. In the same period ethnographers have studied more limited segments of social life – hospitals and schools in particular; they have also written essays on the methods discussed by Hughes and others in the interactionist tradition, without referring to the research experience accumulated in that tradition. See, as examples, Jones (1970), Ablon (1977), and Cassel (1977).

47   I use here, among other testimonies, the still unpublished transcription of a conversation (in Berkeley, probably in 1981 or 1982) between Troy Duster, Howard Becker, Aaron Cicourel, John Kitsuse, Edwin Lemert, and David Matza.

References

Ablon, J. (1977) "Field methods in working with middle class Americans: new issues of values, personality, and reciprocity." Human Organization 36: 69–72.

Adams, R. N. and J. J. Preiss (1960) Human Organization Research. Homewood, IL: Dorsey Press.

Anderson, N. (1923) The Hobo: The Sociology of the Homeless Man. Chicago: Univ. of Chicago Press.

Anderson, N. (1961) "Introduction," in The Hobo: The Sociology of the Homeless Man. Chicago: Univ. of Chicago Press.

Anderson, N. (1982) "Sociology has many faces: part II." J. of the History of Sociology 3: 1–19.

Anderson, N. (1983) "A stranger at the gate: reflections on the Chicago school of sociology." Urban Life 11: 396–406.

Barton, A. H. and P. F. Lazarsfeld (1955) "Some functions of qualitative analysis in social research." Frankfurter Bieträge zur Soziologie 1: 321–61.

Becker, H. S. (1958) "Problems of inference and proof in participant observation." Amer. Soc. Rev. 23: 652–60.

Becker, H. S. (1963) Outsiders: Studies in the Sociology of Deviance. New York: Free Press.

Becker, H. S. (1970) Sociological Work: Method and Substance. Chicago: Aldine.

Becker, H. S. and J. Debro (1970) "Dialogue." Issues in Criminology 5: 159–179.

Becker, H. S. and B. Geer (1957) "Participant observation and interviewing: a comparison." Human Organization 16: 28–32.

Becker, H. S., B. Geer, and E. C. Hughes (1968) Making the Grade: The Academic Side of College Life. New York: John Wiley.

Becker, H. S., B. Geer, E. C. Hughes, and A. L. Strauss (1961) Boys in White: Student Culture in Medical School. Chicago: Univ. of Chicago Press.

Becker, H. S., B. Geer, D. Riesman, and R. S. Weiss (1968) Institutions and the Person: Essays Presented to Everett C. Hughes. Chicago: Aldine.

Bittner, E. (1967) "The police on skid-row: a study of peace-keeping." Amer. Soc. Rev. 32: 699–715.

Bittner, E. (1973) "Objectivity and realism in sociology," pp. 109–25 in G. Psathas (ed.) Phenomenological Sociology: Issues and Applications. New York: John Wiley.

Blumer, H. (1947) "Sociological theory in industrial relations." Amer. Soc. Rev. 12: 271–278.

Blumer, H. (1962) "Society as symbolic interaction," pp. 179–92 in A. M. Rose (ed.) Human Behavior and Social Processes: An Interactionist Approach. London: Routledge & Kegan Paul.

Blumer, H. (1969) Symbolic Interactionism: Perspective and Method. Englewood Cliffs, NJ: Prentice-Hall.

Bruyn, S. T. (1967) "The new empiricists: the participant observer and phenomenologist." Sociology and Social Research 51: 317–22.

Bulmer, M. (1984) The Chicago School of Sociology. Chicago: Univ. of Chicago Press.

Carey, J. T. (1975) Sociology and Public Affairs: The Chicago School. Beverly Hills, CA: Sage.

Cassel, J. (1977) "The relationship of the observer to the observed in peer group research." Human Organization 35: 412–16.

Castells, M. (1972) La question urbaine. Paris: François Maspero.

Cavan, R. (1983) "The Chicago school of sociology." Urban Life 11: 407–20.

Chapoulie, J.-M. (1973) "Sur l'analyse sociologique des groupes professionnels." Revue Française de Sociologie 16: 86–114.

Chicago Commission on Race Relations (1922) The Negro in Chicago: A Study of Race Relations and a Race Riot. Chicago: Univ. of Chicago Press.

Chombart de Lauwe, P.-H. (1952) Paris et l'agglomération parisienne. Paris: Presses Universitaires de France.

Cicourel, A. V. (1968) The Social Organization of Juvenile Justice. New York: John Wiley.

Cicourel, A. V. (1974) Theory and Method in a Study of Argentine Fertility. New York: John Wiley.

Cressey, P. G. (1932) The Taxi-Dance Hall. Chicago: University of Chicago Press.

Cressey, P. G. (1983) "A comparison of the roles of the 'sociological stranger' and the 'anonymous stranger' in field research." Urban Life 12: 102–20.

Dalton, M. (1959) Men Who Manage. New York: John Wiley.

Dalton, M. (1964) "Preconceptions and methods in Men Who Manage," pp. 50–95 in P. Hammond [ed.] Sociologists at Work. New York: Basic Books.

Daniels, A. K. (1972) "The irreverent eye." Contemporary Sociology 1: 402–09.

Davis, F. (1959) "The cabdriver and his fare: facets of a fleeting relationship." Amer. J. of Sociology 65: 158–65.

Davis, F. (1973) "The martian and the convert: ontological polarities in social research." Urban Life and Culture 2: 333–43.

Davis, F. (1974) "Stories and sociology." Urban Life and Culture 3: 310–16.

De Gerando, J.-M. (1800) Considérations sur les diverses méthodes à suivre dans l'observations des peuples sauvages. Paris: Société des Observateurs de l'homme. Republished in J. Copans and J. Jamin [eds.] (1978) Aux origines de l'anthropologie française. Paris: Le Sycomore.

De Gerando, J.-M., (1969) The Observation of Savage Peoples (F.C.T. Moore, ed. and trans.). Berkeley: Univ. of California Press.

Deutscher, I. (1966) "Words and deeds: social science and social policy." Social Problems 13: 235–54.

Deutscher, I. (1973) What We Say/What We Do: Sentiments and Acts. Glenview, IL: Scott, Foresman.

Diner, S. J. (1975) "Department and discipline: the department of sociology at the University of Chicago (1892–1920)." Minerva 13: 514–553.

Douglas, J. D. (1976) Investigative Social Research: Individual and Team Field Research. Beverly Hills, CA: Sage.

Dubin, S. C. (1983) "The moral continuum of deviance research: Chicago sociologists and the dance hall." Urban Life 12: 75–94.

Emerson, R. M. (1969) Judging Delinquents: Context and Process in Juvenile Court. Chicago: Aldine.

Emerson, R. M. (1981) "Observational field research". Ann. Rev. of Sociology 7: 351–78.

Faris, R. E. L. (1962) Chicago Sociology: 1920–32. Chicago: University of Chicago.

Faught, J. (1980) "Presuppositions of the Chicago school in the work of Everett C. Hughes." Amer. Sociologist 15: 72–82.

Fisher, B. M. and A. L. Strauss (1978) "Interactionism," pp. 457–98 in T. Bottomore and R. N. Nisbet [eds.] A History of Sociological Analysis. New York: Basic Books.

Freidson, E. (1971) Profession of Medicine: A Study in the Sociology of Applied Knowledge. New York: Dodd, Mead.

Glaser, B. G. and A. L. Strauss (1967) The Discovery of Grounded Theory: Strategies for Qualitative Research. Chicago: Aldine.

Gohre, P. (1891) Drei Monate Fabrikarbeiter und Hardwerksbursche. Leipzig: Grünow.

Gold, R. L. (1952) "Janitor versus tenant: a status-income dilemma." Amer. J. of Sociology 57: 486–93.

Gold, R. L. (1958) "Roles in sociological field observations." Social Forces 36: 217–233.

Gouldner, A. W. (1954) Patterns of Industrial Bureaucracy. Glencoe, IL: Free Press.

Gurvitch, G. [ed.] (1949) Industrialisation et technocratie. Paris: Armand Colin.

Gusfield, J. R. (1955) "Fieldwork reciprocities in studying a social movement." Human Organization 14: 29–34.

Halbwachs, M. (1932) "Chicago, expérience ethnique." Annales d'histoire économique et sociale 4: 11–49.

Hall, O. (1948) "The stages of a medical career." Amer. J. of Sociology 53: 327–36.

Hall, O. (1949) "Types of medical careers." Amer. J. of Sociology 55: 243–53.

Hayner, N. (1936) Hotel Life. Chapel Hill: University of Carolina Press.

Hughes, E. C. (1931/1979) The Growth of an Institution: The Chicago Real Estate Board. Chicago: Arno Press.

Hughes, E. C. (1943) French Canada in Transition. Chicago: University of Chicago Press. [French trans. J. C. Falardeau, "Rencontre de deux mondes: la crise d'industrialisation du Canada Français." Montréal: Les Editions du Boreal Express.]

Hughes, E. C. (1951a) "Mistakes at work." Canadian J. of Economics and Political Sci. 17: 320–27.

Hughes, E. C. (1951b) "Work and self," pp. 313–23 in J. H. Rohrer and M. Sherif (eds.) Social Psychology at the Crossroads. New York: Harper & Row.

Hughes, E. C. (1952) "The sociological study of work: an editorial foreword." Amer. J. of Sociology 57: 423–6.

Hughes, E. C. (1955) "The early and contemporary study of religion." Amer. J. of Sociology 60: i–iv.

Hughes, E. C. (1956) "Of sociology and the interview: editorial preface." Amer. J. of Sociology 62: 137–42.

Hughes, E. C. (1958) Men and Their Work. Glencoe, IL: Free Press.

Hughes, E. C. (1959) "The study of occupations," pp. 442–58 in R. K. Merton et al. (eds.) Sociology Today. New York: Basic Books.

Hughes, E. C. (1960) "The place of field work in social science," pp. iii–xiii in B. H. Junker (ed.) Field Work: An Introduction to the Social Sciences. Chicago: University of Chicago Press.

Hughes, E. C. (1961) "Tarde's Psychologie Economique: an unknown classic by a forgotten sociologist." Amer. J. of Sociology 66: 553–9.

Hughes, E. C. (1962) "Sociologists and the public." Transactions of the Fifth Congress of Sociology 1. Washington, DC: International Sociological Association.

Hughes, E. C. (1970a) "Teaching as fieldwork." Amer. Sociologist 5: 13–18.

Hughes, E. C. (1970b) "The humble and the proud: comparative study of occupations." Sociological Q. 11: 147–56.

Hughes, E. C. (1971) The Sociological Eye: Selected Papers. Chicago: Aldine.

Hughes, E. C. (1974) "Who studies whom?" Human Organization 33: 327–34.

Hughes, E. C. (1981) Interview by R. S. Weiss. (Unpublished manuscript)

Hughes, E. C. and H. M. Hughes (1952) Where Peoples Meet: Racial and Ethnic Frontiers. Glencoe, IL: Free Press.

Hughes, E. C., H. M. Hughes, and I. Deutscher (1958) Twenty Thousand Nurses Tell Their Story. Philadelphia: Lippincott.

Hughes, H. M. (1980–81) "On becoming a sociologist." J. of the History of Sociology 3: 27–39.

Humphreys, L. (1970) Tearoom Trade. Chicago: Aldine.

Jones, D. J. (1970) "Towards a native anthropology." Human Organization 29: 251–259.

Junker, B. H. (1960) Field Work: An Introduction to the Social Sciences. Chicago: Univ. of Chicago Press.

Kluckhohn, F. R. (1940) "The participant observer technique in small communities." Amer. J. of Sociology 46: 331–43.

Landesco, J. (1929) Organized Crime in Chicago: Part III, Illinois Crime Survey. Chicago: Univ. of Chicago Press.

Langlois, C. and C. Seignobos (1897) Introduction aux études historiques. Paris: Hachette.

Lapiere, R. T. (1969) "Comment on Irwin Deutscher's Looking Backward." Amer. Sociologist 4: 41–2.

LePlay, F. (1855) Les Ouvriers Européens. Paris: Imprimerie Impériale.

Liebow, E. (1967) Tally's Corner. Boston: Little, Brown.

Lofland, L. [ed.] (1980) "Reminiscences of classic Chicago: the Blumer-Hughes talk." Urban Life 9: 251–81.

Lohman, J. D. (1937) "The participant observer in community studies." Amer. Soc. Rev. 2: 890–98.

Malinowski, B. (1922) Argonauts of the Western Pacific. Prospect Heights, IL: Waveland Press.

McCall, G. J. and J. L. Simmons (1969) Issues in Participant Observation: A Text and Reader. Reading, MA: Addison-Wesley.

Manning, P. K. (1973) "Existential sociology." Sociological Q. 14: 200–25.

Manning, P. K. (1979) "Metaphors of the field: varieties of organizational discourse." Administrative Sci. Q. 24: 660–71.

Matthews, F. H. (1977) Quest for an American Sociology: Robert E. Park and the Chicago School. Montreal: McGill-Queen's Univ. Press.

Merton, R. K., G. Reader, and P. L. Kendall (1957) The Student-Physician: Introductory Studies in the Sociology of Medical Education. Cambridge, MA: Harvard Univ. Press.

Miller, S. M. (1952) "The participant observer and over-rapport." Amer. Soc. Rev. 17: 97–99.

Obershall, A. R. (1965) Empirical Social Research in Germany (1848–1914). Amsterdam: Mouton.

Palmer, V. (1928) Field Studies in Sociology: A Student's Manual. Chicago: Univ. of Chicago Press.

Park, R. E. and E. W. Burgess (1921) Introduction to the Science of Sociology. Chicago: Univ. of Chicago Press.

Park, R. E. and E. W. Burgess (1925) The City. Chicago: Univ. of Chicago Press.

Parsons, T. (1970) "On Building social system theory: a personal history." Daedalus 99: 826–81.

Platt, J. (1983) "The development of the 'participant observation' method in sociology: origin myth and history." J. of the History of the Behavioral Sciences 19: 379–93.

Polsky, N. (1969) Hustlers, Beats and Others. Garden City, NY: Doubleday.

Raushenbush, W. (1979) Robert E. Park: Biography of a Sociologist. Durham, NC: Duke Univ. Press.

Rock, P. (1979) The Making of Symbolic Interactionism. London: Macmillan.

Rose, A. M. [ed.] (1962) Human Behavior and Social Processes: An Interactionist Approach. London: Routledge & Kegan Paul.

Roth, J. A. (1956) "The status of interviewing." Midwest Sociologist 19: 8–11.

Roth, J. A. (1963) Timetables: Structuring the Passage of Time in Hospital Treatment and Other Careers. Indianapolis, IN: Bobbs- Merrill.

Roth, J. A. (1966) "Hired hand research." Amer. Sociologist 1: 190–96.

Roth, J. A. (1974a) "Professionalism: the sociologist's decoy." Sociology of Work and Occupations 1: 6–23.

Roth, J. A. (1974b) "Turning adversity to account." Urban Life and Culture 3: 347–361.

Roy D. (1952) "Quota restriction and goldbricking in a machine shop." Amer. J. of Sociology 57: 427–42.

Roy, D. (1954) "Efficiency and 'the fix': informal intergroup relations in a piecework machine shop." Amer. J. of Sociology 60: 255–66.

Schatzman, L. and A. L. Strauss (1973) Field Research: Strategies for a Natural Sociology. Englewood Cliffs, NJ: Prentice-Hall.

Schwartz, M. S. and C. G. Schwartz (1955) "Problems in participant observation." Amer. J. of Sociology 60: 343–54.

Shaw, C. A. (1930) The Jackroller: A Delinquent Boy's Own Story. Chicago: Univ. of Chicago Press.

Shibutani, T. [ed.] (1970) Human Nature and Collective Behavior: Papers in Honor of Herbert Blumer. Englewood Cliffs, NJ: Prentice-Hall.

Shils, E. (1948) The Present State of American Sociology. Glencoe, IL: Free Press.

Shils, E. (1981) "Some academics, mainly in Chicago." Amer. Scholar 50: 179–196.

Snodgrass, J. (1976) "Clifford R. Shaw and Henry D. McKay: Chicago criminologists." British J. of Criminology 16: 1–19.

Spradley, J. P. (1980) Participant Observation. New York: Holt, Rinehart & Winston.

Stein, M. R. (1954) "Field work procedures: the social organization of a student research team," pp. 247–69 in A. W. Gouldner, (ed.) Patterns of Industrial Bureaucracy. Glencoe, IL: Free Press.

Sudnow, D. (1967) Passing On: The Social Organization of Dying. Englewood Cliffs, NJ: Prentice-Hall.

Sutherland, E. H. and C. Conwell (1937) The Professional Thief. Chicago: Univ. of Chicago Press.

Thrasher, F. M. (1927) The Gang: A Study of 1313 Gangs in Chicago. Chicago: Univ. of Chicago Press.

Vidich, A. J. (1955) "Participant observation and the collection and interpretation of data." Amer. J. of Sociology 55: 354–60.

Vidich, A. J. and J. Bensman (1954) "The validity of field data." Human Organization 13: 20–27.

Wax, M. L. (1972) "Tenting with Malinowski." Amer. Sociological Rev. 37: 1–13.

Wax, R. H. (1968) "Participant observation." Intl. Encyclopedia of the Social Sciences 11: 238–41.

Wax, R. H. (1971) Doing Fieldwork: Warnings and Advice. Chicago: Univ. of Chicago Press.

Westley, W. A. (1953) "Violence and the police." Amer. J. of Sociology 59: 34–41.

Whyte, W. F. (1981) Street Corner Society: The Social Structure of an Italian Slum. (originally published in 1943) Chicago: Univ. of Chicago Press.

Wirth, L. (1928) The Ghetto. Chicago: Univ. of Chicago Press.

Zorbaugh, H. H. (1929) The Gold Coast and the Slum. Chicago: Univ. of Chicago Press.

Part II

Qualitative Interviewing, Life History, and Narrative Analysis

INTRODUCTION TO PART II

The following readings consider issues central to qualitative interviewing, life history, and narrative analysis. These methods are among the oldest and most venerable among the qualitative researcher's repertoire. In recent years, however, they have become subject to a great deal of renewed interest and critical debate. Social scientists once prided themselves on a professional ability to use the information they elicited from people to generate superior understandings of those people and of their social worlds. This ability was always somewhat complicated in the case of qualitative researchers, given their professed mandate to faithfully grasp how research subjects themselves orient to things. However, what once seemed just a complication has blossomed into what some have called a full-blown epistemological crisis. These days there remains very little consensus as to whether narratives elicited from those we study are more properly viewed as data to be analyzed, as incisive analyses in their own right, or as complex combinations of the two. The readings that follow offer different takes upon this question and together provide a good sense of the range of issues that are at stake.

Howard Becker's essay, "The Life History and the Scientific Mosaic," was first published in 1966. It was expressly written as an introduction to a reissue of Clifford Shaw's famous life-history study *The Jack-Roller*. Between the first publication of *The Jack-Roller* in 1930, and the reissue for which Becker wrote, quantitative research methods predicated on a positivist philosophy of science had come to dominate academic sociology. In this climate there was little cause to assume that the majority of practicing sociologists appreciated the contribution a document like *The Jack-Roller* makes to the social sciences. Becker's essay is an effort to help them do so. Though it advances a dissident position, this essay plainly reflects the dispute domain into which Becker sought to intervene, a dispute domain saturated with positivist dogma and concerns to fortify sociology's scientific identity. Accordingly, the merits of Shaw's study are asserted above all in terms of its pertinence to "general sociological theory" (p. 63). The life history method is presented primarily as a source of *data* to be appropriated for social scientific analysis, "[the] sociologist who gathers a life history takes steps to ensure it covers everything we want to know . . . [t]he sociologist keeps the subject oriented to the questions sociology is interested in" (p. 64). Hence, while the method is promoted as a resource for faithfully recovering the richly nuanced detail of respondents' "own stor[ies]," the chief purpose of learning these stories is cast in terms of their prospective use in developing formal social theory.

Becker indicates that life histories of particular types of people (delinquents in the case of *The Jack-Roller*) can serve as touchstones to evaluate scientific theories that purport to deal with those types of people. While the life history may not offer definitive proof of any particular theoretical proposition, it may stand as a "negative case," that can be used to falsify theories that do not jibe with it. Life histories may cast light upon the *subjective* side of institutional processes. That is, they can reveal how institutional arrangements are reproduced, sometimes unwittingly, through activities that are locally meaningful to the actors involved. Because they are comparatively sensitive to the temporality of social life, life histories may produce data uniquely suited to formulating theories of general social processes like socialization and social change. Finally, life histories may serve to reveal lifestyles, points of view, and social circumstances we would otherwise never encounter. They may thus serve to expand our social horizons, which cannot but improve our skills as social scientists. Becker's remarks variously indicate how data collected through qualitative interviews and life history documents can be valuable resources for scientific theorizing of the formal hypothesis testing variety. But he also bids for a future when "a fuller understanding of the complexity of the scientific enterprise will restore sociologists' sense of the versatility and worth of the life history" (p. 73). In the future Becker urged, we would not treat life histories merely as data to support formal theorizing, but in their own right as fully-fledged and respected contributions to the scientific mosaic.

Since Becker wrote "The Life History and the Scientific Mosaic," many social scientists have followed the course he proposed. Many have indeed come to more fully understand the complexity of the scientific enterprise and have become a good deal more sophisticated in their regard for the knowledge making potential of qualitative interviews, life histories, and narrative. One major component of this movement has been a growing sensitivity to the details of the interview process itself. No longer seen simply as a window on the worlds of research subjects, the interview has itself become the subject of increasing analytic attention. Marjorie DeVault has been at the forefront of a growing community of researchers who advise greater analytic attention be paid to the *conversational* details of interviews. Drawing upon phenomenology, ethnomethodology, and feminist scholarship, DeVault argues that the *forms* of talk that emerge in interviews may reveal a great deal about how interviewees experience their worlds. In short, *how* things are said can often disclose as much or more than *what* is actually said.

In her essay, DeVault notes that "language itself reflects male experiences, and . . . its categories are often incongruent with women's lives" (p. 96). This creates a methodological challenge for researchers who would hope to use language to learn about women's experiences. DeVault discusses analytic strategies pertaining to four elements of the research process: constructing topics, listening to respondents, transcribing and editing interview material, and writing about respondents' lives. Throughout her essay, DeVault indicates how women might draw upon their own personal experiences as women to help them elicit, interpret, and convey the language and experiences of their respondents. In this she expands upon the professionally motivated strategies of data collection and analysis outlined in Becker's essay. As she writes, "[p]rofessional training as sociologists and the routine practices of the discipline encourage us to abandon . . . traditions of 'woman talk' in favor of a more abstract, controlled, and emotionless discourse. I have meant to suggest that as we construct feminist discourses in sociology, we can instead recognize those distinctively female traditions, borrow from them, and build upon them in our practice as researchers" (p.112). While DeVault still views respondents' talk primarily as data to be analyzed, she has offered a greatly expanded picture of the range of interpretive resources that we might properly bring to the work of data collection and analyses.

Holstein and Gubrium are also interested in the local dynamics of the interview process itself. They explicitly eschew the classic understanding of interviewing which likens the process "to 'prospecting' for the true facts and feelings residing within the respondent" (p. 115). Interviewers are not merely passive recipients of respondents' accounts nor are respondents merely repositories of static memories and experiences that interviewers might selectively excavate. Instead, "[b]oth parties to the interview are necessarily and ineluctably *active*. Meaning is not merely elicited by apt questioning, nor simply transported through respondent replies; it is actively and communicatively assembled in the interview encounter" (p. 114). This perspective advises careful attention to the specific procedures through which interviewers and respondents collaboratively accomplish not only the conversational exchange that is the interview itself, but also the substantive account of things that is the interview's result. Attention to the inevitably active and collaborative nature of interviews and the data we draw from them raises profoundly important questions regarding such age-old distinctions as those between theory and data, analyst and analysand, and, of course, objectivity and subjectivity. While by no means abjuring the notion of scientific objectivity, Holstein and Gubrium call for closer attention to the myriad locally organized activities through which objectivity is honored, not only as a scientific ideal, but as an actual concrete accomplishment.

In the final essay, "Narrative Authenticity," Elinor Ochs and Lisa Capps pick up and elaborate upon the idea that social scientists are not the only social actors concerned to establish the objective validity of their descriptions of social events. Comparative study of how credible description is done across a variety of scientific and non-scientific settings serves to reveal the complex realities of actually doing objectivity as a type of social practice. Drawing from data of a dinner table discussion involving a mother, father, and two young brothers, Ochs and Capps explicate a series of recurrent techniques used in the social accomplishment of narrative authenticity. When narrative reports are presented as valid memories of real events, claimants are often required to furnish such things as authoritative corroborating testimony, further details of the event in question, and various forms of affective evidence which indicate such things as candor, trustworthiness, and certainty. These techniques for doing objectivity are demonstrably evident across a wide array of social settings and figure in very powerful sorts of ways throughout both our public and private lives. Ochs and Capps demonstrate how narrative analysis can be used to illuminate a very great deal about both the importance and the intricacies of achieving and sustaining shared memories, and of how profoundly such work shapes us.

References

Becker, Howard S. 1970. "The Life History and the Scientific Mosaic." In *Sociological Work: Method and Substance*. Chicago: Aldine Publishing Company.

DeVault, Marjorie L. 1990. "Talking and Listening from Women's Standpoint: Feminist Strategies for Interviewing and Analysis." *Social Problems* 37 (1): 96–116.

Holstein, James A. and Jaber F. Gubrium. 1997. "Active Interviewing." In *Qualitative Research: Theory, Method and Practice*. Edited by David Silverman. Thousand Oaks, CA: Sage Publications.

Further Reading on Qualitative Interviewing, Life History, and Narrative Analysis

Bourdieu, Pierre. 1996. "Understanding." *Theory, Culture and Society.* 13(2): 17–37.

DeVault, Marjorie L. 1999. *Liberating Method: Feminism and Social Research.* Philadelphia: Temple University Press.

Douglas, Jack D. 1985. *Creative Interviewing.* Beverly Hills, CA: Sage.

Harding, Sandra. 1991. *Whose Science? Whose Knowledge?: Thinking from Women's Lives.* Ithaca, NY: Cornell University Press.

Holstein, James A. and Jaber F. Gubrium. 1995. *The Active Interview.* Thousand Oaks, CA: Sage.

Josselson, Ruthelen and Amia Lieblich, eds. 1995. *Interpreting Experience: The Narrative Study of Lives.* Thousand Oaks, CA: Sage.

Mishler, Elliot G. 1986. *Research Interviewing: Context and Narrative.* Cambridge, MA: Harvard University Press.

Riessman, Catherine Kohler. 1993. *Narrative Analysis.* Newbury Park, CA: Sage.

Spradley, James P. 1979. *The Ethnographic Interview.* New York: Holt, Rinehart and Winston.

Weiss, Robert S. 1995. *Learning from Strangers: The Art and Method of Qualitative Interview Studies.* New York: Free Press.

4 The Life History and the Scientific Mosaic

Howard S. Becker

The life history is not conventional social science "data," although it has some of the features of that kind of fact, being an attempt to gather material useful in the formulation of general sociological theory. Nor is it a conventional autobiography, although it shares with autobiography its narrative form, its first-person point of view and its frankly subjective stance. It is certainly not fiction, although the best life history documents have a sensitivity and pace, a dramatic urgency, that any novelist would be glad to achieve.

The differences between these forms lie both in the perspective from which the work is undertaken and in the methods used. The writer of fiction is not, of course, concerned with fact at all, but rather with dramatic and emotional impact, with form and imagery, with the creation of a symbolic and artistically unified world. Fidelity to the world as it exists is only one of many problems for him, and for many authors it is of little importance.

The autobiographer proposes to explain his life to us and thus commits himself to maintaining a close connection between the story he tells and what an objective investigation might discover. When we read autobiography, however, we are always aware that the author is telling us only part of the story, that he has selected his material so as to present us with the picture of himself he would prefer us to have and that he may have ignored what would be trivial or distasteful to him, though of great interest to us.

As opposed to these more imaginative and humanistic forms, the life history is more down to earth, more devoted to our purposes than those of the author, less concerned with artistic values than with a faithful rendering of the subject's experience and interpretation of the world he lives in. The sociologist who gathers a life history takes steps to ensure that it covers everything we want to know, that no important fact or event is slighted, that what purports to be factual squares with other available evidence and that the subject's interpretations are honestly given. The sociologist keeps the subject oriented to the questions sociology is interested in, asks him about events that require amplification, tries to make the story told jibe

Thomas and Znaniecki published the first sociological life history document to receive wide attention in *The Polish Peasant*.[1] Clifford Shaw and his associates published several others in the years following: *The Jack-Roller, The Natural History of a Delinquent Career,* and *Brothers in Crime*. During the same period Edwin Sutherland published the still popular *Professional Thief*. And similar documents have appeared occasionally since, most recently *The Fantastic Lodge* and *Hustler!*[2] When *The Jack-Roller* was reissued a few years ago, I was asked to write an introduction and made that the occasion for some thoughts on the place of the life history in contemporary sociology.

with matters of official record and with material furnished by others familiar with the person, event, or place being described. He keeps the game honest for us.

In so doing, he pursues the job from his own perspective, a perspective which emphasizes the value of the person's "own story." This perspective differs from that of some other social scientists in assigning major importance to the interpretations people place on their experience as an explanation for behavior. To understand why someone behaves as he does you must understand how it looked to him, what he thought he had to contend with, what alternatives he saw open to him; you can understand the effects of opportunity structures, delinquent subcultures, social norms, and other commonly invoked explanations of behavior only by seeing them from the actor's point of view.

The University of Chicago sociology department promoted this perspective vigorously during the 1920s. Almost every study made some use of personal documents. Theoretically grounded in Mead's social psychology, its practicality in research attested by *The Polish Peasant*, and its use persuasively urged by Ernest W. Burgess, the life history enjoyed great popularity. It was one of the many research devices that found a place in the research scheme of the department.

The research scheme did not grow out of a well-developed axiomatic theory, but rather from a vision of the character of cities and city life which permeated much of the research done at Chicago in the exciting period after the arrival of Robert E. Park in 1916. *The Ghetto, The Gold Coast and the Slum, The Gang*[3] – all these were part of the research scheme. And so were the ecological studies of the succession of ethnic groups in Chicago and of the distribution of juvenile delinquency, mental illness, and other forms of pathology. Park enunciated the general scheme, as it developed, in occasional papers on the nature of the city and the role of communication in social life, and in introductions to the books his students produced. Everything was material for the developing theory. And studies of all kinds, done by a variety of methods, contributed to its development.[4] The contribution of any study could thus be evaluated in the context of the total enterprise, not as though it stood alone.

When I first went to San Francisco several years ago and began to think about doing research there, I automatically began looking for the Local Community Fact Book, the demographic studies, the analyses of neighborhoods and institutions, and all the other kinds of background material I had come to take for granted when I worked in Chicago. But they were not there; no one had done them. Perhaps it is because no one group of researchers had ever existed there as well organized as the group that got its start under Park during the twenties. That group saw connections among all the various problems they were working on. Above all, they saw that the things they were studying had close and intimate connections with the city, considered in the abstract, and with Chicago itself, the particular city they were working in. For the Chicago group, whatever the particular subject matter under study, the researcher assumed that it took its character in part from the unique character and form of the city it occurred in. He relied, implicitly and explicitly, on the knowledge that had already been gathered, as he contributed his own small piece to the mosaic of the theory of the city and knowledge of Chicago that Park was building.

The image of the mosaic is useful in thinking about such a scientific enterprise. Each piece added to a mosaic adds a little to our understanding of the total picture. When many pieces have been placed we can see, more or less clearly, the objects and

the people in the picture and their relation to one another. Different pieces contribute different things to our understanding: some are useful because of their color,
others because they make clear the outline of an object. No one piece has any great
job to do; if we do not have its contribution, there are still other ways to come to an
understanding of the whole.

Individual studies can be like pieces of mosaic and were so in Park's day. Since the
picture in the mosaic was Chicago, the research had an ethnographic, "case history"
flavor, even though Chicago itself was seen as somehow representative of all cities.
Whether its data were census figures or interviews, questionnaire results or life
histories, the research took into account local peculiarities, exploring those things
that were distinctively true of Chicago in the 1920s. In so doing, they partially
completed a mosaic of great complexity and detail, with the city itself the subject, a
"case" which could be used to test a great variety of theories and in which the
interconnections of a host of seemingly unrelated phenomena could be seen, however imperfectly.

Our attention today is turned away from local ethnography, from the massing of
knowledge about a single place, its parts, and their connections. We emphasize
abstract theory-building more than we used to. The national survey is frequently
used as a basic mode of data collection. Above all, researchers are increasingly
mobile, moving from city to city and university to university every few years,
building no fund of specialized local knowledge and passing none on to their
students. The trend is away from the community study – there will be no more
elaborate programs of coordinated study such as those that produced the *Yankee
City Series*[5] or *Black Metropolis*.[6] And a great loss it will be.

In any case, the scientific contribution of such a life history as *The Jack-Roller* can
be assessed properly only by seeing it in relation to all the studies done under Park's
direction, for it drew on and depended on all of them, just as all the later studies of
that Golden Age of Chicago sociology depended, a little, on it. Much of the background that any single study would either have to provide in itself or, even worse,
about which it would have to make unchecked assumptions, was already at hand for
the reader of *The Jack-Roller*. When Stanley, its protagonist, speaks of the boyish
games of stealing he and his pals engaged in, we know that we can find an extensive
and penetrating description of that phenomenon in Thrasher's *The Gang*. And when
he speaks of the time he spent on West Madison Street, we know that we can turn to
Nels Anderson's *The Hobo*[7] for an understanding of the milieu Stanley then found
himself in. If we are concerned about the representativeness of Stanley's case, we
have only to turn to the ecological studies carried on by Shaw and McKay[8] to see the
same story told on a grand scale in mass statistics. And, similarly, if one wanted to
understand the maps and correlations contained in ecological studies of delinquency,
one could then turn to *The Jack-Roller* and similar documents for that understanding.

I am not sure what the criteria are by which one judges the contribution of a piece
of scientific work considered in its total context, but I know that they are not such
currently fashionable criteria as are implied by the model of the controlled experiment. We do not expect, in a large and differentiated program of research, that any
one piece of work will give us all the answers or, indeed, all of any one answer. What
must be judged is the entire research enterprise in all its parts. (One can, of course,

assess life histories by such criteria as those suggested by Kluckhohn, Angell and Dollard.)[9] Criteria have yet to be established for determining how much one piece of a mosaic contributes to the conclusions that are warranted by consideration of the whole, but these are just the kind of criteria that are needed. In their place, we can temporarily install a sympathetic appreciation of some of the functions performed by life history documents, taking *The Jack-Roller* as a representative case.

What are those functions? In the first place, *The Jack-Roller* can serve as a touchstone to evaluate theories that purport to deal with phenomena like those of Stanley's delinquent career. Whether it is a theory of the psychological origins of delinquent behavior, a theory of the roots of delinquency in juvenile gangs, or an attempt to explain the distribution of delinquency throughout a city, any theory of delinquency must, if it is to be considered valid, explain or at least be consistent with the facts of Stanley's case as they are reported here. Thus, even though the life history does not in itself provide definitive proof of a proposition, it can be a negative case that forces us to decide a proposed theory is inadequate.

To say this is to take an approach to scientific generalization that deserves some comment. We may decide to accept a theory if it explains, let us say, 95 per cent of the cases that fall in its jurisdiction. Many reputable scientists do. In contrast, one can argue that any theory that does not explain all cases is inadequate, that other factors than those the theory specifies must be operating to produce the result we want to explain. It is primarily a question of strategy. If we assume that exceptions to any rule are a normal occurrence, we will perhaps not search as hard for further explanatory factors as we otherwise might. But if we regard exceptions as potential negations of our theory, we will be spurred to search for them.[10]

More importantly, the negative case will respond to careful analysis by suggesting the direction the search should take.[11] Inspection of its features will reveal attributes which differ from those of otherwise similar cases, or processes at work whose steps have not all been fully understood. If we know the case in some detail, as a life history document allows us to know it, our search is more likely to be successful; it is in this sense that the life history is a useful theoretical touchstone.

The life history also helps us in areas of research that touch on it only tangentially. Every piece of research crosses frontiers into new terrain it does not explore thoroughly, areas important to its main concern in which it proceeds more by assumption than investigation.[12] A study of a college, for instance, may make assumptions (indeed, must make them) about the character of the city, state, and region it is located in, about the social class background and experience of its students, and about a host of other matters likely to influence the operation of the school and the way it affects students. A study of a mental hospital or prison will make similarly unchecked assumptions about the character of the families whose members end up in the institution. A life history – although it is not the only kind of information that can do this – provides a basis on which those assumptions can be realistically made, a rough approximation of the direction in which the truth lies.

In addition to these matters of neighboring fact, so to speak, the life history can be particularly useful in giving us insight into the subjective side of much-studied institutional processes, about which unverified assumptions are also often made. Sociologists have lately been concerned with processes of adult socialization and, to take an instance to which Stanley's case is directly relevant, with the processes of degradation and "stripping" associated with socialization into rehabilitative institutions such as prisons and mental hospitals.[13] Although the theories concern themselves with institutional action rather than individual experience, they either assume something about the way people experience such processes or at least raise a question about the nature of that experience. Although Stanley's prison experiences do not, of course, provide fully warranted knowledge of these matters, they give us some basis for making a judgment.

The life history, by virtue again of its wealth of detail, can be important at those times when an area of study has grown stagnant, has pursued the investigation of a few variables with ever-increasing precision but has received dwindling increments of knowledge from the pursuit. When this occurs, investigators might well proceed by gathering personal documents which suggest new variables, new questions, and new processes, using the rich though unsystematic data to provide a needed reorientation of the field.

Beneath these specific contributions which the life history is capable of making lies one more fundamental. The life history, more than any other technique except perhaps participant observation, can give meaning to the overworked notion of *process*. Sociologists like to speak of "ongoing processes" and the like, but their methods usually prevent them from seeing the processes they talk about so glibly.

George Herbert Mead, if we take him seriously, tells us that the reality of social life is a conversation of significant symbols, in the course of which people make tentative moves and then adjust and reorient their activity in the light of the responses (real and imagined) others make to those moves. The formation of the individual act is a process in which conduct is continually reshaped to take account of the expectations of others, as these are expressed in the immediate situation and as the actor supposes they may come to be expressed. Collective activity, of the kind pointed to by concepts like "organization" or "social structure," arises out of a continuous process of mutual adjustment of the actions of all the actors involved. Social process, then, is not an imagined interplay of invisible forces or a vector made up of the interaction of multiple social factors, but an observable process of symbolically mediated interaction.[14]

Observable, yes; but not easily observable, at least not for scientific purposes. To observe social process as Mead described it takes a great deal of time. It poses knotty problems of comparability and objectivity in data gathering. It requires an intimate understanding of the lives of others. So social scientists have, most often, settled for less demanding techniques such as the interview and the questionnaire.

These techniques can, I think, tell us much, but only as we are able to relate them to a vision of the underlying Meadian social process we would know had we more adequate data. We can, for instance, give people a questionnaire at two periods in their life and infer an underlying process of change from the differences in their answers. But our interpretation has significance only if our imagery of the underlying process is accurate. And this accuracy of imagery – this congruence of theoretically posited process with what we could observe if we took the necessary time and trouble – can be partially achieved by the use of life history documents. For the life history, if it is done well, will give us the details of that process whose character we would otherwise only be able to speculate about, the process to which our data must ultimately be referred if they are to have theoretical and not just an operational and predictive significance. It will describe those crucial interactive episodes in which new lines of individual and collective activity are forged, in which new aspects of the self are brought into being. It is by thus giving a realistic basis to our imagery of the underlying process that the life history serves the purposes of checking assumptions, illuminating organization, and reorienting stagnant fields.

But perhaps the most important service performed for sociology by a document like *The Jack-Roller* is one that it also performs for those who are not sociologists. David Riesman has described social science as, in part, a "conversation between the classes."[15] It describes to people the way of life of segments of their society with which they would never otherwise come in contact. The life history, because it is the actor's "own story," is a live and vibrant message from "down there," telling us what it means to be a kind of person we have never met face to face. The United States is fortunate in having fewer barriers, in the form of closed social circles and rules against interaction outside of them, than most societies. Nevertheless, the distances between social classes, between ethnic groups, and between age groups are such that it is hard for most sociologists (let alone others whose work does not push them toward this knowledge) to comprehend what it means to live the life of a Negro junkie or a Polish delinquent.

Johan Galtung suggests the function of this kind of knowledge in the scientific process in his discussion of the causes of the excessive abstractness and formality of Latin American sociology. He argues that Latin American society is more rigidly stratified, both horizontally and vertically, than the societies of northern Europe and North America. This means that the Latin American, when he comes to sociology, will never have had the informal interaction with members of other classes and social segments that young people in other societies gain through travel, through summer employment, and in similar ways. As a result, Galtung says, preconceived ideas of the character of other members of the society are never put to the test of direct confrontation with social reality:

> Sociologists who would never accept the idea that the only thing which has motivated them has been the desire to make money have no difficulty in perceiving the capitalist as interested only in the most money for the least work, or the worker as motivated in a similar manner. A more intimate knowledge of them would invariably reveal shadings, greater identification, greater variety in motives, but the paucity of interaction protects the sociologist from this knowledge. From this comes the great interest in the alienation of the lower classes: without denying its reality, a factor which maintains the image of the alienation of the working class is the alienation of the intellectual himself, with respect to his society in general and certainly with respect to the working class.[16]

By providing this kind of voice from a culture and situation that are ordinarily not known to intellectuals generally, and to sociologists in particular, *The Jack-Roller* enables us to improve our theories at the most profound level: by putting ourselves in Stanley's skin, we can feel and become aware of the deep biases about such people that ordinarily permeate our thinking and shape the kinds of problems we investigate. By truly entering into Stanley's life, we can begin to see what we take for granted (and ought not to) in designing our research – what kinds of assumptions about delinquents, slums, and Poles are embedded in the way we set the questions we study. Stanley's story allows us, if we want to take advantage of it, to begin to ask questions about delinquency from the point of view of the delinquent. If we take Stanley seriously, as his story must impel us to do, we might well raise a series of questions that have been relatively little studied – questions about the people who deal with delinquents, the tactics they use, their suppositions about the world, and the constraints and pressures they are subject to. Such studies are only now beginning to be done. Close study of *The Jack-Roller* and similar documents might provide us with a wide range of questions to put as we begin to look at the dealings of policemen, judges, and jailers with delinquents.

Given the variety of scientific uses to which the life history may be put, one must wonder at the relative neglect into which it has fallen. Sociologists, it is true, have never given it up altogether. But neither have they made it one of their standard research tools. They read the documents available and assign them for their students to read. But they do not ordinarily think of gathering life history documents themselves or of making the technique part of their research approach.

A number of simultaneous changes probably contributed to the increasing disuse of the life history method. Sociologists became more concerned with the development of abstract theory and correspondingly less interested in full and detailed accounts of specific organizations and communities. They wanted data formulated in the abstract categories of their own theories rather than in the categories that seemed most relevant to the people they studied. The life history was well suited to the latter task, but of little immediately apparent use in the former.

At the same time, sociologists began to separate the field of social psychology from that of sociology proper, creating two specialties in place of two emphases within one field, and focused more on "structural" variables and synchronic functional analyses than on those factors that manifested themselves in the life and experience of the person. Again, the life history made a clear contribution to the latter task but seemed unrelated to studies that emphasized group attributes and their interconnections.

But perhaps the major reason for the relatively infrequent use of the technique is that it does not produce the kind of "findings" that sociologists now expect research to produce. As sociology increasingly rigidifies and "professionalizes," more and more emphasis has come to be placed on what we may, for simplicity's sake, call the *single study*. I use the term to refer to research projects that are conceived of as self-sufficient and self-contained, which provide all the evidence one needs to accept or reject the conclusions they proffer, whose findings are to be used as another brick in the growing wall of science – a metaphor quite different than that of the mosaic. The single study is integrated with the main body of knowledge in the following way: it derives its hypotheses from an inspection of what is already known; then, after the research is completed, if those hypotheses have been demonstrated, they are added to the wall of what is already scientifically known and used as the basis for further studies. The important point is that the researcher's hypothesis is either proved or disproved on the basis of what he has discovered in doing that one piece of research.

The customs, traditions, and organizational practices of contemporary sociology conspire to make us take this view of research. The journal article of standard length, the most common means of scientific communication, is made to order for the presentation of findings that confirm or refute hypotheses. The Ph.D. thesis virtually demands that its author have a set of findings, warranted by his own operations, which yield conclusions he can defend before a faculty committee. The research grant proposal, another ubiquitous sociological literary form, pushes its author to state what his project will have proved when the money has been spent.

If we take the single study as the model of scientific work, we will then use, when we judge research and make decisions about how to organize our research, criteria designed to assure us that the findings of our single study do indeed provide a sound basis on which to accept or reject hypotheses. The canons of inference and proof now in vogue reflect this emphasis. Such methodologists as Stouffer, and others who followed him, developed techniques for assessing hypotheses based on the model of the controlled experiment.[17] Compare two groups, those who have been exposed to the effects of a variable and those who have not, before and after the exposure. The multiple comparisons made possible by this technique allow you to test not only your original hypothesis, but also some of the likely alternative explanations of the same results, should they be what you have predicted. This is the approved model. If we cannot achieve it, our study is deficient unless we can devise workable substitutes. If we do achieve it, we can say with assurance that we have produced scientific findings strong enough to bear the weight of still further studies.

Criteria drawn from the experimental model and used to evaluate single studies in isolation, however useful they may be in a variety of contexts, have had one bad by-product. They have led people to ignore the other functions of research and, particularly, to ignore the contribution made by one study to an overall research enterprise even when the study, considered in isolation, produced no definitive results of its own. Since, by these criteria, the life history did not produce definitive results, people have been at a loss to make anything of it and by and large have declined to invest the time and effort necessary to acquire life history documents.

We can perhaps hope that a fuller understanding of the complexity of the scientific enterprise will restore sociologists' sense of the versatility and worth of the life history. A new series of personal documents, like those produced by the Chicago School more than a generation ago, might help us in all the ways I have earlier suggested and in ways, too, that we do not now anticipate.

Notes

1   W. I. Thomas and Florian Znaniecki, *The Polish Peasant in Europe and America* (2d ed., New York, 1927), II, 1931–2244.

2   Clifford R. Shaw, *The Jack-Roller* (Chicago, 1930), *The Natural History of a Delinquent Career* (Chicago, 1931), and *Brothers in Crime* (Chicago, 1936); Chic Conwell and Edwin H. Sutherland, *The Professional Thief* (Chicago, 1937); Helen MacGill Hughes (ed.), *The Fantastic Lodge* (Boston, 1961); Henry Williamson, *Hustler*, edited by R. Lincoln Keiser (Garden City, N.Y., 1965).

3   Louis Wirth, *The Ghetto* (Chicago, 1928); Harvey W. Zorbaugh, *The Gold Coast and the Slum: A Sociological Study of Chicago's Near North Side* (Chicago, 1929); Frederic M. Thrasher, *The Gang: A Study of 1,313 Ganges in Chicago* (Chicago, 1928).

4   See Everett C. Hughes' account of this "great movement of social investigation" in "Robert Park," *New Society*. (December 31, 1964), 18–19; and Robert E. Park, *Human Communities* (Glencoe, Ill., 1952).

5 Published in several volumes by W. Lloyd Warner and his collaborators.

6 St. Clair Drake and Horace Cayton, *Black Metropolis* (New York, 1945).

7 Nels Anderson, *The Hobo* (Chicago, 1923).

8 Clifford R. Shaw and Henry D. MacKay, *Juvenile Delinquency and Urban Areas* (Chicago, 1942).

9 Clyde Kluckhohn, "The Personal Document in Anthropological Science," in Louis Gottschalk *et al., The Use of Personal Documents in History, Anthropology, and Sociology* (New York, 1945), pp. 79–173; Robert Angell, "A Critical Review of the Development of the Personal Document Method in Sociology 1920–1940," ibid., pp. 177–232; John Dollard, *Criteria for the Life History* (New Haven, 1932).

10 See, for instance, George H. Mead, "Scientific Method and Individual Thinker," in John Dewey *et al., Creative Intelligence* (New York, 1917), pp. 176–227, and Alfred Lindesmith, *Opiate Addiction* (Bloomington, 1947), pp. 5–20. Lindesmith turns the strategy into a systematic method of inquiry usually referred to as analytic induction.

11 See, for a similar view growing out of the tradition of survey research, Patricia L. Kendall and Katherine M. Wolf, "The Analysis of Deviant Cases in Communications Research," in Paul F. Lazarsfeld and Frank Stanton (eds.), *Communications Research 1948–1949* (New York, 1949), pp. 152–79.

12 See Max Gluckman (ed.), *Closed Systems and Open Minds* (Chicago, 1964).

13 Harold Garfinkel, "Conditions of Successful Degradation Ceremonies," *American Journal of Sociology* 61 (1956): 420–24; and Erving Goffman, *Asylums* (Garden City, N.Y., 1961), pp. 127–69.

14 See George Herbert Mead, *Mind, Self, and Society* (Chicago, 1934); Herbert Blumer, "Society as Symbolic Interaction," in Arnold Rose (ed.), *Human Behavior and Social Processes* (Boston, 1962), pp. 179–92; and Anselm L. Strauss *et al., Psychiatric Ideologies and Institutions* (New York, 1964), pp. 292–315.

15 David Riesman, *Abundance for What?* (Garden City, 1965), pp. 493–4.

16 Johan Galtung, "Los factores socioculturales y el desarrollo de la sociología en América latina," *Revista Latinoamericana de Sociología* 1 (March, 1965): 87.

17 See the very influential paper by Samuel A. Stouffer, "Some Observations on Study Design," *American Journal of Sociology* 55 (January 1950): 355–61, and any of a large number of books and articles on method which take essentially the same position.

5 Talking and Listening from Women's Standpoint: Feminist Strategies for Interviewing and Analysis

Marjorie L. DeVault

The research generated by academic feminism – involving a new and careful attention to women's experiences – is beginning to "bring women in" to theorizing. But this research also demonstrates how traditional paradigms have been shaped by the concerns and relevances of a relatively small group of powerful men. The dilemma for the feminist scholar, always, is to find ways of working within some disciplinary tradition while aiming at an intellectual revolution that will transform that tradition (Stacey and Thorne 1985). In order to transform sociology – to write women and their diverse experiences into the discipline – we need to move toward new methods for writing about women's lives and activities without leaving sociology altogether. But the routine procedures of the discipline pull us insistently toward conventional understandings that distort women's experiences (Smith 1987, 1989).

Feminist methodology should provide strategies for managing this central contradiction – strategies that will help us with the "balancing act" demanded of any scholar who attempts innovative research within a scholarly tradition. I use the term "strategies" to suggest that feminist methodology will not prescribe a single model or formula. Rather, I think of feminist methods as distinctive approaches to subverting the established procedures of disciplinary practice tied to the agendas of the powerful (Smith 1974). In the discussion that follows, I pursue some implications of feminism for the production and use of interview data. I do not treat questions about the ethics of interviewing or relations with informants, which have been discussed extensively by feminist researchers (e.g., Mies 1983; Oakley 1981; Reinharz 1983; Stacey 1988). In many ways, my approach is solidly grounded in a tradition of qualitative sociological inquiry and in relatively conventional methods for conducting interviews. But I will suggest that feminism gives us distinctive ways of extending the methods of this qualitative tradition.

I begin with an observation central to much feminist thinking: that language itself reflects male experiences, and that its categories are often incongruent with women's lives. This apparent obstacle to expression, I will argue, can be turned to advantage

An earlier version of this paper was presented at the annual meeting of the Society for the Study of Symbolic Interaction, New York, August 1986, and portions of that talk were excerpted in *Women and Language*, 1987, 10:33–36. I am indebted to Arlene Kaplan Daniels and Howard S. Becker for teaching me about interviewing and for helpful comments on this paper; to the late Marianne Paget, Dorothy F. Smith, Darlene Douglas-Steele and Judith Wittner for many discussions of these issues; to the Stone Center for Developmental Services and Studies at Wellesley College, where I began to write this paper; and to Syracuse University, whose assistance enabled me to complete the work.

through attention to research as activity fundamentally grounded in talk. Qualitative researchers of various sorts have become increasingly conscious in recent years of the obvious but mostly taken-for-granted feature of the data they collect: that interviews consist of talk (Paget 1983; Mishler 1986a). This new awareness is related to the insights of phenomenologists, who investigate the production of everyday consciousness (see e.g., Psathas 1973; Darroch and Silvers 1983), and ethnomethodologists, who have taken as problematic the patterns of talk and interaction through which the members of any group constitute a shared reality (Garfinkel 1967; Heritage 1984). I will suggest that this new kind of attention to the language of research should be central to the feminist project. Assuming relatively standard procedures for interviewing, I will examine, as social interaction grounded in language, four aspects of work with interview data: constructing topics, listening, editing, and writing. My aim is to bring into the methodological discussion insights from feminist linguists about women's relation to language and to speech, and to examine, as aspects of social research, the processes of talking and listening "as women." My understanding of what it means to talk or listen "as a woman" is based on the concept of "women's standpoint" (Smith 1987; Hartsock 1981); the approach does not imply that all women share a single position or perspective, but rather insists on the importance of following out the implications of women's (and others') various locations in socially organized activities (see also DeVault 1990).

Women and Language

Language was an early topic for feminist researchers and by now there is a large body of research on women and language (for summaries, see Thorne and Henley 1975; Lakoff 1975; Miller and Swift 1977; Spender [1980] 1985; Thorne, Kramarae, and Henley 1983). These studies demonstrate how linguistic forms (the generic "he," for example) exclude women, and how vocabulary and syntax make women deviant. The names of experiences often do not fit for women. For an example that is simple and immediate, consider the difficulties that arise in an attempt to apply the terms "work" and "leisure" to most women's lives. Many of the household activities so prominent in women's lives do not fit comfortably into either category (see e.g., Smith 1987: 68), and many of women's activities, such as family, community, and volunteer work, are best described as "invisible work" (Daniels 1987). There are other examples – the terms "public" and "private," for example, construct a distinction that obscures women's "multiple crisscrossings" of fluid and constantly shifting boundaries (Saraceno 1984: 7). Such disjunctures between language and women's lives have been central to feminist scholarship; presumably, there are many more to be revealed. Presumably, as well, the lack of fit between women's lives and the words available for talking about experience present real difficulties for ordinary women's self-expression in their everyday lives. If words often do not quite fit, then women who want to talk of their experiences must "translate," either saying things that are not quite right, or working at using the language in non-standard ways.

To some extent, this kind of problem must exist for everyone: language can never fit perfectly with individual experience. My claim, however, is that the problems of what we might call linguistic incongruence must be greater for some groups than for others. Research on gender differences in speech provides some support for this claim, suggesting that, in at least some contexts, women face particular difficulties of speech. In mixed-sex dyads and groups, women are less listened to than men and less likely to be credited for the things they say in groups; they are interrupted more often than men; the topics they introduce into conversations are less often taken up by others; and they do more work than men to keep conversations going. Further, Candace West (1982) suggests that responses to speech are so thoroughly gendered that women cannot overcome these difficulties by simply adopting "male" styles: she found that when women did interrupt male speakers, they were more likely than male interrupters to be ignored, a pattern she speculatively attributes to a male presumption that women's speech can, in general, be treated as trivial. These and similar findings have been presented as effects of power relations between men and women. They can also be seen as manifestations of the special obstacles for women to speaking fully and truthfully.

Dale Spender, in *Man Made Language* ([1980] 1985), reviews and extends these ideas in ways I have found especially helpful. Beginning with the anthropologists Edwin and Shirley Ardener's (1975) idea that women in society are a "muted group," she traces the consequences of various ways that women are denied access to linguistic resources. The concept of "mutedness" does not imply that women are silent: in every culture, women speak, in a variety of forms and settings, and in almost all cultures, women are important transmitters of language, through their care and teaching of children. But just as muted sounds are audible but softened, women speak in ways that are limited and shaped by men's greater social power and control, exercised both individually and institutionally (and exercised to control less privileged men as well as women). Spender argues that distinctive features of women's speech should not be seen as deficiencies in linguistic skill, but as adaptive responses to these constraints on their speech. She also sees in language a potential source of power for women: she argues that woman-to-woman talk is quite different from talk in mixed groups – because women speakers are more likely to listen seriously to each other – and that it affords opportunities for women to speak more fully about their experiences. She argues, in fact, that consciousness-raising, which might be understood as woman-to-woman talk systematized, is at the heart of feminist theorizing (see also MacKinnon 1983).

Spender's discussion of "woman talk" is optimistic; she emphasizes the value of communication among women, and does not give much consideration to its difficulties. In drawing on her discussion, I do not mean to imply that women always (or even usually) understand each other easily. While understanding and familiar comfort are benefits of some of the ways that women have come together, they are not guaranteed by gender alone. Women who are positioned differently learn to speak and hear quite different versions of "woman talk," adapting to distinctive blends of power and oppression. Failures of understanding abound. Statements from feminists of color, for example, reveal not only their difficulties speaking among white feminists (e.g., hooks 1981), but also the costs for feminist research of the exclusion of their voices (e.g., Collins 1986, 1989). At the same time, feminist scholars have begun to experiment with texts that reflect the conflict and messiness of talking and listening together (e.g., Joseph and Lewis 1981; Lugones and Spelman 1983; Bulkin, Pratt, and Smith 1984). Such texts hold the promise that, with careful attention, we can learn from each other about our differences as well as our common experiences.

These ideas from feminist linguistic researchers provide the starting point for my discussion of interview talk, which will focus on the talk that occurs in interviews conducted by women with women. (I do not mean to imply that the label "feminist" can be applied only to research conducted by women and about women, but this category does include most feminist research to date. The reasons for such a pattern deserve attention, but lie beyond the scope of this article.) Below, I discuss the ways that these perspectives on women's talk have influenced my own thinking about interviewing. Though I draw examples primarily from my study of the work that women do within families (DeVault 1984, 1987, 1991), I attempt to indicate as well how these ideas might be relevant to other projects.

Constructing Topics

The categories available from the discipline construct "topics" for research do not necessarily correspond to categories that are meaningful in women's lives. Female researchers, like other women, have become accustomed to translating their experiences into standard vocabulary. But to fully describe women's experiences, we often need to go beyond standard vocabulary – not just in our analyses, but also in the ways that we actually talk with those we interview. By speaking in ways that open the boundaries of standard topics, we can create space for respondents to provide accounts rooted in the realities of their lives.

My research, for example, examines household routines for planning, cooking and serving meals. I thought of it, in the beginning, as a study of housework. But I was also motivated by a sense that the feminist literature on housework didn't fit my experience. Analyses that took the content of household work for granted left things out, and the parts left out were somehow what made the work not only burdensome, but meaningful and compelling as well. I wanted to study a single kind of housework in detail, and for a variety of reasons that were only partly conscious, I was drawn to the work of providing food. The term is awkward and sounds odd, and in fact, there is no term that says precisely what I meant. I meant more than just cooking, more than "meal preparation" (the efficiency expert's term). And "providing," of course, has traditionally been used for what the traditional husband does – it is linked to the wage that a woman transforms into family meals. Though I knew – in at least a preliminary sense – what I wanted to study, I had no concise label for my topic. Eventually, I began to call it "the work of feeding a family," and later, just "feeding." But in the beginning, as I started to conduct interviews, I told my respondents that I wanted to talk with them about "all the housework that has to do with food – cooking, planning, shopping, cleaning up." I used my questions to show them that they should talk very specifically – "Who gets up first?" "What kind of cereal?" and so on – and in spite of my worries about "topic," these interviews were remarkably easy to conduct. Almost all of my respondents, both those who loved to cook and those who hated it, spoke easily and naturally. Looking back, I can see that I identified, in a rough way, a category that made sense to my respondents because it was a category that organized their day-to-day activity. For women who live in families and do this work, feeding is a central task and takes lots of time.

Strategizing about how to do it leads to the development of routines, to frequent rearrangements and improvisations, and to pride in the "little tricks" that make the work easier. The topic is easy for women (and for men who actually do the work) to talk about. Our talk happened in a way that I and my respondents knew and were comfortable with, because such conversations among women are often settings for discussing this kind of work. Chatting about the details of household routines is a way of finding out what someone else does, reflecting on one's own practice, getting and sharing ideas or solutions to common problems. Sometimes, in fact, my respondents were uncomfortable because our talk didn't seem like an interview: several stopped in mid-sentence to ask, "Is this really what you want?" "Are you sure this is helping you?" They were prepared to translate into the vocabulary they expected from a researcher, and surprised that we were proceeding in a more familiar manner.

The point here – that feminist topics go beyond standard labels – applies to other kinds of research as well. Elizabeth Stanko, as follow-up to her book *Intimate Intrusions* (1985a), conceived a study of women's strategies for avoiding assault (Stanko 1985b, 1990). Her aim is to examine a broad range of what we might call "defensive maneuvers" – not just learning self-defense, but choosing places to live, things to wear, routes for walking home, and times to go to the laundromat. There is no label that includes all of these – and the category is probably one that men would be less likely than women to understand. But when Stanko, as a female researcher, says to women that she is concerned with "the things we do to keep safe," she taps into a set of activities informed by knowledge and strategizing that make up a meaningful category for virtually all women in our society. (Though of course, the practices and conditions of the experience vary tremendously – in this instance, urban women are probably more at risk and more vigilant than others; and affluent women certainly find it easier to avoid risk than those with fewer material resources.)

Marianne Paget (1981), as part of a study of the practice of committed artists, has written about a barrier to creative work that she could see in the stories of women artists but not in those of men. She uses the term "ontological anguish" to refer to the conflict between these women's intense commitment to the creation of high art, and their learned sense that, as women, they are not supposed to participate in making culture. The artists themselves do not identify this problem. Paget sees it in their accounts of becoming artists – accounts that they provide in response to her questions about the work they finally came to do. This example suggests that researchers do not have to begin with a conception of expanded topic. Paget began with an interest in how artists do their work; she discovered that in order to explain their art, women artists have to tell about getting over a barrier. Paget allows them to tell their own stories, gives a name to the barrier they describe, and through her analysis makes it a phenomenon that we can examine and discuss.

The household work process that I analyze and the defensive strategies that Stanko studies are activities that most women learn to take for granted, activities that are normally only partly conscious, learned without explicit attention. Similarly, Paget discusses a sort of "problem with no name" for women artists, a problem they experience in various ways and can talk about indirectly, but do not ordinarily label. The promise of feminist ethnography is that we can elicit accounts and produce descriptions of these kinds of practice and thought that are part of female consciousness but left out of dominant interpretive frames, shaped around male concerns. When this kind of topic construction is successful, we recognize the thinking that emerges from the analysis – we know the experience – but we are also surprised and learn something new. The analysis produces the "aha" or "click" of consciousness-raising that has been central to the development of feminist thinking, and that serves as a pointer toward a new way of seeing the world.

Conversation analytic researchers have investigated the construction of "topic" in everyday talk, and their findings help to illuminate the examples I have discussed by demonstrating how topics are produced collaboratively. Boden and Bielby (1986), for example, report that elderly conversation partners use a shared past as the basis for constructing conversational interaction in the present. And Maynard and Zimmerman (1984) report that unacquainted speakers often work at establishing areas of shared experience. In their study, conversation partners often developed topics out of the shared features of their immediate setting (the oddness of an arranged encounter in a social psychology lab). But speakers also investigated each other's categorical memberships (e.g., "sophomore" or "sociology major") and experiences (attending a recent concert) in "pre-topical" talk aimed at constructing a "shared-ness" that could lead to topic development. Paget (1983), emphasizing the "conversational" character of intensive interviewing, discusses how an interviewer and respondent collaborate in a "search procedure." It is the interviewer's investment in finding answers, her own concern with the questions she asks and her ability to show that concern, that serves to recruit her respondents as partners in the search: the things said are responses to these words of this particular researcher. The researcher is actively involved with respondents, so that together they are constructing fuller answers to questions that cannot always be asked in simple, straightforward ways.

I claim here that a feminist sociology must open up standard topics from the discipline, building more from what we share with respondents as women than from disciplinary categories that we bring to research encounters. In order to do this, researchers need to interview in ways that allow the exploration of incompletely articulated aspects of women's experiences. Traditionally, qualitative researchers have conducted interviews that are "open-ended" and "intensive," seeking to avoid structuring the interaction in terms of the researcher's perspectives. But eliciting useful accounts of women's experiences is not simply a matter of encouraging women to talk. Most members of a society learn to interpret their experiences in terms of dominant language and meanings; thus, women themselves (researchers included) often have trouble seeing and talking clearly about their experiences. What researchers can do is to take responsibility for recognizing how the concepts we have learned as sociologists may distort women's accounts. We can return to activities conducted in specific settings as the sources for our studies, and ground our interviewing in accounts of everyday activity – in accounts of how particular women actually spend their time at home, for example, rather than a previously defined concept of "housework". Dorothy Smith (1987: 187–9) suggests that when we ground interviews in this way, we find that social organization is "in the talk" and that we can mine the talk for clues to social relations. This kind of interviewing, which does not begin from topics established in the discipline, will be more like everyday "woman talk" than like survey research.

Listening

I have argued above that since the words available often do not fit, women learn to "translate" when they talk about their experiences. As they do so, parts of their lives "disappear" because they are not included in the language of the account. In order to "recover" these parts of women's lives, researchers must develop methods for listening around and beyond words. I use the term "listening" in this section in a broad sense, to refer to what we do while interviewing, but also to the hours we spend later listening to tapes or studying transcripts, and even more broadly, to the ways we work at interpreting respondents' accounts. (I do not, however, attend to comparative aspects of analysis, which involve bringing together interpretations of multiple interviews.)

Spender's discussion of the special features of "woman talk," cited above, emphasizes the importance of listening. She notes that listening has been neglected in communication research in favor of research on speech, and she suggests that this imbalance results from the fact that those who control knowledge production are more concerned with airing their views than with hearing those of others (Spender [1980] 1985: 121–5). Spender argues that women (like members of other subordinate groups) are highly skilled at listening – to both men and women (see also Miller 1976, 1986) – and that women together can more easily cooperate in understanding each other than speakers in mixed groups. Presumably, these ideas have relevance for woman-to-woman interviewing, even though the interview setting is structured, and more artificial than everyday talk. When women interview women, both researcher and subject act on the basis of understandings about interviewing, and both follow the rules (or negotiate a shared version of the rules) associated with their respective roles. But changes in the role of researcher, based on incorporating rather than denying personal involvements, have been at the heart of many discussions of feminist methodology (Reinharz 1983; Stanley and Wise 1983). In fact, it is sometimes quite difficult for female researchers, and especially feminists, to maintain the role prescribed by traditional methodological strictures. Ann Oakley (1981), for example, explains how impossible it was for her to be an "ideal" interviewer in her discussions with pregnant women: she wasn't willing to respond, "I haven't really thought about it" when interviewees asked questions such as "Which hole does the baby come out of?" or "Why is it dangerous to leave a small baby alone in the house?" Many of these discussions suggest that women interviewing women bring to their interaction a tradition of "woman talk." They help each other develop ideas, and are typically better prepared than men to use the interview as a "search procedure" (Paget 1983), cooperating in the project of constructing meanings together.[1]

When this project involves the recovery of unarticulated experience, as so much feminist research does, researchers have another resource: they can listen for the everyday processes of "translation" that are part of women's speech. When I use the term here – as I have been doing rather loosely so far – I mean to refer to the various ways that women manage to deal with the incongruence of language in their everyday speech. Often, this means using words that are familiar and "close enough" to experience for most purposes, relying on listeners to understand – for example, calling "housework" whatever chores must be done at home. Sometimes, too, translation means trying to develop a more complex meaning, trying to respond more fully to questions that are not quite appropriate. In these cases, it may mean saying part of what is experienced, groping for words, doing the best one can. As an interviewer who is also a woman – who has also learned to translate – I can listen "as a woman," filling in from experience to help me understand the things that are incompletely said. As a researcher, my job is to listen for these translations, and to analyze the disjunctures that give rise to them. These linguistic phenomena provide "clues" to women's experiences (Frye 1983: xii).

In my research on the work of feeding a family, I was concerned to uncover neglected aspects of women's experience of housework. I wanted to examine those parts of the work of planning, cooking and serving meals that women rarely think about, but have learned from their mothers and from ideologies of family life – those parts of housework that actually produce family life day to day. I asked the women in my study (and the few men who took major responsibility for cooking) to describe their daily routines in some detail: what they cooked and why, how they planned and managed family meals, when and where they bought food, and so on. As the interviews progressed, I became increasingly fascinated with some characteristic features of my respondents' talk. They spoke very concretely, about the mundane details of everyday life, but they often said things in ways that seemed oddly incomplete. They connected topics in ways that were sometimes puzzling and they assumed certain kinds of knowledge on my part ("Like, you know, the Thursday section of the newspaper," an implicit reference to the fact that many U.S. newspapers include recipes and features on food and diet in their Thursday editions). I coded my data in the traditional way, noting when respondents mentioned "topics" such as "planning," "nutrition," and so forth. But in many cases, the analysis really began with a particular phrase that seemed to demand investigation. I began to pay more and more attention to the ways things were said. I was especially interested in difficulties of expression – those fascinating moments when respondents got stuck, and worked at articulating thoughts they were not used to sharing: "It's kind of hard to explain . . . ."

One woman, talking about why she worked so hard at organizing regular meals for her family, told me:

> My husband sees food as something you need to live. But – I don't quite know how to describe it – I really have an emphasis on the social aspects. I mean, the food is an important part, but it's kind of in that setting.

As we talked, this woman was trying to formulate the principles that guide her activities. It is difficult because she doesn't have appropriate words. She knows what she means, but expressing it is new. Another woman echoed her idea, in a similar way:

> The initial drudgery is what you dislike. Actually going shopping, doing all the planning, chopping, cutting, what have you. And of course cleaning up. But you do it for the good parts, you know, you get enough of the good part to keep doing it.

There are words for the physical tasks, but not for the interpersonal work that is more important for this woman – the activity she summarizes, somewhat puzzled herself, as "the good part." Again, it is clear that her experiences are inadequately coded in standard vocabulary, and that she must work at saying what she means.

Another example: although most women told me that they didn't really do much "planning," several of my respondents referred to an immediate, improvisational kind of thinking they do while shopping. They did not know quite what to call this process. One told me: "Most of the time, I kind of plan when I'm at the store, you know? Like OK, we have chicken Monday, pork chops Tuesday – I be kind of, you know, figuring out in my mind, as I shop, what's what." Another explained: "My husband likes to just get in and out, and then that's it. Whereas me, I like to look around, and just think, you know."

These kinds of comments do not constitute "good quotes" in the conventional sense: they are halting and rather inarticulate, and seem hardly to have any content. Typically, I think, they would be discarded as containing little information about what these women do. I used these women's words somewhat differently, however: not as straightforward accounts of "what happens," but as hints toward concerns and activities that are generally unacknowledged. Often, I believe, this halting, hesitant, tentative talk signals the realm of not-quite-articulated experience, where standard vocabulary is inadequate, and where a respondent tries to speak from experience and finds language wanting.[2] I tried to listen most carefully to this kind of talk. As I began to understand what these women were saying, I also began to see more clearly how standard vocabulary – the managerial term "planning," for instance – really doesn't describe what they do. I could also begin to see why the term doesn't fit: the concept of planning makes organizational sense where there is a separation of conception and execution, but housework has traditionally been organized so as to join not only conception and execution, but also work and the personality of the one who does it.

As I began to look for these difficulties of expression, I became aware that my transcripts were filled with notations of women saying to me, "you know," in sentences like "I'm more careful about feeding her, you know, kind of a breakfast." This seems an incidental feature of their speech, but perhaps the phrase is not so empty as it seems. In fact, I did know what she meant. I did not use these phrases systematically in my analyses, but I think now that I could have. Studying the transcripts now, I see that these words often occur in places where they are consequential for the joint production of our talk in the interviews. In many instances, "you know" seems to mean something like, "OK, this next bit is going to be a little tricky. I can't say it quite right, but help me out a little; meet me halfway and you'll understand what I mean." (It is perhaps similar to the collaborative use of "Uh huh" to sustain extended stretches of talk, noted by Schegloff [1982].) If this is so, it provides a new way to think about these data. "You know" no longer seems like stumbling inarticulateness, but appears to signal a request for understanding. The request was honored on the woman-to-woman level, as I nodded, "um hmm," making the interview comfortable, doing with my respondent what we women have done for generations – understanding each other. But I fear that the request is too often forgotten when, as researchers, we move from woman talk to sociology, leaving the unspoken behind. In some sense, this is a betrayal of the respondent – I say I understand, but if I later "forget," her reality is not fully there in what I write.

Finally, there were bits of speech that just seemed odd to me, that I wanted to understand. In one interview, for example, I asked what the evening meal was like. The reply was a long one; we had been talking about this woman's own parents and how they ate, and her answer gave information about her own childhood as well as the patterns she and her husband have developed. Eventually, I asked her to explain how their "family style" meals were different from those of her childhood. Again, her answer was long and specific and moved beyond the question. Her husband serves the meat, but not as well as her grandfather and her father did; this bothers her sometimes. Then she went on:

> And the service is important. You know, how the table is set and so forth. We probably, again when I was growing up we never had paper napkins except when my dad was out of town. We do now, have paper napkins, although we have cloth napkins and I like it. What I would like – maybe I will but probably not – but at one point where we lived we had cloth napkins and everybody had their own napkin ring, and that way you didn't have to keep changing the napkins.

She went on to talk about other things, but I was haunted by a fragment of this excerpt: "What I would like – maybe I will but probably not –," which struck me immediately with its off-hand poignancy. The question, for me, was why anyone would say such a thing, what context produces this remark. Later I began to see how this woman was doing her work as we talked; she was, momentarily, musing and strategizing about the kind of meal she wished to produce for her family. What happens in her talk? Telling about her family routine, she mentions napkin rings, and thinks that she would like to use them again. Her wistful, automatic thought that she will do something different (again, not quite planning, but something akin to it) reveals her sense of how the material trappings of meals can become foundations for more emotional aspects of family life. And her brief comment also contains clues to the fate of her own preferences and desires: she plans and wishes, but she also recognizes that she alone is responsible for doing the work, and that in the end she will have limited time and make choices that reflect the priorities of others. I certainly could not see all these things when I noticed this remark, but I knew at least that there was something more to be said about this oddly contradictory phrase. As I thought about it, it brought back the time in my own life when I thought I might save my marriage by making better salads. And when I began to look, I found this kind of thinking in the comments of others as well.

As the last example suggests, researchers' own experiences as women serve as resources for this kind of listening. While other feminists have noted the value of personal involvement in interviewing, even researchers who value involvement have talked of it in a mostly unanalyzed way, as experience rather than as an element of method. If feminist researchers are to move toward a more disciplined use of the personal, we need to make the process one that we can consciously adopt and teach. We need to analyze more carefully the specific ways that interviewers use personal experience as a resource for listening. Here, I briefly discuss my own approach and a related example. What they have in common is a focus on attention to the unsaid, in order to produce it as topic and make it speakable.

My procedure, which I have illustrated above, involves noticing ambiguity and problems of expression in interview data, then drawing on my own experience in an investigation aimed at "filling in" what has been incompletely said. The point is not simply to reproduce my own perspective in my analysis; the clues I garner from this kind of introspection are only a beginning and should lead me back to hear respondents in new ways. What produces the analysis is the recognition that something is unsaid, and the attempt to articulate the missing parts of the account. The interpretive process is analogous to reading a narrative account, placing oneself in the narrator's position and referring to an implied context for the story that is told. It is a process that is being studied by analysts of reading and narrative, and the work of these theorists should provide one way of conceptualizing this kind of listening (for sociologists' discussions of narrative, see e.g., Smith 1983; Mishler 1986a, b; DeVault 1990; Richardson 1990).

A related approach to "personal listening" can be seen in the work of Dorothy Smith and Alison Griffith, who have studied the ways that mothers' activities are shaped by the organization of schooling (Smith 1987; Griffith and Smith 1987). They interviewed mothers about what they do to help their children in school – how they get them dressed and there on time, how they teach them "basic skills," how they manage children's experiences with teachers and the institutions of schooling. Griffith and Smith have written about the ways that they have used their experiences as resources for analysis. They were aware from the beginning that their personal histories as single mothers provided impetus and direction for the study, and that they used a commonality of experience with their respondents to develop interview questions and to establish "rapport" and move the interviews ahead. But they also report that their analysis was furthered by noticing and using a particular sort of emotional response to some of their interviews. Griffith, for example, tells about returning from an interview with a middle-class, full-time mother who deploys an impressive range of material and educational resources to further her children's development. Her field notes ask:

> And where was I in all this? I was feeling that I hadn't done my own mothering *properly*. I had let my children watch T.V.; they'd never been taken to a Shakespearean play; when I was upset with the school, I had never managed to make things better for my children and indeed, at times made it worse; etc. In other words, my mothering, in relation to other women's mothering, appeared to be less than adequate on almost every count. As a consequence, I was finding the interview process very difficult emotionally. (Griffith and Smith 1987: 94)

The reaction is understandable, and might simply be treated, sympathetically, as one of the pitfalls of researching personally meaningful topics. But Griffith and Smith go beyond this kind of recognition to analyze the unnoticed matrix of social organization that constructs both the interview talk and their emotional reaction to it. They report that reflections on this kind of reaction led them to see a "moral dimension" to mothering, and to trace its sources in social organization. Analysis does not end, but rather begins with the recognition of their own emotion: Griffith and Smith went on to look for, and found, other illustrations of this aspect of mothering in the accounts of those they interviewed. But their own experience helped them find these clues to the social organization of mothering (see also Rothman 1986 on deep emotional response and its relation to the analysis of amniocentesis experiences).

Any competent listening depends on various kinds of background knowledge. I have argued above that woman-to-woman listening can be based on a particular type of unspoken knowledge. Of course, this kind of listening is not simple. It is certainly not guaranteed in any woman-to-woman interaction. Riessman (1987), in an analysis of a middle-class Anglo interviewer's misunderstandings of a Puerto Rican respondent, provides a sobering account of one woman's inability to hear another. Asked to explain how her divorce came about, the respondent provides an episodic narrative in which a series of exemplary vignettes answer the question. The interviewer, expecting a story with a linear temporal organization, is confused, and interrupts the account repeatedly in an attempt to elicit the sort of narrative she expects. It is not only a frustrating encounter, but a striking example of how difficult it can be to hear things said in unfamiliar forms, and how damaging when respondents are not heard. But Riessman's analysis of this mishearing also suggests that, with awareness and effort, it is possible to analyze such problems in the service of more skillful listening. The critical point is that feminist researchers can be conscious of listening as process, and can work on learning to listen in ways that are personal, disciplined, and sensitive to differences.

Preserving Women's Speech

I have suggested above that researchers can use women's speech to provide clues to analysis. This kind of analysis proceeds through attention to typically unnoticed features of talk, and is therefore made possible by methods of data collection and recording that preserve such features. In this section, I discuss several issues of "editing," a term I use to refer to the decisions researchers make about recording, transcribing, and excerpting from conversations with informants. Though these are usually thought of (if thought of at all) as mechanical or technical issues, researchers are increasingly aware of their substantive relevance. Each decision about these matters results in saving or losing aspects of interview talk, and some approaches to analysis depend on aspects of talk that are routinely discarded by other analysts. Concretely, the questions include: Should interviews be tape recorded? How should they be transcribed? What would constitute a "complete" transcription? When excerpting from transcripts, what (if anything) are we allowed to change? Should we "clean up" quotations? How? And why or why not? My aim in what follows is not to prescribe any particular version of transcription or presentation. Rather, I want to call attention to the questions, survey some possible answers, and suggest that for feminist researchers, "more complete" representations of talk can provide a resource for analysis built on distinctive features of women's speech.

Standard handbooks on qualitative methods stress the importance of exhaustive recording of conversation in interviews and field settings, but devote relatively little attention to methods of recording conversation or writing about it. Bogdan and Taylor (1975), for example, who discuss such issues in more detail than most authors, recommend that field workers avoid taping; they provide some hints for remembering dialogue, and they suggest including records of "dialogue accessories" such as gesture, tone and accent, but they also reassure the reader that field notes need not include "flawless reproduction of what was said" (Bogdan and Taylor 1975: 60–61). They do suggest that researchers tape-record intensive interviews, because subjects' words are important and the situation is artificial anyway, but they omit discussion of transcription techniques. Presumably, students learn how to deal with these matters through experience and oral teaching, and by reading exemplary texts. The Bogdan and Taylor book, for example, teaches about these matters implicitly through the inclusion of exemplary field notes and finished research reports.

Fieldworkers in the symbolic interactionist tradition adopt a variety of solutions to problems of collecting and representing talk as data: some rely on memory rather than tape recordings (and indeed, some work in settings and adopt roles that make recording impractical), while others advocate taping interviews (often citing, in addition to the analytic utility of this technique, the benefit of easier concentration on the face-to-face interaction instead of on remembering what is said). Transcription, in this tradition, is typically viewed as a mechanical task, often assigned to subordinates in the research enterprise, though many researchers do acknowledge that the transcription process can afford rich insight. While some qualitative researchers insist that transcripts should include everything that is said (often mentioning, for instance, the importance of recording the interviewer's questions), many seem to edit out some material at this stage. Lillian Rubin (1979: Appendix), for example, defends the practice of organizing edited transcripts in terms of previously developed categories of interest rather than as verbatim records of the interview (though she does listen to entire tapes as she proceeds with the analysis). Further, the interactionist tradition in qualitative methods is virtually silent on methods for recording particular features of talk, taking for granted, for the most part, the adequacy of standard English spelling and punctuation. Excerpts in published reports tend to be brief – a few sentences from the respondent surrounded by analytic comment – and usually seem to have been "polished" by the sociologist, since they read more smoothly than most ordinary speech. Researchers routinely indicate that they have changed respondents' names and some details of their lives in order to protect their subjects' anonymity, but they rarely report in detail on which details they have changed and how.

In a rare discussion of these issues, Bob Blauner (1987) discusses the problems of editing "first-person" sociology. He notes that oral history and life history researchers have been more self-conscious about editing than most qualitative sociologists. Perhaps because the talk of informants is so much more prominent in their texts, life history researchers seem more conscious than others that they must make decisions about how to condense long hours of conversation, whether and how to represent dialect and non-standard grammar, and how much commentary to add to their subjects' words. Though Blauner limits his discussion to "personal document" texts – intended to present findings through extended personal narrative rather than through a sociologist-author's analytic discussion – every researcher working with interview data makes these editing decisions.

Blauner argues that the particular features of an individual's speech often have substantive significance. (Interestingly, his example focus mainly on the ways that African-American speakers mix standard and black English, and might be seen as linguistic phenomena corresponding to the ones I have claimed are important in women's speech.) Reporting on his own editing, he describes himself as having "some of the folklorist's purism" with respect to language and expressive style, but also as being "very free as an editor" (Blauner 1987: 50). He almost never changes any words when he quotes his informants (though he sometimes adds or deletes words to clarify meaning), but he condenses and eliminates material in ways intended to bring out the meaning and sociological relevance of a particular story. He also eliminates repetitive speech,[3] and, like most sociologists, changes personal names and details of identity in order to protect the anonymity of informants. Blauner also reports that many life history researchers edit their informants' words in order to encourage more respectful reading. Usually, the worry is that readers will be prejudiced, or simply distracted, by speech that reveals lack of education or a particular regional or class background. Blauner cites the example of Robert Coles, who translates slang and vernacular into standard English in order to highlight the content rather than style of respondents' speech.

These approaches, while emphasizing the importance of respondents' own words, also give the researcher much authority as translator and mouthpiece. The researcher, relying on her understanding of respondents' meanings, represents their words in forms that fit into sociological texts. Typically, this means interpreting, condensing, excerpting, and polishing respondents' talk. One rationale for such transformation emphasizes its benign intent: the researcher's purpose, often, is to secure a hearing for respondents who would not otherwise be heard. The purpose of editing is to cast talk into a form which is easier to read – and more compelling – than raw interview documents, which are often lengthy, rambling, repetitive and/or confusing. Another rationale emphasizes the redundancy of talk: the researcher should include only as much detail as needed to illustrate the analytic points to be made. (Howard Becker, for example, argues that tape recording interviews is usually unnecessary, explaining that he is confident of remembering those details that he needs to make an analysis [personal communication]. My work as Becker's student convinced me that I could remember "enough" from interviews to write sound and interesting sociology, and I repeat his advice to my own students, though with more ambivalence. However, my discussion elsewhere in this article suggests that memory is often inadequate.) Both rationales show that editing, though usually relatively unnoticed, is an essential and consequential part of the routine practice of producing a particular kind of sociological text.

Such "routine practices" must be thought of as the solutions to problems of representation accepted by a community of interpreters (Becker 1986). They are neither right or wrong for all time, but represent solutions that are relatively adequate for the purposes at hand. I have suggested above, however, that feminist researchers – whose purposes often include disrupting routine practice – might do well to adopt a reasoned suspicion of standard solutions to representation problems. I have argued that one purpose of feminist research is to recover and examine unnoticed experience, and that standard language and forms are likely to be inadequate for describing those experiences. Standard practice that smooths out respondents' talk is one way that women's words are distorted; it is often a way of discounting and ignoring those parts of women's experience that are not easily expressed.

Conversation and discourse analysis provide models for representing talk much more completely. Conversation analytic researchers (see e.g., Schenkein 1978; Atkinson and Heritage 1984) aim at discovering the recurring features of talk and interaction that produce the orderliness of social life; they take talk as the primordial grounding of social interaction.

Analysis focuses on the significance of conversational features as minute (and as typically unnoticed) as indrawn breath, elongated vowel sounds and hesitations as short as one-tenth of a second. Discourse analysis (e.g., Fisher and Todd 1983; Mishler 1986a) is typically based on longer stretches of talk, but involves a similarly close attention to the details of talk and storytelling. Feminists working in these traditions (e.g., Fishman 1978; West and Zimmerman 1983; Todd and Fisher 1988) have attended to the significance of gender as it both produces and is produced by the social relations of talk. Their work is especially useful for the kind of analysis I propose here, because they show, explicitly and in detail, the kinds of obstacles to expression that women confront in everyday interaction.

Researchers who rely on these approaches work with very detailed transcripts, which look more complicated than standard text and are usually rather difficult for the uninitiated to read. In the case of conversation analysis, they are based on a system of notation developed by Gail Jefferson (described in Shenkein 1978: xi-xvi); some researchers use other, generally similar notation systems (see e.g., several different levels of detail in the papers brought together by Todd and Fisher 1988). Although the form of such a transcript gives many readers the impression of a technical, "objective" approach to talk, insiders to the tradition view transcripts more provisionally. For these researchers, the talk itself is central; they work primarily from tapes, they play tapes when they present their work to others, and they view transcripts as subject to continual criticism and revision as they "hear the talk" more completely. Transcribing itself is a subtle and difficult craft, learned through apprenticeship and experience, and practiced improvisationally. Notation systems change as researchers attend to previously neglected features of talk.

Conversation and discourse analysts aim to study talk as it actually happens, and they certainly come closer than those who simply translate talk into standard written English. However, one of the important lessons to be drawn from conversation analysis is precisely how difficult it is to hold and study "the talk itself." While these technically sophisticated notation systems capture many features of talk left out of more conventional representations, they cannot be thought of as "complete." So far, most of them leave out gesture and "body language" (but see Goodwin 1979; Goodwin and Goodwin 1989), as well as subtle aspects of talk that have not yet been noticed and notated. They seem most useful (or at least are most used) for studying the form rather than content of speech. In addition, these systems often have the effect of obscuring the individuality of speech. Because transcripts in this form require large investments of both production time and space in articles, analyses are based on relatively short fragments of speech, usually too short to give a sense of a speaker's characteristic style of speech. One might argue that the difficulty of reading a detailed transcript has the beneficial effect of forcing the reader to study respondents' talk more carefully than when it is represented in standard English. But because these transcripts require such concentrated reading, accent and dialect are often less effectively conveyed than through variations on more standard writing.

No transcription technique preserves all the details of respondents' speech, and no technique will be adequate for every analysis. My intention here is not to propose that feminist researchers must follow analytic programs emphasizing the details of talk, but rather to encourage strategic borrowing from these approaches. In my research on housework, for example, I did not begin with the intention of studying women's speech. I was not trained as an analyst of talk, and I did not use any specialized method for transcribing discourse. But I worked carefully from tape recordings. Without the tapes, I would not have been able to reproduce the hesitation and uncertainty of speech that have so interested me since I finished the interviewing. I doubt that I could have reproduced the delightfully individual accounts built around the significance of particular brands of breakfast cereal or particular cuts of meat – these stories contained too much detail about items too ordinary to remember with confidence. I think I would have remembered hesitation as a general phenomenon, or the fact that respondents often referred to particular preferences, but I needed their exact words as evidence, in order to show readers, in some detail, how they spoke about these matters.

As I worked with the interviews, I learned from conversation and discourse analysis to attend to the details of respondents' speech. I did not systematically transcribe details of dialect, pauses, or emphasis. But as I transcribed, I developed the rudiments of a system for preserving some of the "messiness" of everyday talk. I inserted ungrammatical commas to indicate hesitation mid-sentence. I included many (though not all) of my respondents' "um"s and "you know"s; I indicated outright laughter, but I had not yet learned to hear more attenuated out-breaths as signals of emotion. I transcribed the often confusing process of self-correction (e.g., "And I'm a lot more concerned about – well, I shouldn't say concerned, I should say aware, of what I eat."). In these ways, I recorded more of the inelegant features of my respondents' talk than is customary in the kind of interview study I conducted, and the transcripts retained at least some of the distinctiveness of women's talk about housework.

When I began to write about these interviews, I first selected illustrative excerpts that were clear and concise, and I felt free to do minor editing that made them clearer or more euphonious (eliminating a superfluous phrase, for example, when the meaning of a statement was clear). As the analysis developed, however, I became aware of the power of respondents' actual, often puzzlingly complex language. I began to search for more confusing rather than clearer speech and I stopped editing excerpts. The halting, unedited excerpts I produced required more analytic comment, of a different sort than I had previously provided. I began to attend more carefully to the small features of respondents' accounts, and to how their stories were situated in longer stretches of discourse. I returned, sometimes, to the original tapes, listening for and transcribing more details of the talk. Instead of relying on the routine practices of the interactionist tradition I had learned, I developed editing strategies that preserved and exploited distinctive features of respondents' talk.

Paget's work provides another example of strategic borrowing, and suggests that editing actual talk may be one of the ways that conventional sociology has suppressed emotion. In her study of artistic work (Paget 1981, 1983), she relies on a system of notation that preserves many features of naturally occurring speech: false starts and hesitations, rhythm and accent, periods of silence. In the analysis, she uses these features of the talk as signals of emotion. For example: the artist informant tells a story of long, hard times, and finally, some success. Paget presents a long excerpt from the interview transcript, and uses the sound of her respondent's account to pinpoint the artist's account of a turning point in her development: "THHEN . . . . . . sl(h)owly i started to meet other artists . . . ." (Paget 1983: 84). As she develops the analysis, Paget summarizes the artist's story, and also explains how she herself understood its significance: "Then things in general got much better. 'THHEN' (line 1212) is said with special dramatic effect. It is like a beacon" (Paget 1983: 87). Paget attends to both the content and structure of speech. In her approach, features of speech like pauses and emphasis provide clues to emotion and meaning, and these in turn are building blocks for the analysis. Knowledge, Paget says, "accumulates with many turns at talk. It collects in stories, asides, hesitations, expressions of feeling, and spontaneous associations" (Paget 1983: 78). The researcher preserves the emotion in respondents' talk, and displays it for readers. "Had I edited these exchanges," she explains, "freed them of the odd and essential noises of talk's presence, I would have reworked meanings. The transcript would move forward in an orderly and formal manner. But the dynamic construction of what was said would be gone" (Paget 1983: 87).

There is increasing evidence of a fruitful interchange between traditional approaches to qualitative sociology and the newer insights of conversation and discourse analysis (e.g., Mishler 1986; Moerman 1988; Boden 1990). There is also evidence of a heightened awareness of transcription in linguistic research (see e.g., Ochs 1979), and especially at the borders between conversation analysis and other qualitative approaches (e.g., Mishler 1984). Feminist work should be an important site for mutual influence. For conversation and discourse analysts, attention to the characteristic difficulties in women's speaking provides one route toward showing how the primordial "social doings" of talk and interaction form the "scaffolding of social structure" (West and Zimmerman 1987: 129, 147). For feminists working in more conventional qualitative modes, these approaches call attention to the importance of talk and its organized complexity, and provide techniques for capturing and using talk in analyses of interview data.

Writing about Women's Lives

Social scientists have become increasingly aware, during the 1980s, that writing is not a transparent medium with which researchers simply convey "truths" discovered in the field, but itself constructs and controls meaning and interpretation. In anthropology, a well-developed movement has grown up around the analysis of ethnographic texts, and has begun to stimulate its own feminist critique (see Clifford and Marcus 1986; Mascia-Lees, Sharpe, and Cohen 1989). A similar focus has begun to develop in sociology as well (Brown 1977; Richardson 1988; Van Maanen 1988; Hunter 1990; and, with respect to feminist writing specifically, Smith 1989), though it has been less focused and coherent than in anthropology, perhaps because sociologists write in a variety of genres. Here, I will discuss just one aspect of sociological writing, the issue of "labeling" women's experiences. But broader questions about writing should be on a feminist methodological agenda. As we modify traditions for data collection and analysis, we will need to experiment with forms and texts which allow us to fully express the insights arising from transformations in research practice.

Feminists have long been aware that naming is political – the labels attached to activities establish and justify their social worth – and that women's activities have often been labeled in ways that serve the project of controlling and subordinating women (Frye 1983). When researchers write about women's lives, whatever our methods of collecting and analyzing interview data, we confront the dangers of mis-labeling that can result from the use of language that does not fit. A feminist strategy in sociology, then, must extend to the language of our texts: we must choose words carefully and creatively, with attention to the consequences of naming experience.

As housework and child care have become legitimate topics for sociologists, for example, researchers have faced the vexing problem of labeling the unpaid work of raising children. Standard vocabulary forces a set of unsatisfactory choices. Suzanne Peters (1985) discussed these problems when she organized a group of sociologists to meet and share research on "motherwork." By selecting a label that referred to mothers, she chose explicitly to "capture a certain element of present social reality ... (that women mostly raise children)" (Peters 1985: 16). But she also recognized that any vocabulary used to describe these activities should be treated as provisional, and she invited participants in the working group to explore the implications of this and other labels. By using the term "motherwork," for example, with its gender specificity, we might be denying even the possibility that men can do this work. We might be leaving out lesbian and gay couples who raise children. By using a single, coined term, we might be universalizing the experience, implying that an activity exists that is somehow the same everywhere and in all times. And what are the implications of talking about "work"? The concept does for mothers' activities what it had earlier done in research on housework – calls attention to the time and effort involved in mothering, and its social and economic significance. But it might also obscure "important emotional aspects of mothering, which include creating rela-tionships and cherishing individuals" (Peters 1985: 19).

The problem is familiar, perhaps for all researchers, but especially for feminists exploring previously neglected experiences. But the problem is often defined rather narrowly, in terms of choosing a single word or phrase that will serve.[4] The assumption is that the researcher can, with reasonable care, make decisions that are politically or analytically correct, and then forge ahead, armed with the proper concept. I want to argue instead for a strategic imprecision – that researchers are not well served by deciding exactly what to call mothers' work, and that we would do better to use several different labels, sometimes more or less interchangeably, and sometimes to refer to subtle shadings of meaning that we are just beginning to interpret. This strategy recognizes that different labels will capture different parts of the reality we are working to construct. I developed such an approach in my study of housework, though I did not start out to do so. I began with the notion that I would eventually find a term for the neglected, invisible part of housework that I was most concerned with. As my analysis developed, I used a variety of labels – "family work," "caring," "the work of coordination" or "interpersonal work" – trying to indicate how thought and the construction of relationships are part of housework, but stubbornly resisting suggestions that I could capture what houseworkers really do with a term such as "management." Increasingly, as my understandings grew more complex, I gave up the search for a single label, and simply worked at producing a fuller understanding of women's household activity.

Now, I understand this problem as another manifestation of the uneasy fit between language and women's experiences. If the language is "man-made," it is not likely to provide, ready-made, the words that feminist researchers need to tell what they learn from other women. Instead of imposing a choice among several labels, none of which are quite right, feminist texts should describe women's lives in ways that move beyond standard vocabularies, commenting on the vocabularies themselves along the way (see e.g., Reinharz 1988). Instead of agreeing on what to call women's activity, we should make our talk richer and more complex – we should use many words, and put them together in ways that force readers to imagine the reality we're describing in a new way – to taste it, try it out, turn it over, take it apart. In discussions of household and family activity, labels like "work" and "emotion" are words that channel thinking, leading the mind down old, familiar roads. And that should not be the effect of a feminist text.

There are unexpected barriers to putting this strategy of rich and complex description into practice. Many readers of social science, accustomed to more conventional analysis, are confused by a shifting vocabulary. Copy editors, whose job includes checking manuscripts for consistency, enforce the routine practice of obscuring complexity under concepts derived from (or developed in opposition to) disciplinary frames (for some examples of problems with editing and feminist discourse, see Paget 1990). These problems suggest that feminist researchers must continue to discuss these linguistic difficulties very explicitly whenever we write. When using a multi-layered vocabulary, quite different from those typically anchoring sociological analyses, we will need to alert readers to this strategy and intentions informing it. We will need to prepare the reader to read in new ways – not to expect neat re-definitions, but to settle in for a much longer process of shaping new meanings.

These last comments point toward the construction of an audience for feminist research as an aspect of feminist method. Texts work and move because they are read. But audiences must learn how to read texts, especially those that are "different" because they stretch and extend rhetorical convention (DeVault 1990b). This problem pulls writing toward the conventional, as authors strive to communicate effectively with audiences that exist. But a more transformative solution would involve more explicit attention to methods for reading innovative texts. Part of the task of feminist writing, then, should be to instruct a newly forming audience about how to read and hear our words.

Discussion

I have argued that language is often inadequate for women. Its inadequacy surely takes multiple forms for women in different locations. Often, our relations to language are contradictory, because we are both subject to, and also working within, a loosely coordinated ruling apparatus (Smith 1987) with oppressive consequences for others besides women. Talk and interaction are thoroughly gendered, but women do not share a single experience of oppression through talk or a single culture of resistance. Instead, we share multiple versions of both oppression and resistance. There remains in this article an unresolved tension between an insistence on the importance of gender and a recognition of cross-cutting differences among women. I have relied on suggestive metaphors of language as "man-made" and of resistance through "woman talk," both of which are too simple if taken too literally. I acknowledge that difficulty here as a way of pointing to aspects of these methodological projects that need fuller development.

In spite of obstacles to women's expression, language is a resource to be used, and in use, there are many possibilities. While much feminist research in linguistics is designed to show how language and the organization of talk contribute to the subordination of women, it also shows, often, how skillfully and creatively women speakers circumvent and subvert the processes of social control, whether they do so by "talking back" (hooks 1989) or "telling it slant" (Spender [1980] 1985). It is quite difficult for most women to be speaking subjects – harder than for men – and that is true both for women as our research subjects and for us as researchers when we write and talk about our work. But women in different places and positions have long traditions of working at self-expression and understanding, using the language to talk about our lives, and working at listening. Professional training as sociologists and the routine practices of the discipline encourage us to abandon these traditions of "woman talk" in favor of a more abstract, controlled, and emotionless discourse. I have meant to suggest that as we construct feminist discourses in sociology, we can instead recognize those distinctively female traditions, borrow from them, and build upon them in our practice as researchers.

Notes

1   Compare Paget (1983) and Mishler (1986b). Mishler, though without making gender the issue, comments perceptively on the difference between Paget's case and an example from his own interviewing. He notes that their different practices produced quite different results.
2   Carol Gilligan's analysis of women's moral reasoning relies in part on a similar "hearing" of hesitation in women's speech. See Gilligan (1982: 28–9, 31).
3   As an example, he cites the frequent use of "crutch words" such as "you know," though he warns that this kind of repetitiveness should not be confused with "controlled and conscious repetition for rhetorical effect" (Blauner 1987: 51). My discussion of the phrase "you know," above, suggests that such material can be analytically useful precisely because it is not used consciously by respondents toward some end, but rather points toward issues they cannot fully articulate.
4   Another solution to the problem – developing new vocabulary – has produced several experiments with the idea of a feminist dictionary (e.g., Daly and Caputi 1987; Kramarae and Treichler 1986). These books are resources that should encourage feminist sociologists to think about words in new ways. But, while feminists have successfully coined some new words ("sexism," for example), the usefulness of this kind of invention is limited by most of our audiences' impatience with such experimentation.

References

Ardener, Edwin. 1975. "Belief and the problem of women." In *Perceiving Women*, ed. Shirley Ardner, 1–17. New York: John Wiley and Sons.

Ardener, Shirley, ed. 1975. *Perceiving Women*. New York: John Wiley and Sons.

Atkinson, J. Maxwell and John Heritage 1984. Structures of Social Action: Studies in Conversation Analysis. Cambridge: Cambridge University Press.

Becker, Howard S. 1986 *Doing Things Together ("Telling about society")*. Evanston, Ill.: Northwestern University Press.

Blauner, Bob 1987. "Problems of editing 'first-person' sociology." *Qualitative Sociology* 10: 46–64.

Boden, Deirdre. 1990. "People are talking: conversation analysis and symbolic interaction." In *Symbolic Interaction and Cultural Studies*, ed. Howard S. Becker and Michal M. McCall. Chicago: University of Chicago Press.

Boden, Deirdre and Denise D. Bielby. 1986. "The way it was: topical organization in elderly conversation." *Language and Communication* 6: 73–89.

Bogdan, Robert and Steven J. Taylor. 1975. *Introduction to Qualitative Research Methods: A Phenomenological Approach to the Social Sciences*. New York: John Wiley and Sons.

Brown, Richard H. 1977. *A Poetic for Sociology*. Cambridge, Mass.: Harvard University Press.

Bulkin, Elly, Minnie Bruce Pratt and Barbara Smith. 1984. *Yours in Struggle: Three Feminist Perspectives on Anti-Semitism and Racism*. New York: Long Haul Press.

Clifford, James and George E. Marcus, eds. 1986. *Writing Culture: The Poetics and Politics of Ethnography*. Berkeley, Calif.: University of California.

Collins, Patricia Hill. 1986. "Learning from the outsider within: the sociological significance of black feminist thought." *Social Problems* 33: 14–32.

—— 1989. "The social construction of black feminist thought." *Signs* 14: 745–73.

Daly, Mary and Jane Caputi. 1987. *Websters' First New Intergalactic Wickedary of the English Language*. Boston: Beacon Press.

Daniels, Arlene Kaplan. 1987. "Invisible work." *Social Problems* 34: 403–15.

Darroch, Vivian, and Ronald J. Silvers, eds. 1983. *Interpretive Human Studies: An Introduction to Phenomenological Research*. Lanham, Md.: University Press of America.

DeVault, Marjorie L. 1984. "Women and food: housework and the production of family life." Ph.D. Dissertation, Northwestern University, Evanston, Ill.

—— 1987. "Doing housework: feeding and family life." In *Families and Work*, ed. Naomi Gerstel and Harriet Engel Gross, 178–91. Philadelphia: Temple University Press.

—— 1990a. "Novel readings: the social organization of interpretation." *American Journal of Sociology* 95: 887–921.

—— 1990b. "Women write sociology: rhetorical strategies." In *The Rhetoric of Sociology*, ed. Albert Hunter. New Brunswick, N.J.: Rutgers University Press.

—— 1991. *Feeding the Family: The Social Organization of Caring as Gendered Work*. Chicago: University of Chicago Press.

Fisher, Sue, and Alexandra Dundas Todd. 1983. *The Social Organization of Doctor-Patient Communication*. Washington, D.C.: Center for Applied Linguistics.

Fishman, Pamela M. 1978. "Interaction: the work women do." *Social Problems* 25: 397–406.

Frye, Marilyn. 1983. *The Politics of Reality: Essays in Feminist Theory*. Trumansburg, N.Y.: The Crossing Press.

Garfinkel, Harold. 1967. *Studies in Ethnomethodology*. Englewood Cliffs, N.J.: Prentice-Hall.

Gilligan, Carol. 1982. *In a Different Voice*. Boston: Harvard University Press.

Goodwin, Charles. 1979. "The interactive construction of a sentence in natural conversation." In *Everyday Language: Studies in Ethnomethodology*, ed. George Psathas, 97–121. New York: Irvington.

Goodwin, Charles, and Marjorie H. Goodwin. 1989. "Conflicting participation frameworks." Paper presented at the annual meeting of the American Sociological Association, San Francisco.

Griffith, Alison I., and Dorothy E. Smith. 1987. "Constructing cultural knowledge: mothering as discourse." In *Women and Education: A Canadian Perspective*, ed. Jane Gaskell and Arlene McLaren, 87–103. Calgary, Alberta: Detselig.

Hartsock, Nancy M. 1981. "The feminist standpoint: developing the ground for a specifically feminist historical materialism." In *Discovering Reality: Feminist Perspectives on Episte-mology, Metaphysics, Methodology, and Philosophy of Science*, ed. Sandra Harding and Merrill Hintikka, 283–310. Boston: Reidel.

Heritage, John. 1984. *Garfinkel and Ethnomethodology*. Cambridge: Polity Press.

hooks, bell 1981. *Ain't I a Woman: Black Women and Feminism*. Boston: South End Press.

—— 1989. *Talking Back: Thinking Feminist, Thinking Black*. Boston: South End Press.

Hunter, Albert, ed. 1990. *The Rhetoric of Sociology*. New Brunswick, N.J.: Rutgers University Press.

Joseph, Gloria I., and Jill Lewis. 1981. *Common Differences: Conflicts in Black and White Feminist Perspectives*. Boston: South End Press.

Kramarae, Cheris, and Paula A. Treichler. 1986. *A Feminist Dictionary*. New York: Routle-dge, Chapman and Hall.

Lakoff, Robin. 1975. *Language and Women's Place*. New York: Harper and Row.

Lugones, Maria C., and Elizabeth V. Spelman. 1983. "Have we got a theory for you! Feminist theory, cultural imperialism and the demand for 'the woman's voice.'" *Women's Studies International Forum* 6: 573–81.

MacKinnon, Catharine. 1983. "Feminism, marxism, method, and the state: an agenda for theory." In *The Signs Reader*, ed. Elizabeth Abel and Emily K. Abel, 227–56. Chicago: University of Chicago Press.

Mascia-Lees, Frances E., Patricia Sharpe, and Colleen Ballerino Cohen. 1989. "The post-modernist turn in anthropology: cautions from a feminist prespective." *Signs* 15: 7–33.

Maynard, Douglas W. and Don H. Zimmerman. 1984. "Topical talk, ritual and the social organization of relationships." *Social Psychology Quarterly* 47: 301–16.

Mies, Maria. 1983. "Towards a methodology for feminist research." In *Theories of Women's Studies*, ed. Gloria Bowles and Renate Duelli Klein, 117–39. London: Routledge and Kegan Paul.

Miller, Casey and Kate Swift. 1977. *Words and Women*. Garden City, N.Y.: Anchor Double-day.

Miller, Jean Baker. 1976. *Toward a New Psychology of Women*. Boston: Beacon.

—— 1986. "What do we mean by relationships?" Working Paper No. 22, Stone Center for Developmental Services and Studies, Wellesley College, Wellesley, Mass.

Mishler, Elliot G. 1984. *The Discourse of Medicine: Dialectics of Medical Interviews*. Nor-wood, N.J.: Ablex.

—— 1986a. *Research Interviewing: Context and Narrative*. Cambridge, Mass.: Harvard University Press.

—— 1986b. "The analysis of interview-narratives." In *Narrative Psychology: The Storied Nature of Human Conduct*, ed. Theodore R. Sarbin, 233–55. New York: Praeger.

Moerman, Michael. 1988. *Talking Culture: Ethnography and Conversation Analysis*. Phila-delphia: University of Pennsylvania Press.

Oakley, Ann. 1981. "Interviewing women: a contradiction in terms." In *Doing Feminist Research*, ed. Helen Roberts, 30–61. London: Routledge and Kegan Paul.

Ochs, Elinor. 1979. "Transcription as theory." In *Developmental Pragmatics*, ed. Elinor Ochs and Bambi B. Schieffelin, 43–72. New York: Academic Press.

Paget, Marianne A. 1981. "The ontological anguish of women artists." *The New England Sociologist* 3: 65–79.

—— 1983. "Experience and knowledge." *Human Studies* 6: 67–90.

—— 1990. "'Unlearning to not speak.'" *Human Studies* 13(2): 119–45.

Peters, Suzanne. 1985. "Reflections on studying mothering, motherwork, and mothers' work." Paper presented at The Motherwork Workshop, Institut Simone de Beauvoir, Concordia University, Montreal.

Psathas, George. 1973. *Phenomenological Sociology: Issues and Applications*. New York: Wiley and Sons.

Reinharz, Shulamit. 1983. "Experiential analysis: a contribution to feminist research." In *Theories of Women's Studies*, ed. Gloria Bowles and Renate Duelli Klein, 162–91. London: Routledge and Kegan Paul.

——1988. "What's missing in miscarriage?" *Journal of Community Psychology* 16: 84–103.

Richardson, Laurel. 1988. "The collective story: postmodernism and the writing of sociology." *Sociological Focus* 21: 199–208.

——1990. "Narrative and sociology." *Journal of Contemporary Ethnography* 19(1): 116–35.

Riessman, Catherine Kohler. 1987. "When gender is not enough: women interviewing women." *Gender and Society* 1: 172–207.

Rothman, Barbara Katz. 1986. "Reflections: on hard work." *Qualitative Sociology* 9: 48–53.

Rubin, Lillian B. 1979. *Women of a Certain Age: The Mid-Life Search for Self*. New York: Harper and Row.

Saraceno, Chiaro. 1984. "Shifts in public and private boundaries: women as mothers and service workers in Italian daycare." *Feminist Studies* 10: 7–29.

Schegloff, Emanuel A. 1982. "Discourse as an interactional achievement: some uses of 'uh huh' and other things that come between sentences." In *Analyzing Discourse: Text and Talk*, ed. Deborah Tannen, 71–93. Washington, D.C.: Georgetown University Press.

Schenkein, Jim, ed. 1978. *Studies in the Organization of Conversational Interaction*. New York: Academic Press.

Smith, Dorothy E. 1974. "The ideological practice of sociology." *Catalyst* No. 8: 39–54.

——1983. "No one commits suicide: textual analysis of ideological practices." *Human Studies* 6: 309–59.

——1987. *The Everyday World as Problematic: A Feminist Sociology*. Boston: Northeastern University Press.

——1989. "Sociological theory: methods of writing patriarchy." In *Feminism and Sociological Theory*, ed. Ruth A. Wallace, 34–64. Newbury Park, Calif.: Sage.

Spender, Dale. [1980] 1985. *Man Made Language* (2nd ed. with revised introduction). London: Routledge and Kegan Paul.

Stacey, Judith. 1988. "Can there be a feminist ethnography?" *Women's Studies International Forum* 11: 21–27.

Stacey, Judith, and Barrie Thorne. 1985. "The missing feminist revolution in sociology." *Social Problems* 32: 301–16.

Stanko, Elizabeth. 1985a. *Intimate Intrusions: Women's Experience of Male Violence*. Boston: Routledge and Kegan Paul.

——1985b. Presentation at a meeting of the Boston area chapter of Sociologists for Women in Society, November.

——1990. *Everyday Violence*. London: Pandora Press.

Stanley, Liz, and Sue Wise. 1983. "'Back into the personal' or: our attempt to construct 'feminist research.'" In *Theories of Women's Studies*, ed. Gloria Bowles and Renate Duelli Klein, 192–309. London: Routledge and Kegan Paul.

Thorne, Barrie, and Nancy Henley. 1975. *Language and Sex: Difference and Dominance*. Rowley, Mass.: Newbury House.

Thorne, Barrie, Cheris Kramarae, and Nancy Henley, eds. 1983. *Language, Gender and Society*. Rowley, Mass.: Newbury House.

Todd, Alexandra Dundas, and Sue Fisher, eds. 1988. *Gender and Discourse: The Power of Talk*. Norwood, N.J.: Ablex.

Van Maanan, John. 1988. *Tales of the Field: On Writing Ethnography*. Chicago: University of Chicago Press.

West, Candace. 1982. "Why can't a woman be more like a man? An interactional note on organizational game-playing for managerial women." *Work and Occupations* 9: 5–29.

West, Candace, and Don H. Zimmerman. 1983. "Small insults: a study of interruptions in cross-sex conversations between unacquainted persons." In *Language, Gender and Society*, ed. Barrie Thorne, Cheris Kramarae and Nancy Henley, 86–111. Rowley, Mass.: Newbury House.

—— 1987. "Doing Gender." *Gender and Society* 1: 125–51.

6 Active Interviewing

James A. Holstein and Jaber F. Gubrium

In our "interview society" (Silverman, 1993), the mass media, human service providers and researchers increasingly generate information by interviewing. The number of television news programmes, daytime talk-shows and newspaper articles that provide us with the results of interviews is virtually incalculable. Looking at more methodical forms of information collection, it has been estimated that 90 per cent of all social science investigations use interviews in one way or another (Briggs, 1986). Interviewing is undoubtedly the most widely applied technique for conducting systematic social inquiry, as sociologists, psychologists, anthropologists, psychiatrists, clinicians, administrators, politicians and pollsters treat interviews as their "windows on the world" (Hyman et al., 1975).

Interviewing provides a way of generating empirical data about the social world by asking people to talk about their lives. In this respect, interviews are special forms of conversation. While these conversations may vary from highly structured, standardized, quantitatively oriented survey interviews, to semi-formal guided conversations and free-flowing informational exchanges, all interviews are interactional. The narratives that are produced may be as truncated as forced-choice survey answers or as elaborate as oral life histories, but they are all constructed *in situ*, as a product of the talk between interview participants.

While most researchers acknowledge the interactional character of the interview, the technical literature on interviewing stresses the need to keep that interaction strictly in check. Guides to interviewing – especially those oriented to standardized surveys – are primarily concerned with maximizing the flow of valid, reliable information while minimizing distortions of what the respondent knows (Gorden, 1987). The interview conversation is thus framed as a potential source of bias, error, misunderstanding or misdirection, a persistent set of problems to be controlled. The corrective is simple: if the interviewer asks questions properly, the respondent will give out the desired information.

In this conventional view, the interview conversation is a pipeline for transmitting knowledge. A recently heightened sensitivity to representational matters (see Gubrium and Holstein, 1997) – characteristic of poststructuralist, postmodernist, constructionist and ethnomethodological inquiry – has raised a number of questions about the very possibility of collecting knowledge in the manner the conventional approach presupposes. In varied ways, these alternate perspectives hold that meaning is socially constituted; all knowledge is created from the actions undertaken to obtain it (see e.g., Cicourel, 1964, 1974; Garfinkel, 1967). Treating interviewing as a social encounter in which knowledge is constructed suggests the possibility that the interview is not merely a neutral conduit or source of distortion, but is instead a site of, and occasion for, producing reportable knowledge itself.

Sociolinguist Charles Briggs (1986) argues that the social circumstances of interviews are more than obstacles to respondents' articulation of their particular truths. Briggs notes that, like all other speech events, interviews fundamentally, not incidentally, shape the form and content of what is said. Aaron Cicourel (1974) goes further, maintaining that interviews virtually impose particular ways of understanding reality upon subjects' responses. The point is that interviewers are deeply and unavoidably implicated in creating meanings that ostensibly reside within respondents (also see Manning, 1967; Mishler, 1986, 1991; Silverman, 1993). Both parties to the interview are necessarily and ineluctably *active*. Meaning is not merely elicited by apt questioning, nor simply transported through respondent replies; it is actively and communicatively assembled in the interview encounter. Respondents are not so much repositories of knowledge – treasuries of information awaiting excavation, so to speak – as they are constructors of knowledge in collaboration with interviewers. Participation in an interview involves meaning-making work (Holstein and Gubrium, 1995).

If interviews are interpretively active, meaning-making occasions, interview data are unavoidably collaborative (see Alasuutari, 1995; Holstein and Staples, 1992). Therefore, any technical attempts to strip interviews of their interactional ingredients will be futile. Instead of refining the long list of methodological constraints under which "standardized" interviews should be conducted, we suggest that researchers take a more "active" perspective, begin to acknowledge, and capitalize upon, interviewers' and respondents' constitutive contributions to the production of interview data. This means consciously and conscientiously attending to the interview process and its product in ways that are more sensitive to the social construction of knowledge.

Conceiving of the interview as active means attending more to the ways in which knowledge is assembled than is usually the case in traditional approaches. In other words, understanding *how* the meaning-making process unfolds in the interview is as critical as apprehending *what* is substantively asked and conveyed. The *hows* of interviewing, of course, refer to the interactional, narrative procedures of knowledge production, not merely to interview techniques. The *whats* pertain to the issues guiding the interview, the content of questions, and the substantive information communicated by the respondent. A dual interest in the *hows* and *whats* of meaning production goes hand in hand with an appreciation of the constitutive activeness of the interview process.

This appreciation derives from an ethnomethodologically informed social constructionist approach that considers the process of meaning production to be as important for social research as the meaning that is produced (cf. Berger and Luckmann, 1967; Blumer, 1969; Garfinkel, 1967; Heritage, 1984; Pollner, 1987). In many significant ways, this also resonates with methodological critiques and reformulations offered by an array of feminist scholars (see DeVault, 1990; Harding, 1987; Reinharz, 1992; Smith, 1987). In their distinct fashions, ethnomethodology, constructionism, poststructuralism, postmodernism and some versions of feminism are all interested in issues relating to subjectivity, complexity, perspective and meaning-construction. Still, as valuable and insightful as this is, these "linguistically attuned" approaches can emphasize the *hows* of social process at the expense of the *whats* of lived experience. We want to strike a balance between these *hows* and *whats* as a way of reappropriating the significance of substance and content to studies of the social construction process. The aim is not to obviate interview material by deconstructing it, but to harvest it and its transactions for narrative analysis. While the emphasis on process has sharpened concern with, and debate over, the epistemological status of interview data, it is important not to lose track of *what* is being asked about in interviews and, in turn, *what* is being conveyed by respondents. A narrow focus on *how* tends to displace the significant *whats* – the meanings – that serve as the relevant grounds for asking and answering questions.

Taking the meaning-making activity of all interviewing as our point of departure, we will discuss how the interview cultivates its data. We begin by locating the active view in relation to more traditional conceptions of interviewing, contrasting alternate images of the subject behind the interview respondent.

Traditional Images of Interviewing

Typically, those who want to find out about another person's feelings, thoughts or actions believe that they merely have to ask the right questions and the other's "reality" will be theirs. Studs Terkel, the consummate journalistic and sociological interviewer, says he simply turns on his tape recorder and invites people to talk. Writing of the interviews he did for his brilliant study of *Working*, Terkel notes:

> There were questions, of course. But they were casual in nature...the kind you would ask while having a drink with someone; the kind he would ask you.... In short, it was conversation. In time, the sluice gates of dammed up hurts and dreams were opened. (1972: xxv)

As unpretentious as it is, Terkel's image of interviewing permeates the social sciences; interviewing is generally likened to "prospecting" for the true facts and feelings residing within the respondent. Of course there is a highly sophisticated technology that informs researchers about how to ask questions, what sorts of questions not to ask, the order in which to ask them, and the ways to avoid saying things that might spoil, contaminate or otherwise bias the data (Fowler and Mangione, 1990; Hyman et al., 1975). The basic model, however, remains similar to the one Terkel exploits so adroitly.

The image of the social scientific prospector casts the interview as a search-and-discovery mission, with the interviewer intent on detecting what is already there inside variably cooperative respondents. The challenge lies in extracting information as directly as possible. Highly refined interview techniques streamline, systematize and sanitize the process. This can involve varying degrees of standardization (see Maccoby and Maccoby, 1954), ranging from interviews organized around structured, specially worded questions and an orientation to measurement, to flexibly organized interviews guided by more general questions aimed at uncovering subjective meanings. John Madge contrasts what he calls "formative" with "mass" interviews, categorizing them according to whether the respondent "is given some sort of freedom to choose the topics to be discussed and the way in which they are discussed" (1965: 165). Formative interviews include the non-directive interviews favoured in Rogerian counselling (see Rogers, 1945), informal interviews and life histories. Most large-scale surveys fall into the mass interview category. Mainly, classification centres on the characteristics and aims of the interview process, with little attention paid to how interviews differ as occasions for knowledge production.

The Subject Behind the Respondent

Regardless of the type of interview, there is always an image of the research *subject* lurking behind persons placed in the role of interview respondent (Holstein and Gubrium, 1995). Projecting a subject behind the respondent confers a sense of epistemological agency, which bears on our understanding of the relative validity of the information that is reported. In traditional approaches, subjects are basically conceived as passive *vessels of answers* for experiential questions put to respondents by interviewers. They are repositories of facts and the related details of experience. Occasionally, such as with especially sensitive interview topics or with recalcitrant respondents, researchers acknowledge that it may be difficult to obtain accurate experiential information. None the less, the information is viewed, in principle, as held uncontaminated by the subject's vessel of answers. The trick is to formulate questions and provide an atmosphere conducive to open and undistorted communication between the interviewer and respondent.

Much of the methodological literature on interviewing deals with the nuances of these intricate matters. The vessel-of-answers view cautions interviewers to be careful in how they ask questions, lest their manner of inquiry bias what lies within the subject. The literature offers myriad procedures for obtaining unadulterated facts and details, most of which rely upon interviewer and question neutrality. For example, it is assumed that the interviewer who poses questions that acknowledge alternative sides of an issue is being more "neutral" than the interviewer who does not. The successful implementation of neutral practices elicits truths held in the vessel of answers behind the respondent. Validity results from the successful application of the procedures.

In the vessel-of-answers approach, the image of the subject is epistemologically passive, not engaged in the production of knowledge. If the interviewing process goes "by the book" and is non-directional and unbiased, respondents will validly give out what subjects are presumed to merely retain within them – the unadulterated facts and details of experience. Contamination emanates from the interview setting, its participants and their interaction, not the subject, who, under ideal conditions, serves up authentic reports when beckoned to do so.

What happens, however, if we enliven the image of the subject behind the respondent? Construed as active, the subject behind the respondent not only holds facts and details of experience, but, in the very process of offering them up for response, constructively adds to, takes away from and transforms the facts and details. The respondent can hardly "spoil" what he or she is, in effect, subjectively creating.

This activated subject pieces experiences together, before, during and after assuming the respondent role. As a member of society, he or she mediates and alters the knowledge that is conveyed to the interviewer; he or she is "always already" an active maker of meaning. As a result, the respondent's answers are continually being assembled and modified and the answers' truth value cannot be judged simply in terms of whether they match what lies in a vessel of objective knowledge.

From a more traditional standpoint, the objectivity or truth of interview responses might be assessed in terms of reliability, the extent to which questioning yields the same answers whenever and wherever it is carried out, and validity, that is, the extent to which inquiry yields the "correct" answers (Kirk and Miller, 1986). When the interview is seen as a dynamic, meaning-making occasion, however, different criteria apply. The focus is on how meaning is constructed, the circumstances of construction, and the meaningful linkages that are made for the occasion. While interest in the content of answers persists, it is primarily in how and what the active subject/respondent, in collaboration with an equally active interviewer, produces and conveys about the active subject/respondent's experience under the interpretive circumstances at hand. One cannot simply expect answers on one occasion to replicate those on another because they emerge from different circumstances of production. Similarly, the validity of answers derives not from their correspondence to meanings held within the respondent, but from their ability to convey situated experiential realities in terms that are locally comprehensible.

This active image of the interview is best put in perspective by contrasting it with specific traditional approaches. The two approaches we have selected differ considerably in their orientations to the experiential truths held by the passive subject. The first orients to the rational, factual value of what is communicated. Typical of survey interviewing, it focuses on the substantive statements, explanations and reasons with which the respondent articulates experience. We use Jean Converse and Howard Schuman's candid book *Conversations at Random* (1974) as an exemplary text. The second approach orients to the purportedly deeper and more authentic value of the subject's feelings. It emphasizes sentiment and emotion, the ostensible core of human experience. We use Jack Douglas's book *Creative Interviewing* (1985) to illustrate this approach.

Survey Interviewing

While Converse and Schuman attempt to elaborate upon the most standardized of interviewing techniques, their book also considers the survey interview "as interviewers see it" and richly illustrates how interpretively engaging and, relatedly, how difficult and exasperating the survey respondent can be. It describes the interesting and complex personalities and meanings that interviewers encounter while interviewing, depicting them, respectively, as "the pleasure of persons" and "connoisseurs of the particular". But the authors caution the reader that, even though it will be evident throughout the book that the respondent can be quite interpretively active, this does not work against the pursuit of objective information. This information, the reader eventually learns, is derived from the repository of knowledge that lies passively behind the respondent. The authors do not believe that the respondent's conduct implicates his or her subject in the construction of meaning. As lively, uninhibited, entertaining and difficult as the respondent might be at times, his or her passive subject ultimately holds the answers sought in the research.

Converse and Schuman's book is filled with anecdotal reminders of what interviewers must learn in order to keep the subject's vessel of answers in view and the respondent on target. In part, it is a matter of controlling onself as an interviewer so that one does not interfere with what the passive subject is only too willing to disclose. The interviewer must shake off self-consciousness, suppress personal opinion and avoid stereotyping the respondent. Learning the interviewer role is also a matter of controlling the interview situation to facilitate the candid expression of opinions and sentiments. Ideally, the interview should be conducted in private. This helps assure that respondents will speak directly from their vessels of answers, not in response to the presence of others. The seasoned interviewer learns that the so-called "pull of conversation", which might have an interpretive dynamic of its own fuelled by the active subjectivity of both the respondent and the interviewer, must be managed so that the "push of inquiry" (p. 26) is kept in focus. Ideally, the cross-pressures of conducting inquiry that will produce "good hard data" are managed by means of "soft" conversation (p. 22).

Throughout, Converse and Schuman's book provides glimpses of how problematic the image of the passive subject is in practice. The illustrations repeatedly tell us that interviews are conversations where meanings are not only conveyed, but cooperatively built up, received, interpreted and recorded by the interviewer. While the veteran interviewer learns to manage the pressures of conversation for the purposes of inquiry, orienting to an active, meaning-making occasion seems to be a mere epistemological step away.

Creative Interviewing

This is different from the approach exemplified in Douglas's book *Creative Interviewing*, but there are some marked similarities that borrow from traditional images. The word "creative" in Douglas's title refers primarily to the interviewer, not the respondent, and, according to Douglas, derives from the difficulties he encountered attempting to probe respondents' "deep experience". Douglas writes that in his many empirical studies, he repeatedly discovered how shallow the standard recommendations were for conducting research interviews. Canons of rational neutrality, such as those Converse and Schuman espouse, failed to capture what Douglas calls his respondents' "emotional wellsprings" and called for a methodology for deep disclosure.

Douglas's difficulties relate as much to his image of the passive subject as they do to shortcomings of standard interviewing technique. Like the image of the subject behind the survey respondent, Douglas also imagines his subjects to be repositories of answers, but in his case, they are well-guarded vessels of feelings. The respondent authentically communicates from an emotional wellspring, at the behest of an interviewer who knows that mere words cannot draw out or convey what experience ultimately is all about. Standard survey questions and answers touch only the surface of experience. Douglas aims more deeply by creatively "getting to know" the real subject behind the respondent.

Creative interviewing is a set of techniques for moving past the mere words and sentences exchanged in the interview process. To achieve this, the interviewer must establish a climate for *mutual* disclosure. The interview should be an occasion that displays the interviewer's willingness to share his or her own feelings and deepest thoughts. This is done to assure respondents that they can, in turn, share their own thoughts and feelings. The interviewers' deep disclosure both occasions and legitimizes the respondent's reciprocal revelations. This, Douglas suggests, is thoroughly suppressed by the cultivated neutrality of the standard survey interview. As if to state a cardinal rule, he writes:

> Creative interviewing, as we shall see throughout, involves the use of many strategies and tactics of interaction, largely based on an understanding of friendly feelings and intimacy, to optimize *cooperative, mutual disclosure and a creative search for mutual understanding.* (1985: 25)

Douglas offers a set of guidelines for creative interviewing. One is to figure that, as he puts it, "genius in creative interviewing involves 99 percent perspiration" (1985: 27); getting the respondent to deeply disclose requires much more work than obtaining mere opinions. A second admonition for engaging in "deep-deep probes into the human soul" is "researcher, know thyself" (1985: 51). Continual self-analysis on the part of the interviewer, who usually is also the researcher, is necessary, lest the creative interviewer's own defence mechanisms work against mutual disclosure and understanding. A third guideline is to show a commitment to disclosure by expressing an abiding interest in feelings. Referring to a neophyte creative interviewer who "has done some wondrously revealing life studies", Douglas writes that the creative interviewer is "driven by . . . friendly, caring, and adoring feelings, but adds to those an endearing, wide-eyed sense of wonderment at the mysteries unveiled before her" (1985: 29).

The wellsprings tapped by creative interviewing are said to be emotional, in distinct contrast with the preferred rational image of facts that filters through Converse and Schuman's book. As Douglas puts it, knowledge and wisdom are "*partially* the product of creative interactions – of mutual searches for understanding, of soul communions" (p. 55). While Douglas's imagined subject is basically emotional, this subject, in the role of respondent, actively cooperates with the interviewer to create mutually recognizable meanings, paralleling what interviewers' accounts in Converse and Schuman's book suggest. In this regard, the mutuality of disclosure – the "creative" thrust of creative interviewing – mediates, adds to and shapes what is said in its own right. What Douglas does not recognize, however, is that this ideally cooperative subject could alternatively constitute the wellsprings of experience in rational or other terms, not necessarily emotional ones. Thus, the subject behind Douglas's respondent remains an essentially passive, if concertedly emotional, fount of experience, not unlike the respondent who "opens up" while having a drink with Studs Terkel.

The Active Interview

Ithiel de Sola Pool (1957), a prominent critic of public opinion polling, once argued that the dynamic, communicative contingencies of the interview literally activate respondents' opinions. Every interview, he suggests, is an "interpersonal drama with a developing plot" (1957: 193). This metaphor conveys a far more active sense of interviewing than is traditionally conceived, an image of the interview as an occasion for constructing, not merely discovering or conveying, information. As Pool writes:

[T]he social milieu in which communication takes place [during interviews] modifies not only what a person dares to say but even what he thinks he chooses to say. And these variations in expression cannot be viewed as mere deviations from some underlying "true" opinion, for there is no neutral, non-social, uninfluenced situation to provide that baseline. (1957: 192)

The active interview and interpretive practice

Conceiving of the interview as an interpersonal drama with a developing plot is part of a broader image of reality as an ongoing, interpretive accomplishment. From this perspective, interview participants are practitioners of everyday life, constantly working to discern and communicate the recognizable and orderly features of experience. But meaning-making is not merely artful (Garfinkel, 1967); meaning is not built "from scratch" on each interpretive occasion. Rather, interpretation orients to, and is conditioned by, the substantive resources and contingencies of interaction.

Meaning is constituted at the nexus of the *hows* and the *whats* of experience, by way of *interpretive practice* – the procedures and resources used to apprehend, organize and represent reality (Holstein, 1993; Holstein and Gubrium, 1994). Active interviewing is a form of interpretive practice involving respondent and interviewer as they articulate ongoing interpretive structures, resources and orientations with what Garfinkel (1967) calls "practical reasoning". Linking artfulness to substantive contingencies implies that while reality is continually "under construction", it is assembled using the interpretive resources at hand. Meaning reflects relatively enduring interpretive conditions, such as the research topics of the interviewer, biographical particulars and local ways of orienting to those topics (Gubrium, 1988, 1989, 1994; Holstein and Gubrium, 1994, 1995). Those resources are astutely and adroitly crafted to the demands of the occasion, so that meaning is neither predetermined nor absolutely unique.

An Active Subject

The image of the *active interview* transforms the subject behind the respondent from a repository of opinions and reasons or a wellspring of emotions into a productive source of knowledge. From the time one identifies a research topic, to respondent selection, questioning and answering, and, finally, to the interpretation of responses, interviewing itself is a concerted project for producing meaning. The imagined subject behind the respondent emerges as part of the project, not beforehand. Within the interview itself, the subject is fleshed out – rationally, emotionally, in combination, or otherwise – in relation to the give-and-take of the interview process and the interview's broader research purposes. The interview *and* its participants are constantly developing.

Two communicative contingencies influence the construction of the active subject behind the respondent. One kind involves the substantive *whats* of the interview enterprise. The focus and emerging data of the research project provide interpretive resources for developing both the subject and his or her responses. For example, a project might centre on the quality of care and quality of life of nursing home residents (see Gubrium, 1993). This might be part of a study relating to national debates about the organization of home and institutional care. If interviews are employed, participants draw out the substantiality of these topics, linking the topics to biographical particulars in the interview process, and thus producing a subject who responds to, or is affected by, the matters under discussion. For instance, a nursing home resident might speak animatedly during an interview about the quality of care in her facility, asserting that, "for a woman, it ultimately gets down to feelings", echoing Douglas's emotional subject and articulating a recognizable linkage between affect and gender. Another resident might coolly and methodically list her facility's qualities of care, never once mentioning her feelings about them. Offering her own take on the matter, the respondent might state that "getting emotional" over "these things" clouds clear judgement, implicating a different kind of subject, more like the rational respondent portrayed in Converse and Schuman's text. Particular substantive resources – such as the common cultural link between women and feelings or the traditional cultural opposition of clear thought and emotionality – are used to form the subject.

A second communicative contingency of interviewing directs us to the *hows* of the process. The standpoint from which information is offered is continually developed in relation to ongoing interview interaction. In speaking of the quality of care, for example, nursing home residents, as interview respondents, not only offer substantive thoughts and feelings pertinent to the topic under consideration, but simultaneously and continuously monitor who they are in relation to the person questioning them. For example, prefacing her remarks about the quality of life in her facility with the statement "speaking as a woman", a nursing home resident informs the interviewer that she is to be heard as a woman, not as someone else – not a mere resident, cancer patient or abandoned mother. If and when she subsequently comments, "If I were a man in this place", the resident frames her thoughts and feelings about the quality of life differently, producing an alternative subject. The respondent is clearly working at how the interview unfolds.

Narrative Incitement, Positional Shifts and Resource Activation

Interviews, of course, hold no monopoly over interpretive practice. Nor are they the only occasions upon which subjects and their opinions, emotions and reports are interpretively constituted. Why, then, is interviewing an especially useful mode of systematic social inquiry? One answer lies in the interview situation's ability to incite the production of meanings that address issues relating to particular research concerns. In the traditional view of interviewing, the passive subject engages in a "minimalist" version of interpretive practice, perceiving, storing and reporting experience when properly asked. Our active conception of the interview, however, invests the subject with a substantial repertoire of interpretive methods and stock of experiential materials. The active view eschews the image of the vessel waiting to be tapped in favour of the notion that the subject's interpretive capabilities must be activated, stimulated and cultivated. The interview is a commonly recognized occasion for formally and systematically doing so.

This is not to say that active interviewers merely coax their respondents into preferred answers to their questions. Rather, they converse with respondents in such a way that alternate considerations are brought into play. They may suggest orientations to, and linkages between, diverse aspects of respondents' experience, adumbrating – even inviting – interpretations that make use of particular resources, connections and outlooks. Interviewers may explore incompletely articulated aspects of experience, encouraging respondents to develop topics in ways relevant to their own everyday lives (DeVault, 1990). The objective is not to dictate interpretation, but to provide an environment conducive to the production of the range and complexity of meanings that address relevant issues, and not be confined by predetermined agendas.

Pool's dramaturgic metaphor is apt because it conveys both the structuring conditions and the artfulness of the interview. As a drama of sorts, its narrative is scripted in that it has a topic or topics, distinguishable roles and a format for conversation. But it also has a *developing* plot, in which topics, roles and format are fashioned in the give-and-take of the interview. This active interview is a kind of limited "improvisational" performance. The production is spontaneous, yet structured – focused within loose parameters provided by the interviewer, who is also an active participant.

While the respondent actively constructs and assembles answers, he or she does not simply "break out" talking. Neither elaborate narratives nor one-word replies emerge without provocation. The active interviewer's role is to incite respondents' answers, virtually *activating narrative production*. Where standardized approaches to interviewing attempt to strip the interview of all but the most neutral, impersonal stimuli (but see Holstein and Gubrium, 1995, for a discussion of the inevitable failure of these attempts), the consciously active interviewer intentionally provokes responses by indicating – even suggesting – narrative positions, resources, orientations and precedents. In the broadest sense, the interviewer attempts to activate the respondent's stock of knowledge (Schütz, 1967) and bring it to bear on the discussion at hand in ways that are appropriate to the research agenda.

Consider, for example, the ways in which diverse aspects of a respondent's knowledge, perspectives, roles and orientations are activated and implicated in an interview involving an adult daughter who is caring for her mother – a victim of senile dementia – at home. The daughter is employed part-time, and shares the household with her employed husband and their two sons, one a part-time college student and the other a full-time security guard. The extract begins when the interviewer (I) asks the adult daughter (R) to describe her feelings about having to juggle so many needs and schedules. This relates to the so-called "sandwich generation", which is said to be caught between having to raise its own children and seeing to the needs of frail elderly parents. Note how, after the interviewer asks the respondent what she means by saying that she had mixed feelings, the respondent makes explicit reference to various ways of thinking about the matter, as if to suggest that more than one narrative resource (with contradictory responses) might be brought to bear on the matter. The respondent displays considerable narrative control: she not only references possible *whats* of caregiving and family life, but, in the process, informs the interviewer of *how* she could construct her answer.

I: We were talking about, you said you were a member of the, what did you call it?

R: They say that I'm in the sandwich generation. You know, like we're sandwiched between having to care for my mother…and my grown kids and my husband. People are living longer now and you've got different generations at home and, I tell ya, it's a mixed blessing.

I: How do you feel about it in your situation?

R: Oh, I don't know. Sometimes I think I'm being a bit selfish because I gripe about having to keep an eye on Mother all the time. If you let down your guard, she wanders off into the back yard or goes out the door and down the street. That's no fun when your hubby wants your attention too. Norm works the second shift and he's home during the day a lot. I manage to get in a few hours of work, but he doesn't like it. I have pretty mixed feelings about it.

I: What do you mean?

R: Well, I'd say that as a daughter, I feel pretty guilty about how I feel sometimes. It can get pretty bad, like wishing that Mother were just gone, you know what I mean? She's been a wonderful mother and I love her very much, but if you ask me how I feel as a wife and mother, that's another matter. I feel like she's [the mother], well, intruding on our lives and just making hell out of raising a family. Sometimes I put myself in my husband's shoes and I just know how he feels. He doesn't say much, but I know that he misses my company, and I miss his of course. [*Pause*] So how do you answer that?

The interviewer goes on to explain that the respondent can answer in the way she believes best represents her thoughts and feelings. But as the exchange unfolds, it is evident that "best" misrepresents the narrative complexity of the respondent's thoughts and feelings. In the following extract, notice how the respondent struggles to sort her opinions to accord with categorically distinct identities. At one point, she explains that she knows how a wife could and should feel because she gathers from the way her husband and sons act that "men don't feel things the same way". This suggests that her own thoughts and feelings are drawn from a fund of gendered knowledge as well. Note, too, how at several points the interviewer collaborates with the respondent to define her identity as a respondent. At the very end of the extract, the respondent suggests that other respondents' answers might serve to clarify the way she herself has organized her responses, indicating that further narrative contextualizing might encourage even more interpretations of her own experience.

R: I try to put myself in their [husband and sons'] shoes, try to look at it from their point of view, you know, from a man's way of thinking. I ask myself how it feels to have a part-time wife and mama. I ask myself how I'd feel. Believe me, I know he [husband] feels pretty rotten about it. Men get that way; they want what they want and the rest of the time, well, they're quiet, like nothing's the matter. I used to think I was going crazy with all the stuff on my mind and having to think about everything all at once and not being able to finish with one thing and get on to the other. You know how it gets – doing one thing and feeling bad about how you did something else and wanting to redo what you did or what you said. The way a woman does, I guess. I think I've learned that about myself. I don't know. It's pretty complicated thinking about it. [*Pause*] Let's see, how do I really feel?

I: Well, I was just wondering, you mentioned being sandwiched earlier and what a woman feels?

R: Yeah, I guess I wasn't all that sure what women like me feel until I figured out how Norm and the boys felt. I figured pretty quick that men are pretty good at sorting things out and that, well, I just couldn't do it, 'cause, well, men don't feel things the same way. I just wouldn't want to do that way anyway. Wouldn't feel right about it as a woman, you know what I mean? So, like they say, live and let live, I guess.

I: But as a daughter?

R: Yeah, that too. So if you ask me how I feel having Mother under foot all the time, I'd say that I remember not so far back that I was under foot a lot when I was a little girl and Mother never complained, and she'd help Dad out in the store, too. So I guess I could tell you that I'm glad I'm healthy and around to take care of her and, honestly, I'd do it all over again if I had to. I don't know. You've talked to other women about it. What do they say?

I: Well, uh

R: Naw, I don't want to put you on the spot. I was just thinking that maybe if I knew how others in my shoes felt, I might be able to sort things out better than I did for ya.

The respondent's comments about both the subject matter under consideration and how one does or should formulate responses show that the respondent, in collaboration with the interviewer, activates diverse narrative resources as an integral part of exchanging questions and answers. Treating the interview as active allows the interviewer to encourage the respondent to shift positions in the interview so as to explore alternate perspectives and stocks of knowledge. Rather than searching for the best or most authentic answer, the aim is to systematically activate applicable ways of knowing – the possible answers – that respondents can reveal, as diverse and contradictory as they might be. The active interviewer sets the general parameters for responses, constraining as well as provoking answers that are germane to the researcher's interest. He or she does not tell respondents what to say, but offers them pertinent ways of conceptualizing issues and making connections – that is, suggests possible horizons of meaning and narrative linkages that coalesce into the emerging responses (Gubrium, 1993). The pertinence of what is discussed is partly defined by the research topic and partly by the substantive horizons of ongoing responses. While the active respondent may selectively exploit a vast range of narrative resources, it is the active interviewer's job to direct and harness the respondent's constructive storytelling to the research task at hand.

Implications for Analysis

Compared to more conventional perspectives on interviewing, the active approach seems to invite unacceptable forms of bias. After all, far more is going on than simply retrieving the information from respondents' repositories of knowledge. "Contamination" is everywhere. This criticism only holds, however, if one takes a narrow view of interpretive practice and meaning construction. Bias is a meaningful concept only if the subject is a preformed, purely informational commodity that the interview process might somehow taint. But if interview responses are seen as products of interpretive practice, they are neither preformed, nor ever pure. Any interview situation – no matter how formalized, restricted or standardized – relies upon the interaction between participants. Because meaning construction is unavoidably collaborative (Garfinkel, 1967; Sacks et al., 1974), it is virtually impossible to free any interaction from those factors that could be construed as contaminants. All participants in an interview are inevitably implicated in making meaning.

While naturally occurring talk and interaction may appear to be more sponta-neous, less "staged" than an interview, this is true only in the sense that such interaction is staged by persons other than an interviewer. Resulting conversations are not necessarily more "realistic" or "authentic". They simply take place in what have been recognized as indigenous settings. With the development of the interview society, and the increasing deprivatization of personal experience (see Gubrium and Holstein, 1995a, 1995b, 1995c; Gubrium et al., 1994), the interview is becoming more and more commonplace, also making it a "naturally occurring" occasion for articulating experience.

Nevertheless, discussion of some topics, while being deeply significant, may none the less be relatively rare in the normal course of everyday life, even in the interview society. For example, as seemingly ubiquitous as is talk about family and domestic life, we have found it useful to study "family discourse" in a relatively circumscribed range of settings, most of which intentionally provoke talk about family as an integral part of conducting routine business, such as in a family therapy agency, for example (see Gubrium, 1992; Gubrium and Holstein, 1990). Active interviews can thus be used to gain purchase on interpretive practice relating to matters that may not be casually topical, yet which are socially relevant. By inciting narrative production, the interviewer may provoke interpretive developments that might emerge too rarely to be effectively captured "in their natural habitat", so to speak.

Given the unconventional nature of active interviewing, how does one make sense of its data? Analysing data concerning interpretive practice is something of an "artful" matter in its own right. This does not mean that analysis is any less rigorous than that applied to traditional interview data; on the contrary, active interview data require disciplined sensitivity to both process and substance.

Interviews are traditionally analysed as more or less accurate descriptions of experience, as reports or representations (literally, re-presentations) of reality. An-alysis entails systematically coding, grouping or summarizing the descriptions, and providing a coherent organizing framework that encapsulates and explains aspects of the social world that respondents portray. Respondents' interpretive activity is subordinated to the substance of what they report; the *whats* of experience over-whelm the *hows*.

In contrast, active interview data can be analysed to show the dynamic interrelatedness of the *whats* and the *hows*. Respondents' answers and comments are not viewed as reality reports delivered from a fixed repository. Instead, they are considered for the ways that they construct aspects of reality in collaboration with the interviewer. The focus is as much on the assembly process as on what is assembled. Using sociologically oriented forms of narrative and discourse analysis, conversational records of interpretive practice are examined to reveal reality-constructing practices as well as the subjective meanings that are circumstantially conveyed (see DeVault, 1990; Gubrium and Holstein, 1994; Holstein and Gubrium, 1994; Propp, 1968; Reissman, 1993; Silverman, 1993). The goal is to show how interview responses are produced in the interaction between interviewer and respondent, without losing sight of the meanings produced or the circumstances that condition the meaning-making process. The analytic objective is not merely to describe the situated production of talk, but to show how what is being said relates to the experiences and lives being studied.

Writing up findings from interview data is itself an analytically active enterprise. Rather than adhering to the ideal of letting the data "speak for themselves", the active analyst empirically documents the meaning-making process. With ample illustration and reference to records of talk, the analyst describes the complex discursive activities through which respondents produce meaning. The goal is to explicate how meanings, their linkages and horizons, are constituted both in relation to, and within, the interview environment. The analyst's reports do not summarize and organize what interview participants have said, as much as they "deconstruct" participants' talk to show the reader both the *hows* and the *whats* of the narrative dramas conveyed, which increasingly mirrors an interview society.

References

Alasuutari, P. (1995) *Researching Culture: Qualitative Method and Cultural Studies*. London: Sage.

Berger, P. L. and Luckmann, T. (1967) *The Social Construction of Reality*. New York: Doubleday.

Blumer, H. (1969) *Symbolic Interactionism*. New York: Prentice Hall.

Briggs, C. (1986) *Learning How to Ask: A Sociolinguistic Appraisal of the Role of the Interviewer in Social Science Research*. Cambridge: Cambridge University Press.

Cicourel, A. V. (1964) *Method and Measurement in Sociology*. New York: Free Press.

Cicourel, A. V. (1974) *Theory and Method in a Study of Argentine Fertility*. New York: Wiley.

Converse, J. M. and Schuman, H. (1974) *Conversations at Random: Survey Research as Interviewers See It*. New York: Wiley.

DeVault, M. (1990) "Talking and listening from women's standpoint: Feminist strategies for interviewing and analysis", *Social Problems*, 37: 96–117.

Douglas, J. D. (1985) *Creative Interviewing*. Beverly Hills, CA: Sage.

Fowler, F. J. and Mangione, T. W. (1990) *Standardized Survey Interviewing*. Newbury Park, CA: Sage.

Garfinkel, H. (1967) *Studies in Ethnomethodology*. Englewood Cliffs, NJ: Prentice-Hall.

Gorden, R. L. (1987) *Interviewing: Strategy, Techniques, and Tactics*. Homewood, IL: Dorsey.

Gubrium, J. F. (1988) *Analyzing Field Reality*. Beverly Hills, CA: Sage.

Gubrium, J. F. (1989) "Local cultures and service policy", in J. F. Gubrium and D. Silverman (eds), *The Politics of Field Research*. London: Sage. pp. 94–112.

Gubrium, J. F. (1992) *Out of Control*. Newbury Park, CA: Sage.

Gubrium, J. F. (1993) *Speaking of Life: Horizons of Meaning for Nursing Home Residents*. Hawthorne, NY: Aldine de Gruyter.

Gubrium, J. F. (1994) "Interviewing", in *Exploring Collaborative Research in Primary Care*. Thousand Oaks, CA: Sage. pp. 65–76.

Gubrium, J. F. and Holstein, J. A. (1990) *What is Family?* Mountain View, CA: Mayfield.

Gubrium, J. F. and Holstein, J. A. (1994) "Analyzing talk and interaction", in J. F. Gubrium and A. Sankar (eds), *Qualitative Methods in Aging Research*. Newbury Park, CA: Sage. pp. 173–88.

Gubrium, J. F. and Holstein, J. A. (1995a) "Biographical work and new ethnography", in R. Josselson and A. Lieblich (eds), *The Narrative Study of Lives*, Vol. 3. Newbury Park, CA: Sage. pp. 45–58.

Gubrium, J. F. and Holstein, J. A. (1995b) "Life course malleability: Biographical work and deprivatization", *Sociological Inquiry*, 65: 207–23.

Gubrium, J. F. and Holstein, J. A. (1995c) "Qualitative inquiry and the deprivatization of experience", *Qualitative Inquiry*, 1: 204–22.

Gubrium, J. F. and Holstein, J. A. (1997) *The New Language of Qualitative Method*. New York: Oxford University Press.

Gubrium, J. F., Holstein, J. A. and Buckholdt, D. R. (1994) *Constructing the Life Course*. Dix Hills, NY: General Hall.

Harding, S. (ed.) (1987) *Feminism and Methodology*. Bloomington: Indiana University Press.

Heritage, J. (1984) *Garfinkel and Ethnomethodology*. Cambridge: Polity.

Holstein, J. A. (1993) *Court-Ordered Insanity: Interpretive Practice and Involuntary Commitment*. Hawthorne, NY: Aldine de Gruyter.

Holstein, J. A. and Gubrium, J. F. (1994) "Phenomenology, ethnomethodology, and interpretive practice", in N. K. Denzin and Y. Lincoln (eds), *Handbook of Qualitative Research*. Newbury Park, CA: Sage. pp. 262–72.

Holstein, J. A. and Gubrium, J. F. (1995) *The Active Interview*. Thousand Oaks, CA: Sage.

Holstein, J. A. and Staples, W. G. (1992) "Producing evaluative knowledge: The interactional bases of social science findings", *Sociological Inquiry*, 62: 11–35.

Hyman, H. H., Cobb, W. J., Feldman, J. J., Hart, C. W. and Stember, C. H. (1975) *Interviewing in Social Research*. Chicago: University of Chicago Press.

Kirk, J. and Miller, M. L. (1986) *Reliability and Validity in Qualitative Research*. Beverly Hills, CA: Sage.

Maccoby, E. E. and Maccoby, N. (1954) "The interview: A tool of social science", in G. Lindzey (ed.), *Handbook of Social Psychology*. Reading, MA: Addison-Wesley. pp. 449–87.

Madge, J. (1965) *The Tools of Social Science*. Garden City, NY: Anchor Books.

Manning, P. L. (1967) "Problems in interpreting interview data", *Sociology and Social Research*, 51: 301–16.

Mishler, E. G. (1986) *Research Interviewing*. Cambridge, MA: Harvard University Press.

Mishler, E. G. (1991) "Representing discourse: The rhetoric of transcription", *Journal of Narrative and Life History*, 1: 255–80.

Pollner, M. (1987) *Mundane Reason*. Cambridge: Cambridge University Press.

Pool, I. de S. (1957) "A critique of the twentieth anniversary issue", *Public Opinion Quarterly*, 21: 190–8.

Propp, V. I. (1968) *The Morphology of the Folktale*. Austin: University of Texas Press.

Reinharz, S. (1992) *Feminist Methods of Social Research*. New York: Oxford University Press.

Reissman, C. K. (1993) *Narrative Analysis*. Newbury Park, CA: Sage.

Rogers, C. R. (1945) "The non-directive method as a technique for social research", *American Journal of Sociology*, 50: 279–83.

Sacks, H., Schegloff, E. A. and Jefferson, G. (1974) "A simplest systematics for the organization of turn-taking for conservation", *Language*, 50: 696–735.

Schütz, A. (1967) *The Phenomenology of the Social World*. Evanston, IL: Northwestern University Press.

Silverman, D. (1993) *Interpreting Qualitative Data: Methods for Analysing Talk, Text and Interaction*. London: Sage.

Smith, D. E. (1987) *The Everyday World as Problematic: A Feminist Sociology*. Boston: Northeastern University Press.

Terkel, S. (1972) *Working*. New York: Avon.

7 Narrative Authenticity

Elinor Ochs and Lisa Capps

Narrators of personal experience work to make their stories sound credible. As Labov (1982) noted:

> Reportable events are almost by definition unusual. They are therefore inherently less credible than nonreportable events. In fact, we might say that the more reportable an event is, the less credible it is. Yet credibility is as essential as reportability for the success of a narrative. (p. 228)

Credibility depends in part upon the plausibility of a chain of objective events and whether they can be corroborated. Narrators, however, couch these events within subjective events that can not be contradicted. The narrators studied by Labov (1972, 1982, 1986) threaded their narratives with subjective events such as thinking ("I thought he was gonna *hit* me"), knowing ("I didn't know what it was"), talking to oneself ("I said to myself, 'There'll be times I can't put up with this...'"), intending ("I was about to hit him"), and feeling ("boy that was an *eery* night for me comin' home").

Remembering is also a subjective event. However, although remembering itself is an unobservable and therefore unverifiable mental state, a thought cast as remembered is presented as true. *Remember* is a factual mental verb (Chafe & Nichols, 1986) that presupposes the certainty of a proposition. Thus: "I remember going to the House of Fabrics with you in my red corduroy pants" presupposes that the speaker went "to the House of Fabrics with you in my red corduroy pants." Remembering, then, is an authenticating act: Rememberers publicly claim to have brought to conscious awareness a state, event, or condition that is real in their eyes; they believe it to be true.

In this sense, acts of remembering are attempts to seize authority with respect to a topic of concern. For the presupposed truths to become recognized as such, however, these acts require validation by others. When such validation is not forthcoming, the authenticity of the remembered experience and by implication the reliability of the rememberer is called into question (Taylor, 1995). Contested memories can concern personal and collective events of consequence for groups and nations. Contestation of memory, however, can also concern events of import only to family members or acquaintances directly involved. In the following family encounter between three-year-old Evan, his older brother Dick, and their parents, the event contested concerns whether or not Dad promised Evan ice cream for dessert if he ate a good dinner. Towards the end of dinner, Evan attempts to remind Dad about the promise (Ochs, 1994, p. 116):

Evan: YOU '*MEMBER* I COULD HAVE A –

Dad is occupied talking to Dick and Evan has to repeat his reminder to Dad and then to Mom:

DADDY? YOU ('**MEMBER**) IF I EAT A *GOOD* DINNER I –

... ((*Evan is tapping Dad's arm for attention*))

MO:MMY Mommy. – you – you '*member* – (um) if I eat a good ...*din*ner I could have a *ice* cream

At this point Dad contests Evan's memory, while the rest of the family side with Evan:

Dad:	An ice cream? – Who said that
Evan:	You
Dick:	*You* (0.4 pause)
Mom:	Ooooooooo *((laughing))hehe*
Dad:	*I* didn't say that
Dick:	**Remember**? – he – you said "Daddy – could I have a i:cecrea:m?" ...
Dad:	Where *was* I? ...
Dad:	I don't even **remember** telling you that – What was I doing when?
Dick:	Daddy I'll tell you the *exact* words you said.
Dad:	Tell m-What was I doing – where *was* I first of all?
Dick:	You were sitting right in that chair where you are now. (0.4 pause)
Mother:	*((laughing))* hehehaha – It's *on* film – they have you.

In this exchange, it is not enough for Evan to have remembered Dad's promise or for Evan to have the supported recall of his older brother. Dad denies the remembered event and demands the exact details as positive proof. In the face of Dad's challenge, the children supply further evidence of the remembered event. Dick tells him he can quote his exact words and cites the precise locale of the promise: "You were sitting right in that chair where you are now." Mom, who first signals Dad's sinking position with her incriminating "Ooooooooo" and snickering, provides the clinching source of evidence, namely, that the researchers have captured this entire episode on film. Her comment "They have you" may be interpreted to mean both that the researchers have Dad on tape and that the children have Dad boxed into a corner.

In this family interaction, a child's memory prevails, but often this is not the case, particularly when children are unable to garner support from more mature persons: In dyadic adult—child encounters, for example, children's rememberings often give way to adult reformulations, backed by their authoritative status in the family. This phenomenon is the object of focus in family therapies, in which parental accounts frequently prevail over those of children (Aronsson & Cederborg, 1994; Cederborg, 1994; Minuchin & Fishman, 1981). In their study of Swedish family therapy, Aronsson and Cederborg articulated the linguistic and interactional resources that family members routinely bring to their talk to display authoritative stance, including evidential adverbs like *actually* and *absolutely* and recruitment of authoritative support, as in the following narrative dispute between adolescent Sam and his father (Cederborg, 1994, p. 126):

> *Father*: Your clothing allowance was suspended for five months because you consistently spent it on things other than clothes, and then went and asked your mother to buy you clothes.
>
> *Sam*: That's **not actually** *true*.
>
> *Father*: *That's* **ABSOLUTELY true, ask your mother.**

Another consistent marker of high certainty is reference to *exact numbers*. For instance, Sam and his father conflict in their accounts of the amount of time that Sam devoted to studying, Sam supports his position that he has indeed studied hard by specifying the exact time he spent on this task:

> *Sam*: The week before I went back I did **2.5** hours every day revising for my exams.

Of note here is that not only does he use numbers, he formulates the number as a statistic – 2.5 – as if he had arithmetically calculated average time per day across number of days studied. Sam's father is not to be outdone by such displays. He himself gets into the numbers game, claiming:

> *Father*: Three days you didn't do anything AT ALL. You were watching television all day and went off to Tom's in the afternoon.

Sam and his father continue to clash over the truth:

> *Sam*: That just **ISN'T true**
>
> *Father*: It **IS true**,
>
> *Sam*: No.

At this point, father not only appeals to other authorities, he specifies the exact number who he believes will back him up:

> *Father*: Well **three** people will **tell** you it is.

Displays of relative certainty and displays of positive and negative affect are the building blocks of identities. Each display of high certainty in the dispute between Sam and his father may be seen as an attempt to establish themselves as authorities and at the same time establish the addressee as a liar or culprit. Sam and his father become gridlocked in their unwillingness to accept the identities they have attempted to assign one another. Therapists work to establish a more balanced dialogue between parental and child perspectives on past events. This process involves helping family members relinquish their sense of absolute certainty about what they remember, in part through the therapist's modeling of less absolute stances and in part through making explicit the subjectivity and malleability of memory.

Sam and his father are not alone in their sense that their narrative tells the true story. Eyewitness testimonies, for example, are used in court to establish what actually happened. Research, however, suggests that memory of eyewitnessed events is affected by prior life experiences and biases and by postevent experiences, reflections, and conversations, including the testimony of others and the displayed dispositions of lawyers (Loftus, 1979). Loftus and her colleagues (Loftus, 1979, 1980; Loftus & Ketcham, 1991) conducted *misinformation* experiments, in which participants (generally college students) are shown videos of simulated accidents and crimes. These studies demonstrated that witnesses are highly suggestible and can be led into modifying their perceptions through questioning techniques that contain presuppositions (e.g., "Did you see *the* dent in the car?", rather than "Did you see a dent?").

The issue of veracity versus subjectivity of narrative and memory plagues clinicians, litigators, and philosophers, among others. For those who believe there is a truth to recall, an important question is: Can a past truth ever be accessed? Kundera (1995, pp. 128–9) airs perhaps the most despairing response to this issue:

> Try to reconstruct a dialogue from your own life, the dialogue of a quarrel or a dialogue of love. The most precious, the most important situations are utterly gone. Their abstract sense remains.... perhaps a detail or two, but the acousticovisual concreteness of the situation in all its continuity is lost... And not only is it lost but we do not even wonder at this loss. We are resigned to losing the concreteness of the present... Remembering is not the negative of forgetting. Remembering is a form of forgetting... We die without knowing what we have lived.

For those who are more optimistic about the recoverability of memory, a driving question is: How can we ascertain the accuracy of a memory? Is resistance to suggestion and refusal to modify one's account indicative of truth? The resistance displayed by Sam and his father suggests that being impervious is no assurance of accurate recall. Is implicit memory in the form of, for example, somatic sensations, fragmented flashbacks, or dreams indexical of the true occurrence of a past event? Unanswered, this question remains hotly contested (Sarbin, 1995). Although some believe that therapists or clients themselves can induce implicit memories (creating false memories) and that behavioral manifestations can be feigned, others insist on their unequivocal authenticity (e.g., Loftus, 1980; Terr, 1994). The issue has profound emotional and legal consequences for the lives of would-be victims and perpetrators. What are the consequences for one's sense of reality and self-identity when one's memory of even seemingly insignificant events is repeatedly overruled? Or when one becomes convinced that an emotionally significant event did not happen or happened in a radically different manner than one's memory? The risks can include social isolation, persecution, and excruciating self-doubt, which are frequently associated with psychiatric disorders.

There is no simple resolution of the tension between subjectivity and truth of a remembered past. This tension may be an inherent property of selfhood. As Bergson (1911) noted, and others like Kundera (1981, 1985, 1995) and Ricoeur (1988) later concurred, we can't reflect upon ourselves in the present, as we experience the moment. Rather, the nonpresent – the past and the possible – is the modality for self-making. As Bruner (1987) noted: "We seem to have no other way of describing 'lived time' save in the form of a narrative" (p. 12). Knowledge of past and potential selves in turn is grounded in beliefs about the past and the possible and in our assumption that these beliefs are true. The activity of self-reflection, however, also engenders the awareness that beliefs vary in certainty, can be contested, and are vulnerable to change. As such, the process of grounding ourselves is infused with doubt and motion. Havel (1988, p. 225) alluded to this dynamic when he reflected: "man is the only creature who is both a part of being (and thus a bearer of its mystery), and aware of that mystery as a mystery. He is both the question and the questioner, and cannot help being so." We come to define ourselves as we grapple with our own and others' ambiguous emotions and events. As a result, uncertainty as well as certainty plays an important role in configuring selves. Paradoxically, we are perhaps most intensely cognizant of ourselves when we are unsure of ourselves, including our memories. The tension between certainty and doubt drives narrative activity in pursuit of an authentic remembered self.

References

Aronsson, K. and Cederborg, A. -C. (1994). Co-narration and voice in family therapy: Voicing, devoicing and orchestration. *Text, 14*, 345–70.

Bergson, H. (1911). *Creative evolution.* Boston, MA: University Press of America.

Bruner, J. (1987). Life as narrative. *Social Research, 54*(1), 11–32.

Cederborg, A.-C. (1994). *Family therapy as collaborative work.* Unpublished doctoral dissertation, Linkoping University, Sweden.

Chafe, W., and Nichols, J. (1986). *Evidentiality: The linguistic coding of epistemology.* Norwood, NJ: Ablex.

Havel, V. (1988). *Letters to Olga* (Paul Wilson, Trans.). New York: Henry Hold.

Kundera, M. (1981). *The book of laughter and forgetting.* Harmondsworth, England: Penguin.

Kundera, M. (1985). *The unbearable lightness of being.* New York: Harper & Row.

Kundera, M. (1995). *Testaments betrayed.* New York: HarperCollins.

Labov, W. (1972). The transformation of experience in narrative syntax. In *Language in the inner cities: Studies in Black English Vernacular* (pp. 354–96). Philadelphia: University of Pennsylvania Press.

Labov, W. (1982). Speech actions and reactions in personal narrative. In D. Tannen (Ed.), *Georgetown University round table on languages and linguistics 1981: Analyzing discourse: Text and talk* (pp. 219–47). Washington, DC: Georgetown University Press.

Labov, W. (1986, March 10). *On not putting two and two together: The shallow interpretation of narrative.* Pitzer College Invited Lecture, Claremont, CA.

Loftus, E. F. (1979). *Eyewitness testimony*. Cambridge, MA: Harvard University Press.

Loftus, E. F. (1980). *Memory*. Reading, MA: Addison-Wesley.

Loftus, E. F., and Ketcham, K. (1991). *Witness for the defense*. New York: St. Martin's Press.

Minuchin, S., and Fishman, C. H. (1981). *Family therapy techniques*. Cambridge, MA: Harvard University Press.

Ochs, E. (1994). Stories that step into the future. In D. F. Biber and E. Finegan (Eds.), *Perspectives on register: Situating register variation within sociolinguistics* (pp. 106–35). Oxford, England: Oxford University Press.

Ricoeur, P. (1988). *Time and narrative* (Vol. 1–3; K. Blarney and D. Pellauer, Trans.). Chicago: University of Chicago Press.

Sarbin, T. (1995). A narrative approach to "repressed memories." *Journal of Narrative and Life History, 5*, 51–66.

Taylor, C. E. (1995). *Child as apprentice-narrator: Socializing voice, face, identity, and self-esteem amid the narrative politics of family dinner*. Doctoral dissertation, University of Southern California, Los Angeles.

Terr, L. (1994). *Unchained memories*. New York: Basic Books.

Part III

Observational Fieldwork

INTRODUCTION TO PART III

This section of the book concerns observational fieldwork. This method involves, quite basically, placing oneself in direct personal contact with the social group one is intent to study as they go about their affairs. In contrast to interview techniques, wherein we ask people to tell us about their experiences and activities, observational fieldwork entails witnessing people's lives and circumstances firsthand. For quite some time, researchers made little distinction between qualitative interviewing and observational fieldwork. Both were subsumed under the general rubric "ethnographic fieldwork." Ethnographers were advised to find and foster relationships with particular "key informants," while at the same time observing for themselves the round of activities that engaged the locals. While combining methods remains pervasive (and is very often extremely useful), researchers have in recent years been more inclined to explicitly distinguish the methods of observational fieldwork, or what is frequently called "participant observation," from interview and life history methods.

One reason for this is simply that interviewing and observation require different sorts of skills. Good interviewers are not necessarily good observers and vice versa. However, beyond merely technical considerations, important theoretical considerations also figure in this distinction. If we accept the theory that *describing* is itself an interactional and goal-oriented activity, we will expect people to describe things differently in different social contexts. For instance, how someone describes their group's activities to other group members often differs quite dramatically from how they describe those activities to outsiders. Therefore, when we interview people we must always contemplate *what* is being included and what is being left out, *how* it is being included and how it is being left out and, of course, *why*. When we observe directly, however, our encounter with local meanings and practices is not mediated by our respondents' personal judgments regarding what should and should not be discussed. There are other benefits to direct observation as well. Much of what we might find interesting and distinctive about local life simply does not occur to locals as interesting or worthy of mention at all. Furthermore, as the old saying goes, actions often speak louder than words – what people do may indicate how they orient to certain things better than what they explicitly tell us. Often what people consider meaningful and important they nonetheless find difficult to put into words. Indeed, sometimes people find certain things hard to discuss precisely because they consider those things so profoundly meaningful. Firsthand observation can often help us to grasp such matters in ways that other research methods cannot.

In the first essay, "The Place of Fieldwork in the Social Sciences," Everett Hughes offers his thoughts on the importance of what he calls the "observation of people *in situ*" (p. 496). This essay was written to introduce a volume entitled *Fieldwork: An Introduction to the Social Sciences*, a classic collection of ethnographic studies edited by Buford Junker and published in 1960. Hughes begins the essay with a brief genealogy of the readings that comprise the collection. He then moves on to discuss the genealogy of the method itself, noting a debt to anthropology, to Robert Park's background in journalism, and to the early "survey method" developed among British social reformers like Charles Booth. Like Becker in "The Life History and the Scientific Mosaic," Hughes makes certain to note the unduly modest regard for observational fieldwork that was common among his colleagues at the time and endeavors to promote the method to higher scientific standing. Perhaps most importantly, Hughes writes,

> the sample survey...must work on the assumption that some very large population speaks so nearly the same language, both in letter and in figure of speech, that the differences in answers will not be due in significant degree to differences in the meaning of words in the questions. This is a condition hard to meet even in Western literate countries; in many parts of the world it cannot be met at all. The survey method...must work with small variation in the midst of great bodies of common social definition...Very often, groups of people not in the common social world have to be left out of consideration...It is part of the merit of field work...that it does not have to limit itself to minor variations of behavior within large homogeneous populations. (p. 501)

In addition to noting its invaluable sensitivity to large variations in the meanings research subjects find in their worlds and to the singularity of smaller or culturally distinctive groups, Hughes notes the value of observational fieldwork for both informing the design of larger sample surveys and for empirically grounding theoretical explanations of observed statistical variations, "[t]here is a tendency for the statistical concentrations and relationships found in a questionnaire survey to be explained in a text which merely presents alternative speculations. It is at that point that good field work, instead of getting 'soft' data, would give firmer stuff" (p. 502). Finally, Hughes remarks on the trend toward researching subjects closer to home. Particularly in sociology, fieldworkers increasingly share much in common with those they study. Hence, they must dedicate more attention and creative negotiation to sustaining a suitable balance between participating in, and analyzing, social worlds. Given the intricacies of achieving this balance, it is unwise to reify our recipes for conducting effective observational fieldwork. It is not through adherence to some fixed scheme, but through sensitive and intelligent adjustment to unfolding events that we will succeed as researchers in the field.

In his remarks, Goffman similarly highlights the massive variety of ways in which fieldwork can yield interesting and important insights. He advises immersion in the widest possible sense. Observational fieldwork does not end with firsthand observation of people going about their business. It entails trying,

> to subject yourself...to their life circumstances...to accept all of the desirable and undesirable things that are a feature of their life. That 'tunes your body up' and with your 'tuned up' body and with the ecological right to be close to them...you are in a position to note their gestural, visual, bodily response to what's going on around them and you're empathetic enough – because you've been taking the same crap they've been taking – to sense what it is they're responding to. (p. 126)

Goffman emphasizes the bodies of both the researcher and those researched. Researchers should draw upon all of their senses to observe and they should observe a good deal more than what their research subjects say to each other. That is, watch everything that people are doing with their bodies and do so with every faculty that your own body provides. Likewise, in addition to immersing oneself completely in the research setting, as fieldworkers we should also strive to detach ourselves from the worlds from which we have come. Goffman is a good deal more emphatic on this point than many, but the gist of his advice is sound. To the extent we do not cut our ties to the world outside our research setting, we will be distracted from that setting. Additionally, Goffman advises meticulous attention to the initial experiences we have on the first day in the field. It is on this day that our setting will appear most unfamiliar, and distinctive, to us. In time the setting may come to seem more ordinary but trust your initial instincts. Complete your notes as soon as you can. The longer you wait to record what you have observed the more you will forget. Write up your notes as thoroughly and lushly as possible. You can't possibly know in advance what ultimately might prove useful.

In their essay, "Difference and Dialogue: Members Readings of Ethnographic Texts," Robert Emerson and Melvin Pollner provide an incisive examination of how best to interpret the responses our research receives from those it is about. Some have insisted that confirmation by those whose lives have been studied is the indisputable benchmark of ethnographic validity. Emerson and Pollner paint a picture that is at once more theoretically nuanced and better grounded in empirical materials. By and large, ethnographers strive to produce fairly general accounts of characteristic aspects of the people or settings studied. Because the people we study are not routinely required to think in such terms, our analyses may often appear alien or unnatural to them. Furthermore, members may not be inclined to assess ethnographic accounts for their specifically *scientific* validity. More likely, they will be assessed for their relevance to concerns more routinely encountered in the setting itself. Hence, members' readings of ethnographic texts are not pristine. Like the texts themselves, these readings reflect the complex relationships that both link and separate members' worlds and the worlds of researchers. And because they reflect these relationships, members' readings of ethnographic texts may be used not only to eliminate differences between social scientific knowledge and local knowledge, but to reveal the complex nature of those differences in the first place.

Phillipe Bourgois' essay "In Search of Horatio Alger: Culture and Ideology in the Crack Economy," is a masterful exemplar of the ethnographic genre not only for his exceptional writing skills, but for the combination of lush descriptive detail and pointed theoretical purchase. Bourgois takes us to the mean streets of Spanish Harlem and allows us to experience its distinctive ecology and inhabitants, and its place in the larger historical and cultural context. He then proceeds by a deft tacking back and forth between descriptive example and theoretical exegesis to demonstrate what we might learn about drug dealing, urban street life, and our communities in general from a close consideration of the world in and around "the botanica." Though perhaps not all of us are up to such feats, Bourgois makes it clear that it is possible to effectively write for different audiences simultaneously. His style of composition is inclusive, at once inviting to those of us interested in being transported into other worlds and other ways of life, and those of us taken with the study of society as such.

References

Goffman, Erving. 1989. "On Fieldwork." *Journal of Contemporary Ethnography* 18: 123–32.
Hughes, Everett C. 1960. "The Place of Field Work in Social Science." In *Field Work: An Introduction to the Social Sciences*. Edited by Buford H. Junker. Chicago: University of Chicago Press.

Further Reading on Observational Fieldwork

Atkinson, Paul. 1990. *The Ethnographic Imagination: Textual Constructions of Reality*. London: Routledge.
Burawoy, Michael, Alice Burton, Ann Arnett Ferguson, Kathryn J. Fox, Joshua Gamson, Nadine Gartrell, Leslie Hurst, Charles Kurzman, Leslie Salzinger, Josepha Shiffman, and Shiori Ui. 1991. *Ethnography Unbound: Power and Resistance in the Modern Metropolis*. Berkeley: University of California Press.
Clifford James, and George E. Marcus, eds. 1986. *Writing Culture: The Poetics and Politics of Ethnography*. Berkeley: University of California Press.
Denzin, Norman K., and Yvonna S. Lincoln, eds. 1994. *The Handbook of Qualitative Research*. Thousand Oaks, CA: Sage.
Ellis, Carolyn, and Michael G. Flaherty, eds. 1992. *Investigating Subjectivity*. Newbury Park, CA: Sage.
Emerson, Robert M., ed. 1988. *Contemporary Field Research: A Collection of Readings*. Prospect Heights, IL: Waveland Press.
Emerson, Robert M., Rachel I. Fretz, and Linda L. Shaw. 1995. *Writing Ethnographic Fieldnotes*. Chicago: University of Chicago Press.
Geertz, Clifford. 1973. *The Interpretation of Culture*. New York: Basic Books.
Glaser, Barney G. and Anselm Strauss. 1967. *The Discovery of Grounded Theory: Strategies for Qualitative Research*. Chicago: Aldine.
Gubrium, Jaber F. and James A. Holstein. 1997. *The New Language of Qualitative Method*. New York: Oxford University Press.
Katz, Jack. "Ethnography's Warrants." *Sociological Methods & Research* 25(4): 391–423.
Lofland, John and Lyn H. Lofland. 1995. *Analyzing Social Settings*. Belmont, CA: Wadsworth.
Sanjek, Roger, ed. 1990. *Fieldnotes: The Making of Anthropology*. Ithaca, NY: Cornell University Press.
Schatzman, Leonard and Anselm Strauss. 1973. *Field Research: Strategies for a Natural Sociology*. Englewood Cliffs, NJ: Prentice-Hall, Inc.
Silverman, David. 1993. *Interpreting Qualitative Data: Methods for Analyzing Talk, Text and Interaction*. London: Sage.
Silverman, David, ed. 1997. *Qualitative Research: Theory, Method, and Practice*. Thousand Oaks, CA: Sage.
Smith, Dorothy E. 1987. *The Everyday World as Problematic*. Boston: Northeastern University Press.
Van Maanen, John. 1988. *Tales of the Field: On Writing Ethnography*. Chicago: University of Chicago Press.
Van Maanen, John, ed. 1995. *Representation in Ethnography*. Thousand Oaks, CA: Sage.
Warren, Carol A. B. 1988. *Gender Issues in Field Research*. Newbury Park. CA: Sage.

8 The Place of Field Work in Social Science

Everett C. Hughes

Field work refers to observation of people *in situ;* finding them where they are, staying with them in some role which, while acceptable to them, will allow both intimate observation of certain parts of their behavior, and reporting it in ways useful to social science but not harmful to those observed. It is not easy to find a suitable formula in the best case; it may be impossible in some cases: say, a secret society devoted to crime or revolution or simply espousing "dangerous" ideas. But most people can be studied and most can do more field work than they believe. It is a strenuous, but exciting and satisfying business to expand one's own social perceptions and social knowledge in this way, and to contribute thereby to general social knowledge. Learning to do it – both parts of it, observing and reporting – can have some of the quality of a mild psychoanalysis. But, as in other kinds of self-discovery, one cannot learn more about one's self unless he is honestly willing to see others in a new light, and to learn about them, too.

But perhaps I should say something of the history of the project out of which this volume* came. Dr. Junker, a man of much and varied field experience – in Yankee City, in a prison, in southern and midwestern communities, in various professions and institutions, among various racial and ethnic groups, in the United States Army both at home and in Europe – has thought about this subject for a good many years. He has done field work on field work. In 1951 he joined me in a project whose aim was to do just that.[1]

How did I come to initiate such a project? Certainly not because I ever found field observation easy to undertake. Once I start, I am, I believe, not bad at it. But it has always been a torture. Documents are so much easier to approach; one simply blows the dust off them, opens them up, and may have the pleasure of seeing words and thoughts on which no eye has been set these many years. Yet, in every project I have undertaken, studying real estate men, the Catholic labor movement in the Rhine-land, and newly industrialized towns in Quebec, the time came when I had to desert statistical reports and documents and fare forth to see for myself. It was then that the real learning began, although the knowledge gained in advance was very useful; in fact, it often made possible the conversations which opened the field. One who has some information and asks for more is perhaps less likely to be refused than one who has no advance information; perhaps the best formula is to have advance knowledge, but to let it show only in the kind of questions one asks. But if I have usually been hesitant in entering the field myself and have perhaps walked around the block

* This chapter was originally published in Buford H. Junker, *Field Work: An Introduction to the Social Sciences* (Chicago: University of Chicago Press, 1960).

getting up my courage to knock at doors more often than almost any of my students (I have been doing it longer), I have sent a great many students into the field. Listening to them has given me sympathy with their problems; it has also convinced me that most students can learn to do field observation and will profit from it.

When I came to the University of Chicago in 1938, my colleagues assigned me an introductory course in sociology. It was a course taken mainly by young people who had two or more years of social science in the College of the University of Chicago. They were probably better read in the social sciences than their peers in any other college on this continent. But many of them had not yet come to that point in education where one sees the connection between small things and great. They liked everything to be great – events as well as ideas. They were inclined to be impatient with the small observations which, accumulated, are the evidence on which theories of culture and society are built. To quite a number of them real life seemed banal, trivial, and often misguided.

I used various devices to get some of the students to collect social data themselves, in the hope that the experience would give them a livelier sense of the problems of gathering social data and turning them, by analysis, into social facts. Eventually I took a bolder step. Since there was no danger that these students would miss adequate exposure to social theories, I, with the approval of my colleagues, replaced the general course with a full term of introduction to field work.

While we never set the form of the course in any inflexible way, there was a general pattern which did not change greatly. Each student, alone or with another, made a series of observations in a Census Tract or other small area of Chicago outside his everyday experience and reported on these observations almost week by week. We discussed the problems the students met in the field. They were asked to notice especially whom they were taken for by people in the areas where they studied and to find an explanation for the peculiar roles attributed to them. When they had done the several assigned kinds of observation, they were asked to draw up a proposal for a study which might be done in such an area, by a person of small resources.

After some years in which nearly all students of sociology, many students of anthropology, and some others went through this experience, I asked for and received a small grant to be used in putting together what we had learned from these several hundred students about the learning and doing of field work and to learn how people of greater experience and sophistication had gone about field observation.

Dr. Junker took charge of the project. Dr. Ray Gold interviewed the current crop of students about their field experiences. Together we held a seminar in which people who had done field observation on a great variety of problems and in many different situations reported on their experiences. A record was kept of their reports. Miss Dorothy Kittel, a bibliographer, helped us in finding documents which reported experiences of people in the field. We put some of the resulting material into a privately circulated document, "Cases on Field Work." What Dr. Junker has put into the present book is in part a more succinct and readable distillate of that volume. But it is more than that. This book has evolved through eight more years of his thought and work.

Those of us who had a part in this project have been strengthened in our conviction that field work is not merely one among several methods of social study but is paramount. It is, more than other methods of study, itself a practice, consciously undertaken, in sociology itself – in the perceiving and predicting of social roles, both one's own and those of others. It consists of exchanges of tentative social gestures, to use the terms of George Herbert Mead. That theme is developed by Dr. Junker. I shall confine myself to some general remarks on the place of field work in the social sciences.

Field work, when mentioned as an activity of social scientists, calls to mind first of all the ethnologist or anthropologist far afield observing and recording the ways, language, artifacts, and physical characteristics of exotic or primitive people. He is presumably there because the people he is interested in have never written down anything about themselves or because, if they do write, they have not had the habit of recording the things the ethnologist wants to know. The early manuals issued to aid ethnologists told the prospective observer what to look for, not how to look for it. Later anthropologists – Malinowski, Margaret Mead, and others – have told of their field experiences in a penetrating way.

Until a generation ago the phrase field work might also have brought to mind what was then called the "social survey." At the turn of the century the social surveyors were going to the slums of the great cities of Britain and North America to observe the "conditions" in which the new urban industrial poor lived. They then reported them in simple statistical tables on consumption of food and clothing, on wages, housing, illness and crime. But they also described what they found, "fully, freely, and bitterly," as Robert E. Park used to say, in the hope that an aroused public would change things. Their work had its journalistic and literary counterpart in "muck-raking." The seventeen volumes of Charles Booth's *The Life and Labour of the People of London* report several years of observation of the kind known then and for several decades afterwards as "social survey." Among Booth's collaborators were school "visitors," who went from door to door to see conditions and to talk to people. They also visited churches, clubs, public houses, parks, and pawnshops. They got acquainted with the factories, docks, and other places of work of the poor of East London. The work continued for several years; when at last they did the field work for a series of volumes entitled *Religious Influences*, they described not merely the feeble religious institutions of East London, but also the recreational institutions – including public houses – which seemed to have supplanted the church in the lives of working people. They had become rather more sympathetic reporters than muck-rakers. They had also established a tradition of social observation with two facets: (1) the kinds of data which were thought important to description of the social life of the poor, and (2) a way of gathering them. In North America, the tradition was carried on and developed; the Pittsburgh Survey (Kellogg, 1909–14), reporting the conditions of life and work of immigrant steelworkers, was the most voluminous and notorious of such projects in this country. LePlay, in France, had gone about getting data from families concerning their incomes and expenditures. In all of these enterprises, investigators went among the industrial and urban poor to gather information which was not, at that time, to be found in the censuses taken by public authorities. In many of them, the surveyors were betrayed by their humanity and curiosity into noting other kinds of information, into becoming, in effect, the ethnologists of social classes and other social groups than their own.

For the older social surveys discovered and described customs and institutions as well as opinions. Bosanquet, in the course of surveying the standards of living in London, learned the peculiar functions of the pawnshop among the poor of London.[2] Booth described the institutions of East London and came to the conclusion that no recreational or religious institution could survive there without a subsidy: it might be from gambling or the sale of beer, or it might be subsidy from the middle classes in other parts of town. He also described in detail the habits of drinking, by age and sex, among working people, and came to the conclusion that the sending of children to fetch a bucket of beer for their father's tea did not have the horrible consequences the middle class attributed to it.[3]

Although the surveys were not, in Europe, associated with the name of sociology, in England and America the survey movement became part of the peculiar sociological mix. Social workers, important in the earlier surveys, turned more and more to individual case work and seemed to lose interest in communities, groups, and styles of life. "Professionalized" social work abandoned the social survey for psychiatry, which uses a quite different research role and collects information of a different kind.

The unique thing about the early department of sociology at the University of Chicago was that it brought together Albion W. Small, who was both a devotee of German theoretical sociology and of the American social gospel of reform, and a number of people who were even more closely identified with social surveys, social problems, and social reform. W. I. Thomas, who inspired and carried out the great study of *The Polish Peasant in Europe and America* with the collaboration of Florian Znaniecki, was following the tradition of the social survey, but he was also leading it in a new direction, that of a more self-conscious and acute theoretical analysis. Robert E. Park, who eventually joined the department, combined even more than the others, the two facets of American sociology. For he had a Heidelberg degree in philosophy, got by writing a theoretical treatise on collective behavior in the crowd and the public.[4] His interest in the behavior of crowds and publics was, however, developed during twelve years of work as a newspaper reporter and city editor. He did more perhaps than any other person to produce the new American sociology in which people went out and did field observations designed to advance theoretical, as well as practical, knowledge of modern, urban society.

Under his influence, and that of his colleagues, hundreds of students of sociology at the University of Chicago went to the field in various areas of Chicago. Their work was co-ordinated, for some years, by Dr. Vivien Palmer, who then published a book on how to do such observation.[5] With the development of better quantitative methods of handling social data, the practice of field work declined. It became known, with a certain condescension, as the "anthropological" method. Eventually the very term "survey" took on a new meaning. "Survey research" now means the study of political or other opinions, including consumers' preferences, by interviewing, with set questions, individuals so chosen as statistically to represent large populations about which the information is wanted. Going to the field means getting out to interview the sample. Some place is given to less formal field observation, but it is called "pilot study" or "exploratory study," and is considered preparatory to the main business of getting a questionnaire on the road. Its aim is to learn how to standardize the questions one wants to ask, not generally to learn what questions to ask. Great ingenuity is sometimes shown in such exploration and pretesting, but it is usually done with a certain impatience, since it delays the real work of "administering" the questionnaire. Once the questionnaire is settled upon, any doubts about the questions must be explained away, as it is too expensive and too disturbing to change anything at that point. The survey research of today, valuable as it is, conceives of field observation in quite a different way from that presented in this book.

For one thing, the sample survey still must work on the assumption that some very large population speaks so nearly the same language, both in letter and figure of speech, that the differences in answers will not be due in significant degree to differences in the meaning of words in the questions. This is a condition hard to meet even in Western literate countries; in many parts of the world, it cannot be met at all. The survey method, in this new sense of the term, must work with small variation in the midst of great bodies of common social definition. The preparatory field work is used to determine the limits of common meaning within which one can conduct the survey. Very often, groups of people not in the common social world have to be left out of consideration. In this country many surveys omit Negroes and other "deviant" groups. It is part of the merit of field work of the kind we are discussing in this book that it does not have to limit itself to minor variations of behavior within large homogeneous populations. But even within such populations, field observation is more than a preparatory step for large statistical surveys. It is an ongoing part of social science. Most surveys, again in the new sense, would be much more useful if they were followed by even more intensive field work than that which precedes them. There is a tendency for the statistical concentrations and relationships found in a questionnaire survey to be explained in a text which merely presents alternative speculations. It is at that point that good field work, instead of getting "soft" data, would give firmer stuff. In fact, this is what was done in a recent study of anxiety among college professors.[6] A field team followed the interviewers. The social science of today requires, in fact, a great many arts of observation and analysis. Field observation is one of them.

There were some important differences between the field work of the ethnologists and that of the sociologists who followed the tradition of the social survey. The ethnologist was always an exotic to the people he studied; clearly a stranger in every way except his humanity, and perhaps he had to establish even that. The sociologist observed and reported upon a segment of his own world, albeit a poverty-stricken and socially powerless one. He was usually a class stranger to the people he studied; often, in some measure, an ethnic, religious, or racial stranger. Still, he was among people of kinds whom he might see any day in public places and who might read the same newspaper as himself. In due time, some of the sociologists themselves came from the segments of society which had been, or still were, objects of study and began to report on the very minorities – racial, sectarian, ethnic – of which they were members. The sociologist came to be less and less a stranger studying strangers and reporting to still other strangers. Student, object of study, and member of audience for the study tended to overlap and merge more and more. The sociologist was now reporting observations made, not as a complete stranger, but in some measure as a member of an in-group, although, of course, the member becomes something of a stranger in the very act of objectifying and reporting his experiences.

The unending dialectic between the role of member (participant) and stranger (observer and reporter) is essential to the very concept of field work. It is hard to be both at the same time. One solution is to separate them in time. One reports, years later and when one is at a distance in mind and spirit, what he remembers of social experiences in which he was a full participant.

It is doubtful whether one can become a good social reporter unless he has been able to look, in a reporting mood, at the social world in which he was reared. On the other hand, a person cannot make a career out of the reporting of reminiscenses unless he is so far alienated from his own background as to be able to expose and exploit it before some new world with which he now identifies himself. One has to learn to get new data and to get them in a great variety of settings as demanded by new problems he wants to solve. Other ways of solving this dialectic include being a part-time participant and part-time reporter, privately participant and publicly reporter, or publicly participant and secretly reporter. All these are practiced. All have their moral, personal, and scientific pitfalls. But the dialectic is never fully resolved, for to do good social observation one has to be close to people living their lives and must be himself living his life and must also report. The problem of maintaining good balance between these roles lies at the very heart of sociology, and indeed of all social science.

Each of the two disciplines, anthropology and sociology, which have made most use of field work, has its own history. In each, the field situation has tended to be different from that of the other. The ethnologist reported upon a whole community; the sociologist generally observed and reported only upon people of some segment, usually a poor and socially powerless one, of a community. In due time, it came about that some of the sociologists themselves came from odd and less-known corners of society or from minorities and began to report upon their own people to their new associates in the academic and larger society. This introduced a new element of distinction from the older ethnology. For the sociologist was now reporting upon observations made, not in the role of the stranger, but as a full member of the little world he reported on. He observed as a member of an in-group but, in the act of objectifying and reporting his experience, became of necessity a sort of outsider.

As one reads into the analyses and the documents included herein, he will see the meaning of this. For it comes out clearly, I believe, that the situations and circumstances in which field observation of human behavior is done are so various that no manual of detailed rules would serve; it is perhaps less clear, but equally true, that the basic problems are the same in all situations. It is the discovery of this likeness inside the shell of variety that is perhaps the greatest and most important step in learning to be an effective and versatile observer.

In the foregoing I have said nothing about the logic of field observation in social science. One reason I have not done so up to this point is that I wanted to emphasize that the departments of social science are as much historic institutions as logical divisions. Each one is the product either of social movements inside the academic world or of movements outside which later got into the academic world. While some of the departments have or claim a peculiar subject matter which sets them off from the others, this subject matter is perhaps more often a product of history, become convention and prerogative, than of pure logic. One might imagine a university in which there would be no divisions of subject matter except those dictated by clear differences of method. Economists would study all phenomena which could profitably be studied by the methods developed for analysis of the behavior of men playing the game of maximizing their share of scarce, but desired, goods. Some other branch would study all phenomena which yield well to analyses based upon skilled observation of power relations among men, and so on. I think it is obvious that this is not the situation at present. Each branch of social science appears to be some mixture of a concern with a basic logic or method with a somewhat monopolistic and jealous concern with some set of institutions or practical problems.

One should add that each, whatever its basic logic or method, has its favorite kinds of data. The historian loves to get his hands on a manuscript that no one has seen before. He wants to sit down in a quiet and musty corner of the archives and copy out parts of it by hand. He is preoccupied with manuscripts and prides himself on his skill in reading both the lines and what is between the lines. The political scientist shares this interest or preoccupation somewhat, with the variation that he especially loves a secret rather than merely rare document. The psychologist has, more than others engaged in the study of social behavior, set himself the model of the natural scientist making stylized observations in a prepared situation, that is, in a laboratory. The economist and some sociologists like to get their data already in quantitative form and in massive numbers. Their love is the manipulation of such data to create situations with a maximum of chance and then to discover departures from it.

Now there may be some relation between the number of possible fruitful kinds of data and ways of getting and handling them and the number of departments of social science in an American university, but I doubt it. We may discover in due time that there are only a few basic ways of getting human data and a few basic skills for analyzing them. While it may for a long time be true that the departments will be distinguished more by their preoccupations than by their method, conceived in terms of pure logic, it may also be that we can sort out these basic skills of observation and analysis and work on them irrespective of conventional disciplinary lines.

One of these areas of skill will be that of observing and recording the behavior of human beings "on the hoof." Men deposit some of their thoughts and actions in artifacts and documents which historians learn to read with consummate skill. Some of their actions yield to analysis of small items of behavior recorded in astronomical numbers of cases. But others, I am convinced, yield only to close observation at the time, observation sometimes of the passive bystander, sometimes of the active participant, sometimes of the active intervener, as in the case of the group experimenter and of the psychoanalyst who rends painful hidden memories from the unwilling patient. It is observation "on the hoof" that we refer to as field observation.

It is a method increasingly used by students of many modern institutions (unions, industries, hospitals, armies) as well as by students of communities, near or far from home. The outstanding peculiarity of this method is that the observer, in greater or less degree, is caught up in the very web of social interaction which he observes, analyzes, and reports. Even if he observes through a peephole, he plays a role: that of spy. And when he reports his observations made thus he becomes a kind of informer. If he observes in the role of a member of the group, he may be considered a traitor the moment he reports. Even the historian, who works upon documents, gets caught in a role problem when he reports, unless there is no person alive who might identify himself with the people or social group concerned. The hatred occasionally visited upon the debunking historian is visited almost daily upon the person who reports on the behavior of people he has lived among; and it is not so much the writing of the report, as the very act of thinking in such objective terms that disturbs the people observed. It is a violation of apparently shared secrets and sentiments. The reader will see that in the discussions and documents which follow we have all become very much occupied with the dimensions of this problem, of the on-going social and personal dilemmas of the man who observes and analyzes, more than is necessary for survival and good participation, the behavior of people about him and reports it to some audience.

The usefulness of field observation is not confined to one institution or aspect of life – religious conduct, economic, familial, political, or any other institutional aspect of behavior will yield in some measure to field observation. Insofar as it does, the observer, no matter what his formal field or academic fraternity, will share problems of skill, role, and ethic with all others who use the method. The aim of the project from which this book grew was not to sell this idea to people in sociology or in other fields, but to assemble what knowledge and insight we could on problems of learning and using the method of field observation, without limiting ourselves to any conventional confines.

If there is any sense in which field method is peculiarly sociological it is in this. If sociology is conceived as the science of social interaction and of the cultural and institutional results of interaction (which become factors conditioning future inter-action), then field observation is applied sociology. Insofar as the field observer becomes a conscious observer and analyst of himself in the role of observer, he becomes also a pure sociologist. For the concepts which he will need for this observation of the observer are the very concepts needed for analysis of any social interaction. The very difficulties of carrying out field observation – the resistance of his subjects, the danger that his very success as a participant may later prevent him from full reporting, even the experience of getting thrown out of town – are facts to be analyzed sociologically. It was the realization of these points that made our little research group exclaim one day, almost as one man, "We are studying the sociology of sociology."

This has a peculiar corollary. The problem of learning to be a field observer is like the problem of learning to live in society. It is the problem of making enough good guesses from previous experience so that one can get into a social situation in which to get more knowledge and experience to enable him to make more good guesses to get into a better situation, ad infinitum.

The problem of any field observer is to learn how he, even he, can keep expanding this series as long as possible and in what situations he can do so. The part of theoretical analysis and the part of insightful experience, and the relation of the two to each other, are, in a sense, what we set out to discover.

Notes

1   The project was supported from a grant made by the Ford Foundation to the Division of the Social Sciences of the University of Chicago. The late professors W. Lloyd Warner and Robert Redfield served as advisers.

2   Helen D. Bosanquet, *The Standard of Life and Other Studies* (London: Macmillan & Co., 1895).
3   For an account of the further development of the social survey in Great Britain see D. Caradog Jones, *Social Surveys* (London: Hutchinson's University Library, 1949); also his article, "Evolution of the Social Survey in England since Booth," *American Journal of Sociology*, XLVI, 818–25.
4   *Masse und Publikum, eine methodologische und soziologische Untersuchung* (Bern, Back, and Grunau, 1904).
5   *Field Studies in Sociology* (Chicago: University of Chicago Press, 1928).
    The Webbs wrote a classic in this field under the title, *Methods of Social Study* (London: Longmans, Green & Co., 1932).
6   Paul F. Lazarsfeld and Wagner Thielens, Jr., *The Academic Mind: Social Scientists in a Time of Crisis* (New York: Free Press, 1958), with a field report by David Riesman.

9 On Fieldwork

Erving Goffman

Transcribed and Edited by Lyn H. Lofland

Editor's Introduction

What follows is a transcription of a tape-recorded talk given by Erving Goffman during the 1974 Pacific Sociological Association Meetings, where he was a member of a panel of successful fieldworkers discussing their data collection and analysis procedures. John Lofland, who organized the session, had invited Sherri Cavan, Fred Davis, and Jacqueline Wiseman, as well as Goffman, to talk candidly and informally about how they went about doing their work. Somewhat revised versions of the Cavan, Davis, and Wiseman talks, along with an additional piece by Julius Roth, were published in this journal in a special section of the October 1974 issue. Claiming that his own remarks had been too informal to warrant publication, Goffman asked not to be included.

Erving Goffman liked neither to be photographed nor to be "taped" and, very much in keeping with his usual practice, at the beginning of his talk he asked that no recordings be made. However, appropriate to an overflow audience composed heavily of enthusiastic, if not totally ethical, fieldworkers, surreptitious recordings were, in fact, made and the transcription that follows is one result.

While Goffman was alive, there was every reason to hope he might eventually turn these informal remarks into a published piece. With his premature death in 1982, however, this hope was shattered. For oddly enough, despite the many students whose fieldwork he supervised and despite his own numerous experiences, Goffman never published anything on the topic. He had a great deal to say about the matter, as his many students can certainly attest, but what he had to say was communicated orally and remains only in the memories of a small number of social scientists. What he said that day in March 1974 may not be earthshaking. He was, in this instance, a creative carrier of a tradition, not its inventor. But what he had to say was, as one would expect from Goffman, thoughtful, uniquely insightful, and, in places, eloquent. I am grateful to his widow, Gillian Sankoff, who agreed with us that the value of this "oral essay" overrode Goffman's expressed wish that it not be preserved, and who gave permission for its publication.

A final word about the accuracy and editing of the transcription. Unsurprisingly, given the "undercover" manner in which it was recorded, the quality of the tape is poor. Despite the use of techniques that improved that quality somewhat, portions of the talk are not sufficiently intelligible to include. Fortunately, it *is* clear from the tape that these portions consist entirely of "asides," brief forays into topics that are mentioned and then dropped, and their loss does not detract from the substance of what Goffman had to say. As I hope will be apparent to people who knew him well and/or who were present at the panel session, my editing of the transcription has been light. I have certainly not attempted to translate "spoken Goffman" into written prose (in fact, I have tried, with punctuation, to convey the cadence of his speech), but I have, for purposes of clarity, dropped an extraneous word here and there, added an occasional word (in brackets), and, in one or two instances, slightly altered sentence structure.

I am going to report on what I conclude from studies of this kind that I've done. And I can only begin by repeating John Lofland's remarks that what you get in all of this [attempt to articulate techniques] is rationalizations,[1] and we're in the precarious position of providing them. The only qualification of that precariousness is that ordinarily people go into the field without any discussion at all, so we can't be damaging the situation too much.

I think there are different kinds of fieldwork: going on digs, experiments, observational work, interviewing work, and the like, and these all have their own characters. I only want to talk about one kind and that's one that features participant observation – observation that's done by two kinds of "finks": the police on the one hand and us on the other. It's us that I want to largely talk about, although I think in many cases they do a quicker and better job than we do.

By participant observation, I mean a technique that wouldn't be the only technique a study would employ, it wouldn't be a technique that would be useful for any study, but it's a technique that you *can* feature in some studies. It's one of getting data, it seems to me, by subjecting yourself, your own body and your own personality, and your own social situation, to the set of contingencies that play upon a set of individuals, so that you can physically and ecologically penetrate their circle of response to their social situation, or their work situation, or their ethnic situation, or whatever. So that you are close to them while they are responding to what life does to them. I feel that the way this is done is to not, of course, just listen to what they talk about, but to pick up on their minor grunts and groans as they respond to their situation. When you do that, it seems to me, the standard technique is to try to subject yourself, hopefully, to their life circumstances, which means that although, in fact, you can leave at any time, you act as if you can't and you try to accept all of the desirable and undesirable things that are a feature of their life. That "tunes your body up" and with your "tuned-up" body and with the ecological right to be close to them (which you've obtained by one sneaky means or another), you are in a position to note their gestural, visual, bodily response to what's going on around them and you're empathetic enough – because you've been taking the same crap they've been taking – to sense what it is that they're responding to. To me, that's the core of observation. If you don't get yourself in that situation, I don't think you can do a piece of serious work. (Although, if you've got a short period of time, there would be all kinds of reasons why you wouldn't be able to get in that situation.) But that's the name of the game. You're artificially forcing yourself to be tuned into something that you then pick up as a witness – not as an interviewer, not as a listener, but as a witness to how they react to what gets done to and around them.

Now there are two main issues following from that. What you do after you get the data, which Jackie [Wiseman] has addressed herself to. And the other is, how you go about acquiring the data. And I think that, in turn, divides up into two general problems, that of *getting into place* so that you're in a position to [acquire data] and the second is the *exploitation of that place*. There's a minor phase of getting out – of "getting out" in your head – which we could look at later on if you want to.

Getting into Place

I want to talk very briefly – a few minutes each – on those two major phases: that of getting into place and that of exploiting place once you get into it. There are certain rules in the trade about getting into place: You do a survey, you mess up some field situations that you're not going to use to find a little bit out about their life, you develop rationales for why you should be there. You have to anticipate being questioned by the people whom you study so you engage in providing a story that will hold up should the facts be brought to their attention. So you engage in what are sometimes called "telling" practices. (In the early years of this business, we frowned upon total participant observation, that is total passing in the field, because people had very fancy notions about what it would be like to be discredited. I don't mean moral issues, I mean concerns about the fact that they would be discovered and be humiliated. I think, at least in my experience, it's proven to be a fact that that's much exaggerated and that you can act as though you're somebody you're not and get away with it for a year or two. Whether you want to do that, of course, is another issue, one that bears on the ethical and professional issues attached to participant observation. I would be happy to talk about that, but I'm not talking about that right now.) So you have to get some story that will be – I like a story such that if they find out what you are doing, the story you presented could not be an absolute lie. If they don't find out what you're doing, the story you presented doesn't get in your way.

Now the next thing you have to do is cut your life to the bone, as much as you can afford to cut it down. Except for a few murder mysteries or something you can bring along in case you get really depressed, remove yourself from all resources. One of the problems of going in with a spouse, of course, is that while you can get more material on members of the opposite sex (especially if you go in with a kid), it does give you a way out. You can talk to that person, and all that, and that's no way to make a world. The way to make a world is to be naked to the bone, to have as few resources as you can get by with. Because you can argue – just as Jackie argued that every world makes sense to people – you can argue that every world provides substance for the people, provides a life. And that's what you're about, [that's what you're] trying to get quickly, you see. So, the way to get it is to need it. And the only way to need it is to not have anything of your own. So you should be in a position to cut yourself to the bone. But lots of people don't do that too much – partly because of the contingencies of getting a degree and all that.

Then there is the other issue, which I'll only remark on briefly and then go on to a little bit on note taking and the like, and that's the self-discipline required. As graduate students, we're only interested in being smart, and raising our hands, and being defensive – as people usually are – and forming the right associations, and all that. And if you're going to do good fieldwork, it seems to me, that's got to go by the board. You've got to really change your relationship to the way you manage [the] anxieties and stresses of the social networks around you. For one thing, you have to open yourself up to any overture. Now, you can't follow up these overtures because you may early associate yourself with the wrong person. You've got to be disciplined enough with the people to find out what the various classes of individuals are that are involved in the place. You've got to then decide which class you're going to study. Once you do that you've got to find out about the internal cleavages within the class, and then decide which internal cleavage you're going to accept as your own. So, you shouldn't get *too* friendly. But you have to open yourself up in ways you're not in ordinary life. You have to open yourself up to being snubbed. You have to stop making points to show how "smart assed" you are. And that's extremely difficult for graduate students (especially on the East Coast, especially in the East!). Then you have to be willing to be a horse's ass. In these little groups, the world consists of becoming very good at doing some stupid little things, like running a boat, or dealing, or something like that, you see. And you're going to be an ass at that sort of thing. And that's one reason why you have to be young to do fieldwork. It's harder to be an ass when you're old. And you have to engage in a strategy with respect to costume. People don't like to cut their hair, for example,[2] so they retain something of their own self, which is nonsense. On the other hand, some people try to mimic the accents of the people they're studying. People don't like to have their accents mimicked. So you have to get a mix of changing costume, which the natives will accept as a reasonable thing, that isn't complete mimicry on the one hand, and that isn't completely retaining your own identity either.

Then, there's the issue, again, as part of the way in which you discipline yourself, of what you do with confidants. People like to find a friend where [they're doing their study] and tell the friend the "true things" and discuss with their friend what's going on. Unless that friend is in a structural position of not being able to retell the stories – and there are ways in which you could find such a friend – then I don't think you should talk to anybody.

Now there are also tests that you can run on whether you've really penetrated the society that you're supposed to be studying and I'll mention some of these briefly in passing. The sights and sounds around you should get to be normal. You should be able to even play with the people, and make jokes back and forth, although that's not too good a test. People sometimes assume that if they're told strategic secrets, that's a sign that they're "in." I don't think that's too good a sign. One thing is, you should feel you could settle down and forget about being a sociologist. The members of the opposite sex should become attractive to you. You should be able to engage in the same body rhythms, rate of movement, tapping of the feet, that sort of thing, as the people around you. Those are the real tests of penetrating a group.

Exploiting Place

Let me talk for one minute before I quit on what you do *after* you get in the situation. First, I'll review this business of "getting in." Remember, your job is to get as close to some set of individuals as possible. So you've got to see that they're aligned against some others that are around. There's no way in which, if you're dealing with a lower group, you can start from a higher group, or be associated with a higher group. You've got to control your associations. If you get seen in any formal or informal conversation with members of a superordinate group, you're dead as far as the subordinate group is concerned. So you've got to really be strategic and militant about the way you handle these social relationships.

Now about exploitation of the place you're in. I think you should spend at least a year in the field. Otherwise you don't get the random sample, you don't get a range of unanticipated events, you don't get deep familiarity. It's deep familiarity that is the rationale – that, plus getting material on a tissue of events – that gives the justification and warrant for such an apparently "loose" thing as fieldwork.

Then there is the affiliation issue. You can't move down a social system. You can only move up a social system. So, if you've got to be with a range of people, be with the lowest people first. The higher people will "understand," later on, that you were "really" just studying them. But you can't start at the top and move down because then the people at the bottom will know that all along you really were a fink – which is what you are.

Note taking: two minutes or a minute on note taking. There is a freshness cycle when moving into the field. The first day you'll see more than you'll ever see again. And you'll see things that you won't see again. So, the first day you should take notes all the time. By the way, about note taking, obviously you find corners in the day when you can take notes. And every night you should type up your fieldnotes. [And] you have to do it every night because you have too much work to do and you'll begin to forget. Then there are various devices you can use. You can start penetrating by going to open socials where, indeed, people might allow you to take open notes. If you put your notebook on a larger piece of paper, people won't see your notebook. It's masked. They won't be disturbed by it. [Learn to] fake off-phase note taking. That is, don't write your notes on the act you're observing because then people will know what it is you're recording. Try to discipline yourself to write your notes before an act has begun, or after it has started so that people won't be able to detect from when you start taking notes and when you stop taking notes what act you're taking notes about.

There's an issue about when to stop taking notes. Usually when you are merely duplicating what you've already got. Remember, you'll get, in a year, between 500 and 1,000 pages of single-spaced typed notes and this will be too much to read more than once or twice in your lifetime. So don't take *too* many notes.

Then there's [the matter of] what to do with information. Jackie takes seriously what people say. I don't give hardly any weight to what people say, but I try to triangulate what they're saying with events.

There's the issue of seeking multi-person situations. Two-person situations are not good because people can lie to you while they're with you. But with three people there, then they have to maintain their ties across those two other persons (other than yourself), and there's a limit to how they can do that. So that if you're in a multi-person situation, you've got a better chance of seeing things the way they ordinarily are.

Now, a point that I think is very important is this. We tend, because of our peculiar training, to try to write defensible statements, which is language written in Hemingway-type prose, defensible prose. That's the worst possible thing you can do. Write [your fieldnotes] as lushly as you can, as loosely as you can, as long as you put yourself into it, where you say, "I felt that." (Though not to too great a degree.) And as loose as that lush adverbialized prose is, it's still a richer matrix to start from than stuff that gets reduced into a few words of "sensible sentences." I'm now not [supporting] unscientific [practices] or anything like that. I'm just saying that to be scientific in this area, you've got to start by trusting yourself and writing as fully and as lushly as you can. That's part of the discipline itself, too. I believe that [other] people shouldn't read [your] fieldnotes, partly because it's a bore for them. But if they are going to read your fieldnotes, you'll tend not to write about yourself. Now don't *just* write about yourself, but put yourself into situations that you write about so that later on you will see how to qualify what it is you've said. You say, "I felt that," "my feeling was," "I had a feeling that" – that kind of thing. This is part of the self-discipline.

Now, these are comments on note taking. There are issues about getting out, about leaving the field so you can come back to it, [but] I think we can leave that, and – I'm going to stop right now.

Notes

1   In his introductory remarks, John Lofland had commented that it was likely difficult for fieldworkers to "know" exactly what it is they do to generate their analyses.
2   Recall that the year is 1974 and, especially for younger men, long hair was still both stylish and a symbol of distance from the "establishment."

10 Difference and Dialogue: Members' Readings of Ethnographic Texts

Robert M. Emerson and Melvin Pollner

Ethnography moves between two worlds. The desire to describe "the social and cultural worlds of a particular group ... [in ways that] are sensitive to the interpretations recognized and acted on by members of that group" (Emerson 1988, p. 19) drives ethnography toward the life world of participants. Seeking the lived meaning of social worlds, ethnography strives to overcome difference and distance. Although particular ethnographers may resist total surrender (Wolff 1964), the ethnographic project – at least in its more phenomenological expressions – invites a virtual merger between researcher and participant.

Yet the lifeworld of participants is but one domain to which ethnography responds. Grounded in the academy and the human sciences, ethnography is oriented to a professional readership as the primary audience of its texts. Thus, the observations and experiences of the field are formed and transformed in accord with the criteria and concerns of disciplinary discourse. Indeed, professional ethnography's mere explication, as well as its renderings of experience into textualized forms (e.g., Stoddart 1986; Marcus and Cushman 1982), may deeply transform what would otherwise be tacitly experienced. Mediated through discipline-directed explication and textualization, the final ethnographic rendering may be different from and even alien to participants' endogenous accountings.

In these ways, ethnography's concern with participants' life worlds encourages proximity and merger, as its embeddedness within the social sciences require distance and difference. Yet ethnography is not necessarily riven by these potentially conflicting demands. The typical fate of ethnography is to be read or heard by other ethnographers and only rarely (if at all) by those whose lives are represented. Thus, the ethnographer is able to move in one direction at one time, and in a different direction at another. Audience segregation, however, is not always possible. Indeed strong, principled objections have been voiced regarding the ethical and methodological appropriateness of such segregation (e.g., Barnes 1967; Nash and Weintraub 1972).

Ethically, the failure to return to the field with findings or descriptions exacerbates an imbalance inhering in the ethnographer's relation with participants. Often, the ethnographer secures access to the life worlds of participants for little more than the promise of a non-obstructive presence. The return to the field with text, it has been argued, makes partial payment for the gift of access (although given some ethnography, the return of the ethnographer might be considered yet another burden).[1]

More comprehensive efforts to rectify the imbalance suggest co-participatory research in which participants are not only consumers of the ethnographic text but fully involved in its construction (Whyte 1979).

More common, however, are limited calls for dialogue which emphasize its methodological value. Group members would seem to have special, even privileged claims for evaluating the accuracy, meaning and relevance of ethnographers' accounts. Indeed, some ethnographers have suggested that the response of those with the most insight into the lived experience of a social world – participants – can be used as a source of verification to affirm, qualify, or dispute research findings. Douglas (1976, p. 131), for example, recommended taking findings and descriptions back to the field to determine "if the members recognize, understand and accept one's descriptions of the setting." Similar procedures, variously termed "member verification," "member tests of validity," "host verification" and "respondent validation," have been recommended and used by a number of field researchers (e.g., Bloor 1978; Gould, Walker, Crane, and Lidz 1974; Lincoln and Guba 1985; Schatzman and Strauss 1973; Wiseman 1970).

Yet the significance of participants' response to ethnographers' accounts is problematic. Some ethnographers contend that to regard members' responses as though they provided a correct or definitive version of a setting or the experience of a setting overlooks several problematic features of these responses. Bloor (1988), for example, found that physicians' responses to his ethnographic accounts of their diagnostic procedures often reflected a variety of situational and organizational considerations that precluded straightforward determination of their meaning. Similarly, in prior work we suggested that "the significance of member response itself has to be considered in terms of the relational context in which it is proffered," pointing, for example, to how friendship ties between researchers and researched made assessment of even affirmative and positive responses problematic (Emerson and Pollner 1988, p. 193).

Others intimate more severe and perhaps irremediable limitations. Schutz (1962) in particular has suggested that the observing scientist and participating member are separated by an unbridgeable gulf. While participants' knowledge and formulations of activities are situated within the on-going practical activity of the group, the system of relevances of the researcher originates in the scientific community.[2] Thus, owing to their radically different existential positions and projects, researchers' accounts necessarily differ from those of participants and the researcher qua researcher cannot engage members in a direct and meaningful way.

In sum, despite the proliferation of explicit programmatic claims and implicit theoretical critiques of their possibility, the literature provides few detailed descriptions of actual responses to ethnographic representations.[3] In their absence, the celebration or denigration of participant responses seems premature. Furthermore, the possibilities of and procedures for promoting dialogue between members and ethnographer remain unrealized. In this paper, we begin to fill these gaps by describing and commenting upon one encounter in which we elicited participant reactions to our ethnographic account of the practices of psychiatric emergency teams. Although our project was not explicitly motivated by co-participatory or member-validation initiatives, in the course of preparing for a major presentation we asked a key participant to read and respond to two fairly finalized papers. Following an overview of the project and synopsis of the texts, we describe the major reactions to our paper – and our reactions to his reactions. We conclude by considering the significance of such dialogue for ethnography.

Setting and Methods

In the 1970s, we conducted field research on the management of psychiatric emergencies in a regional community mental health clinic in Southern California. Serving a catchment area population of almost 700,000 people, the clinic was operated by a staff of about 45, including psychiatrists, psychologists, psychiatric social workers, public health nurses, and psychiatric technicians (psych techs). Organized to provide crisis intervention, much of the staff remained in the clinic, providing short-term help for both walk-in patients and patients scheduled for office appointments. Part of the clinic staff worked regularly on the psychiatric emergency team (PET team), that made field trips on emergency calls received by the clinic for either crisis intervention or evaluation for hospitalization. Over a period of six months we observed the operations of these PET teams, in the office as incoming calls were processed, as the teams selected cases to be seen and organized to go out, and in the field as "clients" were sought out, interviewed and evaluated, and some disposition of the case was made.

About one year after the end of our field research, we had completed drafts of two papers on PET. The first (published in revised form as Emerson and Pollner 1978) addressed the procedures by which PET workers reviewed accumulated calls in selecting those to visit and evaluate on that particular shift. We suggested that in many instances PET workers selected cases in ways that would accord with a maxim, "do the worst first," where "worst" reflected assessed psychiatric "seriousness." In other instances, case selection proceeded on the basis of other maxims, including "do the easiest first," "do the nearest first," and "any case will do."

The second paper examined PET teams' use of the term "shit work" to designate at least some of their own activities. To quote from the abstract of the subsequently published version of this paper (Emerson and Pollner, 1976, p. 243):

"Shit work" characterizations emerged when team members felt not only unable to do something for clients in a therapeutic sense, but compelled to do something to them in a coercive sense (in particular, to order involuntary hospitalization). It is suggested that not only are dirty work designations the product of reviewing work performance through a particular perspective, but they also function publicly to reaffirm performance criteria, to express moral distance from a particular performance, and to tutor an observer into the preferred interpretation of a particular transaction.

We used these two papers as the primary mechanism to carry through with our long-planned effort to take back our ethnographic accounts to the PET workers we had accompanied and observed. We had, of course, continually discussed our evolving understandings of specific events and general "patterns" with PET workers as part of the ongoing field research.[4] To explicitly "take back" research "results" to those that are depicted in those results is interactionally a project of a very different order. First, ethnographic accounts present some *overall* characterization of the members' world or activities (or of some portion thereof), rather than a more partial account of some specific incident. For example, we sought to characterize "PET case selection" *as such*, not to elicit further accounts of specific decisions or incidents that we had observed. "Taking back" thus tends to trade in *formulations* (Garfinkel and Sacks 1970) of the setting or activity per se, rather than in talk about the meaning or grounds for particular incidents. The meanings of such accounts for members are thus very different. Second, in a taking back procedure the researcher must necessarily make an explicit commitment to a particular version of what she or he "observed," "found," and so forth. This explicitness often contrasts with checking procedures, where the fieldworker can ask for additional information from a stance that proposes ignorance, partial or incomplete knowledge, a stance that empowers the observed as the ultimate authority and that allows quick and easy retreat if the research formulation is challenged.

While we had spent a great deal of time with a number of PET workers in the office we studied, we had developed the closest ties with and felt the most respect for Art, a social worker with a strong commitment to PET. Slightly more than a year after our field work ended, we gave copies of the papers to Art, asked him to read them over and show them to his coworkers if he desired, and then meet to discuss them with us. We met with Art over lunch two days prior to a more public presentation of our research on PET we had agreed to make to the County Mental Health Department, which provided a second occasion for presenting participants with our ethnographic findings (see Emerson and Pollner 1988). In our talk with Art, which we tape recorded, we were concerned not only with how he as a PET insider evaluated our accounts, but also with identifying anything in the papers that would embarrass or create trouble for him or the other workers in his office if presented to the County.

While Art reported "recognizing" and even "endorsed" many of our findings (but see the deeply problematic character of such endorsements as discussed in Emerson and Pollner 1988, pp. 191–3), he delivered a number of direct blows to our ethnographic pretensions. Specifically,

1   while we understood our descriptions to provide an "inside view" of PET decision-making, Art repeatedly characterized our accounts as "an outside view";
2   while we thought we had been sensitive to the concrete practical concerns that gave PET decision making its own rational character, Art insisted that our accounts were inaccurate or unfair in portraying PET as "inconsistent" or "irrational";
3   while we thought we were simply describing PET activities in ways devoid of obvious practical import, Art read our accounts with a view toward their likely local organizational and political uses.

In what follows, we will examine each of these reactions and the issues they raise for members' understandings of ethnographic accounts.

"An Outside View"

Despite our commitment to describe PET activities "from the inside," from the very start Art reported experiencing our writings as having presented a *"different"*, *an "outside point of view"* of PET work. This sense of having been looked at from the "outside" surfaced in comments about reading accounts of PET activities that, at least at first glance, seemed startlingly off base. Art, for example, noted a number of points at which he had a "that's not true" reaction, but which was immediately followed by a corrective "but it is true." In some instances Art invoked this "but it is true" response to fault his own prior understanding of PET, suggesting that our "outside view" allowed him to now "see" matters he had previously failed to appreciate or misperceived because his very closeness to them:

> It was interesting. At one point you made a note about the social workers thinking that it was really below them, beneath them, to do this work, to do the PET work. That was interesting. I didn't realize that. I said that's not true. But it probably is. Most of them did feel they shouldn't do that. It was only a couple of us working on it, at the time. It was Barry and I, basically, I guess, and Ted, but Ted didn't like it. Barry didn't either. So that's ... it's – that's not true. But it is true.

Here Art's reaction of surprise and recognition seems to reflect our ethnographic focus upon what actors had come to experience as background, as taken for granted.[5]

In other instances Art explicitly framed this conflict between what he knew and what we had written as a matter of *differential perspectives*. For example, after initially praising the dirty work paper as having "captured a lot of PET" (and implying that the worse first paper failed to do so), Art commented:

> The other thing too, it's interesting to read about yourself (food gulp) working, from somebody else's point of view. [Right, yeah] I thought wow! That's probably true! That's an outside view.

Here Art depicts his initial reaction of startled surprise giving way – in part – to an appreciation of our accounts as resting on a "different perspective" on these PET activities. It is not so much that he had misperceived, but that he now encountered a different version and understanding of these events.

In part, Art attributed this difference to the "abstract" or "theoretical" character of our accounts. In the following, for example, he seemed to be saying that on mulling over the worst first paper, its descriptions (presumably of the "inconsistency" of PET decision-making) appear not so much wrong or inaccurate as "theoretical" – that is, foreign and in some respects irrelevant to his concerns as a PET team member:

> M: Any place where you had the sense like, were those guys here? Or were they just dreaming it up?
>
> A: Well, except in the first paper. But as you say, I suppose, it's theoretical. I mean you were coming from a certain familiar background, some sociological theory, in past

articles. Only there. But when I think about it, I think it's true. But I have to think about it in different contexts. I mean, certainly when you describe something, it's easy to recognize when that's described if you've had that experience . . . theoretically given something, it's a little more difficult. It's a whole different frame of reference.

Also at issue here is the very attempt to describe "PET decision-making" as such. When we discussed "PET hospitalization decision-making" or "PET case selection decision-making," for example, we were engaging projects that were neither common nor primary projects for PET members. To characterize an overall pattern of PET activity (i.e., how and why "decisions" in general get made) is a very different matter from describing how a specific PET team selected an actual case for a home visit (although even the latter is not without its problematic features). Such an account not only rests upon massive selectivity, but also summarizes or formulates actual ongoing activities in ways that will almost necessarily be foreign to those engaged in them (Garfinkel and Sacks, 1970). From an earlier point in our discussion:

> I got – become very confused. But I said that's true, we operate that way. [um hum, um hum] Only thing it lacks which the other one gives it somehow – the second paper, the paper on shit work – is (pause) the administrative realities, . . . the surrounding parts to PET, those tangential things that it would hinge upon all the time. The first paper didn't have that. It was more – I guess it was more abstract in the sense of trying to search out – maybe that was my difficulty – what are the absolute ways in which one makes the decision? What are the ————? And you try to pin to hang it on certain (I guess) theories or what would pass (for theories).

In this respect, the distinctively sociological "scope" of the descriptions of PET activities we sought to provide appeared "strange" to an insider. In the midst of doing, what is relevant to actors are matters of concrete, specific scope; almost any effort to provide an "overview description" will invoke other purposes or relevances, and is therefore apt to seem strange, or at least "outside," to an insider. These sorts of descriptions, moreover, may almost inevitably be heard as "evaluative," because one occasion when something like this would be done arises when you or someone else is evaluating your "overall" performance.

Art's reflections on these moments of startled surprise also conveyed the sense that our accounts of PET activities had direct, personal meaning to him. At one point, for example, he mused that our papers made PET seem "fucked up," not only to any disinterested observer, but even to himself. In this respect, on encountering this "outside view" of his own work activities, Art's reaction involved self-questioning and self-doubt along the lines, "Is that the kind of enterprise I am engaged in?"

Finally, we would call attention to the importance of "differential perspectives" in preserving the sense that ethnographers and member had indeed been viewing the same world (Pollner 1987). On the one hand, Art regularly appealed to the notion of "perspective" to account for discrepancies between what he knew and what we had described; in so doing, of course, he avoided making fundamental challenges to the accuracy or validity of our accounts, as well as dissolving any such challenges that our ethnography might pose to this world. Indeed, Art even used "perspective" as a device to gain new "insight" from our descriptions; in particular, encountering versions of his work as seen by sympathetic outsiders brought on concern about the fundamental nature of the whole PET enterprise. On the other hand, our efforts to describe the meanings and relevances that PET workers themselves assigned to events committed us to a "perspectival" position; these efforts assumed, after all, that these meanings and relevances were *assigned* rather than simply there. For example, we were not saying simply that PET work *was* "dirty work," but that it became dirty work through the meanings, concerns, and commitments that PET workers infused into it. Only *some* PET workers at that! As a result, we came to depict as "seen" what to PET workers simply "was." In this way, "capturing the member's point of view" may assume a point of view; such descriptions, while ostensibly eschewing a "point of view," in fact impose point-of-viewism, imbuing what is seen by members as factual, objective, "there" with qualities of subjectivity and choice (Bittner 1973).

"PET's Portrayed 'Inconsistency' is Inaccurate"

At a number of places Art suggested that our descriptions and accounts rendered PET decision-making activities inconsistent, irrational, even "crazy." As he explained at the very beginning of our session:

> Read the paper on – not the one on it's being shit work – the one on decision-making [right], the "worst first." When I finished with it – I'd run through it real quick one night when I got home – my first impression was Jeez, PET's really fucked up. . . . It doesn't know what the hell it's doing. Which is true, to some degree. But I had to go back and try to put the pieces together.

Art identified several domains of PET work in which our accounts depicted PET as acting "inconsistently," as not knowing "what the hell it's doing." One involved PET decisions on involuntary hospitalization (an important but not central focus of the dirty work paper). Whereas the recently enacted Lanterman–Petris–Short (LPS) Act held that the mentally ill could be hospitalized only if they were dangerous to self or to others, or gravely disabled, our accounts indicated that PET did not always attend to these criteria in deciding to hospitalize. As Art reflected at one point:

> I get a sense that we were crazy in the way we made our decisions. [he he] Because, we begin with, ah – I mean, it's a psychiatric thing as opposed to a legal thing. But then it becomes a legal thing as opposed to a psychiatric thing. You know, a person's crazy but they're not LPS. But then another time it's because they're crazy or because certain behaviors indicate certain things, and they're crazy, and they're not LPS but they're crazy, so we hospitalize em. Then other times we hospitalize them because they're LPS. They're *legally* dangerous and . . .

Secondly, Art noted that our accounts of PET procedures for selecting (and not selecting) cases for field visits (the focus of the worst first paper) conveyed a sense of inconsistency, providing the following illustration:

> In some ways maybe the first paper (just) tried to describe the decision-making process. So what you do, you try to record the actual event of decision making. One point, a

social worker walks in, picks up a paper, and says I know this client, it's not so bad. The doctor comes in and picks it up and says, that's very bad. She shrugs her shoulders and says PET (shouldn't be done), I guess.

On both these substantive issues, Art seemed torn: On the one hand, he insisted that our renderings made PET decision making seem *more* inconsistent than it really was, producing a sense of randomness or "irrationality" that was unnecessary and inaccurate. On the other hand, he seemed to concede, on reading our accounts, that PET decision making was indeed inconsistent at times. These tensions are reflected in the following comments on the relevance of diagnostic and legal criteria in hospitalization decisions:

> I mean, I guess in some senses I become very confused on what basis we make a decision after reading the paper. I mean which is true. We make it different – Sometimes it's for psychiatric reasons; a catatonic goes to the hospital because catatonic – that's a psychiatric diagnosis, that's a psychiatric thing. All catatonics act the same. That's a body of knowledge, supposedly, that you can deduce certain facts from, and you say one thing and it's [tight]. Okay. Then other times you say, well-l-l, this person's a little dangerous, you send him to the hospital. Legally dangerous. Regardless of what he is. When the – on the one time you make the basis legally, on the legal thing, on another time to – There is no coherent or integrated knowledge – [in other words] no consistency to – to the way we make decisions.

On another point, however, Art insisted unequivocally that our accounts inaccurately characterized PET as irrational or inconsistent: We had "missed" key "administrative realities" that lay behind and informed specific PET decisions. Our accounts of PET case selection, he emphasized, omitted "the surrounding parts to PET, those tangential things that it would hinge upon all the time." He elaborated these concerns in the following comments:

> I guess like for example, when you say, when you pick up a call in the Sunset area, for a number of reasons. Then the second call you pick up is in the Sunset area, too, because they're close to one another. That's true! That's exactly how you do it! The only reason you do that is because of pressures of administrative . . . But what it really gets down to is it's insane to try to service [a] 750,000 population area with two people, you know, in the City of LA. That part's missing, okay.

By neglecting the larger, structural context – the administratively and politically created "insanity" of having to cover a huge population area – our descriptions were restricted and circumscribed, in this sense attributing "irrationality" to PET workers rather than to the environing political system where it belonged.

Art's critique on this count points toward one aspect of the inherent micropolitics of descriptions; specifically, the kind and degree of *context* indicated as relevant to some particular event or incident is rife with implications for the depicted meaning and rationality of members' actions. We had contexted case selection decisions within the narrow parameters of what PET workers explicitly talked about in picking cases. In so doing we neglected factors implicitly informing such decisions and talk – that there were more cases than could ever be handled by the available staff, and that organizational and political factors, not low worker productivity, produced this overload. As a result we depicted as purely personal (e.g., PET workers selecting second cases in order to finish early, or at best, to get the work done) decisions which were actually shaped by broader administrative and political contexts.

On this count in particular we found compelling Art's critique that we had ignored or not given enough prominence to key "practicalities" underlying PET work. We sought to give greater prominence to such practicalities and broader contexts in subsequent published accounts. As others have noted (Heritage 1984), then, "context" is not a fixed and invariant feature of descriptions, but is an interactionally sensitive and accomplished matter. Indeed, we would suggest farther that our exchanges with Art reveal how relevant context can become an explicitly attended to and negotiated process.

"And Somebody Reads That and Says, Wow!"

Even at the time, Art's "outside perspective" criticisms effected us, feeling as we did that we not only were cognizant of but also had highlighted and honored the order and rationality of PET activities from the "inside." Several times we sought to reassure Art that we wanted to accent the internal logic of PET practices. These efforts failed:

> M: ... The central theme is not that things, in a sense, were inconsistent, although it might look like that from the point of view of the outside. From the point of view of the inside, there are changing grounds of making the decision. On a day to day basis, it looks inconsistent, but there is that line at the end. It is not as though PET is using a roulette wheel ... situation [Yeah, I know] as they know it, as PET understands it. Here are the good grounds for making the decision as they're made.
>
> A: What if they're bad grounds?

A telling response! In our stance as non-evaluative ethnographers we assumed that any and all "grounds" that PET workers might have for choosing one case over another, or for hospitalizing one patient but not another, were acceptable and valid. If on some shift PET workers avoided cases that looked overly "dangerous" or too "time consuming," we were perfectly willing to acknowledge such considerations as "adequate grounds" for decisions. In pointing out that these might be "bad grounds," Art raised the issue of how those directly concerned with these activities – Art himself and other PET workers, their immediate supervisors, and administrators and politicians involved in setting County policy – might evaluate and use our ethnographic accounts.

The key issue here involved the presumed audiences of our accounts. Whereas we were writing for relatively anonymous and far-removed audiences, Art read our descriptions with an eye toward how specific local, concerned audiences might use them. His immediate supervisors and administrators comprised one such audience. For example, later in the session Art veered in the following direction in response to an earlier question as to whether there was anything in the papers "that we should hold back on":

The only thing I wouldn't give them – It's true, it's absolutely true [that's not true] persons who are making their PET calls near the bank, and calling – [chuckle] That is absolutely true. That's not true! I wouldn't give the administration that. They're always accusing me of that anyway, whether you do it or not. You never do enough work in their eyes.

To a concerned, front-line sympathizing ethnographer, making time to go to the bank allows personal automomy and flexibility within a bureaucratically constrained work world. As Art pointed out, administrators could not be counted on to react with such understanding.

But Art was attentive to broader audiences than simply his immediate supervisers. Almost from the start of this session Art referred to PET's uncertain political and organizational future. Indeed, as we pressed him to tell us what to be on guard for in our upcoming presentation to the County, he sketched the following bleak picture:

I'm not [so sure] that what is ever said about PET is going to save very much, at this point.... Things happen so quickly. Health Department took over everything and [is switching its regional] directors, and chopped things up. They're movin' quick. And I think whatever decisions are to be made about PET we simply don't know about, and they've been made. And they're too costly. The only way they can make it reasonable is make it a small neighborhood area. They're gonna cut it. They have to. Cos they are cutting and health, education and welfare gets cut all the time. During a depression. And they are tightening up... Getting grams like, prove that you're worth it. Write up what you do, how many cases you carry. PET's so expensive... It cost something like $300, $400 a PET call, was the average cost, given the mechanical problems with the car, and gas, and personnel. And that's too expensive! That's a hell of a lot of money... Unless you do... and you turn out more work and do more calls and prove that it's worth going out – concretely, financially, that it showed you saved the County money, I think they're going to cut it.

Despite his initial statement that nothing we or anyone said could effect PET's future, Art returned a number of times to emphasize that our work would be read for its relevance to just these issues. For example, with regard to our neglect of "pressures of administrative reality" in discussing PET's tendency to select a second case independently of seriousness near a first case, Art noted:

And somebody reads that and says, wow! I think, anyway. You know, that's no good, I mean, what? What are they making decisions like that for? Well, the reason is, it's many, many miles apart....

Here Art implicitly seemed to be reviewing our accounts from the point of view of administrators evaluating PET with distinctive organizational and policy concerns. On this score, our accounts did not help PET but just the reverse; as Art commented at one point, "there's every grounds for discontinuing."

Furthermore, Art insisted that our attempts to provide an "inside" view of PET activities grounded in situational practicalities – even where successful – would not be heard in the ways we intended. And this was a matter not simply of our legitimating PET practices where others would not, but more fundamentally, of our having assumed a stance of "neutrality" that others would not and indeed could not honor. Specifically, Art pointed out that our descriptions and accounts failed to draw conclusions and make evaluations that would be obvious to and inevitably made by PET practitioners and administrators. For example, with regard to our description of the "inconsistencies" in PET's case selection procedures, Art noted the sort of questions he – and others – would ask of such an account:

> But I guess what I was doing in the [papers] – and now I have to draw conclusions from it – I have to say, that's really bad. It's really bad, that some calls lay in the box cos they're dangerous, cos we might get hurt, but that's the call you're supposed to respond to. I mean all these k – the way – But you didn't draw any conclusions from it. You didn't say – And you had all these – And there's a thousand different ways, that's true, of making those decisions. On another day the psych tech might pick up the thing and argue with the guy about the call. And that decides the decision.

Indeed, we would further suggest that the very concern with our accounts as depicting "inconsistencies" in PET decision making was motivated by concern with the practical, organizational and political uses of these accounts. Simply put, as ethnographers we were not concerned with "inconsistencies," but with local, situated meanings. For example, we had emphasized the varied skills and informing assumptions brought to bear in reading slips to decide which to select. That social workers and psychiatrists might draw upon different skills and bodies of knowledge, and so come to different interpretations of a case's "seriousness," simply stood as evidence of different rationalities at work. When actors without this sort of detached neutrality turned to our accounts, such "differences" stood out as "inconsistencies"; it was not "interesting" (sociologically, theoretically), but positively disturbing, to hear, as Art put it, that a social worker might read one slip and conclude "it's not so bad" and a doctor read the same slip and decide "that's very bad." In this respect it was Art himself who initially recognized and formulated PET "inconsistencies" in our accounts.

These sorts of reactions suggest that while the descriptions of ethnographically-observed scenes and events may be framed or conceived as "neutral," their neutrality is in fact an achieved matter, and one that is easily dispelled and recast.[6] In large part the sense that ethnographic descriptions (and sociological accounts more generally) are "neutral" derives from the conditions that those whom these accounts are about (1) rarely see these accounts and (2) if they do see them and argue with or otherwise dispute them, are disenfranchised as legitimate critics because of their own partial self interests. That is, the authoritativeness of ethnographic accounts derives in part from the assumption that the ethnographer has no particular practical axe to grind with respect to the events described, in part from the ways these accounts are not only privileged but also isolated from the settings that they are about. When these conditions are disrupted, the framework of neutrality around sociological knowledge and around even "mere sociological description" itself becomes tenuous. Whereas cracks in the aura of neutrality are common matters in the lore of evaluation research, they are less recognized with respect to field research and to the descriptions and accounts that such research produces.

Dialogue and Difference

In the effort to penetrate and portray the lifeworld of members, dialogue offers itself as an indispensible resource. Indeed, it is difficult to envision ethnography of any depth and seriousness succeeding without consulting participants about their interpretations and assessments of their social worlds. Within the realm of phenomenological ethnography, proposals have suggested developing dialogue further by presenting participants with researchers' accounts in order to secure feedback about the adequacy of a researcher's formulations.

As ethnography strives to penetrate one social world it is already deeply embedded in another – the academic/social science community. The dual committment makes problematic the ostensible ease and attractiveness of eliciting and interpreting the response to the ethnographic text. The elicitation procedure is predicated on the possibility of a cognitive utopia (Tyler 1986) in which differences in discourse and structures of relevance are overcome or discounted allowing researcher and participant to speak openly, honestly, and deeply. Yet, as we have suggested elsewhere (Emerson and Pollner 1988), such transactions are themselves deeply embedded in relational and organizational contexts and thus as charged, ambiguous and managed as other episodes in the field. Although the researcher may desire responses which transcend the particular contexts in which they are elicited, the responses often prove to be deeply oriented to and shaped by those contexts.

If participants do not transcend their contexts, researchers do not transcend theirs. The very quest to produce a veridical textual account of taken for granted practices, processes, and perspectives originates not within the immediate lifeworld of members but within the lifeworld of the ethnographer. The explication and textualization of the tacit domain are already intrusive transformations. The novelty of the project is heightened by the suffusion of structures of relevance that also derive from the lifeworld of the ethnographer.

Schutz (1962) suggested some of the substantive and structural differences between an ethnographer and participants which emerge as a consequence of ethnography's extrinsic origins and concerns:

> Having no "Here" within the social world the social scientist does not organize this world in layers around himself as the center. He can never enter as a consociate in an interaction pattern with one of the actors on the social scene without abandoning, at least temporarily, his scientific attitude. The participant observer or field worker establishes contact with the group studied as a man among fellowmen; only his system of relevances which serves as the scheme of his selection and interpretation is determined by the scientific attitude, temporarily dropped in order to be resumed again. (Schutz, 1962, p. 40)

The account of the ethnographic observer, Schutz implied, entailed a transformation if not deformation, of participants' experiences and interpretations.

Ironically, although appropriate as a characterization of some forms of social science research, Schutz's analysis does not fully capture the more complex concerns of the very kind of research to which his insistence upon the significance of commonsense constructs in the organization of social action contributed. For phenomenologically oriented ethnography especially, the goal is to explicate the bodies of knowledge, and structure of relevancies through which members organize and experience the social world. Thus, one might retort to Schutz that the explication of the structure of relevancies is one of the points of ethnography.

Yet Bittner suggests that even the effort to describe the member's perspective, bodies of knowledge, and structure of relevancies may lend itself to a peculiar distortion. The very stance and attitude of ethnography encourage, perhaps even assures, a slippage into a distorting subjectivism (Bittner 1973, pp. 121–2):

> The paramount fact about the reality bounded by an ethnographic field work project is that it is not the field worker's own, actual life situation. This is so not because he might disdain accepting it as his own world, nor because he somehow fails in his attempts to make it his world, but because he cedes it as not being his world. He has deliberately undertaken to view it as the world of others . . . Since the field worker, as field worker of course, always sees things from a freely chosen vantage point – chosen, to be sure, from among actually taken vantage points – he tends to experience reality as being of subjective origin to a far greater extent than is typical in the natural attitude. Slipping in and out of points of view, he cannot avoid appreciating meanings of objects as more or less freely conjectured.

Given the distinctive stance and attitude of ethnography, the ethnographic text could prove to be an irremediably anomalous rendering of the tacit practices and perspectives of the lifeworld. Further, the prospect of extrinsic, if not incommensurable, structure of relevancies suggests that efforts at member validation risk unintelligibility from the outset. These considerations, together, with the problematics posed by the organizational and interactional processes which suffuse the situated construction of member responses (Emerson and Pollner 1988) suggest that efforts to solicit member responses to ethnographic texts are likely to be ambiguous, difficult, and uncertain efforts for both participants and researchers.

These daunting prospects, however, are not grounds for dismissing dialogue regarding textual versions. On the contrary, the difficulties, differences, and ambiguities make such dialogical efforts invaluable. The dialogue is not merely a medium for resolving substantive differences – although it is that – but an occasion for revealing the suppositions, structure of relevancies, and practices of two forms of life: that of participants and of researchers. The very effort to resolve differences begins to reveal and elaborate the forms of life in relation to one another.

Our discussion with Art, for example, suggests the contestability of our conception of a "neutral" account. Despite the fact that we understood our own representation to be primarily descriptive and impartial, Art apprises us that our account is partisan and incriminating and will be responded to as such in the local organizational context – as indeed our subsequent experience bore out. Such disjunctures have the potential to throw into relief how the researcher's organizational here and now is indeed not that of the member and that the difference may infect virtually every aspect of ostensibly descriptive discourse including the sense that it is merely "descriptive." Similarly, we learn that our conception of the "inside" we generally sought to portray may be so askew that Art characterizes it as a view from the "outside." To be sure, the significance of such characterizations is highly ambiguous and may even be constructed as such – perhaps it is a euphemized way of saying to friends that they are wrong – but the direct encounter with such a characterization is cognitively stunning, and precipitates a rethinking as to what we could have been doing.

If our position is both delineated and shaken through dialogue, so too is Art's. Some of the displacing consequences of the text and dialogue can only be surmised. Over the course of our experience with Art, as well as with other respondents, we noticed features of the response – some explicit, some less so – that had to do not just with whether PET work had been correctly described (although that was a strong and pervasive concern) but the fact that PET had been described at all. The sheer production of an organizationally detached description and the invitation to respond seemed to be a novel, perturbing, and significant event. Relatedly, the very elicitation procedure transforms the definition and dynamic of the researcher-participant relation that had previously existed: instead of the ethnographer asking to listen to the participant, the ethnographer now asks to be listened to (or read) by participants. In a certain sense, the elicitation procedure bids the member to become a participant-observer of the social world of the researcher.

Art also appears to see PET with new eyes. Only on reading our accounts does he seem to appreciate, for example, his minority status in liking to do PET work (Emerson and Pollner 1988, pg. 11). Furthermore, characterizing what we have done as a view from the "outside," Art expresses chagrin over the apparent inconsistency of PET selection procedures. Although he indicates that we have understated the practical and economic constraints which necessitate the practices described in this paper, he seems to recognize in a fresh way "inconsistency" in PET selection practices. Indeed, there are moments when it appears that our accounts threaten to shake his personal faith in PET's value and integrity. As he reported his reactions to the papers at an early point in our meeting:

> My initial impression, I really felt bad. I really said, God, PET is really in bad shape. I mean . . . then I said to myself, there's every grounds for discontinuing, as is. It's irrational.

The inclusion of participant's reaction to the text provides an opportunity for differences of view about substantive features and for disjunctures between observer and participant lifeworlds to emerge.[7] Inclusion of the dialogue in the final text assures that members' voice will be heard in a relatively unmediated fashion (as will that of the ethnographer him/herself) in response to a version of the very text encountered by the reader. The ethnographer need hardly defer to the participant's version – nor does participant affirmation of the text translate into validation – but through inclusion of participant reaction all parties to the ethnography are forced to explicitly confront the possibility and significance of difference. The dialogical response to the text, we suggest, is not so much a way of bridging the chasm between researcher and participant – though it may contribute to reducing the gap – but an occasion for making its dimensions and depth visible to participant, researcher, and reader.

Concluding Remarks

The significance of the reactions of participants to an ethnographic text is indeterminate and ambiguous (Emerson and Pollner 1988). Each utterance is shaped in response to many features of the on-going situation other than the matter at hand, that is, the text. Was Art really oscillating between perspectives? Or was it a nice way of saying that we had missed the mark? These and other equivocalities multiply in this transaction just as they can in other aspects of ethnography and, indeed, in everyday life. Together with the other disjunctures and problematics it would seem that dialogue regarding the text is a hopelessly uncertain and ambiguous enterprise. We cannot suggest a methodological remedy – and we do not think there is one. But what presents itself as a problem may in fact be an opportunity. Ambiguity, uncertainty, and difference are endemic to ethnography. As such, we would suggest, they are not to be suppressed or overcome, but displayed – to participants, researchers, and readers. The inclusion of dialogue about the text between researcher and participant is a powerful method for displaying "an understanding of the *differences between* two worlds, that exists between persons who are indeterminately far apart, in all sorts of different ways, when they started out in their conversation" (Tedlock 1979, p. 388, cited in Handler 1985).

Notes

1   This reaction was most dramatically expressed when the citizens of *Small Town in Mass Society* (1968) featured a large scale copy of the jacket of this book on a float in their Fourth of July parade. Following the float came "a manure- spreader filled with very rich barnyard fertilizer, over which was bending an effigy of 'The Author'" (Vidich and Bensman 1968, p. 466; the quotation comes from a local newspaper account).

2   Bloor (1988, p. 157), following Schutz, has advanced a similar position, insisting that members' and researchers' accounts cannot be simply juxtaposed to determine their correspondence:

> (W)hile laymen produce their own distinctive sociological accounts of their social worlds, these accounts will inevitably differ from the accounts provided by sociological researchers since each is formulated in light of different purposes at hand. A member's sociological account will only have that degree of clarity, consistency, and elaborateness required by the member's purpose at hand, and hence cannot be directly compared with a sociologist's description compiled for different purposes.

3   The paucity of studies stands in contrast to other disciplines and endeavors such as psychiatry and journalism, where the reaction of those analyzed and described has received descriptive and analytic attention.

4   Blumer (1969, p. 41) provides an informative account of "checking out" ethnographic observations by using a group of well-informed informants.

5   Bloor (1978, p. 549) provides a parallel instance in the reaction of a surgeon to an ethnographic account of his patterns of referral:

> I think it was a fair assessment, a fair summary. It put into words many of the things to do which are more second nature I think. You know, I think you've done quite well summarizing (laughs) me; some of these things, "Well, I think, you know, that is right", when I see it written down. And when you're doing it, well, I suppose you have these things in the back of your mind but... (p. 549) Bloor also suggests that these specialists "were perhaps only marginally interested in the content of the

reports" (p. 550), since as surgeons, "clinical assessment, especially for a routine surgical procedure like adenotonsillectomy, is not a central interest" (p. 551).

6   See Pollner and Emerson (1988) for an analysis of the interactional processes whereby an ethnographer and those being observed collaborate in producing – at least for a moment – a sense of observer neutrality through what we termed "nonconsequential presense."
7   Including participant response is also a way of discharging ethical responsibility to participants while not ceding control of the text. The ethnographer can assure participants that their responses to the ethnographic rendering will itself be included as part of the text although objections and disagreements are hardly assured of being credited as definitive or privileged.

References

Barnes, J. A. 1967. "Some Ethical Problems in Modern Field Work." Pp. 193–213 in *Anthropologists in the Field*, edited by D. C. Jongsman and P. Gutkind. Assen, The Netherlands: Van Gorcum.
Bittner, E. 1973. "Objectivity and Realism in Sociology." Pp. 109–28 in *Phenomenological Sociology: Issues and Applications* edited by G. Psathas. New York: Wiley.
Bloor, M. J. 1978. "On the Analysis of Observational Data: A Discussion of the Worth and Uses of Inductive Techniques and Respondent Validation." *Sociology* 12: 545–52.
——1988. "Notes on Member Validation." Pp. 156–172 in *Contemporary Field Research: A Collection of Readings*, edited by Robert M. Emerson. Prospect Heights, IL: Waveland.
Blumer, H. 1969. *Symbolic Interactionism*. Englewood Cliffs, NJ: Prentice Hall.
Douglas, J. D. 1976. *Investigative Social Research: Individual and Team Field Research*. Beverly Hills, CA: Sage.
Emerson, R. M. 1988. *Contemporary Field Research: A Collection of Readings*. Prospect Heights, IL: Waveland.
Emerson, R. M. and M. Pollner. 1976. "Dirty Work Designations: Their Features and Consequences in a Psychiatric Setting." *Social Problems* 23: 243–55.
——1978. "Policies and Practices of Psychiatric Case Selection." *Sociology of Work and Occupations* 5: 75–96.
——1988. "On the Uses of Members' Responses to Researchers' Accounts." *Human Organization* 47: 189–98.
Garfinkel, H. and H. Sacks. 1970. "On Formal Structures of Practical Actions." Pp. 338–66 in *Theoretical Sociology*, edited by J. C. McKinney and E. A. Tiryakian. New York: Appleton Century Crofts.
Gould, L., A. L. Walker, L. E. Crane, and C. W. Lidz. 1974. *Connections: Notes from the Heroin World*. New Haven, CT: Yale University Press.
Handler, R. 1985. "On Dialogue and Destructive Analysis: Problems in Narrating Nationalism and Ethnicity." *Journal of Anthropological Research* 41: 171–82.
Heritage, J. 1984. *Garfinkel and Ethnomethodology*. Cambridge, MA: Polity Press.
Lincoln, Y. S. and E. G. Guba, 1985. *Naturalistic Inquiry*. Beverly Hills, CA: Sage.
Marcus, G. and R. Cushman. 1982. "Ethnographies as Texts." *Annual Review of Anthropology* 11: 25–69.
Nash, D. and R. Weintraub 1972. "The Emergence of Self-Consciousness in Ethnography." *Current Anthropology* 13: 527–42.
Pollner, M. 1987. *Mundane Reason*. Cambridge, MA: Cambridge University Press.
Pollner, M. and R. M. Emerson. 1988. "The Dynamics of Inclusion and Distance in Fieldwork Relations." Pp. 235–52 in *Contemporary Field Research: A Collection of Readings*, edited by R. M. Emerson. Prospect Heights, IL: Waveland.

Schatzman, L. and A. Strauss. 1973. *Field Research: Strategies for a Natural Sociology.* Englewood Cliffs, NJ: Prentice-Hall.

Schutz, A. 1962. "Common-Sense and Scientific Interpretation of Human Action." Pp. 3–47 in *Collected Papers, Vol. I: The Problem of Social Reality*, edited by Maurice Natanson. The Hague: Martinus Nijhoff.

Stoddart, K. 1986. "The Presentation of Everyday Life: Some Textual Strategies for 'Adequate Ethnography.'" *Urban Life* 15: 103–21.

Tedlock, D. 1979. "The Analogical Tradition and the Emergence of Dialogical Anthropology." *Journal of Anthropological Research* 35: 387–400.

Tyler, S. A. 1986. "Post-Modern Ethnography: From Document of the Occult to Occult Document." Pp. 122–140 in *Writing Culture: The Poetics and Politics of Ethnography*, edited by J. Clifford and G. E. Marcus. Berkeley: University of California Press.

Vidich, A. J. and J. Bensman. 1968. *Small Town in Mass Society.* Rev. Ed. Princeton, NJ: Princeton University Press.

Whyte, W. F. 1979. "On Making the Most of Participant Observation." *American Sociologist* 14: 56–66.

Wiseman, J. P. 1970. *Stations of the Lost: The Treatment of Skid Row Alcholics.* Englewood Cliffs, NJ: Prentice-Hall.

Wolff, Kurt H. 1964 "Surrender and the Community Study: The Study of Loma." Pp. 233–63 in *Reflections on Community Studies*, edited by A. J. Vidich, J. Bensman and M. R. Stein. New York: Wiley.

11 In Search of Horatio Alger: Culture and Ideology in the Crack Economy

Phillipe Bourgois

The heavyset, white undercover cop pushed me across the ice cream counter, spreading my legs and poking me around the groin. As he came dangerously close to the bulge in my right pocket, I hissed in his ear – "it's a tape recorder." He snapped backwards, releasing his left hand's grip on my neck, and whispered a barely audible "sorry." Apparently he thought he had clumsily intercepted an undercover from another unit instead of an anthropologist, because before I could get a look at his face, he had left the bodega[1] grocery store-*cum*-numbers-joint. Meanwhile the marijuana sellers stationed in front of the bodega that Gato and I had just entered to buy beer saw that the undercover had been rough with me and suddenly felt safe and relieved. They were finally confident that I was a white addict rather than an undercover.[2]

I told Gato to grab the change on my $10 bill from the cashier as I hurried to leave this embarrassing scene. At the doorway, however, I was blocked by Bennie, a thin teenager barging through the door to mug us. Bennie pushed me to the side and lunged at the loose dollar bills in Gato's hand, the change from the beers. "That's my money now Gato – give it to me," he shouted. I started in with a loud "Hey! yo, what are you talking about, that's my money! Get away from it." But one look at the teenager's contorted face and narrowed eyes stopped me halfway through the sentence. Gato's underbreath mutter of "be careful – my man is dusted" was redundant. I was ready to give up the eight bills – and more if necessary – to avoid any out-of-control violence from a mugger high on angel dust.

Cautiously, Gato went through some of the motions of struggling with the angry dust head to whom – I found out later – he really did owe money to cover his share of the supply of marijuana confiscated in a drug bust last week in front of the same bodega. Gato tried two different tacks. One was gentle: staring deeply into his mugger's face – which was two inches from his own – pulling at the fistful of bills, "Yo Bennie, chill out. I know how much I owe you. I'll take care of you tomorrow. This ain't my money. *Please* don't take this money." A second time, a little tougher and louder: "I told you this ain't my money; get off of it! It ain't my money!" Bennie just got tougher; he knew Gato was "pussy" and wrenched at the bills, hissing about the $60 still owed him from last week. They had been selling marijuana together for several weeks on the corner next to the bodega, and he knew that Gato would not fight back. As the bills were about to rip, Gato finally let go, looking back at me helplessly.

As we stepped out the bodega's door, Bennie kept yelling at Gato about the $60 he still owed him, warning him that he better pay up tomorrow. At this point Bennie let out a whistle and a dented Vega came roaring down the block, careening to the curb, cutting us off in the direction we were walking. A young man in the passenger seat tried to open his door and jump skillfully onto the sidewalk before the car stopped, but instead he fell on his face in the gutter. He jumped back to his feet unsteadily, his nose bleeding, and a baseball bat waving in his right hand. The driver, who was steadier, apparently not high on angel dust like his companions, also rushed out of the car and was running at us. Bennie called out that all was "cool," that he already had the money, and they slowed down, walking toward us with puffed backs, one with the baseball bat resting on shoulder.

I ran back to the bodega door, but Gato had to stand firmly because this was the corner he worked, and those were his former partners. They surrounded him, shouting about the money he still owed, and began kicking and hitting him with the baseball bat. Gato still did not turn and run; instead he jumped up and down, prancing sideways along the sidewalk toward the corner on the main avenue in the hopes that the new colleagues he was steering crack customers to at the bogus "botanica"[3] around the corner might be able to catch sight of what was happening to him. He was knocked down two times before reaching the corner; they could have done Gato much more damage but backed away, walking back to the car with deliberate slowness, pretending not to notice me. The two who had driven up in the Vega had not seen the policeman frisk me, and they evidently did not think it wise to pick a fight with an unknown "white boy" who was just the right age to be an undercover. They pulled at Bennie's elbow and hopped into the Vega to drive off. Their attempt at burning rubber merely resulted in whining the car's gears.

By the time I caught up with Gato half a block down the avenue, he had already finished telling the story to a cousin of his who was on her way to the botanica crack house. His cousin was a woman in her late twenties, dressed "butch" in a long-sleeved jean jacket despite the midsummer midnight heat. Her emaciated face and long sleeves left no doubts as to her being a coke mainliner. When I arrived, she was waiving her skinny arms and stamping on the ground, whining hoarsely at Gato, telling him he couldn't just run off like that, that he had to "go down swinging like a man," that he couldn't just let people chase him around like that, that he had to show them who's who, and did he know who he was and where he was? Now what did he expect to do? Where was he going to work? And finally, she needed back right away the money (which he had spent on crack instead) she had lent him yesterday to buy a new supply of marijuana, and she was disgusted with him.

After we finished telling the story at the crack/botanica house where I had been spending most of my evening hours this summer, Chino, who was on duty selling that night with Julio, jumped up, excitedly calling out "What street was that on? Come on, let's go, we can still catch 'em. How many were they?" I quickly stopped this mobilization for a revenge posse, explaining that it was not worth my time and that we should just forget about it. Chino looked at me disgustedly, sat back down on the milk crate in front of the botanica's door, and turned his face away from me, shrugging his shoulders. Julio, whom I had become quite close to, jumped up in front of me to berate me for being "pussy." He also sat back down shortly afterwards, feigning exasperated incredulity with the comment, "Man, you still think like a blanquito." A half dozen spectators – some empty pocketed ("thirsty") crack addicts, most sharply dressed, drug-free teenage girls competing for Chino's and Julio's attentions – giggled and snickered at me.

To recuperate some minimal respect, I turned on Gato, telling him he owed me the $8 Bennie the dust head had stolen, and I ordered him to empty his pockets. Grinning, he pulled out a dollar and promised he would come by tomorrow with seven more. He told me not to worry; he would pay me back first. Of course, I knew he would not because he knew that I was one of the few individuals on the street even more "pussy" than he.

Seeing my feeble attempt, and perhaps hoping to give me a second chance, Julio came up to Gato at this point. Making sure I saw what he was doing, he dropped a vial of crack in Gato's shirt pocket in payment for the half dozen customers he had steered to the crack house that evening. I was supposed to grab the vial – worth $5 – from Gato's pocket as partial compensation for the seven he still owed me. But I could not bring myself to rip Gato's shirt pocket open and grab the vial, knowing that Gato was "thirsty" and might get violent with me. He might have been "pussy" in the confrontation with Bennie, but he certainly was not going to be "pussy" with me.

A few minutes later Chino and Julio told everyone it was time to close shop. It had just turned 12:30 a.m, and they had to turn in the evening's receipts to their boss. They hurriedly pulled down the metal gates over the botanica entrance, eager to leave work and get on with an evening of partying. As he was walking away, Julio turned around to tell me "good night – I guess you're staying around here tonight, verdad [right]?" For the first time he was not going to invite me up to his girlfriend Jackie's apartment in the nearby projects (which she shared with her adopted grand-father and three children) to drink beer while he and Chino and whoever else was around snorted coke and ate dinner. He had to come home before 1 o'clock because Jackie was due at "the Candy Store" down the avenue to sell twenties of "rock." Jackie's husband Papito, who used to own the botanica crack site that Julio and Chino worked at, was now "upstate" serving two to five years for his second conviction for selling cocaine and possessing firearms. Two nights before Papito was scheduled to go to jail, as he was closing down the botanica, Jackie, who was eight months pregnant at the time, shot him in the stomach right in the doorway of the botanica in front of all his workers and everyone else hanging out that evening. She was furious because, instead of leaving money for her before beginning his jail sentence, Papito had been running around spending thousands of dollars on young women and bragging about it at the crack house.

Ten months later Jackie was doing much better, especially following the problem-free birth of her third daughter. Jackie was relieved that the infant had come out "normal" despite the fact that she had been snorting large quantities of cocaine during the final months of her pregnancy. Papito's cousin Big Pete had taken over the crack franchise at the botanica while Papito was serving time. He had witnessed the shoot-out and had been impressed by Jackie's "balls." Consequently, shortly after the birth of her daughter, Big Pete hired Jackie to sell "twenties of rock" at another sales point that he owned in the neighborhood that doubled as a candy store.

Incidentally, not everyone was impressed by Jackie's shooting of her husband Papito. After starting up a relationship with Julio shortly after her husband's hospi-talization and jailing, Jackie had told Rose, a fifteen-year-old former girlfriend of Julio's, to stop hanging around the crack house or else. I happened to be present one evening when Rose was discussing this threat with the crowd hanging around the crack house. Someone was warning Rose that Jackie meant business and began retelling the story of Jackie's shooting Papito when Aida, the seller on shift at the crack house that evening, looked up from the pink baby blanket she was knitting to interrupt: "Big deal! Anybody can buy a fucking gun. What's the big deal? You just stay here Rose. You can come visit me any time you want. That woman's just a nasty, loud-mouthed bitch. She can't tell me or you or anyone else what to do here. She don't own the place. I'll tell Big Pete to set her straight."

Rose did indeed keep hanging around until another violent complication arose. Another ex-boyfriend of Rose's who claimed he still loved her out of control threatened to kill Julio and commit suicide if she kept hanging out at the crack house. This still did not keep Rose away. Instead, Julio was obliged to call on some friends and have them hang out with him at the crack house for extra protection. Rose's jilted lover did indeed return a few days later with two big friends, but they just kept walking by when they saw the crowd protecting Julio. Julio was exasperated with the whole issue because he had lost all interest in Rose last summer after he had gotten her pregnant (she had been fourteen at the time). She had had a big argument with him when he refused to pay for her abortion.

For the past few weeks we had baby-sat Jackie's children along with her sixty-five-year-old alcoholic grandfather-in-law while Jackie worked selling the twenties of crack. Baby-sitting involved first eating everything in the refrigerator, sending one of the children out for beer, keeping the grandfather from drinking any hard liquor, shouting at the young children if they quarreled, playing tenderly with the nine-month-old, and accompanying Chino and Julio into the bedroom to keep "conversating" with them as they ground up and sniffed cocaine. By daybreak Jackie had usually returned from work with fresh coke for Julio and Chino to sniff and "break night." They would sleep from midmorning until late afternoon, careful to arrive on time for their evening shift (4:00 p.m. to 12:30 a.m.) at the botanica crack house.

Culture and Material Reality

The foregoing summary of my fieldwork is merely a personalized glimpse of the day-to-day struggle for survival, *and for meaning*, by the people who comprise the extraordinary statistics on inner-city crack and crime.[4] These are the very same Puerto Rican residents of Spanish Harlem whom Oscar Lewis in *La Vida* declared to be victims of a "culture of poverty," mired in a "self-perpetuating cycle of poverty" (Lewis, 1966: 5). The culture-of-poverty concept has been severely critiqued for its internal inconsistencies, its inadequate understanding of culture and ethnicity, its ethnocentric/middle-class bias, and especially its blindness to structural forces and blame-the-victim implications (cf. Eames and Goode, 1980; Leacock, 1971; Stack, 1974; Valentine, 1968; Waxman, 1977). Despite the negative scholarly consensus on Lewis's theory, the alternative discussions either tend toward economic reductionism (Ryan, 1986; Steinberg, 1981; Wilson, 1978) or else ultimately minimize the reality of profound marginalization and destruction – some of it internalized – that envelop a disproportionate share of the inner-city poor (cf. Stack, 1974; Valentine, 1978; see critiques by Harrison, 1988; Maxwell, 1988; Wilson, 1987). More important, the media and a large proportion of the inner-city residents themselves continue to subscribe to a popularized blame-the-victim/culture-of-poverty theory that has not been adequately rebutted by scholars.

The media now refer to the inner-city residents described in my ethnographic vignette as "the underclass," the "hard-core unemployed," and the "unemployables." These pariahs of urban industrial society seek their income, and subsequently their identity and the meaning in their lives, through what they perceive to be high-powered careers "on the street." They partake of ideologies and values and share symbols that, it could be argued, add up to an "inner-city street culture" that is completely excluded from the mainstream economy and society but ultimately derived from it. Most of them have few direct contacts with non-inner-city residents; and when they do, it is usually in a position of domination: teachers in school, bosses, police officers, and later parole or probation officers.

How can the complicated ideological dynamic accompanying inner-city poverty be understood without falling into an idealistic culture-of-poverty and blame-the-victim interpretation? Scholars who offer structural, political-economic reinterpretations of the inner-city dynamic emphasize historical processes of labor migration in the context of institutionalized racism. They dissect the structural transformations in the international economy, which they see as destroying the manufacturing sector in the U.S. while leading to a burgeoning low-wage, low-prestige service sector (cf. Davis, 1987; Sassen-Koob, 1986; Steinberg, 1981; Tabb and Sawers, 1984; Wilson, 1987). These sorts of theories have the virtue of addressing the structural confines of the inner-city dynamic but also a vice: they tend to see the actual actors involved as passive. In my view, such interpretations fail to grasp fully the complex relationship between ideological processes and material reality, and between culture and class.

To explain fully the dynamic I saw day in and day out on New York's mean streets, we have to understand its relationship to the larger structural processes of international labor migration in the world economy. But the inner-city residents I hung out with in Spanish Harlem are more than mere victims of historical transformations or of the institutionalized racism of a perverse political-economic system. They do not passively accept their fourth-class citizen fate. They are struggling determinedly – just as ruthlessly as the corporate robber barons of the nineteenth century and the yuppie investment bankers of today – to earn money, demand dignity, and lead meaningful lives. And in this lies the tragic irony that is at the heart of their existence: their very struggle against – yet within – the system exacerbates the trauma of their community and helps destroy thousands of individual lives (Bourgois, 1992, 1995).

In the day-to-day experience of the street-bound inner-city resident, unemployment and personal anxiety over the impossibility of providing a minimal standard of living for one's family translate into intracommunity crime, intracommunity drug abuse, intracommunity violence. The objective, structural desperation of a population without a viable economy and facing the barriers of systematic discrimination and marginalization gets channeled into self-destructive cultural practices.

Most important, the "personal failure" of those who survive on the street is articulated in the idiom of race. The racism of the larger society becomes internalized on a personal level. Once again, although the individuals in the ethnographic fragment at the beginning of this chapter are the victims of long-term historical and structural transformations, they do not interpret their myriad difficulties in political-economic terms. In their struggle to survive and even to succeed, they daily enforce the details of the trauma and cruelty of their lives on the others who inhabit the excluded margins of urban America.

Cultural Reproduction Theory

Education theorists have developed a literature on the processes by which structures and cultures of privilege and power are made and remade in daily life. They have tried to understand how society is "reproduced" by studying the ideological domination of the poor and the working class in school settings (*e.g.*, Giroux, 1983). Some of these theories of social reproduction tend toward an economic reductionism or a simple, mechanical functionalism (see, *e.g.*, Bowles and Gintis, 1977). More recent variants emphasize the complexity and contradictory nature of the dynamic of ideological domination (Willis, 1983). There are several ethnographies that document how the very process whereby working-class students resist the imposition of middle-class norms in school ends up channeling them into marginal roles in the economy for the rest of their lives (cf. Foley, 1990; Macleod, 1987; Willis, 1977). Other ethnographically based interpretations show that for inner-city African-American students to achieve traditional academic success, they must reject their ethnic identity and cultural dignity; when such students do well in school, they are often seen by their peers as caving in to the demands of white institutions, the educational equivalent of an "Uncle Tom" (Fordham, 1988; Zweigenhaft and Domhoff, 1991).

Beyond school settings, cultural reproduction theory has great potential for shedding light on how structurally induced cultural resistance and self-reinforced marginalization interact at the street level in the inner-city experience. Rather than a culture of poverty, the violence, crime, and substance abuse of the inner city can be understood as manifestations of a "culture of resistance," a culture defined by its stance against mainstream, white, racist, and economically exclusive society. This culture of resistance, however, results in greater oppression and self-destruction. More concretely, resisting the outside society's racism and refusing to accept demeaning, low-wage, entry-level jobs contributes to the sorts of crime, addiction, and intracommunity violence for which crack has become an emblem.

Most of the individuals in my earlier vignette are *proud* that they are not being "exploited" by "the white man," although they also feel "like fucking assholes" for being poor. Contrary to popular images, all of them have previously held numerous jobs in the legal economy. Most of them hit the street in their early teens, working odd jobs as delivery boys and baggers in supermarkets and bodegas. Most have held the jobs that are objectively recognized as among the least desirable in U.S. society. Virtually all of these street participants have had deeply demeaning personal experiences in the minimum-wage labor market due to abusive, exploitative, and often racist bosses or supervisors. They see the illegal, underground economy as offering not only superior wages, but also a more dignified workplace.

Gato, for example, had worked for the ASPCA, cleaning out the gas chambers where stray dogs and cats are killed. Bennie had been fired six months earlier from a night-shift job as security guard on the violent ward for the criminally insane on Wards Island. Chino had been fired a year ago from a job installing high-altitude storm windows on skyscrapers after an accident temporarily blinded him in the right eye. Upon being disabled, he discovered that his contractor had hired him illegally through an arrangement with a corrupt union official who had paid him half the union wage, pocketing the rest, and who had no health insurance for him. Chino also claimed that his foreman was a "Ku Klux Klanner" and had been especially abusive to him because he was a black Puerto Rican. While recovering from the accident, Chino had become addicted to crack and ended up in the hospital as a gunshot victim before landing a job at Big Pete's crack house.

Julio's last legal job before selling crack was as an off-the-books messenger for a magazine catering to New York yuppies. He had gotten addicted to crack, began selling his household possessions, and finally was thrown out by his wife, who had just given birth to his son (the second generation "Julio Junior" to be raised on public assistance). Julio had quit his messenger job in favor of stealing car radios for a couple of hours at night in the very same neighborhoods where he had been delivering messages for ten-hour days at just above minimum wage. After a close encounter with the police, Julio begged his cousin for a job in his crack house. Ironically, the sense of responsibility, success, and prestige that selling crack provided enabled him to kick his crack habit and substitute for it a considerably less expensive powder cocaine and alcohol habit.

The underground economy is the ultimate "equal opportunity employer" for inner-city youth (cf. Kornblum and Williams, 1985). As Mike Davis has noted for Los Angeles, the structural economic incentive to participate in the drug economy is overwhelming: "With 78,000 unemployed youth in the Watts-Willowbrook area, it is not surprising that the jobless resort to the opportunities of the burgeoning 'crack economy' or that there are now 145 branches of the rival Crips and Bloods gangs in south-central L.A." (Davis, 1987: 75). In fact, what *is* surprising is how few inner-city youths become active in the underground economy; most still enter the legal economy and accept low-wage jobs.

In contrast, individuals who "successfully" pursue careers in the "crack economy" or any other facet of the underground economy are no longer "exploitable" by legal society. They speak with anger at their former low wages and bad treatment. They make fun of friends and acquaintances – many of whom come to buy drugs from them – who are still employed in factories, in service jobs, or in what they (and most other people) would call "shitwork." Of course, many others are less self-conscious about the reasons for their rejection of entry-level, mainstream employment. Instead, they internalize societal stereotypes and think of themselves as lazy and irresponsible, quitting their jobs to have a good time on the street. Many still pay lip service to the value of a steady, legal job. Still others cycle in and out of legal employment, supplementing their entry-level jobs with part-time crack sales in a paradoxical subsidy of the low wages of the legal economy by the illegal economy.

The Culture of Terror in the Underground Economy

The culture of resistance and the underground economy that have emerged in opposition to demeaning, underpaid employment in the mainstream economy often engender violence. Anthropologist Michael Taussig (1984: 492) has shown that in the South American context of extreme political repression and racism against Amerindians and Jews, "cultures of terror" emerge to become "a high-powered tool for domination and a principle medium for political practice." But unlike the Putumayo massacres in the early twentieth century and the Argentine torture chambers of the 1970s, which Taussig writes about, domination in the inner city's culture of terror is self-administered, even if the root causes are generated externally. With the exception of the occasional brutal policeman or the bureaucratized repression of the social welfare and criminal justice institutions, the physical violence and terror of the inner city are carried out largely by inner-city residents themselves.

Regular displays of violence are necessary for success in the underground economy – especially the street-level, drug-dealing world of crack. Violence is essential for maintaining credibility and for preventing rip-offs by colleagues, customers, and holdup artists. Indeed, as I learned the hard way in my fieldwork, upward mobility in the crack sector of the underground economy requires a systematic and effective use of violence against one's colleagues, one's neighbors, and to a certain extent, oneself. Behavior that appears irrationally violent and self-destructive to middle-class (or working-class) outside observers can be more accurately interpreted according to the logic of the underground economy as judicious public relations, advertising, rapport building, and long-term investment in one's "human capital."

This can be seen very clearly in the fieldwork summary at the beginning of this chapter. Gato and I were mugged because Gato had a reputation for being "soft" or "pussy" and because I was publicly unmasked as *not being* an undercover cop and hence safe to attack. Gato had tried to minimize the damage to his future ability to sell on that corner by not turning and running. He had pranced sideways down the street while being beaten with a baseball bat and kicked to the ground twice. Nevertheless, the admonishments of his cousin, the female coke mainliner to whom he told the story, could not have been clearer: where was he going to work after such a public fiasco? Significantly, I found out later that this was the second time this had happened to Gato this year. Gato was not going to be upwardly mobile in the underground economy because of his "pussy" reputation; he was simply not as effectively violent as his "chosen" occupation required. One's "street rep" is as valuable an asset in the world of crack dealers as professional reputations are among stockbrokers, physicians, and business people.

Employers or new entrepreneurs in the underground economy look for people who can demonstrate their capacity for effective violence and thus terror. This is clearly illustrated by Big Pete's hiring of Jackie to sell cocaine at his candy store shortly after he witnessed her shooting Papito, her husband (his cousin). Similarly, Marco, another one of Big Pete's primary street-level sellers, had a "bionic leg." He had been shot through the thigh in a previous crack confrontation ("when I thought I was Superman") by a "dum dum" bullet. His leg had been rebuilt, leaving him with a pronounced limp but quick coordination. He frequently referred to his rebuilt limb in conversation; it was a source of pride and credibility for him. He was considered an effective crack dealer.

For Big Pete, the owner of a string of crack and cocaine franchises, the ability of his employees to hold up under gunpoint was crucial because stickups of dealing dens are not infrequent. In fact, during the first thirteen months of my fieldwork, the botanica was held up twice. Julio happened to be on duty both times. He admitted to me that he had been very nervous when they held the gun to his temple and asked for money and crack. Nevertheless, not only did he withhold some of the money and crack that was hidden behind bogus botanica merchandise, but he also later exaggerated to Big Pete the amount that had been stolen in order to pocket the difference. The possibility of being held up was constantly on Julio's mind. Several times when more than two people walked into the botanica at once, Julio stiffened as if expecting them to pull out weapons. On another occasion, he confided to me that he was nervous about a cousin of his who all of a sudden had started hanging out at the crack house/botanica, feigning friendship. Julio suspected him of casing the joint for a future stickup.

In several long conversations with active criminals (a dealing den stickup artist, several crack dealers, and a former bank robber), I asked them to explain how they were able to trust their partners in crime sufficiently to ensure the longevity and effectiveness of their enterprise. To my surprise, I was not given righteous raps about blood brotherhood trustworthiness or boyhood loyalty. Instead, in each case, in slightly different language, I was told somewhat aggressively, "What do you mean how do I trust him? You should ask, 'How can he trust me?!'" In each case, their point was unmistakable: *their own ruthlessness is their only real security* (e.g., "My support network is me, myself, and I"). The vehemence with which they made these assertions suggests that they felt threatened by the idea that their security and success might depend upon the trustworthiness of a partner or employee. They were claiming – in one case angrily – that they were not dependent upon trust because they were tough enough to command respect, willing to engage in enough violence to enforce all contracts they entered into.

For example, at the end of the summer, Chino was forced to flee out of state to a cousin's because his own cocaine use had gotten sufficiently out of hand that he snorted merchandise he was supposed to sell. When he was unable to turn in the night's receipts to Big Pete, he left town, certain that a violent reprisal was coming. In the same way, my own failure to display a propensity for violence in several instances cost me the respect of the members of the crack scene that I frequented. This was very evident when I turned down Julio and Chino's offer to chase down the three men who mugged Gato and me. Julio despaired that I "still [thought] like a blanquito" and was genuinely disappointed in my lack of common sense and self-respect.

These concrete examples of the need to cultivate a public reputation for violence are extreme but common among the individuals who rely on the underground economy for their income. Their survival and success are dependent upon their capacity for terror. Individuals involved in street crack sales and other sectors of the underground economy cannot turn to lawful means for conflict resolution and so cultivate the culture of terror in order to intimidate competitors, maintain credibility, develop new contacts, cement partnerships, and ultimately have a good time. For the most part, they are not conscious of this process; the culture of terror has become a myth replete with a set of roles, rules, and satisfactions all its own.[5]

Significantly, the pervasiveness of the inner-city culture of terror does not apply solely to crack sellers or to street criminals; to a certain extent, all individuals living in the neighborhood who want to maintain a sense of autonomy (*i.e.*, who do not want to have to rush out of their houses during daylight hours only or quadruple lock their doors at sunset) find it useful to participate to some limited extent in some corner of the culture of terror. In this manner, the culture of terror seeps into the fabric of the inner city, impinging upon its residents – including the majority of the population who work nine to five plus overtime in mainstream jobs just above poverty-level wages.

A powerful ideological dynamic, therefore, poisons interpersonal relations throughout much of the community by legitimizing violence and mandating distrust. On a more obvious level, the culture of terror is experienced physically by anyone who spends time on the street. All who frequent the streets will be exposed to the violence of the underground economy even if they do not participate in it. For example, during just the first thirteen months of my residence in Spanish Harlem, I witnessed a series of violent events: (1) a deadly shooting of the mother of a three-year-old child outside my window by an assailant wielding a sawed-off shotgun (the day before the victim had slashed her future murderer with a razor blade when he complained about the quality of the $5 vials of crack that she sold); (2) a bombing and a machine gunning of a numbers joint by a rival faction of the local "mafia," once again within view of my apartment window; (3) a shoot-out and police car chase scene in front of a pizza parlor where I happened to be eating a snack; (4) the firebombing of a heroin house by an unpaid supplier around the block from where I lived; (5) a dozen screaming, clothes-ripping, punching fights; (6) at least bi-weekly sightings of an intravenous drug-using mother with visible needle "tracks" on her arms walking down the street with a toddler by her side, or a pregnant woman entering and leaving a crack house; (7) almost daily exposure to broken-down human beings, some of them in fits of crack-induced paranoia, some suffering from delirium tremens, and others in unidentifiable pathological fits, screaming and shouting insults to all around them.

Of course, as a street fieldworker, I was looking for these events. They are not, strictly speaking, random samples of inner-city experience. Had I been a typical Spanish Harlem resident intent upon making it on time to my nine to five job every morning, I would not have noticed at least half of these events, and I would not have had the time or the interest to find out the details on most of the other half. I surely would not have paid any attention to the broken-down human beings walking the streets, begging change, and mumbling or shouting to themselves. Nevertheless, these examples do not include the dozens of additional stories of accounts of killings and beatings told to me by eyewitnesses and sometimes even by family members and children of the victims or the perpetrators.

Perhaps the most poignant expression of the pervasiveness of the culture of terror was the comment made to me by a thirteen-year-old boy in the course of an otherwise innocuous, random conversation about how he was doing in school and how his mother's pregnancy was going. He told me he hoped his mother would give birth to a boy "because girls are too easy to rape." He was both sad and bragging when he said this, matter-of-factly asserting his adulthood and "realistic" knowledge of the mythical level of terror on the street where he was growing up.

In order to interact with people on the street, one has to participate at least passively in this culture of destruction and terror. Small children already talk about it in grade school. I overheard the story of a boy whose mother told him never to fight. Not long into the school year a classmate mugged him of his mid-afternoon snack and pocket money. By not fighting back, according to his mother's dictates, the child quickly developed a "pussy" reputation. During the ensuing weeks, he lost his snack and money every single day until finally, when he complained to his mother, she berated him, "What's the matter with you? Can't you fight back?"

The Horatio Alger Myth Revisited

It is important to understand that the underground economy and the violence emerging out of it are not propelled by an irrational cultural logic distinct from that of mainstream America. On the contrary, *street participants are frantically pursuing the American Dream.* The assertions of the culture-of-poverty theorists that the poor have been badly socialized and do not share mainstream values is simply wrong. In fact, ambitious, energetic inner-city youths are attracted to the underground economy precisely *because* they believe in Horatio Alger's version of the American Dream. They are, in true American fashion, frantically trying to get their piece of the pie as fast as possible. In fact, they often follow the traditional U.S. model for upward mobility to the letter: aggressively setting themselves up as private entrepreneurs. They are the ultimate "rugged individualists," braving an unpredictable free-market frontier where fortune, fame, and destruction are all just around the corner.

Hence Indio, a particularly enterprising and ambitious young crack dealer who was aggressively carving out a new sales point, shot his brother in the spine and paralyzed him for life while he was high on angel dust in a battle over sales rights. His brother now works for him, selling on crutches. Meanwhile, the shooting has cemented Indio's street reputation, and his workers are awesomely disciplined: "If he shot his brother, he'll shoot anyone."

For many of the people I met, the underground economy and the culture of terror are seen as the most *realistic* routes to upward mobility. Contrary to the pious preachments of politicians and the privileged, who claim that with hard work anyone can make it in America, they know from their own lived experience that "straight" entry-level jobs are not viable channels to upward mobility, especially for high school dropouts. Drug selling or other illegal activity appears as the most effective and rational option for getting rich within one's lifetime.

Many of the street dealers are strictly utilitarian in their involvement with crack, and they snub their clients despite the fact that they usually ingest considerable amounts of alcohol and powder cocaine themselves. They refer to their merchandise as "this garbage" and often openly make fun of crack heads as they arrive "on a mission" to "see Scotty"[6] with fistfuls of money. Sometimes they even ask their "respectable looking" clients with incredulity, "You don't do this shit do you?" Chino used to chant at his regular customers "Come on, keep on killing yourself; bring me that money; smoke yourself to death; make me rich." On another occasion, I witnessed an argument between a crack seller and two young men who were drug-free and virulently opposed to the underground economy. The crack seller essentially won the argument by deriding the drug-free young men for missing out on a smart, easy opportunity to make good money.

The Search for Dignity

Even though the average street seller is employed by the owner of a sales point for whom he has to maintain regular hours, meet sales quotas, and be subject to being fired, the street seller has a great deal of autonomy and power in his daily (or nightly) schedule. His boss comes only once or twice a shift to drop off drugs and pick up money. Frequently, a young messenger is sent instead. Sellers are often surrounded by a bevy of "thirsty" friends and hangers-on – often young teenage women in the case of male sellers – willing to run errands, pay attention to conversations, give support in arguments and fights, and provide sexual favors because of the relatively large amounts of money and drugs passing through their hands. In fact, even youths who do not use drugs will hang out and attempt respectfully to befriend the dealer just to be privy to the excitement of people coming and going, copping and hanging; money flowing, arguments, detectives, and stick-up artists – all around danger and excitement. Other nonusers will hang out to be treated to an occasional round of beer, Bacardi, or on an off night, Thunderbird. Crack dealers attain "status" on the street that they would be hard-pressed to find in any "legit" job open to them.

The channel into the underground economy is by no means strictly economic. Besides wanting to earn "crazy money," people choose "hoodlum" status in order to assert their dignity by refusing to "sling a mop for the white man" for "chump change" (cf. Anderson, 1976: 68). Employment – or better yet, self-employment – in the underground economy accords a sense of autonomy, self-worth, and an opportunity for extraordinarily rapid, short-term upward mobility that is only too obviously unavailable in entry-level jobs in the licit economy. To be able to live opulently without "visible means of support" – like, say, the "idle rich" in the Hamptons – is considered the ultimate expression of success for many Americans. For residents of Spanish Harlem, however, this is a viable option only in the underground economy. The proof of this is visible to everyone on the street as they watch teenage crack dealers drive by in convertible Suzuki Samurai jeeps with the stereo blaring, "beam" by in impeccable BMWs, or – in the case of the middle-aged dealers – glide along in well-waxed Lincoln Continentals. Nor are these material achievements unimaginable, for anyone can aspire to be promoted to the level of seller, perched on a twenty-speed mountain bike with a beeper on one's belt. In fact, many youths not particularly active in the drug trade run around with beepers on their belts just pretending to be "big time." It is no coincidence that Julio was able to quit crack only after getting a job selling it.

The feelings of self-actualization and self-respect that the dealer's lifestyle offers cannot be underestimated. A former manager of a coke-shooting gallery who had employed a network of a half-dozen sellers, lookouts, and security guards and who had grossed $7000–$13,000 per week for over a year before being jailed explained to me that the best memories of his drug-dealing days were of the respect he received from people on the street. He described how, when he drove up in one of his cars to pick up the day's receipts, a bevy of attentive men and women would run to open the door for him and engage him in polite small talk, not unlike what happens in many licit businesses when the boss arrives. Others would offer to clean his car. He said that even the children hanging out in the street who were too young to understand what his dealings involved looked up to him in awe. He would invite a half-dozen friends and acquaintances out to dinner in expensive restaurants almost every night.

He also noted that his shooting gallery had enabled his wife and two children to get off welfare. Accepting welfare as an adult head of household had been particularly humiliating for him. Significantly, after coming out of jail, he had been unable to reunite with his wife and children, who were living at his wife's mother's apartment. His mother-in-law would not let him in the house, and his new legit job as a messenger for a Wall Street brokerage firm paid far too little for him to afford an apartment of his own for his family. Consequently, he roomed illegally in the apartment of a woman with two children supported by public assistance who took in boarders to supplement her income off the record. He was determined not to reenter the underground economy for fear of being detected by his parole officer and sent back to jail.

Conjugated Oppression

The dynamism of the multibillion-dollar underground economy, the rejection of demeaning exploitation in the mainstream economy, and the dignity offered by illegal entrepreneurial activity explain only a portion of the violence and substance abuse in the inner city. They do not account for the explosive appeal of a drug like crack. It is necessary to examine the structural dynamic of the inner-city experience on a deeper level to explain why so many people would be so attracted to crack today (or heroin only a half-dozen years ago). This involves the conflation of ethnic discrimination with a rigidly segmented labor market, and all the hidden injuries to human dignity that this entails, especially in a place like New York City. It involves, in other words, the experience of many forms of oppression at once, or what I call "conjugated oppression" (cf. Bourgois, 1988, 1989).

A casual, random stroll through Spanish Harlem will expose one to cohorts of emaciated coke and crack addicts. Many will be begging for their next vial; others will be "petro" – crashing from the high and intensely paranoid of everyone around them – shivering, mumbling to themselves in agitated angst with their eyes wide and jaws tense. If the stroller should happen upon a "copping corner," it will look like a street fair, especially late at night – cars driving by, people coming and going, building doors opening and closing, people hanging out all over. Most likely, a hail of whistles and shouts will accompany the stroller's arrival as the lookouts warn the "pitchers" who carry the drugs that a potential undercover has entered the scene.

Conjugated oppression consists of an ideological dynamic of ethnic discrimination that interacts explosively with an economic dynamic of class exploitation to produce an overwhelming experience of oppression that is more than the sum of the parts. It offers insight into why hordes of "petro" crack heads, teenagers and grandparents alike, will continue to fry their brains and burn up their bodies in a hysteria of ecstatic substance abuse. It helps explain why the former heroin mainliners turned coke shooters continue poking their veins into abscesses while sharing HIV-infected needles.

In the Puerto Rican community, there is the added problem of confused and frustrated national identity due to the ambiguous "colonial/commonwealth" status of their homeland (even if they are third generation born on the mainland). When they venture out of El Barrio through the streets of Manhattan, they are confronted everywhere by a rigidly segmented ethnic/occupational hierarchy. In fact, it could be argued that Manhattan sports a de facto apartheid labor market, because a close look at the minute differences in job categories and prestige shows that they generally correlate with ethnicity.

Furthermore, in New York City, the insult of working for entry-level wages amidst extraordinary opulence is especially painful for Spanish Harlem youths who have been raised in abject poverty only a few blocks from all-white neighborhoods commanding some of the highest real estate values in the world. As messengers, security guards, or Xerox machine operators in the corporate headquarters of the Fortune 500 companies, they are brusquely ordered about by young white executives who often make as much in a month as they do in a year and who do not even have the time to notice that they are being rude.

Confronting Manhattan's ethnic/occupational hierarchy drives the inner-city youths depicted in this chapter deeper into the confines of their segregated neighborhood and the underground economy. They prefer to seek out meaning and upward mobility in a context that not only values their skills, but does not constantly oblige them to come into contact with people of a different, hostile ethnicity wielding arbitrary power over them. In the underground economy, especially in the world of substance abuse, they never have to experience the silent, subtle humiliations to which they are routinely subjected in the entry-level labor market or even during a mere subway ride downtown.

In this context, the fleeting relief offered by the crack high and the meaning provided by the rituals and struggles around purchasing and using the drug resemble millenarian religions. Such religious cults have swept colonized peoples attempting to resist oppression in the context of accelerated social trauma – whether it be the Ghost Dance of the Great Plains Amerindians, the "cargo cults" of Melanesia, the Mamachi movement of the Guaymi Amerindians in Panama, or even religions such as Farrakhan's Nation of Islam and the Jehovah's Witnesses in the heart of the inner city (cf. Bourgois, 1986, 1989). Substance abuse in general and crack in particular offer an inverted equivalent to the purification of a millenarian metamorphosis. Users are instantaneously transformed from unemployed, depressed high school dropouts, despised by the world – and secretly convinced that their failure is due to their own inherent stupidity, "racial laziness," and disorganization – into masses of heart-palpitating pleasure, followed only minutes later by a jaw-gnashing crash and wide awake alertness that fills their life with concrete and compelling purpose: get more crack – fast!

Notes

This is an abbreviated and revised version of an article originally published in *Contemporary Drug Problems* (volume 16, 1989). Another article with a similar theme was published in *Anthropology Today* (volume 5, number 4, 1989).

1   A bodega is a small grocery store.
2   All the names have been changed, as have some of the descriptions of settings, to protect confidentiality. This research was undertaken with the cooperation of the individuals

appearing in the chapter. Several of them read – or were read – earlier drafts and provided useful critical comments. I thank them for their help and understanding.

3 A botanica is an herbal pharmacy and utility store for religious objects used in santeria.

4 Fieldwork for this research during the 1985–90 period was funded by the Wenner-Gren Foundation for Anthropological Research, the U.S. Bureau of the Census, two Washington University junior faculty summer research grants, lottery funds, an Affirmative Action grant from San Francisco State University, the Committees for Research on the Urban Underclass and for Public Policy Research on Contemporary Hispanic Issues, the Harry Frank Guggenheim Foundation, and the National Institute on Drug Abuse. Any errors of interpretation are, of course, my responsibility.

5 For an ethnopsychological perspective on the logic of violence among Chicano youth gang members in Southern California, see Vigil, 1988.

6 A code language around the television series *Star Trek* has emerged among crack users in New York City (as in "Beam me up, Scotty" for getting high).

References

Anderson, Elijah. *A Place on the Corner.* Chicago: University of Chicago Press, 1976.

Bourgois, Philippe. "The Miskitu of Nicaragua: Politicized Ethnicity." *Anthropology Today* 2: 4–9 (1986).

—— "Conjugated Oppression: Class and Ethnicity Among Guaymi and Kuna Banana Workers." *American Ethnologist* 15: 328–48 (1988).

—— *Ethnicity at Work: Divided Labor on a Central American Banana Plantation.* Baltimore: Johns Hopkins University Press, 1989.

—— "From Jibaro to Crack Dealer: Confronting the Restructuring of Capitalism in Spanish Harlem," in Jane Schneider and Rayna Rapp, eds., *Articulating Hidden Histories.* Pp. 125–41. Berkeley: University of California Press, 1992.

—— *In Search of Respect: Selling Crack in El Barrio.* Cambridge, England: Cambridge University Press, 1995.

Bowles, Samuel, and Herbert Gintis. *Schooling in Capitalist America.* New York: Basic Books, 1977.

Davis, Mike. "Chinatown, Part Two? The 'Internationalization' of Downtown Los Angeles." *New Left Review* 164. ᴜᴜ–86 (1987).

Eames, Edwin, and Judith Goode. "The Culture of Poverty: A Misapplication of Anthropology to Contemporary Issues," in George Gmelch and Walter Zenner, eds., *Urban Life: Readings in Urban Anthropology.* Pp. 320–33. Prospect Heights, IL: Waveland Press, 1980.

Foley, Doug. *Learning Capitalist Culture.* Philadelphia: University of Pennsylvania Press, 1990.

Fordham, Signithia. "Racelessness as a Factor in Black Students' School Success: Pragmatic Strategy or Pyrrhic Victory?" *Harvard Educational Review* 58: 54–84 (1988).

Giroux, Henry. "Theories of Reproduction and Resistance in the New Sociology of Education: A Critical Analysis. *Harvard Educational Review* 53: 257–93 (1983).

Harrison, Faye. "Introduction: An African Diaspora Perspective for Urban Anthropology." *Urban Anthropology* 17: 111–41 (1988).

Kornblum, William, and Terry Williams. *Growing Up Poor.* Lexington MA: Lexington Books, 1985.

Leacock, Eleanor Burke, ed. *The Culture of Poverty: A Critique.* New York: Simon and Schuster, 1971.

Lewis, Oscar. "The Culture of Poverty," in *Anthropological Essays.* Pp 67–80. New York: Random House, 1966.

Macleod, Jay. *Ain't No Makin' It.* Boulder, CO: Westview Press, 1987.

Maxwell, Andrew. "The Anthropology of Poverty in Black Communities: A Critique and Systems Alternative." *Urban Anthropology* 17: 171–91 (1988).

Ryan, William. "Blaming the Victim," in Kurt Finsterbusch and George McKenna, eds., *Taking Sides: Clashing Views on Controversial Social Issues.* Pp. 45–52. Guilford, CT: Dushkin Publishing Group, 1986.

Sassen-Koob, Saskia. "New York City: Economic Restructuring and Immigration." *Development and Change* 17: 87–119 (1986).

Stack, Carol. *All Our Kin: Strategies for Survival in a Black Community.* New York: Harper & Row, 1974.

Steinberg, Stephen. *The Ethnic Myth: Race, Ethnicity, and Class in America.* New York: Atheneum, 1981.

Tabb, William, and Larry Sawers, eds. *Marxism and the Metropolis: New Perspectives in Urban Political Economy.* New York: Oxford University Press, 1984.

Taussig, Michael. "Culture of Terror – Space of Death, Roger Casement's Putumayo Report and the Explanation of Torture." *Comparative Studies in Society and History* 26: 467–97 (1984).

Valentine, Bettylou. *Hustling and Other Hard Work.* New York: Free Press, 1978.

Valentine, Charles. *Culture and Poverty.* Chicago: University of Chicago Press, 1968.

Vigil, James Diego. "Group Processes and Street Identity: Adolescent Chicano Gang Members." *Ethos* 16: 421–45 (1988).

Waxman, Chaim. *The Stigma of Poverty: A Critique of Poverty Theories and Policies.* New York: Pergamon, 1977.

Willis, Paul. *Learning To Labor: How Working Class Kids Get Working Class Jobs.* Aldershot, England: Gower, 1977.

—— "Cultural Production and Theories of Reproduction," in Len Barton and Stephen Walker, eds., *Race, Class and Education.* Pp. 107–38. London: Croom-Helm, 1983.

Wilson, William J. *The Declining Significance of Race.* Chicago: University of Chicago Press, 1978.

—— *The Truly Disadvantaged: The Inner City, the Underclass, and Public Policy.* Chicago: University of Chicago Press, 1987.

Zweigenhaft, Richard L., and G. William Domhoff. *Blacks in the White Establishment: A Study of Race and Class in America.* New Haven, CT: Yale University Press, 1991.

Part IV

Conversation and Discourse Analysis

INTRODUCTION TO PART IV

The study of language has always occupied a central position within the sciences of meaning and human practice. For many it was language that decisively distinguished humanity from the animal kingdom and thereby set the primordial boundaries for the subject matter of the human sciences. Due to the definitive importance that was placed on language, comparative linguistics emerged early on as the very foundation of comparative ethnology. Early research sought to classify languages and dialects and to link their variations to the environmental factors that might explain them. Analytic challenges attendant to distinguishing dialects eventually gave rise to a conceptual fission between phonetics (or the study of the spoken sounds that demarcate different languages and dialects) and phonemics (or the study of how spoken sounds are perceived by language users as features of meaningful utterances). With the rise of Ferdinand de Saussure's structural semiology, phonemic studies of comparative grammar and language usage deposed and encompassed regard for the sonic characteristics of speech itself.

Saussurian structuralists held that speech was impossible if it did implicitly rely on preexisting, and relatively stable, systems of signs. The work of linguistics was thus construed as the investigation of empirical instances of language use for what they revealed about the general structure of the sign system they instantiated. This approach to analysis dominated not only the study of language but the study of culture more generally well through the mid-twentieth century. Saussure's ideas were picked up by legions of social scientists including such profoundly influential figures as Claude Lévi-Strauss, Roland Barthes, Talcott Parsons, and Clifford Geertz. However, beginning in the 1950s, structuralism suffered some rather crippling defeats. By demonstrating acute problems in structuralist accounts of language *acquisition*, Noam Chomsky, and other proponents of his theory of generative grammar, were instrumental in dethroning structuralism. But due to its focus on *innate* linguistic faculties, social scientists did not find the theory of generative grammar especially useful and it was never widely appropriated by social scientists. Social scientists dissatisfied with the serious limitations of structuralist accounts of language have looked elsewhere for analytic inspiration.

During the sixties, innovators in linguistics, anthropology, and sociology like William Labov, John Gumperz, Dell Hymes, Harvey Sacks, Emanuel Schegloff, Gail Jefferson and others showed that the investigation of naturally occurring instances of talk reveals a subtle orderliness to language use that stems neither from fixed sign systems nor innate human faculties. This research demonstrated that language use is *interactively* organized with respect to the specific practical activities that engage participants in conversation. For instance, partners in conversation exhibit nuanced abilities to collaborate in securing and reformulating the *topic* of conversation as conversation unfolds. Hence, "the context" of talk is something that is not only mutable, but also subject to ongoing negotiation by parties to conversations themselves. By changing the topic from work to sports, for example, co-workers may change the frame of their interaction from one which quite likely implicates their status as co-workers and the more general context of their work relationship to a frame that renders the work context quite irrelevant. Moreover, it is precisely by tracking each other's discursive movements in this regard that people discern the meaning in each other's talk. By empirically demonstrating that the achievement of inter-subjective meaning is context dependent, and that the context of talk is not fixed but specified and respecified over the temporal course of talk, conversation and discourse analysts have profoundly humbled the prospects of any theorist who would hope to explain language use exclusively with respect to invariant sign systems or innate human faculties.

In addition to demonstrating the fundamentally negotiated nature of inter-subjective meaning, conversation and discourse analysts have also doggedly insisted that language use be analyzed as social *action*. Language use cannot be grasped without reference to the forms of life within which it participates, and likewise those forms of life must inevitably bend to the practical demands that the use of language itself exerts. This understanding of language use as social action puts conversation and discourse analysts in company with the likes of linguistic philosophers Ludwig Wittgenstein, John Austin, John Searle, and Paul Grice. However, in contrast to the philosophers, conversation and discourse analysts insist that analysis be confined to instances of naturally occurring talk-in-interaction. Conversation and discourse analysts are resolutely empirical in their styles of work, and generally eschew even the mnemonic reproduction of talk in ethnographic fieldnotes for its corruption of talk's details as originally produced. For this reason, one of the defining characteristics of this approach to analysis is its nearly exclusive reliance on data captured in the form of audio and video tape recordings.

In the first essay, "Activity Types and Language," Stephen Levinson defends Wittgenstein's view that the *meaning* of linguistic utterances must always be understood with respect to the concrete practicalities of language *usage*. To do so he introduces the term *activity type*, which he defines as follows, "any culturally recognized activity, whether or not that activity is co-extensive with a period of speech or indeed whether any talk takes place in it at all ... I take the notion of activity type to refer to a fuzzy category whose focal members are goal-defined, socially constituted, bounded, events with *constraints* on participants, settings, and so on, but above all on the kinds of allowable contributions" (p. 368). Activity types are, then, socially organized occasions of talk which exercise constraints on who is entitled to speak and how they are entitled to speak. The point of Levinson's discussion is to critique speech act theorists who would presume to explain the meaning and practical consequences of certain kinds of utterances *in vacuo*, or without reference to the practical activity within which that utterance is made. Through demonstrations of the various speech activities that can be accomplished through the use of questions, Levinson makes a powerful case against speech act theory and for what he calls "a thorough-going pragmatic theory" (p. 366) of meaning and linguistic activity.

In his essay, "Reflections on Talk and Social Structure," Emanuel Schegloff describes how an analyst of conversational materials might address the prospective relevance of "social structure" to talk-in-interaction. In this essay, Schegloff seeks "to formulate and explore the challenges faced by those attracted to the interaction/social structure nexus" (p. 48) and suggests,

A solution must be found to the analytic problems which obstruct the conversion of intuition, casual (however well informed) observation, or theoretically motivated observation into demonstrable analysis. For without solutions to these problems, we are left with "a *sense* of how the world works," but without its detailed explication. (p. 48)

If we hope to *analyze* data comprised of talk-in-interaction, rather than extrapolate theories drawn from other sorts of data to talk-in-interaction, we must remain cognizant of three specific issues: the problem of relevance, the issue of procedural consequentiality, and the competing attentional and analytic claims of conversational structures and social structures respectively. The problem of relevance is to show that parties to a conversation are themselves, at the moment under investigation, somehow oriented to features of their identities and environments that the analyst would hope to invoke to explain their conversation. The issue of procedural consequentiality refers to the challenge of showing that beyond being oriented to particular features of their identities and environments, people's orientations in this regard actually influenced the course of their interaction. The last issue refers to the potential eclipse of insights regarding the nature of talk-in-interaction that may arise from too quickly extrapolating analyses from distributional, institutional, or social structures of the traditional sort. Beyond limiting our understanding of talk-in-interaction, such foreclosure on conversation analysis (CA) itself may in the long run harm the social sciences generally,

> one might argue that the study of talk should be allowed to proceed under its own imperatives, with the hope that its results will provide more effective tools for the analysis of distributional, institutional, and social-structural problems later on than would be the case if the analysis of talk had, from the outset, to be made answerable to problems extrinsic to it. (p. 64)

As Schegloff argues, it is entirely inappropriate to require of conversation analysts that they license their research with respect to theoretical interests other than the explication of talk-in-interaction. What social scientist could suggest that fathoming the anatomy of human verbal communication is not more than warrant enough for this line of scientific inquiry? However, one should by no means surmise from this insistence on analytic autonomy that CA has nothing to contribute to social theory's classic concerns. In his essay, J. Maxwell Atkinson turns the analytic resources of CA on a topic that has fascinated social scientists at least since Weber – charismatic authority. But rather than simply formulating the characteristics of the charismatic leader as a social type, Atkinson educates us as to specific empirically demonstrable practices through which charismatic oratory is accomplished. Moving beyond general and/or speculative observations, his essay is a beautifully crafted, fine-grained empirical analysis of the work of doing being a charismatic leader in the context of the public speech.

References

Levinson, Stephen C. 1979. "Activity Types and Language." *Linguistics* 17. Berlin: Mouton de Gruyter.

Schegloff, Emanuel A. 1991. "Reflections on Talk and Social Structure." In *Talk & Social Structure: Studies in Ethnomethodology and Conversation Analysis*. Edited by Deirdre Boden and Don H. Zimmerman. Berkeley: University of California Press.

Further Reading on Conversation and Discourse Analysis

Atkinson, J. Maxwell, and John Heritage, eds. 1984. *Structures of Social Action: Studies in Conversation Analysis*. Cambridge: Cambridge University Press.

Boden, Deirdre and Don H. Zimmerman, eds. 1991. *Talk and Social Structure: Studies in Ethnomethodology and Conversation Analysis*. Berkeley: University of California Press.

Bourdieu, Pierre. 1991. *Language & Symbolic Power.*, edited and introduced by John B. Thompson. Translated by Gino Raymond and Matthew Adamson. Cambridge, MA: Harvard University Press.

Drew, Paul and John Heritage, eds. 1992. *Talk at Work: Interaction in Institutional Settings*. Cambridge: Cambridge University Press.

Duranti, Allessandro and Charles Goodwin, eds. 1992. *Rethinking Context: Language as an Interactive Phenomenon*. Cambridge: Cambridge University Press.

Heritage, John. 1984. *Garfinkel and Ethnomethodology*. London: Polity Press.

Levinson, Charles C. 1983. *Pragmatics*. Cambridge: Cambridge University Press.

Sacks, Harvey. 1992. *Lectures on Conversation, volumes I & II*. Edited by Gail Jefferson. Introduced by Emanuel A. Schegloff. Oxford, UK: Blackwell.

Van Dijk, Teun A., ed. 1985. *Handbook of Discourse Analysis*. London: Academic Press
—— 1997. *Discourse Studies: a multidisciplinary introduction*. London: Sage.

12 Activity Types and Language

Stephen C. Levinson

1 Introduction

Wittgenstein in a number of places (*The Brown Book, Philosophical Investigations* I: 23) suggests that understanding a language, and by implication having a grasp of the meaning of utterances, involves knowing the nature of the activity in which the utterances play a role. This of course is part of the well-known doctrine of "language games", which by the later writings had "come to mean the study of any form of use of language against a background context of a form of life" (Kenny, 1973: 166).

Now part of what Wittgenstein was getting at has since been captured in the concept of speech acts, although there is of course considerable disagreement about how to handle speech acts theoretically. Some (Searle, for example) would try to reduce the rest of language to speech acts. Others would try to reduce speech acts to the frameworks of analysis that handle the propositional core of language (e.g. Lakoff, 1975; Lewis, 1972; Sadock, 1974). Yet others would accept a fundamental distinction between speech acts and propositional content, and apply Wittgenstein's "language games" mode of analysis only to the former (for an elegant version of such an account see Stennius, 1972). In any case the majority of linguists, and philosophers too, would reject the later Wittgenstein's reduction of meaning to usage in favour of the earlier Wittgenstein's semantical theory, complimented if needs be by a pragmatic theory of speech acts.

But there is more implied in Wittgenstein's language games analogy than can be captured in a theory of speech acts: the list of language games given by Wittgenstein in *Philosophical Investigations* includes describing objects, giving measurements, constructing an object from a measurement, telling jokes, acting plays, praying, guessing riddles, greeting and so on (see also Kenny, 1973: 165).

The intuitions that underlay Wittgenstein's emphasis on the embedding of language within human activities have not been accounted for in any modern theory of how language is used and understood. The purpose of this paper is to document from empirical materials that Wittgenstein's intuitions have a basis in fact, and moreover that his failure to make the distinction between speech acts and speech activities was not just an oversight – the two are interconnected in such fundamental ways that only a thorough-going pragmatic theory will be adequate to describe both phenomena.

To see the force of Wittgenstein's pre-occupations with the matrix activity within which language usage takes place, consider a simple case that should jog the intuitions. In a game of cricket there is a general rule of silence during play, but there are a number of distinct cries that punctuate the proceedings, for example "howzat",

"L.B.W.", "over" (there are also appreciations of play, and instructions from the captain to the team, of the sort "John, the slips"). Now it would be simply and straightforwardly impossible to describe the meaning or the function of these cries without referring to aspects of the game and their role within the game – so for example "howzat" functions as a claim directed to the umpire by one of the fielding side that one of the batsmen is "out", while "over" functions as both a statement that six turns at bowling have now transpired since the last such cry and as an instruction to reverse the direction of bowling, and so on.

The immediate reaction to such cases will no doubt be that they are exceptional, in no way typical of language usage or indeed of language, and parasitic on more ordinary uses of language. And certainly the reduction of meaning to moves within a language game is not going to provide us with any account of the key intuition that sentences have meanings partially independent (not totally of course) of the circumstances in which they are used. But holding a more conservative and traditional theory of meaning (of the sort that pairs meanings with well formed formulae, *in vacuo*) is not going to rescue us from the dilemma that many, indeed probably most, situations in which language is used have an aspect precisely similar to the cricket case. The common feature of course is the extent to which the understanding of what is said depends on understanding the "language game" in which it is embedded, over and beyond whatever meaning the words or sentences may have *in vacuo*.

As an intermediate case consider the following utterances recorded during a basketball game:

(1)   1.   A: Alright Peter.
      2.   B: Here!
      3.   C: Farewell people.
      4.   A: C'mon Peter.
      5.   B: Beautiful tip!
      6.   A: Right over here.

Now understanding these utterances seems to require two things in particular: we need to know the meaning of the words, and we need to know the kind of utterances that typically occur in such a game. It would be helpful of course to have a visual picture of the state of play at each utterance, but lacking this we can still reconstruct the probable function given the two kinds of knowledge above. So utterances 1, 2, 4 and 6 could function as claims that the speaker is in a good position to have the ball passed to him, and thus as requests to do so; while utterance 5 is an appreciation of another player's move, and 3 something more like a war-cry, a shout of defiance by the player with the ball.[1] In assigning functions to the utterances (signals to pass, exhortations, applauds and so on) we depend both on the meaning of the words which serve to differentiate the utterances, and on the possible roles that utterances can play within such a game. In this case we can see that the main reason that we have to rely on information about the game is massive ellipsis, but as we shall see this is only one source of such contextual dependence.

But before proceeding let us turn to clarify a concept that will be basic to what is to follow.

2 Activity Types

I want to introduce as a term of art the notion of an "activity type". There are various terms that are employed by sociologists and anthropologists engaged in the study of language usage which are roughly equivalent, especially "speech event" and "episode" (see e.g. Hymes, 1972; Gumperz, 1972). My notion is to be preferred for present purposes because it refers to any culturally recognized activity, whether or not that activity is coextensive with a period of speech or indeed whether any talk takes place in it at all (see Sacks, Schegloff and Jefferson, 1974 for some useful distinctions here). In particular I take the notion of an activity type to refer to a fuzzy category whose focal members are goal-defined, socially constituted, bounded, events with *constraints* on participants, setting, and so on, but above all on the kinds of allowable contributions. Paradigm examples would be teaching, a job interview, a jural interrogation, a football game, a task in a workshop, a dinner party and so on.

The category is fuzzy because (as with bad examples of the colour red – see Berlin and Kay, 1969) it is not clear whether it includes a chat (probably) or the single telling of a joke (probably not). It appeals to the intuition that social events come along a gradient formed by two polar types, the totally pre-packaged activity on the one hand (for example, a Roman Mass) and the largely unscripted event on the other (for example a chance meeting on the street). There is some (incomplete) correspondence between this gradient and another, that between the poles of a highly formal activity on the one hand and a very informal one on the other. However formality is properly described (and see here Irvine, 1978; Keenan, 1977), it certainly seems to involve greater levels of pre-planning both in action and in speech together with greater social distance between participants. The evidence for this is that style changes accordingly – for example the more elaborate higher diglossic varieties of a language with diglossia (Ferguson, 1964), or address forms conventionally implicating social distance (see Levinson, 1977) will tend to occur in formal situations. Thus my colleagues may address me as *Steve* in the common room, *Dr. Levinson* in a faculty meeting. So style or mode of address can be one index of a change of activity.

A further dimension on which activities vary clearly cross-cuts the other two: this is the degree to which speech is an integral part of each activity. On the one hand we have activities constituted entirely by talk (a telephone conversation, a lecture for example), on the other activities where talk is non-occurring or if it does occur is incidental (a game of football for instance). Somewhere in between (though this dimension of variation is not simply a linear scale like the other two) we have the placing of bets, or a Bingo session, or a visit to the grocers. And there are sometimes rather special relations between what is said and what is done, as in a sports commentary, a slide show, a cookery demonstration, a conjuror's show, and the like. Then there are the peculiarities of rituals, where words and acts are related and integrated in most complex ways (the best descriptions of exotic cases are still those of Malinowski in *Coral Gardens and Their Magic*, Volume II).[2]

There is one discipline that has set itself the task of describing the different uses to which speech is put in different activities in different societies, namely the Ethnography of Speaking as conceived originally by Hymes (1962) and exemplified by the collection of essays in Bauman and Sherzer (1974) (see also Blount and Sanches [eds], 1975). Hymes suggested eight key variables that would function as a classificatory grid for cross-cultural comparison: each activity should be described he suggests as particular constraints on setting, participants, ends (or goals) acts (including specified sequences), key (or tone), instrumentalities (the varieties of language employed, in particular), norms (concerning, for example, attenuation or interruption), and genre (poetic, mythic, prosaic etc.).

The results of such investigations are important for anyone interested in giving Wittgenstein's intuitions about "language-games" some flesh. But there is a drawback to Hymes's taxonomic approach, for not all of the variables he adduces are of equal significance or importance. I would choose to divide the pie a little differently, making a first distinction between the *structure* of the event in question, and the *style* in which it is conducted. Only the former is germane to the issues raised in this paper, and I deal with the latter elsewhere.

Elements of the structure of an activity include its subdivision into a number of sub-parts or episodes as we may call them (for example, a seminar usually involves first a presentation, followed by a discussion, while a court case is divided into a statement of the case, cross-examinations, the passing of sentence etc.), and within each any prestructured sequences that may be required by convention, the norms governing the allocation of turns at speaking, and so on. There may further be constraints on the personnel and the roles they may take, on the time and the place at which the activity can properly take place. There are also more abstract structural constraints, having to do with topical cohesion and the functional adequacy of contributions to the activity.

In general wherever possible I would like to view these structural elements as rationally and functionally adapted to the point or *goal* of the activity in question, that is the function or functions that members of the society see the activity as having. By taking this perspective it seems that in most cases apparently *ad hoc* and elaborate arrangements and constraints of very various sorts can be seen to follow from a few basic principles, in particular rational organization around a dominant goal. This analytic approach is distinct from the taxonomic and descriptive one employed in the Ethnography of Speaking. The dangers of the latter can be most clearly seen in the extreme atomism and particularism in applications to problems of second language teaching, where it is considered necessary to teach the pupil studying the foreign language in its culture each and every structural detail of some activity, even though these details are often direct and simple means of achieving the relevant goals. (See for example Munby, 1978).

But for present purposes our interest in the structure of activities can be confined to one particular important question: *in what ways do the structural properties of an activity constrain (especially the functions of) the verbal contributions that can be made towards it?* This will be one dominant theme of the succeeding discussion, and it will be useful to have a paradigm case in mind. A simple example is provided by Labov's (1972) description of the activity of "sounding" among the Black community of New York. Essentially this consists in the competitive exchange of ritual insults governed by structural constraints of two types. The first of these is that "sounds" or turns at ritually insulting should be constructed in a specific fashion which Labov (1972: 153) represents as follows:

$$T(B) \text{ is so } X \text{ that } P$$

where T is the target of the sound, normally a relative (typically the mother) of B, the addressee, X is a pejorative attribute like "fat" "poor" "dirty" etc. and P is some proposition that must when applied to T be false (otherwise the ritual insult would become a genuine insult). The second type of structural constraint governs appropriate sequencing: if A sounds on B, B should reply with a sound based on A's sound but which "tops" it (i.e. is considered more ingenious), and if possible A should then try to top that, or alternatively try another kind of sound. After each stage the audience makes a vocal assessment of the sound (ibid.: 146). So an exchange might begin as follows:

(2) A: your mother so old she got spider webs under her arms.
     C: awwww!
     B: your mother so old she fart dust.
     C: Ho lawd!

The point here is that there are strict constraints on what counts as a sound: the target should not be the addressee directly nor should the proposition describing the target be true, for example. Moreover sounds should relate to prior sounds in specific ways if they are to be positively evaluated. If these constraints are not met the activity breaks down.

3 Activity Types and Inference

One important fact about activity types then is that there are constraints on what will count as allowable contributions to them.[3] Now there is another important and related fact, in many ways the mirror image of the constraints on contributions, namely the fact that to each and every clearly demarcated activity there is a corresponding set of *inferential schemata*. These schemata are tied to (derived from, if one likes) the structural properties of the activity in question.

Let us start with some straightforward examples. As Turner (1972) has pointed out, the possible ways of starting an activity are contingent, on aspects of its structural organization. So an utterance like:

(3) It's five past twelve.

can serve to start proceedings just in case the activity is scheduled to begin by then and all necessary personnel are present. Notice that if the activity was a university lecture then (3) could only function as the initial utterance of the activity if it was uttered by the lecturer (or his introducer if he was a visitor), who we can designate the "pivotal person" in this activity; in addition there would have to be at least some partial complement of listeners. Now contrast:

(4) We seem to all be here.

which could only serve to initiate a different kind of activity, namely one in which a full complement of persons is required (for example, a committee meeting). Now as

Turner points out, if activities were bounded by silence there would be no problem: the first turn at talking would initiate the proceedings. But such is not the case; normally there is talk of another kind right up to the moment the activity begins. The problem then is to account for the fact that utterances like (3) and (4) have the FORCE of announcing the beginning of an activity, and whatever the details of the account it will clearly have to refer to the mutual knowledge among participants of the particular conditions that must be met in order for the specific activity to begin. Exactly the same sort of remarks of course can be made about ways of terminating a given activity. The following three utterances could function as ways of ending a seminar, a lecture and a committee meeting respectively:

(5) It's one o'clock.
(6) Next week I'll be looking at another approach to the same problem.
(7) Jim's got to go.

These examples are both like and unlike the initial and terminal whistles in a soccer game; they are alike because they have the same sort of force, and they are unlike in that they do so via referring to the necessary pre-requisites of the activity in question, thereby making a knowledge of those pre-requisites essential for the understanding of their function.

Now let us consider an example of a slightly different kind, that can be found in the following exchange recorded in a grocer's shop (where S is the shop-assistant and C the customer):

(8) S: (to last customer): Bub-bye.
    C: Some apples please. Just help myself is that alright?
    S: Yes they're all fine.
    C: Yes they look good.
    S: // // There, that's eighteen, orright?
    C: uhuh. You've just got the one kind of lettuce?
    S: Yes. Cos.
    C: That's a nice one.
    S: Yes. They are getting proper now aren't they. Thirty six please. // // thank you very much.
    C: Thanks. Goodbye.

The utterance of interest here is C's "That's a nice one", which was accompanied by a gesture of pointing. The interesting thing is that this utterance COUNTED AS selecting a lettuce, requesting that it be wrapped, and undertaking to pay for it. As one can see there were no further negotiations about the lettuce. How did the utterance function in the way that it did? The answer is that it had the force that it had by virtue of the expectations governing the activity of shopping in small stores, here specifically the expectation that the customer will only pick out and select goods that he intends to buy. The corollary is that the shop-assistant can take any identification of a piece of merchandise as a selection with intent to purchase, unless there are contrary indications.

With these examples in mind let us turn to the theoretical implications of these observations. There are at least four main approaches to the study of inference in discourse which are worth reviewing as a background to this study. The first of these is Grice's (1975) attempt to isolate some basic background assumptions of co-operation that underlie talk across differing situations. These general assumptions are so strong that apparent violations give rise to inferences that would preserve them. Another approach, in part inspired by Grice's, has been current in linguistics, where to handle inferences to indirect illocutionery force specific rules for formulating indirect expressions of particular kinds have been proposed (see e.g. Gordon and Lakoff, 1971; Heringer, 1972; Fraser, 1975). In fact, as suggested by Searle (1975) and Brown and Levinson (1978), these specific principles can generally be reduced to Grice's more general principles. A third distinct approach is current in Artificial Intelligence, where the emphasis is on using massive amounts of detailed factual knowledge about the world as extra premises to derive inferences made in discourse (see e.g. Charniak, 1972). A problem that then has to be solved is how to bring the relevant facts in at the right moment, a solution to which seemed to be Minsky's idea of a "frame" or block of knowledge that could be called up (see articles in Schank and Nash-Webber [eds], 1975). And finally the fourth and very different approach comes from analyses of conversation by Ethno-methodologists, and especially by Sacks, Schegloff and their associates (see e.g. Turner [ed.], 1974; Schegloff, 1976; Sacks, Schegloff and Jefferson, 1974). The emphasis here is on structural information about conversational organization, and the way in which such information predisposes participants to see utterances as fulfilling certain functions by virtue of their structural location. There are inferences then from the structure of a conversation to the role that any one utterance plays within it.

I suspect that with the possible exception of the second, each of these approaches catches some aspects of the nature of inference in discourse. On methodological grounds though there are reasons to prefer the approaches favoured by Grice and Sacks and Schegloff to that favoured by workers in Artificial Intelligence. For the former focus on structural properties of talk as the source of inferences, while the latter concentrate on the substantive content of background beliefs. And there is reason to presume that such structural properties are fewer and simpler than participants' general belief and knowledge of the world, and thus both more con-ducive to study and more likely to be the sort of thing that participants have to learn initially in order to converse. (Of course there is no reason why these structural kinds of knowledge cannot be subsumed within Artificial Intelligence, and in particular the frames, approach, provided that the special role they play in inferences can be captured; but so far this has not been done.)

Let us return now to the kinds of inferences that are tied to the structural organization of particular activities. The knowledge that is required to make the appropriate inferences is clearly not provided by Grice's maxims alone, for these are (implicitly) supposed to hold across different kinds of activity. Nor is it provided by the general structural expectations that have on the whole been the focus of work by Sacks, Schegloff and their colleagues. The knowledge in question rather seems to be a distinct and further kind of structural expectation that lies behind inference in discourse. The knowledge is much more specific than the kind that Grice had in mind, but much more general than the immense array of facts that workers in Artificial Intelligence generally assume to be involved in inference.

Now there may in fact be some relation between Grice's maxims of conversation and particular expectations associated with particular activities. Grice's maxims of quality, quantity, relevance and manner are supposed to outline preconditions for the rational co-operative exchange of talk. But one thing we can observe is that not all activity types are deeply co-operative. Consider an interrogation: it is unlikely that either party assumes the other is fulfilling the maxims of quality, manner and especially quantity (requiring that one say as much as is required by the other). Inferences that in fully co-operative circumstances would go through (namely conversational implicatures) may no longer do so. Consider the following extract from Haldeman's testimony before the Senate committee that conducted the Watergate hearing (New York Times, 1973: 577):

(9)   Q: You saw all of the papers that were being reviewed, did you not?
      A: Not all the working papers of the committee. I saw the recommendations that went to the President.
      Q: Did you read the recommendations that went to the President?
      A: I am not sure I did or not. If I did it was not in any detail.

Now I take it that in more co-operative and perhaps more normal circumstances the following exchange is bizarre (or has specific implicatures different from those in (9)):

(10) A: Did you see last week's *Newsweek*?
      B: Part of it.
      A: Did you read that part of it?
      B: I'm not sure whether I did or not.

What is strange about (10) of course is that if X says he *saw* some reading matter then he generally implicates that he *read* it, the rationale for a stronger reading being that the questioner is much more likely to be interested in whether the respondent knows something about the content rather than the visual form of the reading matter, and this being mutually assumed it would be uncooperative to understand the question in the other way, so that an answer to the question can be taken to be an answer as to whether or not the respondent *read* the material in question. Hence A's second question is redundant, and thus conversationally bizarre by Grice's maxim of quantity; while B's response to the second question treats it as non-bizarre, thus doubly confusing the reader trying to understand this as an ordinary conversation.

Now the point is that strange as (10) is, it is precisely parallel to (9). So that in understanding (9) we have to cancel the implicature from X *saw* some reading matter to X *read* it. And we understand the implicature to be cancelled because given our understanding of legal enquiries we know it is often not in the interests of a defendant to co-operate beyond the minimum required to escape contempt of court.[4] In particular we know that he may try to avoid committing himself to any definite statement of fact; knowing which, the interrogator cannot be content with implicatures that can later be denied – hence he has to ask the second question, that seeks assent for the inference from *saw* to *read*. That the inference is not assented to by Haldeman is further indication of the extent to which these proceedings are more like zero-sum games than games of pure co-ordination (see Luce and Raiffa, 1957; Lewis, 1969, respectively).

The example indicates that there could be some quite interesting relations between Grice's maxims and different kinds of activities, of a sort where some of the maxims are selectively relaxed to varying degrees in activities of specific types. To take another simple, but rather extreme example consider the kind of talk that takes place in group therapy sessions. Here's an extract from Perls (1969: 189):

(11) M: I said within myself "You know, you don't matter so what are you talking to me for?" And the other one was I felt.
      F: What was the sentence "You don't matter?"
      M: I felt I didn't talk directly to you.
      F: You said some words like, "You don't matter".
      M: Yes. This is what I said to myself.
      F: I know. Can you say it again, "You don't matter?"
      M: Yes. You don't matter.
      F: Say this again.
      M: You don't matter at all.
      F: Say it again.
      M: You don't matter at all.
      F: Say it to a few more people.
      M: You don't, you don't really matter…

There are a number of features that make this very different from ordinary conversation. The repetition of "You don't matter" is a violation of the non-redundancy required by Grice's maxim of quantity. More complex is some violation of ordinary notions of relevance; for example the third utterance is in no way directly tied to the preceding query. And there seem in fact to be for such activities some rules of precedence that allow statements about feelings, especially feelings about what has been said, to supersede direct responses. In other cases the notion of relevance may be preserved intact while complex additional premises (the therapeutic theory) that are unstated link what are apparently unconnected utterances.

Now although these may be extreme examples, paler things of the same sort seem to go on in ordinary everyday activities. For example, in a casual encounter harmless simplifications may be untruths that strictly speaking violate the maxim of quality (see e.g. Sacks, 1975). And at the dinner table a question may be responded to with an unrelated "would you like some more soup". These "violations" are principled in the sense that the degree of cooperation, the ranking or precedence of topics, and so on are intrinsically related to the nature of the activity in question. Must we then reject Grice's attractive and influential theory on the grounds that it does not apply to the empirical facts about the way in which talk is organized? I think that would be hasty: it has already given us a preliminary way of talking about some of the ways in which talk is different in different activities. There are two ways in which the conflict between Grice's general principles of conversation and the particular expectations of specific activities can be reconciled. The first is to seek for a more sophisticated statement of Grice's principles that will allow differing degrees of application of each maxim and the corresponding adjustment of implicatures. The second is to accept Grice's maxims as specifications of some basic *unmarked* communication context, deviations from which however common are seen as special or *marked*. And there are various observations that suggest that the notion of basic unmarked communication context may be essential to pragmatics: for example it seems required by the facts of deixis (where the unmarked deictic centre seems to be the speaker, and his temporal-spatial location at coding time; see Fillmore, 1975), and by the way in which turn-taking is organized in conversation (where the system seems organized around or biased toward two party conversation without pre-allocation of turns – see Sacks, Schegloff and Jefferson, 1974), and by a number of other pragmatic factors. In any case more empirical work on activity types will be required to settle the issue.

Let us turn to a final issue concerning special inferences due to activity types, which was raised at the beginning of the section when we claimed that particular modes of inference were the "mirror image", as it were, of the structural constraints on each activity. What exactly is the relation between the structure of an activity and the inferences special to it? Presumably exactly the same kind of relation that holds between Grice's maxims and the inferences they generate. In that case the maxims set up specific expectations such that if they are apparently violated an inference that would preserve them is derived, and if contributions are adequate they are strongly interpreted as cooperative (the latter is the kind of inference involved in the transition from *five* to *only five* in the exchange: A: How many children does John have? B: five. See Horn, 1972).

In a similar fashion the structural properties of specific activities set up strong expectations. Because there are strict constraints on contributions to any particular activity, there are corresponding strong expectations about the functions that an utterance at a certain point in the proceedings can be fulfilling. For example in a basketball game it is understood that utterances will relate only to the game, and moreover will be restricted to a limited set of functions including for example applause/abuse, exhortations, directions positioning players, and signals to pass the ball. Given these constraints an utterance like "Here! Peter" or "Right over here" can (with appropriate prosodics) be understood best as a signal to pass the ball in the direction of the caller. The inference from the elliptical expression to the instruction or request relies on the constraints on the functions that utterances should have within that activity. Exactly the same kind of remarks hold for example (8) above, where the utterance "That's a nice one" counted as selecting a lettuce for purchase by virtue of the strong expectations about the sorts of things that utterances in such a shop are doing.[5]

4   Some Activities Where Questions Have a Focal Role

There are some activities where questions play a central role, for example an interview, a press conference, a legal case, greeting sequences, classroom teaching, seeking advice from a bureau and so on. It is worth looking at some of these activities in detail to see precisely what role questions play in each.

The focus on questions has been chosen with some design. It is possible, (but mistaken I believe), to view many other kinds of illocutionary force with their associated paradigmatic linguistic forms as having no interactional component. Austin (1962) would have disagreed of course: he stressed the role of "uptake" – the recognition by the other party of the force in question – in the felicity of illocutionary acts. For him a threat, an order, a statement, a bet made to the winds are simply defective even if other felicity conditions are met; if I bet you sixpence that I can outrun you, but you fail to hear, I cannot be said truthfully to have betted you sixpence. In any case with questions (and imperatives too of course), the case is clearer: the force of a question is (on the whole) an attempt to elicit a particular kind of answer. And a question – answer pair is an interactional sequence; such an important one in fact that it plays a special role in the ontogeny of verbal interaction (Keenan, Schieffelin and Platt, 1978) and in the organization of adult discourse (Sacks, n.d. passim; Merritt, 1976; Pope, 1975). So in the case of questions anyway the concept of illocutionary force takes us beyond the bounds of a sentential utterance into a consideration of the role that such utterances can play in a discourse.

It is worth pointing out that even the formal, that is logical, treatment of questions leads in the same direction. A simple way to treat questions logically is to think of them as open sentences, closed by an appropriate answer; so a question–answer pair can denote a truth value just like an indicative sentence, (see e.g. Hull, 1975). Alternatively one can think of them as the declarative disjunction of their possible answers (see e.g. Harrah, 1961; Belnap, 1963).[6] But if questions can only be characterized in relation to their answers, and question–answer pairs are normally distributed across parties to a conversation, then we are back to the essentially interactional nature of questions. Even if we allow that questions can be answered by their poser, we are still irrevocably beyond the sentence and involved in the characterization of sentence properties by reference to their discourse properties.

Our purpose now is to show that the discourse properties involved in the definition of a question are subject to the nature of the activities in which questions are used: in short that the role, and thus the nature, of a question is in part dependent on the matrix "language game".

By way of introduction let us consider the different roles that questions play in an exotic society – among the Gonja of West Africa as reported by E. Goody (1978). This is not simply a catalogue of all the indirect usages to which questions are put; although the interrogative form and its uses are the focus of the report, all the uses described have some family resemblance to the illocutionary force that we paradigmatically associate with questions, more so, I understand, than English questions like "can you please pass the salt". There are strong social constraints in Gonja in the use to which questions can be put in various circumstances; some of these constraints derive from the activity type in which the questions are being used, others are related more closely to the social relations between the interlocutors. Taking those uses of questions that are clearly constrained by the nature of the activity, we may note the following special uses. In greetings, questions are asked about activities and the health of relatives, but the "information that can pass is minimal, for the statement or question is standardized, as is the reply", for "in Gonja a single answer can suffice for all these salutations: awo 'it is cool'. This is the equivalent of 'all right', 'fine', 'ok'" (Goody, 1972: 47). Further examples of such special treatment of questions in greetings can be found in other societies of course – see for example Irvine (1974) on greetings among the Wolof, and Sacks (1975) on greetings between (American) English speakers.

Another special usage in Gonja is the use of rhetorical questions in court cases. An elder may say in such circumstances things like "is it one parent only who creates a child?"; this is interpreted as an attempt to establish the relevance of norms associated with co-parenthood to the judicial case in process. If other elders presiding do not think the norms referred to have relevance to this particular case, they do not answer; on the other hand if they concur with the questioner they provide an affirmative answer of the sort "no, it is not only one parent who creates the child", thereby conceding the judicial point in question (Goody, 1978: 30). There are also special uses of questions in divination, although we are not told much about them; from my own fieldwork in South India I am familiar with a system of questioning restricted to yes/no questions that could be answered by configurations in the divinatory objects, and perhaps in Gonja divination works in the same sort of way.

Other uses of questions in Gonja are more closely related to types of social relationship than to activities. Perhaps intermediate is the use of questions to express what anthropologists call a "joking relationship" as typically holds between potential affines. In Gonja, a man may say to a visiting marriageable girl things like the following:

Man: Have you prepared your trousseau yet?

Girl: How can I? You haven't given me anything towards it.

where the man's question refers to the possibility that the girl could be his next wife, and her reply jokingly "chides him for not having courted her" (Goody, 1978: 28).

Now each of these uses are understood as questions in some sense, indeed in a primary sense because the response to each is or can be an answer in logical terms. But if like Searle (1969) we hoped to capture a common feature, the illocutionary force of questioning, in terms of a set of shared felicity conditions, we should be rudely disappointed. We shall return to this point below.

I now wish to look in detail at two special uses of questions in English, and I shall try and show that the particular uses are closely tied to – indeed derived from – the overall goals of the activities in which they occur.

The following extract comes from the cross-examination of a rape victim by the defendant's lawyer in an English court of law (this and other extracts are reprinted in B. Toner, 1977: 156ff).

(12) 1. Your aim that evening then was to go to the discotheque?
2. Yes.
3. Presumably you had dressed up for that, had you?
4. Yes.
5. And you were wearing make-up?
6. Yes.
7. Eye-shadow?
8. Yes.
9. Lipstick?
10. No I was not wearing lipstick.
11. You weren't wearing lipstick?
12. No.
13. Just eye-shadow, eye make-up?
14. Yes.
15. And powder presumably?
16. Foundation cream, yes.
17. You had had bronchitis had you not?

18. Yes.
19. You have mentioned in the course of your evidence about wearing a coat?
20. Yes.
21. It was not really a coat at all, was it?
22. Well, it is sort of a coat-dress and I bought it with trousers, as a trouser suit.
23. That is it down there isn't it, the red one?
24. Yes.
25. If we call that a dress, if we call that a dress you had no coat on at all had you?
26. No.
27. And this is January. It was quite a cold night?
28. Yes it was cold actually.

Now this is a dialogue constructed of questions and answers. Our initial question is: what exactly are the nature of these questions? An immediate puzzlement is that many, in fact most, of these questions request details that are already known to the questioner. This is clearer perhaps in the second extract:

(13) 1. ... you have had sexual intercourse on a previous occasion haven't you?
      2. Yes.
      3. On many previous occasions?
      4. Not many.
      5. Several?
      6. Yes.
      7. With several men?
      8. No.
      9. Just one.
      10. Two.
      11. Two. And you are seventeen and a half?
      12. Yes.

Here the girl's age is asked, even though the basic facts of the case including this one would be known to all parties. The point of the question is not to learn something from the answer, although it is in part to obtain the answer, to get the witness to state the answer. What can be the point of getting the witness to state what is already known to all present? It could be to obtain a confession, but in this case a statement of one's age is hardly a confession. We could spin the conundrum out, but the point of course is that the function of the question does not lie within utterance 11 (or the answer in 12), but in its JUXTAPOSITION with what has gone before. By careful juxtaposition 11 does the job of suggesting that a girl of seventeen who has already slept with two men is not a woman of good repute.

Turning back to extract (12) we see that juxtaposition there too provides our understanding of what some of these questions are doing. Take utterance 17 for example: here a question about the girl's health follows those about her make-up on the night of the crime, and is succeeded by questions about whether on that occasion she had a coat and how cold the weather was. Again the fact questioned in 17 was known to both questioner and respondent, as indicated by its form – a tagged assertion; the point of asking the question was to obtain an acknowledgement of the fact AT THIS PARTICULAR LOCUS in the cross-examination.

In what kinds of discourse is it appropriate, and perhaps necessary, to state things that may already be known in a certain order or sequence? One answer is: in the presentation of an argument of course. And now we are in a position to state succinctly what our intuitions have already told us about extracts (12) and (13): *the functions of the questions here are to extract from the witness answers that build up to form a "natural" argument for the jury*. The argument that is thus extracted from the girl's answers in (12) goes something like this: the victim was dressed to go dancing, she was heavily made-up – something of a painted lady in fact, and despite the fact that she had been ill she was wearing no coat on the cold winter's night. The implicit conclusion is that the girl was seeking sexual adventures.

But to obtain this argument, or anything like it, we have had to make some basic assumptions about the intentions of the questioner – namely that he wishes to convey an argument, and moreover an argument that will show the facts of the case in a certain light. We can make these assumptions with surety because the nature of the activity – the cross-examining of the victim by the defendant's lawyer – assigns a particular role, a class of intentions in fact, to the questioner. To see the connections between these different levels of discourse organization, first note that if the questions were randomly picked out of a hat, then we could not understand the sequence of questions as an argument designed by the questioner. Secondly note that if the sequence of questions is understood as designed to convey an argument, the conclusion of the argument could be different in different activities. If (13) for example was constructed from the questions posed by a concerned auntie to her modern niece, the implicit conclusion might be something like "well I do disapprove of modern mores". Or even if the roles in the courtroom were reversed, and the respondent in (12) was the defendant accused of luring lorry-drivers into deserted lay-bys where accomplices could hijack the goods, the implicit conclusion would again be different – what else could the siren be doing on a January night under-dressed?

I hope then to have established that our understanding of these extracts as designed to elicit an argument of a certain kind with specific conclusions rests on our knowledge of the kind of activity the talk occurs within. We know that in a rape case it is the job of the defendant and his lawyer to show that the girl asked for it, and the goal of the victim and her counsel to resist this and establish that the defendant committed the crime intentionally and against the girl's resistance. Each of these conflicting goals specifies a class of strategies, and it is the location of these that gives us our understanding of what is going on.[7] For example it will be in the defendant's best interests to obtain the most damaging admissions from the victim; his counsel will therefore ask the strongest version of the relevent question first, and failing to obtain assent, will come down one notch and so on. A structure of this sort can be seen in (13), where the cross-examiner first asks whether the girl has had sexual intercourse on many occasions, to which there is dissent, falls back on several, which is again resisted, and so on. We understand too of course why the girl resists: her understanding like ours rests on a reconstruction of the intended line of argument, and given the goals that the activity assigns to her she must try to thwart that line of argument. In the case in question she was sometimes relatively successful at this, as indicated by the following extract (B. Toner, 1977: 158):

(14) 1. ... you guessed by then this was a man who wanted to make advances to you, didn't you?

2. Well, I didn't think of it straight away.

3. I know you didn't think of it straight away. I am now asking you about the time when you missed the turning and started talking, according to you, about going to Taunton?

4. Well, I thought about it, but I just sort of kept it at the back of my mind. You know, I didn't really want to think about it.

5. You thought about it, and your evening having fallen flat you were not adverse to it, were you?

6. I don't understand what you mean.

7. Well, you didn't mind?

8. Of course I minded.

9. I want to make this quite clear. You did not say, "Stop the car" because you didn't want the car stopped?

10. I did.

This example should make clear the way in which our understanding of what is going on requires reference to the underlying strategies or plans employed by both parties, which in turn are derived from the nature of the activity and the goals that it assigns the various participants. There is a way in which the question-answer format is invariant and insensitive to all of this; together with an assignment of questioner/answerer roles it constructs a turn-taking organization that gives control of topical organization entirely to the questioner, thus making the format a possible vehicle for the expression of an argument. But there is another way in which the role and the function of each question is relative to the goals and strategies of the participants: the questioner hopes to elicit a response that will count as part of an implicit argument, the answerer will try to avoid such a response. The questions may be rhetorical, in the sense that both know the answer (cf. utterance 23 in (12), 11 in (13)); they may appear to seek information when in fact the information is already known (as perhaps in 25 in (12)), or they may appear to merely seek confirmation when in fact they seek information, and so on. In each case the particular role that we see them playing is established by reference to the strategies we assume the questioner to be utilizing by virtue of the role he is playing in particular kind of activity.

Let us turn now to another activity type where questions play an important role: teaching children in the classroom. Interestingly questions are not integral to the teaching process in all cultures; Gonja society again provides some useful cross-cultural perspective here (see Goody, 1978: 40–41). Nevertheless it is clear that questions are an invaluable resource in the classroom: firstly, because they require answers they enjoin participation; secondly, because they provide feedback they can be used to test for knowledge acquired in particular; and thirdly, because they allow the pupil to express the location of any puzzlement he may feel. But in what follows we shall be particularly concerned with questions uttered by the teacher, and with the larger discourse structures that are involved with these questions.

We may start with a piece of constructed data (T denotes teacher, C_1 first child and so on):

(15) T: What are the names of some trees?
      C_1: There are oaks.
      C_2: Apples!
      T: Apple-trees, yes.
      C_3: Yews.
      T: Well done Johnny!
      C_4: Oak trees!
      T: No Sally, Willy's already said that.

The example illustrates that to participate properly in this activity you have to know more than just how to answer questions. For C_4's utterance was a valid and truthful answer to T's question, but the response by T indicates that it was not a valid move in this particular language game. Note too that T's rejoinder does not entirely make explicit the language-game: the game could still consist of uttering any tree-name Willy hasn't already said. T is merely alluding to the rules of the game, not stating them.

Now let us turn to a piece of real data that will illustrate the same sort of thing in greater detail and veracity. The data and some of the insights come from a study of classroom interaction by Gumperz and Herasimchuk (1975: 109 ff).

(16) T: J, how do you spell Ann?
      J: A, N, N.
      T: A,N,N. What kind of an A?
      J: Capital.
      T: Why is it capital?
      J: Cause it's a name.
      T: Of a?
      J: Girl.
      T: OK, I, do you see a name on that page you know?
      I: Ann.
      T: That's the one that J just named. How do you spell Ann?
      I: A,N,N.
      T: How do we say A?
      I: (no response).
      T: J, do you want to help her?
      C: I know.
      J: The letter capital A.
      T: Capital A, N, N. Why do we say "capital", I?
      I: (no response).
      T: Why should we put a capital A on Anne, E?
      E: Because it's someone's name.
      T: It's the *name* of someone, I. So we make it special.
      E: A girl, the name of a girl.
      T: Would you see any other name, I, that you know?
      C: I see a name, a Ben.
      T: (to I): ... any other name? Let I find one. D'you see a name you know there?
      I: (pause) Ken?
      T: All right, Ken. That's right. How do you spell Ken? Don't forget what you'd say to that first letter. How do you spell Ken?
      A: Where is Ken? K, C, K, E, er...

> T: A, I is spelling it. Capital K –
> I: Capital K.
> C: (to other child) You messin up the raser already!
> T: E.
> I: N.
> T: Right. Ken. Do you see any word that you know there, B, anyone's name?
> B: Pat.
> T: Where do you see Pat? do you see an *ae* sound in there?
> B: No.
> T: What sound do you see?
> B: Pat.
> T: Do you see an *ae* sound?
> B: No.
> T: What sound do you see?
> B: Pet.
> I: Peter?
> T: Is there an *er* on the end?
> I: Is it Peter?
> T: I's helping you. She's given you a clue. But is there an *er* on the end of that?
> C: (inaudible).
> T: What's the word?
> C: (inaudible).
> T: What?
> C: Pete.
> T: That's right. How do you spell it?

In this extract I think it is clear that the teacher's questions are REQUESTS TO FOLLOW A PROCEDURE. The procedure in question, which is recursively applied, has three parts: first one should identify names in the text, then one should spell them, and thirdly one should attend to the capitalization of the first letter. The teacher, in getting the children to go through the procedure, also requires that the children's contributions must PROVE (a) that they can identify names, (b) that they can spell them, and (c) that they know about capital letters.

It is because it is necessary in this language game to prove that one can identify a name or spell it, that one cannot repeat an identification or spelling, since one might do that by imitation. And this explains the particular role that we understand T's utterances like the following to be playing: "That's the one that J just named"; "A, I is spelling it". Notice that as in the prior constructed example the rules of the language game are presumed even in these corrections, and not taught. In order to understand these two utterances of the teacher as having the force of dismissing the prior contribution one would need already to know what the rules of the language game are. We are left with what is here, and elsewhere I think throughout the range of activities in a culture, a genuine puzzle: how are the rules of a language game ever learnt?

Even within our culture teaching styles and methods vary a great deal, partly of course in relation to subject-matter, educational ideology within the school, and approaches favoured by particular teachers. Let us take another example of a rather different type, where questions play a different role. The following extract from a science lesson comes from a large corpus gathered by the Birmingham discourse project.[8]

	Teacher		Children
(17)	1. Now tell me: why do you eat all that food? Can you tell me why do you eat all that food? Yes		
		2. To keep strong.	
	3. To keep you strong. Yes. To keep you strong. Why do you want to be strong?		
		4. Sir, – muscles.	
	5. To make muscles. Yes. Well what would you want to do with your muscles?		
		6. Sir, use them.	
	7. You'd want to –	8. Use them.	
	9. You'd want to use them. Well how do you use your muscles?		
		10. By working.	
	11. By working. Yes. And when you're working, what are you using apart from your muscles? What does that food give you? What does the food give you?		
		12. Strength.	
	13. Not only strength; we have another word for it. Yes.		
		14. Energy.	
	15. Good girl. Yes. Energy. You can have a team point. That's a very good word. We use——we're using——energy. We're using——energy. When a car goes into the garage, what do you put in it?		
		16. Petrol.	
	17. You put petrol in. Why do you put petrol in?		
		18. To keep it going.	
	19. To keep it going; so that it will go on the road. The car uses the petrol, but the petrol changes to something, in the same way that your food changes to something. What does the petrol change to?		
		20. Smoke.	
		21. Water.	
		22. Fire.	
	23. You told me before.	24. Smoke.	
		25. Inaudible.	
	26. Again.	27. Inaudible (Energy).	
	28. Energy. Tell everybody.	29. Energy.	
	30. Energy. Yes. When you put petrol in the car, you're putting another kind of energy in the car from the petrol. So we get energy from petrol and we get energy from food. Two kinds of energy.		

Despite the fact that this extract shares with (16) the fact that it is structured primarily by the teacher's use of questions, it is clearly a very different "language-game" in the sense that there are different strategies and procedures in employment. Specifically the discourse in (17) appears to be a variant of the Socratic method: the teacher attempts to make explicit a selected part of the implicit knowledge that he assumes pupils to have, by means of a dialogue of questions and answers. The selected knowledge that the teacher hopes to make explicit is an analogy or parallelism, best expressed by the proportion:

(18)   food:humans::petrol:cars

where the underlying symmetry is that the first part of each pair is the energy source for the second part. There is a parallel here to the way in which in the courtroom questions were used to extract answers that would amount to a specific argument. One difference of course is that whereas in the courtroom a cross-examination is more like a zero-sum game, where one party's losses are the other party's gains, here it is at least the hope of the teacher that the game is perceived as more like one of pure coordination, where both parties stand to lose or gain together. That is, the teacher hopes that by directing questions and selecting answers he will get the pupils to see in what direction he wants them to answer. And there is a presumption of cooperation. The game then consists in trying to get the pupils to see the proportion in (18) and to state the underlying rationale for it.

It is important to note to what extent the procedure here is cooperative and dependent on the pupils foreseeing the KIND of answer that the teacher has in mind. The answer to the teacher's first question for example ("can you tell me why do you eat all that food?") could equally well have been "hunger" or "mother cooks it" or a host of other responses in the wrong direction. Nevertheless these might be truthful answers. Similarly, to the question in 15 ("when a car goes into the garage, what do you put in it?") there would be many correct but useless answers – useless in that they would not advance the game – like air, water, oil and so on. The game could not proceed efficiently, if at all, simply by a selection of randomly produced answers. To play the game the pupils must know the kind of thing the teacher is trying to do, they must foresee the general line of reasoning, and they must cooperatively help to build it.

The discussion so far has in fact oversimplified the nature of the game in (17), and thus the amount of knowledge that the children require in order to play it effectively. Consider how the children are meant to come to a realization of the proportion in (18), and what will count as a display of that realization. They are meant to use the same linguistic category to express the relation between humans and food and between cars and petrol. We see from the apparent inadequacy of the word volunteered in 12 ("strength") and rejected in 13, that the relation must be expressed by the word "energy" to count as a winning move in the game. The game has then a meta-linguistic element. An interesting thing about this element is that it seems to commit the teacher to holding a special view of the relation between language and the world, something approximating to that held by Wittgenstein in the *Tractatus Logico-philosophicus*. For only on such a view would the activity of placing two events, objects, or relations under the same linguistic description amount to saying something about the relationship between those two events, objects or relations in the real world. This Tractarian assumption then seems to underlie the insistence on the use of the word "energy".[9]

We are now in a position to state the knowledge that the child needs in order to play in this particular language-game. He must know that not just any truthful answer to the teacher's questions will count as a valid move; he must attempt to foresee the line of argument so that his answer will contribute towards it. Moreover he needs to see that not just any expression of his contribution will do, and specifically here that parallelisms should be expressed under an identical verbal relation. To do this, he must be able to recognize sameness of linguistic description, and his understanding of the relevance of this will certainly be aided by a grasp of the teacher's Tractarian views (without this grasp the activity will appear to be a purely linguistic game rather than a science lesson).

I have talked loosely of "language-games" at two levels: on the one hand one has the activity type which in part determines the role that language will play, and on the other hand one has particular strategies or procedures within the activity – like teaching spelling in a particular way, or drawing out the pupils' implicit knowledge about energy sources of various sorts. Does the existence of these lower order structures indicate that the notion of activity alone is not predictive of (or explanatory with regard to) the rules of language use in an interesting way? I think not, because there are intrinsic connections between the two layers of organization. For example there are certain goals that seem to be taken as central to teaching. One of these is to impart knowledge, but more importantly to organize knowledge, especially by drawing out important parallels – let us call this the gnomic function. Another is to impart abilities, or knowledge of procedures, like spelling, counting and so on. Now given some other aspects of the activity, especially that one functionary (the teacher) has control both in task-setting and turn-taking while the rest must try to do whatever task the teacher assigns, various detailed features of the teaching strategies or procedures can be seen to follow – in the sense that they seem to be rationally adapted to achieving the overall goals. For example the procedure used in (16) where each child was called upon to demonstrate the ability to identify and spell proper names was a rational way of testing whether that ability had been acquired, and perhaps of enhancing that ability by practice. So it is ultimately against the background of the goals of the activity as a whole and the derivative structures and pedagogical strategies that detailed features of the organization make sense. So an utterance of the form "A, B is spelling it" can function as a command for A to shut up, because it is understood that the teacher T schedules the events, that T has asked B to spell it in order to ascertain whether B has learned the relevant procedure, and that T is therefore not now interested in A's ability.[10]

It seems then that the various levels of organization within an activity cohere, and can be seen to derive as rational means from overall ends and organizational conditions. It may be that the means chosen only SEEM rational to the participants at the time, or are assumed to be on the basis of received wisdom, or more often are rational but turn out to be ineffective because other conditions have not been taken into account. In any case the coherence of the different levels seems to reside in a general tendency towards rational organization.

In the light of the very different usages of questions in these examples, let us return to examine the definition and characterization of a question. Our basic problem is this: can we factor out from all these different usages a common core which we can continue to think of as part of the semantics of questions? Or is there no such core, but rather only a set of language games in which they play roles related by "family-resemblance"?

One influential way of thinking about the properties that individuate different illocutionary forces is to factor out the set of necessary and sufficient conditions for the non-defective performance of the relevant speech act. This is the characterization of speech acts by means of the specification of their "felicity conditions" as advocated by Austin (1962) and Searle (1969, 1976). After stating that "there are two kinds of questions (a) real questions, (b) exam questions" (Searle, 1969: 66), Searle produces the following felicity conditions for "real questions" (the corresponding ones for exam questions are presumably as I have indicated in brackets):

(19) Propositional content condition: any proposition or propositional function.

Preparatory conditions:	(i)	S does not know "the answer" (Exam Q: S knows the answer but doesn't know whether H knows it).
	(ii)	It is not obvious to both S and H that H will provide the information at that time without being asked.
Sincerity condition:		S wants this information (Exam Q: S wants to know if H knows the information).
Essential condition:		Counts as an attempt to elicit this information from H.

It is clear that in line with Searle's method one could go on elaborating the conditions; for instance for real questions there seem to be other preparatory conditions to the effect that S has reason to think that H might know the answer, that S expects H to provide a response, and so on. The notion of "answer" can be independently characterized as an assent or dissent to the proposition of a yes/no question, or the completion of the open proposition in the case of Wh-questions.

The problem for us is that many of the questions that we have examined do not fit into this schema as either "real" or "exam" questions. For example, the utterance 11 in the courtroom example (13) ("And you are seventeen and a half?"),[11] does not fit the first preparatory condition, the sincerity condition or the essential condition: both parties know the answer and know that they know the answer, the speaker doesn't want the information nor does he want to know whether the hearer knows it, nor is he attempting to elicit the information although he is attempting to elicit a response (namely the answer). We could say that this is a rhetorical question, in that these properties are typical of such questions, and that rhetorical questions are "really" statements (see Sadock, 1974, for one such line). However the fact that a response that is an answer is expected and given distinguishes this question from rhetorical questions where responses are inappropriate or optional.

Take another of our questions, utterance 1 in example (17) ("Why do you eat all that food?"). Again both parties know a wide range of truthful answers to this question and know that they do – so it does not fall within Searle's category of exam questions. The questioner doesn't want the information, nor does he want the children to show that they know it, he merely wants a response drawn from the pupils' tacit knowledge that will advance and make explicit his argument about a specific analogy.

Most of the other questions in our examples will also fail to fit Searle's schema in one way or another. Consider the questions in greetings ("How are you?"), where the answers are more or less prescribed so that all the felicity conditions concerning knowledge, information and desire for it must be wrong. Consider too the special uses in Gonja between joking relatives, or in law courts, as described at the beginning of this section. It is really hard to see a common core to all these kinds of questions, except that they elicit responses of specific kinds. But that will hardly distinguish questions from bets, offers and so on. Moreover some questions do not seem intended to elicit responses, unless we consider silence a response – consider the use of sentences like "how could you do that to me?" in a quarrel. Nor will the usual stategy for the rescue of the concept of speech act from the diversity of discourse – namely to identify a paradigmatic type and then consider other usages "indirect speech acts" (see Gordon and Lakoff, 1971; Searle, 1975) – work very well here: the questions in the courtroom for example are not easily understood as other kinds of speech acts masquerading in question form. Nor is the distinction between direct and indirect speech acts so clear in practice: consider the first utterance in (16) for example ("J, how do you spell Ann?"): is this an imperative ("Go through the procedure of spelling Ann!") in question form? But how else would you answer the question except by demonstrating how to spell Ann?[12] Sometimes it is easier to demonstrate an "answer" than to describe it.

Other linguistic approaches to the analysis of questions tend to accept the existence of well-defined felicity conditions; the problem is then where in a linguistic description these should be accommodated. If one accepts the performative analysis (Ross, 1970; Sadock, 1974; Lakoff, 1975), then they can be seen as presuppositions of the higher verb of saying. Even those who have avoided that analysis have tended to see their job as dismantling the hybrid theory of speech acts and parcelling out the felicity conditions to either the semantic or pragmatic component where they are thought more properly to belong (see e.g. Katz, 1977). But if felicity conditions are variable in relation to discourse context, then none of them are the sort of thing one wants in an orderly semantics in any case.

Is there anything left that one could claim to be the semantics of questions? Note that if one rejects the performative analysis, and there are now a great number of arguments why one should (see e.g. Gazdar, 1976 and references therein), then there is reason to think that illocutionary force has nothing to do with semantics, and should rather be handled entirely in pragmatics. Not all linguists seem to see this. Katz (1977) for example while rejecting the performative analysis argues that because one has to provide the semantics for *ask* in such statements as "John asked Mary what the time was", one should assimilate the same semantics to the QUESTION FORM in direct questions. But the argument seems confused: one might as well argue that because one has to provide the semantics for *kick* in sentences like "John kicked Bill", one should provide the same semantics for the action of kicking. Reports of acts have semantic characterizations, acts do not.

If there is a role for semantics to play in the characterization of questions it is probably in the characterization of the logical relation between questions and answers. But since there are also pragmatic constraints on adequate answers (of the sort outlined by Grice, 1975, as well as the sort specific to activities), and since there are many appropriate responses to questions that are not answers, the precise role that this relation will play in the definition of a question is certainly not clear to me.

If on the other hand the illocutionary force associated with questions is an entirely pragmatic affair (as for example in Stennius's 1972 account), then there is no reason to resist the fact that the nature of questions can vary in relation to the particular language games in which they play a role. In that case Wittgenstein's failure to make a distinction between speech acts and the activities they are used in would have a more principled basis than is currently thought.

5 Conclusions

We have argued that types of activity, social episodes if one prefers, play a central role in language usage. They do this in two ways especially. On the one hand they constrain what will count as an allowable contribution to each activity, and on the other hand they help to determine how what one says will be "taken" – that is, what kinds of inferences will be made from what is said. Both of these issues are of some theoretical and practical interest. For example knowing the constraints on allowable contributions will be an important part of what Hymes (1962) has called *communicative competence*, the knowledge required to use language appropriately in cultural situations. The inferential side to these constraints adds an important further element to our understanding of, and appreciation of the importance of, inference in discourse. In addition to the very general principles outlined by Grice (1975), and the very specific organizations of background knowledge emphasized by workers in Artificial Intelligence, there are *activity-specific rules of inference*. Again having a grasp of the latter will play an important role in the reception side of communicative competence, the ability to understand what one hears. And because these activity-specific rules of inference are more culturally-specific than other sorts, they are likely to play a large role in cross-cultural or inter-ethnic miscommunications, an area of growing interest (see e.g. Gumperz, 1977). Computer models of language understanding are also likely to prove disappointing if such bases for inference are not taken into account.

The apprehension will no doubt be that a full understanding of the ways language usage is inextricably entangled with social activities will require the description of a heterogenous mass of arbitrarily varied, culturally determined language games. Certainly compared to simple over-arching principles of a Gricean sort, this is something of a Pandora's box. Nevertheless as we proceeded through the examples we were able to show that many features of these language games are not unprincipled. Rather there seems to be a healthy tendency towards the rational construction of language games as organizations functionally adapted to achieving certain goals – the main purposes of the activity in question. A very good idea of the kind of language usage likely to be found within a given activity can thus be predicted simply by knowing what the main function of the activity is seen to be by participants. If that is the case, then all the details of constraints on language usage within each activity need not be taught to the foreign-language learner, or incorporated into a language understanding program; it will suffice to specify the general goals and any special unpredictable constraints.

And finally we have tried to show that Wittgenstein's abstention from a distinction between speech acts and speech events, both of which fell under the rubric of "language-games", was more principled than speech act theorists would have us believe. To quote him:

But how many kinds of sentence are there? Say assertion, question, and command? – There are *countless* kinds: countless different kinds of use of what we call "symbols", "words", "sentences". And this multiplicity is not something fixed, given once for all; but new types of language, new language-games, as we may say, come into existence, and others become obsolete and get forgotten.... Here the term "language-*game*" is meant to bring into prominence the fact that the speaking of language is part of an activity, or of a form of life. (*Philosophical Investigations*, 1.23.)

We explored this doctrine through an analysis of questions and their usages in various activities. And we may take as an epitaph to that investigation another quote:

If you do not keep the multiplicity of language-games in view you will perhaps be inclined to ask questions like: "What is a question?" – Is it the statement that I do not know such-and-such, or the statement that I wish the other person would tell me...? Or is it the description of my mental state of uncertainty? (*Philosophical Investigations*, 1.24.)

Notes

An earlier version of this article appeared in Pragmatics Microfiche Volume 3, Fiche 3–3, pages D.1-G.5, May, 1978.

My thanks are due to Jay Atlas, Terence Moore and Gerald Gazdar for reading and commenting on an almost illegible first draft; some of the suggestions have been incorporated without further acknowledgement, so not all errors are necessarily my own!

1   Those more familiar with basketball tell me that I have assigned the wrong functions to some of these utterances, on a mistaken analogy to soccer. They tell me that (1)1. is obviously a commendation, (1)4. a critical encouragement. But my mistake only illustrates the point – how specialized the uses of language can be to the particular activities within which they are employed.

2   I have in mind distinctions like Searle's "Word to World" versus "World to Word" fit: a sports commentary mirrors a non-speech event, but magical rites are often held to create the world they describe. Another distinction can be made between cases where concurrent actions describe or illustrate the words, and cases where the words describe the actions. Consider for instance how the same set of photographic slides of, say, Venice could be used to illustrate a lecture on architecture or to describe a holiday trip: in the one case the slides merely illustrate the talk, in the other talk merely amplifies the slides.

3   Recollect that I have confined my remarks to the structural rather than the stylistic properties of speech events: here the constraints on contributions that I have in mind are especially those on the functions that utterances will be understood – if possible – to have.

4   It may be argued, incorrectly I think, that the implicature from *saw x* to *read x* (where x is reading matter) is *particularized* in Grice's sense, that is only holds in certain special circumstances. Its cancellation might then not be dependent on certain levels of cooperation, but due simply to the absence of those special circumstances. However precisely analogous arguments to those I am making here can be made from other examples that have indubitably *generalized* conversational implicatures. For example "three" generally implicates "no more than three", and so the following exchange is expectable only in non-cooperative situations like legal settings:

A: How many men were with you?
B: Three.
A: No more than three?
B: Well, perhaps as many as five.

5 A final issue that arises in connection with inference can be a very real interactional problem that faces conversationalists: how does one ascertain *which* activity one is in at any one point in an on-going interaction? Sometimes the gross facts of physical setting, time, copresent personnel etc. are insufficient to determine the activity. Then one may work backwards, so to speak, from the nature of verbal contributions to a determination of what kind of activity the other participants, at least, think they are in. The need for this kind of inference frequently arises where one kind of activity comes embedded within another, for example joking sequences within work-talk, or business transactions conducted at a cocktail party. A good locus for the study of such activity-identifying processes is where misunderstandings arise due to different cultural or subcultural origins of participants: John Gumperz and associates have done some important work in this area (see e.g. Gumperz and Tannen, 1979; Gumperz, 1977). My lack of attention to this problem of "frame invocation" is a gross oversimplification if it is taken to imply that the determination of the activity one is in is unproblematic, but that is not my intention. In this paper my main aim is to establish that the activities within which utterances occur play a central role in the assignment of function or import to those utterances. If this can be established, the question of how activities are recognized becomes, of course, all the more important.

6 More recently we have the formal treatment of questions as the sets of possible, or true, answers by Hamblin (1973) and Karttunen (1977). Another long-standing tradition of course is to think of questions as imperatives to tell specific answers; there is a rather sophisticated treatment along these lines by Hintikka (1974) incorporating an epistemic element – a yes/no question gets paraphrased essentially as "bring it about that I know that p or not-p". The interactional element here is also clear: an answer will only be adequate relative to the asker's epistemic state. The problem with this line of attack is that it assigns a very specific pragmatic function to questions, while empirically they seem to have a very wide range of functions as will be fully documented below.

7 I am reminded by Carlotta Smith that it would be useful here to distinguish and relate *constraints* on activities from the *strategies* that may flourish within them. We may take constraints to be normatively imposed, and maintained at least in part by the fact that failure to conform may yield quite unintended misinterpretations. Strategies on the other hand may be seen as optimal or self-maximizing patterns of behaviour available to participants in particular roles, UNDER the specific constraints of the relevant activity.

8 The example is cited here by kind permission of Malcolm Coulthard. These and other materials are to appear in a book by D. Brazil. M. Coulthard and C. Johns, *Discourse Intonation and Language Teaching*.

9 It is a Tractarian game, Jay Atlas points out to me, insofar as the syntax of language is MADE to mirror the structure of the world. The emphasis on the metalinguistic element in this game derives directly from Jay Atlas's comments on a version of this paper given to a seminar in Cambridge.

10 Much of this discussion ties into the controversy over the nature of indirect speech acts; for some discussion and many references see Brown and Levinson (1978: 137ff). The classic articles are reprinted in Cole and Morgan (1975).

11 I have not always distinguished between what are syntactically questions and what are only prosodically marked as questions, although there are clearly some pragmatic differences here. But in most cases we could substitute syntactic questions for those marked by

other means in our examples without changing those aspects of the text that we are interested in here. In any case the argument here could be conducted equally well with syntactic questions, drawn from a wider range of data.

12　Let us ignore the other readings of the manner adverbial implicit in *how*, as revealed in such joke answers (this one produced by Jay Atlas) as "Correctly every time".

References

Austin, J. L. (1962). *How to Do Things with Words*. Oxford: Clarendon Press.

Bauman, R. and Sherzer, J. (1974). *Explorations in the Ethnography of Speaking*. Cambridge: Cambridge University Press.

Belnap, N. D. (1963). An analysis of questions. Systems Development Corporation, TM – 1287.000.00. Santa Monica, California.

Berlin, B. and Kay, P. (1969). *Basic Color Terms*. Berkeley and Los Angeles: University of California Press.

Blount, B. and Sanches, M. (1975). *Sociocultural Dimensions of Language Use*. New York: Academic Press.

Brown, P. and Levinson, S. C. (1978). Universals in language usage: politeness phenomena. In E. Goody (ed.), *Questions and Politeness*. Cambridge: Cambridge University Press.

Cole, P. and Morgan, J. (1975). *Syntax and Semantics 3: Speech Acts*. New York: Academic Press.

Charniak, E. (1972). *Towards a Model of Children's Story Comprehension*. Massachusetts Institute of Technology. Artificial Intelligence Laboratory: A1 TR–266.

Ferguson, C. (1964). Diglossia. In D. Hymes (ed.), *Language in Culture and Society*. New York: Holt, Rinehart and Winston.

Fillmore, C. (1975). *Santa Cruz Lectures on Deixis*. Bloomington: Indiana University Linguistics Club Papers.

Fraser, B. (1975). Hedged performatives. In P. Cole and J. Morgan (eds).

Gazdar, G. (1976). On performative sentences. *Semantikos* 1(3): 37–62.

Goody, E. (1972). "Greeting", "begging" and the presentation of respect. In La Fontaine (ed.), *The Interpretation of Ritual*. London: Tavistock Publications.

——(1978). Towards a theory of questions. In E. Goody (ed.), *Questions and Politeness*. Cambridge: Cambridge University Press.

Grice, H. P. (1975). The logic of conversation. In P. Cole and J. Morgan (eds).

Gordon, D. and Lakoff, G. (1971). Conversational postulates. Reprinted in P. Cole and J. Morgan (eds), *Syntax and Semantics 3: Speech Acts*. New York: Academic Press.

Gumperz, J. (1972). Introduction. In J. Gumperz and D. Hymes (eds), *Directions in Sociolinguistics*. New York: Holt, Rinehart and Winston.

——(1977). The conversational analysis of inter-ethnic communication. In E. Lamar Ross (ed.), *Interethnic Communication*. Proceedings of the Southern Anthropological Society, University of Georgia Press.

Gumperz, J. and Herasimchuk, E. (1975). The conversational analysis of social meaning: a study of classroom interaction. In B. Blount and M. Sanches (eds), *Sociocultural Dimensions of Language Use*. New York: Academic Press.

Gumperz, J. and Tannen, D. (1979). Individual and social differences in language use. In W. Wang and C. Fillmore (eds), *Individual Differences in Language Ability and Language Behavior*. New York: Academic Press.

Hamblin, C. L. (1973). Questions in Montague English. *Foundations of Language* 10, 41–53.

Harrah, D. (1961). A logic of questions and answers. In *Philosophy of Science* 28.

Heringer, J. T. (1972). *Some Grammatical Correlates of Felicity Conditions*. Ohio State University Working Papers in Linguistics II, 1–110.

Hintikka, J. (1974). Questions about questions. In M. K. Munitz and P. K. Unger (eds), *Semantics and Philosophy*. New York: New York University Press.

Horn, L. (1972). *On the Semantic Properties of Logical Operators in English*. Unpublished Ph.D. dissertation, University of California, Los Angeles.

Hudson, R. A. (1975). The meaning of questions. *Language* 51(1), 1–31.

Hull, R. D. (1975). A semantics for superficial and embedded questions in natural language. In E. Keenan (ed.), *Formal Semantics of Natural Language*. Cambridge: Cambridge University Press.

Hymes, D. (1962). the ethnography of speaking. In T. Gladwin and W. Sturtevant (eds), *Anthropology and Human Behavior*. Washington. D.C.: Anthropological Society of Washington.

—— (1972). Models of the interaction of language and social life. In J. Gumperz and D. Hymes (eds), *Directions in Sociolinguistics*. New York: Holt, Rinehart and Winston.

Irvine, J. (1974). Strategies of Status manipulation in the Wolof greeting. In R. Bauman and J. Sherzer (eds), *Explorations in the Ethnography of Speaking*. Cambridge: Cambridge University Press.

—— (1978). Formality and informality in speech events. *Texas Working Papers in Sociolinguistics*. Number 52. Austin, Texas: South West Education Development Laboratory.

Katz, J. (1977). *Propositional Structure and Illocutionary Force*. Sussex: The Harvester Press.

Karttunen, L. (1977). Syntax and semantics of questions. *Linguistics and Philosophy* 1, 3–44.

Keenan, E. O. (1977). Why look at unplanned and planned discourse? In E. O. Keenan and T. L. Bennett (eds), *Discourse Across Time and Space*. Southern California Occasional Papers in Linguistics, Number 5, Department of Linguistics, Univ. of S. California, Los Angeles.

Keenan, E. O., Schieffelin, B. and Platt, M. (1978). Questions of immediate concern. In E. Goody (ed.), *Questions and Politeness*, Cambridge: Cambridge University Press.

Kenny, A. (1973). *Wittgenstein*. Harmondsworth: Penguin.

Labov, W. (1972). Rules for ritual insults. In D. Sudnow (ed.), *Studies in Social Interaction*. New York: Free Press.

Lakoff, G. (1975). Pragmatics in natural logic. In E. Keenan (ed.), *Formal Semantics of Natural Language*. Cambridge: Cambridge University Press.

Levinson, S. (1977). *Social Deixis in a Tamil Village*. Unpublished Ph.D. dissertation. University of California, Berkeley.

Lewis, D. (1969). *Convention: a Philosophical Study*. Cambridge, Mass.: Harvard University Press.

—— (1972). General semantics. In G. Harman and D. Davidson (eds), *Semantics for Natural Language*. Dordrecht: Reidel.

Luce, R. D. and Raiffa, H. (1957). *Games and Decisions: Introduction and Critical Survey*. New York: John Wiley & Sons.

Merritt, M. (1976). On questions following questions. *Language in Society* 5(3).

Munby, J. (1978). *Communicative Syllabus Design*. Cambridge: Cambridge University Press.

New York Times (1973). *The Watergate Hearings: Break-in and Cover-up*. Toronto: Bantam Books.

Perls, F. (1969). *Gestalt Therapy Verbatim*. Lafayette, California: Real People Press.

Pope, E. (1975). Questions and answers in English. Indiana University Linguistics Club Mimeo.

Ross, J. (1970). On declarative sentences. In R. A. Jacobs and P. S. Rosenbaum (eds), *Readings in English Transformational Grammar*. Waltham, Massachusetts: Ginn & Co.

Sacks, H. (n.d.). *Transcribed Lectures, 1967–73*. Mimeo, University of California, Irvine.

—— (1975). Everyone has to lie. In B. Blount and M. Sanches (eds), *Sociocultural Dimensions of Language Use*. New York: Academic Press.

Sacks, H., Schegloff, E. and Jefferson, G. (1974). A simplest systematics for the organization of turn-taking in conversation. *Language* 50(4), 696–735.

Sadock, J. (1974). *Toward a Linguistic Theory of Speech Acts*. New York: Academic Press.

Schank, R. and Nash-Webber, B. L. (eds), (1975). *Theoretical Issues in Natural Language Processing*. Cambridge, Mass.: duplicated conference proceedings.

Schegloff, E. (1976). On some questions and ambiguities in conversation. *Pragmatics Microfiche* 2.2., D8–G12.

Searle, J. (1969). *Speech Acts*. Cambridge: Cambridge University Press.

——(1975). Indirect speech acts. In P. Cole and J. Morgan (eds), *Syntax and Semantics 3: Speech Acts*. New York: Academic Press.

——(1976). The classification of illocutionary acts. *Language in Society* 5(1).

Stennius, E. (1972). Mood and language game. In D. Hockney (ed.), *Essays in Philosophical Logic*. Dortrecht: Reidel.

Toner, B. (1977). *The Facts of Rape*. London: Arrow Books.

Turner, R. (1972). Some formal properties of therapy talk. In D. Sudnow (ed.), *Studies in Social Interaction*. New York: The Free Press.

Turner, R. (ed.), (1974). *Ethnomethodology*. Harmondsworth: Penguin.

Wittgenstein, L. (1921). *Tractatus Logico-Philosophicus*. London: Routledge & Kegan Paul.

——(1958). *Philosophical Investigations*. Oxford: Blackwell.

——(1958). *The Blue and Brown Books*. Oxford: Blackwell.

13 Reflections on Talk and Social Structure

Emanuel A. Schegloff

Whether starting from a programmatic address to the structure of face-to-face interaction or from a programmatic concern with the constitutive practices of the mundane world, whether in pursuit of language, culture or action, a range of inquiries in several social science disciplines (most relevantly anthropology, sociology and linguistics) have over the past 25 to 30 years brought special attention to bear on talk-in-interaction. It is not unfair to say that one of the most focused precipitates of this broad interest has been that family of studies grouped under the rubric "conversation analysis." It is, in any case, with such studies of "talk" that I will be concerned in reflecting on "talk and social structure."

Although itself understandable as a sustained exploration of what is entailed in giving an analytic account of "a context" (as in the phrase "in the context of ordinary conversation"), various aspects of inquiry in this tradition of work have prompted an interest in neighboring disciplines in relating features of talk-in-interaction to "contexts" of a more traditional sort – linguistic contexts, cultural contexts, and institutional and social structural contexts. At the same time, investigators working along conversation analytic lines began to deal with talk with properties which were seemingly related to its production by participants oriented to a special "institutional" context; and, wishing to address those distinctive properties rather than ones held in common with other forms of talk (as Sacks had done in some of his earliest work based on group therapy sessions), these investigators faced the analytic problems posed by such an undertaking.

The interest in the theme "talk and social structure" comes, then, from several directions – the most prominent being technical concerns in the analysis of certain forms of talk on the one hand, and an impulse to effectuate a rapprochement with the concerns of classical sociology, and to do so by relating work on talk-in-interaction to those social formations which get referred to as "social structures," or generically as "social structure," on the other hand. My reflections will have this latter impulse as their point of departure, but will quickly seek to engage it by formulating and confronting the analytic problems which it poses.

Of course, a term like "social structure" is used in many different ways. In recent years, to cite but a few cases, Peter Blau (1977) has used the term to refer to the distribution of a population on various parameters asserted to be pertinent to interaction, claiming a derivation from Simmel and his notion of intersecting social circles. Many others have in mind a structure of statuses and/or roles, ordinarily thereby building in an inescapable normative component, of just the sort Blau wishes to avoid. Yet others intend by this term a structured distribution of scarce resources and desirables, such as property, wealth, productive capacity, status, knowledge, privilege, power, the capacity to enforce and preserve privilege, etc.

Still others have in mind stably patterned sets of social relations, whether formalized in organizations or more loosely stabilized in networks.

The sense of "social structure" intended in the thematic concern with "talk and social structure" does not range across all these usages. But almost certainly it includes a concern with power and status and its distribution among social formations such as classes, ethnic groups, age grade groups, gender, and professional relations. It is this sense which has animated, for example, the work by West (1979) and Zimmerman and West (1975) on gender and interruption, and West's work (1984) on doctor/patient interaction. And it includes as well a concern with the structured social relations which comprise organizations and occupational practice and the institutional sectors with which they are regularly identified (as, for example, in Atkinson and Drew's treatment of the courts (1979), in the work of Zimmerman and his associates on the police (for instance, Zimmerman 1984; Whalen and Zimmerman 1987), Maynard's work (1984) on the legal system, that of Heritage (1985a) on mass media news, or Boden's (1995) on organizations). Mehan's studies of decision making in the context of educational bureaucracies (Mehan, Hertweck and Meihls 1986; and Mehan, 1991) touch on both usages (as of course do some of the other studies which I have invoked to exemplify one or the other).

The work which engages with these classical sociological themes and incorporates reference to and treatment of them in studying talk-in-interaction has revived for me some concerns which were deep preoccupations some 25 years ago when work on the analysis of talk-in-interaction, of the sort now referred to as "conversation analytic," was getting underway. In these reflections, I want among other things to review, restate and update some of those considerations, and ask how contemporary efforts to engage these topics stand with respect to some of these older concerns. Do the old concerns still have the force they once had, or have they faded in felt significance? Are there now solutions to the problems as once formulated? Or can the results of current work at the interface of conversation and social structure be usefully enriched or constrained by engaging these issues?

Whatever answers we arrive at to these questions, there is one point I want to make before taking them up. Whatever substantive gains there are to be had from focusing on the relationship between talk and social structure in the traditional sense, this focus is not needed in order to supply conversation analysis with its sociological credentials. The work which is focused on the organization of talk-in-interaction in its own right – work on the organization of turn-taking, or on the organization of sequences, work addressed to the actions being done in turns and the formats through which they are done, work on the organization of repair, and work directed to the many discrete practices of talking and acting through talk which do not converge into domains of organization – this work is itself dealing with social organization and social structures, albeit of a different sort than in the received uses of those terms, and is no less sociological in impulse and relevance (Schegloff 1987b).

For some, the fact that conversation analysis (henceforth, CA) concerns itself with the details of talking has meant that it is a form of linguistics. Perhaps so, but certainly not exclusively so. If it is not a distinctive discipline of its own (which it may well turn out to be), CA is at a point where linguistics and sociology (and several other disciplines, anthropology and psychology among them) meet. For the target of its inquiries stands where talk amounts to action, where action projects consequences in a structure and texture of interaction which the talk is itself progressively embodying and realizing, and where the particulars of the talk inform what actions are being done and what sort of social scene is being constituted. Now, from the start, one central preoccupation of sociology and social theory has been with the character of social action and what drives it (reason, passion, interest, utility) – this is familiar enough. Another concern has been with the character of interaction in which action is embedded, for it is observations about some aspects of the character of interaction that motivated such hoary old distinctions as those between *Gemeinschaft* and *Gesellschaft*, between status and contract, and the like. "Action in interaction" is, then, a longstanding theme of social analysis.

CA's enterprise, concerned as it is with (among other things) the detailed analysis of how talk-in-interaction is conducted as an activity in its own right and as the instrument for the full range of social action and practice, is then addressed to one of the classic themes of sociology, although to be sure in a distinctive way. Of the several ways in which CA shows its deep preoccupation with root themes of social science and sociology in particular, these standing conversation analytic preoccupations resonate more with the title of the recent Atkinson/Heritage collection (1984): they are concerned with "structures of social action" – structures of single actions and of series and sequences of them. Atkinson and Heritage's title is, of course, a thoroughly unveiled allusion to the title of Talcott Parsons's first major work, *The Structure of Social Action* (1937), the work which launched the enterprise of Parsonian action theory. The difference between Parsons's title and the Atkinson/ Heritage allusion, "*The Structure* of Social Action" versus "*Structures* of Social Action," may suggest some of the distinctiveness.

Parsons's tack was conceptual and global. For him there was "*the* structure," and it was arrived at by theoretic stipulation of the necessary components of an analytical unit – the "unit act," components such as "ends," "means," "conditions." This was a thoroughly conceptual enterprise on a thoroughly analytic object. The Atkinson/Heritage "structures of" suggests not only multiplicity of structures, but the empirical nature of the enterprise. The units are concrete activities, and the search for their "components" involves examination and description of empirical instances.

But with all the differences in conception, mode of working, etc., there is a common enterprise here, and it has long been a central one for sociology and the social sciences more generally – to try to get at the character of social action and social interaction. In CA's addressing of this theme and the varied problems and analytic tasks to which it gives rise, it is itself engaged in "*echt*" sociology, even without the introduction of traditional sociological concerns such as "social structure." But the claim that the problems which have preoccupied conversation analysis *are* sociological in impulse and import is without prejudice to our engagement with the work which tries to relate talk to more traditional conceptions of social structure. That engagement is already underway.

The reasons for thinking about the relationships of talk and social structure are ready to hand. Both our casual and our studied examination of interaction and talk-in-interaction provide a lively sense of the occasions on which who the parties are relative to one another seems to matter, and matter to *them*. And these include senses of "who they are" that connect directly to what is ordinarily meant by "social structure" – their relative status, the power they differentially can command, the group affiliations they display or can readily have attributed to them such as their racial or ethnic memberships, their gender and age-grade status, their occupational status and its general standing and immediate interactional significance, and the other categories of membership in the society which can matter to the participants and which fall under the traditional sociological rubric "social structure."

The issue I mean to address is not: is there such a thing as gender/class/power/status/organization/etc.? Or: does it affect anything in the world? Rather, the question is: whatever observations we initially make about how such features of social organization as these work and bear on interaction, how do we translate them into defensible, empirically based analyses that help us to get access to previously unnoticed particular details of talk-in-interaction, and appreciate their significance. For the lively sense we may all share of the relevance of social structure along the lines I have mentioned needs to be converted into the hard currency (if you'll pardon the cash nexus) of defensible analysis – analysis which departs from, and can always be referred to and grounded in, the details of actual occurrences of conduct in interaction.

Again, I do not mean to be addressing myself to two apparently neighboring stances, although there may well be implications for them. I am not centrally concerned with those investigators whose primary analytic commitment is to social structure in the received senses of that term, and who mean to incorporate examination of talk into their inquiries because of the role attributable to it in the "production" of social structure – although I do later comment on them (see pp. 236–7). And I do not take up the position (apparently embraced in Goffman 1983) in which the prima facie relevance of social structure to the organization of interaction is in principle to be disputed (although I do suggest that some received notions may not be sustainable when required to come to terms with the details of actual occurrences). Rather, I mean to formulate and explore the challenges faced by those attracted to the interaction/social structure nexus. A solution must be found to the analytic problems which obstruct the conversion of intuition, casual (however well-informed) observation, or theoretically motivated observation into demonstrable analysis. For without solutions to these problems, we are left with "a *sense* of how the world works," but without its detailed explication.

So what *were* those problems? Or, rather: what *are* those problems? My discussion will be organized around three issues: the problem of relevance, the issue of "procedural consequentiality," and a concern for the competing attentional and analytic claims of conversational structures and "social structure" respectively in the analysis of the data of talk-in-interaction.[1]

The Problem of Relevance

First, *relevance*. Here I draw directly from among the earliest contributions to conversation analysis, the first systematically developed work of Harvey Sacks, now over 20 years old (1972a, 1972b, but the arguments were developing as early as the lectures in Sacks 1964–5). Let me remind you of some issues he raised with respect to how "members" characterize, identify, describe, refer to, indeed "conceive of" persons, in talking to others.

The original focus of the work by Sacks which I mean to recall was the way in which persons engaged in talk-in-interaction did their talk, specifically with respect to reference to persons. Sacks noted that members refer to persons by various category terms – as man/woman, protestant/catholic/jew, doctor/patient, white/black/chicano, first baseman/second baseman/shortstop, and the like. He remarked that these category terms come in collections. In presenting them above, they are inscribed in groups: [man/woman], [protestant/catholic/jew], and so on; and that is the correct way to present them. It is not [man/woman/protestant], [catholic/jew]. This is what is being noted in the observation that the category terms are organized in *collections*.

Some of these collections Sacks called "Pn adequate;" they were adequate to characterize or categorize any member of any population, however specified, whether or not it had been specified (for example, counted, characterized or bounded) in some fashion (1972a:32–3). Other collections were not Pn adequate. [Male/female] *is* Pn adequate; [first baseman/second baseman/shortstop...] is *not* Pn adequate, because the latter is only usable on populations already specified or characterized as "baseball teams," whereas the former is not subject to such restrictions.

One of Sacks's main points was that there demonstrably are many Pn-adequate category collections. The collection of category terms for gender/sex and age are the most obvious ones, and these two alone serve to allow the posing of the problem of relevance. The point is that since everyone who is an instance of some category in one of those collections is necessarily (for that is the import of Pn adequacy) also an instance of some category in the other, or *an* other, the fact that someone *is* male, or *is* middle aged, or *is* white, or *is* Jewish is, by itself, no warrant for so referring to them, for the warrant of "correctness" would provide for use of any of the other reference forms as well. Some principle of relevance must underlie use of a reference form, and has to be adduced in order to provide for one rather than another of those ways of characterizing or categorizing some member. That is the problem of relevance: not just the descriptive adequacy of the terms used to characterize the objects being referred to, but the relevance that one has to provide if one means to account for the use of some term – the relevance of that term relative to the alternative terms that are demonstrably available.

Now, this problem was developed by Sacks initially in describing how members talk about members. It showed the inadequacy of an account of a conversationalist's reference to another as a "cousin" by reference to the other "actually being a cousin." But, once raised, the point is directly relevant to the enterprise of *professional* analysts as well. Once we recognize that whoever can be characterized as "male" or as "protestant," or as "president" or whatever, can be characterized or categorized in other ways as well, our scholarly/professional/scientific account cannot "naively" rely on such characterizations, that is, cannot rely on them with no justification or warrant of their relevance.

Roughly speaking, there are two types of solution to this problem in the methodology of professional analysis. One type of solution can be characterized as the "positivist" stance, in one of the many senses in which that term is currently used. In this view, the way to warrant one, as compared to another, characterization of the participants (for example, in interaction) is the "success" of that way of characterizing them in producing a professionally acceptable account of the data being addressed. "Success" is measured by some "technology" – by statistical significance, a preponderance of historical evidence, and so forth. Sometimes there is an additional requirement that the characterization which produces "successful" analysis be theoretically interpretable; that is, that the selection of descriptive terms for the participants converge with the terms of a professional/scientific theory relevant to the object of description. In this type of solution, which I am calling "positivistic," it does not matter whether or not the terms that are used to characterize the participants in some domain of action, and which have yielded "significant" results, are otherwise demonstrably oriented to or not by the participants being described. That is what makes this solution of the problem "positivist."

The alternative type of solution insists on something else, and that is that professional characterizations of the participants be grounded in aspects of what is going on that are demonstrably relevant *to* the participants, and at that moment – at the moment that whatever we are trying to provide an account of occurs. Not, then, just that we see them to be characterizeable as "president/assistant," as "chicano/black," as "professor/student," etc. But that for them, at that moment, those are terms relevant for producing and interpreting conduct in the interaction.

This issue should be of concern when we try to bring the kind of traditional sociological analysis that is implied by the term "social structure" to bear on talk-in-interaction. Much of what is meant by "social structure" in the traditional sense directly implicates such characterizations or categorizations of the participants as Sacks was examining. If the sense of social structure we are dealing with is the one that turns on the differential distribution of valued resources in society, whether status or power or money or any of the other "goods" whose distribution can be used to characterize social structure, then that implies a characterization or categorization of the participants on that occasion as one relevantly to be selected from that set of terms. But then the problem presents itself of the relevance of those terms to the participants for what they are doing. Without a show of that warrant, we are back to a "positivistic" stance, even though the animating concerns may be drawn from quite anti-positivistic theoretical sources or commitments.

Now let us be clear about what *is* and what is *not* being said here. The point is not that persons are somehow *not* male or female, upper or lower class, with or without power, professors and/or students. They may be, on some occasion, demonstrably members of one or another of those categories. Nor is the issue that those aspects of the society do not matter, or did not matter on that occasion. We may share a lively sense that indeed they do matter, and that they mattered on that occasion, and mattered for just that aspect of some interaction on which we are focusing. There is still the problem of *showing from the details of the talk or other conduct in the materials* that we are analyzing that those aspects of the scene are what the *parties* are oriented to. *For that is to show how the parties are embodying for one another the relevancies of the interaction and are thereby producing the social structure.*

The point here is not only methodological but substantive. It is not just to add a methodological apparatus supporting analyses already in hand. It is rather to add to, and potentially to transform, the analysis of the talk and other conduct itself by enriching our account of it with additional detail; and to show that, and how, "social structure" in the traditional sense enters into the production and interpretation of determinate facets of conduct, and is thereby confirmed, reproduced, modulated, neutralized or incrementally transformed in that actual conduct to which it must finally be referred.

This is not, to my mind, an issue of preferring or rejecting some line of analysis, some research program or agenda. It is a problem of analysis to be worked at: how to examine the data so as to be able to show that the parties were, with and for one another, demonstrably oriented to those aspects of who they are, and those aspects of their context, which are respectively implicated in the "social structures" which we may wish to relate to the talk. If we treat this as a problem of analytic craft, we can use it as leverage to enhance the possibility of learning something about how talk-in-interaction is done, for it requires us to return again to the details of the talk to make the demonstration.

So, one issue posed by the theme "talk and social structure" is relevance.

The Issue of Procedural Consequentiality

The issue just discussed with respect to the characterization of the participants in some talk-in-interaction also is relevant to a characterization of "the context" in which they talk and interact. "Context" can be as much a part of what traditionally has been meant by "social structure" as attributes of the participants are. So, for example, remarking that some talk is being conducted "in the context of a bureaucracy," "in a classroom," "on a city street," etc. is part of what is sometimes intended by incorporating the relevance of social structure.

Such characterizations invoke particular aspects of the setting and not others. They involve selections among alternatives, and among subalternatives. For example, one type of formulation of context characterizes it by "place," and this is an alternative to various other sorts of context characterization. But within that context type, various forms of place formulation are available, all of which can be correct (Schegloff 1972). So, although the details of the argument have not been fully and formally worked out for the characterization of context or setting in the way that Sacks worked them out for the characterization of participants, it appears likely that the issue of relevance can be posed in much the same way for context as it has been for person reference.

What I want to do here is add something to this relevance problem for contexts. It concerns what I am calling the "procedural consequentiality" of contexts.

Even if we can show by analysis of the details of the interaction that some characterization of the context or the setting in which the talk is going on (such as "in the hospital") is relevant for the parties, that they are oriented to the setting so characterized, there remains another problem, and that is to show how the context or the setting (the local social structure), *in that aspect*, is procedurally consequential to the talk. How does the fact that the talk is being conducted in some setting (say, "the hospital") issue in any consequences for the shape, form, trajectory, content, or character of the interaction that the parties conduct? And *what is the mechanism by which the context-so-understood has determinate consequences for the talk?*

This is a real problem, it seems to me, because without a specification of such a linkage we can end up with characterizations of context or setting which, however demonstrably relevant to the parties, do little in helping us to analyze, to explain, to understand, to give an account of how the interaction proceeded in the way in which it did, how it came to have the trajectory, the direction, the shape that it ended up having.[2] When a formulation of the context is proposed, it is *ipso facto* taken to be somehow relevant and consequential for what occurs in the context. It is the analyst's responsibility either to deliver analytic specifics of that consequentiality or to abjure that characterization of the context. Otherwise, the analysis exploits a tacit feature of its own discursive format, but evades the corresponding analytic onus. A sense of understanding and grasp is conveyed to, and elicited from, the reader, but is not earned by the elucidation of new observations about the talk.[3]

So, this is an open question, somewhat less formally stated than the other: how shall we find formulations of context or setting that will allow us (a) to connect to the theme that many want to connect to – social structure in the traditional sense, but (b) that will do so in a way that takes into account not only the demonstrable orientation of the participants, but, further, (c) that will allow us to make a direct "procedural" connection between the context so formulated and what actually happens in the talk. Otherwise we have a characterization that "hovers around" the interaction, so to speak, but is not shown actually to inform the production and grasp of the details of its conduct.

As with the issue of "relevance," I am here putting forward not principled objections to the invocation of social structure as context, but jobs to be taken on by those concerned with the intersection of talk and familiar senses of social structure. They challenge us to be alert to possible ways of showing such connections. I will just mention a few possible directions here.

Some formulations of setting do the sort of job I have in mind because they capture features of the setting that fall under the general rubric of "speech exchange systems" (Sacks, Schegloff and Jefferson 1974: 729ff.). They satisfy this concern because they characterize a setting or context both in ways that connect to our general notions of social structure and in ways which directly refer to aspects of the practices by which the participants organize their talk. Some such settings carry with them as well a set of relevant identifications for the participants.

Consider, for example, the case of the courtroom in session (cf. Atkinson and Drew 1979; my remarks here rest on a much looser, vernacular and unstudied sense of the setting). To focus just on the turn-taking organization, it *is* the "courtroom-ness" of courtrooms in session which seems in fact to organize the way in which the talk is distributed among the persons present, among the *categories* of persons present, in the physical setting. So, for example, onlookers (members of the "audience") are not potential next speakers, as the official proceedings go on. And among the others who *are* potential next speakers at various points – the judge, the attorneys, the witness and the like, there are socially organized procedures for determining when they can talk, what they can do in their talk, and the like. It could be argued, then, that to characterize some setting of talk-in-interaction as in "a court-in-session" characterizes it with a formulation of context which can not only be claimed to connect to the general concern for "social structure" (for it certainly relates to institutional context), but can be shown to be procedurally consequential as well. Insofar as members of the audience sitting behind the bar never get up and talk but rather whisper to one another in asides, whereas the ones in front of the bar talk in defined and regular ways, by the very form of their conduct they show themselves to be oriented to the particular identities that are legally provided by that setting and show themselves to be oriented to "the-court-in-session" as a context.[4]

We have to be careful here to see what sorts of characterizations of context will satisfy these requirements. It is clear to me that vernacular accounts or formulations of context, even if informed by social scientific considerations, will not necessarily do it, if they do not specify how the talk is organized. One example, one not uncommon kind of proposed context description of talk-in-interaction is "an experiment" or "in a laboratory setting." Those terms sound like an adequate formulation of a kind of setting, and for some concerns perhaps they are. But these characterizations do not satisfy the concerns we have been discussing; under the rubrics "laboratory" or "experiment" very different sorts of organization of talk-in-interaction can be conducted.

Consider, for example, a study of repair recently published by the Dutch psycholinguist Willem Levelt (1983). Levelt had conducted an experiment on the so-called "linearization problem" (organizing a mass of simultaneously presented information into a temporally organized, hence linearized, format in talk). He asked a number of subjects to look at a screen on which were projected different shapes – circles, triangles, and the like, which were connected by lines of various sorts. Their job was to describe these figures so that someone else (not present) would be able to retrieve the figure from the description. The descriptions were all tape recorded. Levelt noticed that in the course of producing the descriptions, people regularly "mispoke;" they started to say one thing, cut themselves off and went back and "fixed" it. Levelt recognized these as self-repairs (Schegloff, Jefferson and Sacks 1977), and he wrote up a separate paper on various aspects of the placement and organization of self-repair and the evidence it gives about processes of self-monitoring by speakers.

But it seems to me that the findings of this work, at least with respect to the organization of repair, have an equivocal status at the present time. Why? Not simply because the talk was produced in a laboratory or experimental context. That the data come from laboratory-produced protocols does not tell us what consequences for the character of the talk are entailed. For example, it does not tell us what the speech exchange system was in which this talk was produced. As it happens, this *was* consequential, and has a bearing on the topic of the research report.

The speech exchange system in which this talk was produced was one whose turn-taking organization denied anyone else the right to talk besides the experimental subject. That is to say, within the boundaries of "the experiment," there was no possibility of a sequence in which current speaker's turn (that is, the subject's) is followed by a next turn in which some recipient (that is, the experimenter or a lab assistant) could have initiated repair. That is, this speech exchange system's turn-taking organization transforms the familiar organization by which opportunities to initiate repair are ordered (Schegloff, Jefferson and Sacks 1977). In fact, one of the classical rationales for the insistence on the methodology of experiments, *formal* experiments, is precisely to exclude the talk or other "extraneous" conduct of the experimenter. The whole point was to hold everything (except the variables of interest) constant. And one part of holding everything constant is to keep the experimenter or the experimenter's agent from talking in potentially varying ways to the different subjects, thereby introducing extraneous, and unmeasured, effects into the experimental results. So the whole point of this sort of experimental format *requires* the denial of the possibility of a next turn in which recipient/experimenter could talk.

We have then a very different turn-taking organization that seems to be subsumed by the formulation of context that we call "laboratory" or "experiment," with various sorts of consequences for the organization of repair. Aside from general organizational considerations that relate next-turn repair to same-turn repair (Schegloff 1979b), more specific analytic issues are implicated, only one of which can be mentioned in passing here. It is that the sequential possibility of a next turn by another participant, and orientation to such a possibility, adds a wholly different *sort* of position for initiating repair to the ones incorporated into Levelt's account. He describes the positions in which repair is initiated *within* a turn in terms of their relationship to that which is being repaired (as do Schegloff, Jefferson and Sacks 1977 with respect to the initiation of repair *across* turns). However, he does not (and with his materials he *can* not) formulate the placement of the initiation of repair relative to the structure of the turn in which it occurs. For example, the initiation of repair cannot be formulated relative to possible completion of the ongoing turn by current speaker and possible start of a next turn by another (the relevance of which is analytically instantiated in Schegloff 1987b: 111), a matter we would expect to be strategic if there is a "preference for self-correction."[5]

Until someone does a parallel analysis on talk from ordinary interaction, and sees whether the findings about same-turn repair come out the same way or not, we will not know the status of Levelt's findings about how same-turn repair is organized (where repair is initiated relative to the trouble source, how far back people go when they are going to reframe the trouble source and the like) – how substantial a contribution to our understanding of repair it can be.

In this case, I think the notion of "the laboratory as context" raises some serious concerns about particular research that was conducted under its auspices. But this is by virtue of the particular speech exchange system which composed it on that occasion, which provides the link of procedural consequentiality to the particular features of the talk being focused on in the research.

Compare with this the data addressed in such work as that reported in Zimmerman and West (1975) and Maynard and Zimmerman (1984). These data are also referred to as occurring in a "laboratory" context. But the speech exchange system involved here is a wholly different one. That speech exchange system provided for the parties (in this case, two "subjects") to talk to each other. The organization of the talk did not render any speaker free of the contingency of someone talking next (with the opportunity, in principle, of initiating repair). Were one to use those tapes to study self-repair, I do not think the results would be subject to the concerns raised above about Levelt's results, even though both of those settings can be characterized by a single context descriptor: "laboratory." The vernacular terms do not do the work. In one case "laboratory" is, and in the other case it is not, procedurally consequential *for the particular phenomena being studied.*[6]

In the search, then, for characterizations of context which will link talk to social structure, we cannot necessarily rely on the social-structural terms we have inherited from the past. Some of them will be procedurally consequential, and some of them will not, just as some will be demonstrably relevant to the participants and some will not. We have to find those terms for formulating context which are both demonstrably relevant to the participants and are procedurally consequential for the aspects of the conduct being treated, *on any given occasion*.

But it is not necessarily our *loss* that we cannot just appropriate terms from the traditional lexicon of "social structure" to understand talk. For we come thereby to use our data as a test of the relevance and viability of our sociological inheritance. We should be prepared to find that some of what we have received from the past, however cherished theoretically, culturally, politically, or ideologically, will not pass this test, and must therefore not be incorporated in our analysis. Rather, we should exercise our capacity to address the details of conduct, and exploit our data as challenges to our theoretical and analytic acumen, to enhance and expand our understanding of what "social structure" could consist of, as a robust and expanding tool of analysis rather than as an inheritance from the disciplinary past.

Social Structure or Conversational Structure?

The third concern mobilized by the present theme is for the balance between the focus on social structure and the focus on conversational structure in studying talk-in-interaction. These two thematic focuses (we would like to think) are potentially complementary. But are they really? We must figure out how to make them complementary, because they can also be alternatives in a more competitive sense. Each makes its own claims in organizing observation and analysis of the data, and one can preempt the other. In particular, the more familiar concerns with social structure can preempt new findings about conversational phenomena.

Let me offer some illustrations of this tension, and exemplify them from a recent paper of Zimmerman's, "Talk and its occasion" (1984), whose object of interest is "calls to the police" (an object with which I have also had some experience, cf. Schegloff 1967). The paper's enterprise appears directed specifically to attending both to the concerns of social structure and to the concerns of conversational structure. It offers a full account of this type of talk-in-interaction, and it does so with a sensitivity not only to the social structure involved, but also to the conversational structure of these occurrences. For example, the paper begins with an account of the kind of overall structural organization of the calls, and then focuses on the particular sequence type that makes up most of the calls, namely, an extended request or complaint sequence.[7]

Despite this commitment to both concerns, it seems to me, there is a tendency for the formulated social-structural context to "absorb" and "naturalize" various details of the talk. These features of the talk are thereby made unavailable, in practice if not in principle, for notice and analysis as accountable details of the talk. Their character as aspects of the talk produced by reference to some conversational or interactional organization is vulnerable to being slighted, in favor of assimilation to some social-structural, institutional, or vernacularly contextual source. How to balance these competing claims on our attention, when the competition takes this form, will be a matter to which analysts who are concerned with the thematics of talk-and-social structure will have to remain sensitive. Let me mention just three instances of the tension of which I speak which come up in Zimmerman's paper, and their consequences, to alert investigators to some of the forms which the issue can take.

One form which this issue takes concerns the proper analytic locus of some observed conversational phenomenon. There is, for example, the treatment of requests by organizations, and service agencies in particular. The police are clearly a service agency, and Zimmerman provides data on animal control services, emergency services, and an airline company, to support the claim that it is the "service agency organization" aspect of the setting which matters. Zimmerman's point is that the requests that callers introduce can involve contingencies, and specifically *organizational* contingencies, that are unknown to the caller. "Social structure" is thus doubly oriented to here, first in the institutional locus of "the police," and second in the fact that one of the parties to the conversation can be characterized as "an organization."

Zimmerman points out that in many of these calls a fair amount of talk intervenes between the request or complaint and its remedy. Regularly this takes the form of a series of question–answer sequences, which Zimmerman terms an "interrogative series." He notes that, sequentially speaking, it is a form of "insertion sequence" (Schegloff 1972), but stresses another aspect of this talk, namely that a number of inquiries get made by the recipient-of-the-request which reflect on the *organizational* contingencies and considerations which the request has occasioned. For example, the police have to decide whether the request is something actionable by the police, and that is not something the caller can be supposed to have the technical information to assess. Zimmerman's discussion (1984: 220–2) links the occurrence of extensive insertion sequences or interrogative series to the contingencies generated by the fact that one of the parties to the request sequence is an *organization*.[8] If this were so, this might be a type case in which we would *have* to invoke the social-structural characteristics of one party to the conversation in order adequately to understand features of the talk (Levinson 1979).

But there are many occurrences in which non-organizational, non-service agency recipients of a request go through a quite similar insertion sequence before responding. One example with which I am familiar in detail is a telephone call involving a 15-year-old boy who has been asked by his 14-year-old "sometimes girlfriend" whether she can borrow his "gun." The request sequence itself goes on for four pages of transcript, and he takes her through a series of considerations – an "interrogative series," if you will: what do you want it for? what kind of gun? why that kind? etc. It turns out that there are considerations that apparently never entered her mind in making this request – should it be the longest one? the best one? the best looking one? the best shooting one? Indeed, when he asks "which gun," it is unclear that she knows the "right" terms with which to characterize which one she wants. (The sequence is discussed in Schegloff 1990).

The point is that we have here a long insertion between request and response. Neither participant is an organization or a service agency. The insertion is addressed to such matters as the warrant for the request and its consequent "actionability" by its recipient. It is not clear, then, what distinctively turns on the participation of *organizations* in request or complaint sequences. We seem to have here a regular expansion property of request/complaint sequences (including, perhaps, some recurrent insert types, such as warrant seeking). Perhaps there are particular features of the conduct of insert expansions which are distinctive when organizations are parties to the talk, but this needs to be shown by analysis which juxtaposes request sequences from organizational settings with request sequences (or their cognates) from other settings: that is, what is distinctive to this talk must be spelled out, and it needs to be shown that for the parties it has to do with "doing organizational talk," or with adapting the talk to their organizational exigencies.[9]

The problem to which I am trying to call attention is the cooptation or preemption of a sequential feature of the talk by a social-structural formulation of its context. In this case, if expansions of the sort here illustrated are endemic to request or complaint sequences, if they are part of the methodic practices for doing *sequences of that sort*, then there is no warrant for introducing *social structures of that sort* into the account. They are not "needed." Further, to introduce the social-structural specification of context is to risk missing the potentially general relevance of insertions to sequences of this type. The attributions to social structure, then, can be *at the expense of* increments to our understanding of conversational organization.[10]

A second issue concerning the tension between the social-structural and the conversation-specific is its persistence within a particular analysis. An illustration is provided by the discussion of a call to the police in which, after the police clerk opens the call with a self-identification as police, the caller says, "Yes, I'd like tuh report a loud party." Zimmerman writes:

> What is being made focally relevant in the opening segment of the call is the division of labor in our society with regard to matters of social control. In Sharrock and Turner's terms ... a socially organized resource – police power – is being mobilized to deal with a problem that others cannot or choose not to deal with by other means. This mobilization raises certain issues, i.e., the policeable nature of the problem and its urgency... *The point to be noted here is that the hearability of an utterance as a "complaint" draws on its location within an institutional framework – that of policing – which touches the interactional realm through the organization of the call.* That organization provides a place, just after the alignment of identities in the opening sequence, the "first topic" slot ... which is where the reason for the call is ordinarily provided. (1984: 213, emphasis added)

There is an intended mutual resonance and grounding between the point of this paragraph and the cited instance – that is, between the caller's utterance being a complaint and having been said in what is "in fact" a call to the police. Again, then, institutional context seems criterial to conversational outcome. Indeed, this seems to be an almost ideal case in point, where the articulation of different components of social structure (via the division of labor with respect to police power) is localized and specified in conversation-structural terms – first-topic position after the opening section.

But how is the bearing of the institutional context – its relevance and procedural consequentiality – provided for here as a resource for analyzing the talk? Well, the police have self-identified as police; that appears to certify the relevance of the institutional context, at least for the police participant. But how about the caller? In a corpus of calls to the police with which I worked some years ago, some callers were not "controlled" by the self-identification by the answerer as "Police," but in the very next turn initiated a transformation of the relevant identities of the participants into personal acquaintances (Schegloff 1967: ch. 5; this happens in Zimmerman's corpus as well, cf. Whalen and Zimmerman 1987: 177). The fact that the call is on the "police line," and has been answered by a "police" self-identification, does not *ipso facto* guarantee that is the orientation relevant to the caller.

This issue does not remain unaddressed. Zimmerman points out that callers/ complainants ordinarily begin their first turns with a response token ("yes" or "yeah") which registers the police self-identification and reconciles it "with the caller's sense of who the recipient of the upcoming complaint or report should properly be" (1984: 218). When the initial response by the police (or other service agency) presents some problem in this regard, the caller's first turn does not begin with such a token. Thus, Zimmerman concludes that these initial bits of utterance, "in aligning their situated identities, provide a working framework which commits participants to the nature of the occasion summoned up by the initiation of the call and thereby *provides for the presumptive hearability of utterances as relevant to the purposes of that occasion of talk*" (1984: 219, emphasis added). This is the basis for the earlier cited claim that "the hearability of an utterance as a 'complaint' draws on its location within an institutional framework." The opening utterances establish that framework, on which the subsequent talk may then "draw."[11]

It is, however, in point to observe that the understanding of the caller's initial utterance as a request or complaint is not provided for solely by the institutional context which the opening may have shown to be mutually relevant. The caller, in the call whose examination is at issue here, has constructed the talk in his/her first turn ("Yes, I'd like tuh report a loud party") not only to *be* "calling the police," but to *do* "calling the police." The format employed for the turn, "I'd like to report . . . " appears to be a format for "reporting to the authorities," and perhaps even for "reporting to the police" specifically.[12] A complaint to the landlord is not, I think, done in this way. In this case, it could be argued, the hearability of the utterance as a complaint most proximately draws on *its conversational construction* as "a complaint to the police." Invoking its "factual" institutional location distracts from the method of its conversational accomplishment.[13]

Here again, the social-structural formulation masks the practices of the talk, in this case as *conversationally constituting* the context for the interaction. Once the identification talk in the opening has been invoked to establish the relevance of the institution for the participants, that institutional locus serves to "naturalize" the mode of talk, to provide a tacit covering principle that normalizes the particular way the participants construct the talk. The vernacular characterization "absorbs" the details of the talk as an unnoticed "of course" in such a "formulated-as-institutional" setting, and does not prompt one to note and explicate how the talk enacts "doing being in that setting". There is a mutually grounding relationship between the details of the talk (here, the "I'd like to report . . . " format) and the global provision that this is a "call to the police," with the former having not been explicitly noted at all, and with the latter shown to be relevant by the police opening self-identification. Relevance having been shown by that, concern for the issue is relaxed. The question is not pressed: how is the next (and *any* next) utterance constructed so as to show/do "calling the police"?

A methodological canon is suggested: establishing relevance and establishing procedural consequentiality should not be "threshold" issues, in the sense that once you have done "enough" to show it, you are finished. Rather they are questions for continuing analysis. And not necessarily in the "loaded" form of "how are they now doing 'calling the police'?", but in "open" form – "what does the form of the talk show about recipient design considerations and about orientation to context (institutional, social-structural, sequential, or whatever)." Because we "know" that not everything said *in* some context (institutional or other) is relevantly oriented to that context.

If the focus of inquiry is the organization of conduct, the details of action, the practices of talk, then every opportunity should be pressed to enhance our understanding of any available detail about those topics. Invoking social structure at the outset can systematically distract from, even blind us to, details of those domains of event in the world.

If the goal of inquiry is the elucidation of *social structure*, one might think that quite a different stance would be warranted, and one would want to give freer play to the effective scope of social structure, and to do so free of the constraints I have been discussing. Though this stance has much to recommend it, it could as well be argued that one does not best serve the understanding of social structure by attributing to it properties which are better understood as the products of other aspects of organized social life, such as interactional structure, or by failing to explicate how social structure is accomplished *in* the conduct. In any case, the understanding of social structure will be enhanced if we explicate how its embodiment in particular contexts on particular occasions permeates the "membrane" (Goffman 1961) surrounding episodes of interaction to register its stamp within them.

A third expression of the tension between social-structural and conversation structural interests in talk data concerns the direction in which analysis is pursued; it can distract pursuit of otherwise inviting analytic tacks on the structure of the talk. For example, Zimmerman reports (1984: 219–20) that most of his data accord with the Sharrock and Turner finding that callers package their complaints in a "single utterance format" (Sharrock and Turner 1978), but he displays as well an instance in which the complaint is presented in a multiple utterance format. It appears that this multiple utterance format (or multiple "turn – constructional unit" turn, Sacks, Schegloff and Jefferson 1974) is a structural alternative to the insertion sequence (the "interrogative series") which occurs in the more common cases. For example, the response to the request which ordinarily follows only after an interrogative series here follows directly after completion of the multi-unit request/complaint turn itself.

This relationship (as possible structural alternatives) between [single-utterance request + interrogative series + response] on the one hand, and [multi-unit request + no interrogative series + response] on the other hand, presents some attractive possibilities for analysis. What varies regularly between organization of a story in a multi-unit, single-turn format as compared to a sequence (that is, multi-turn) format? What are the consequences of the contrasting divisions of labor involved in the two formats, especially the differing "steering" potentials? What is added to or subtracted from or modified in the talk by the imposition of sequence structure on it, or by its preemption by single speaker organization? These questions may be put while "holding constant" that the callers are soliciting police action by the telling.[14]

Of course, such questions may remain unaddressed because inquiry is addressed to other matters, equally conversation relevant, and because one cannot do everything in a single paper. But it is possible that the focus on showing how conversations are articulated with, and shaped by, social and institutional structure diverts attention from the questions about conversation structures which particular details of the talk might otherwise prompt.

What then shall be the balance between the claims of conversational structure, with its stress on the methodic ways of talking in which turns and sequences have ways of developing anonymously, whoever the parties are, as aspects of particular structures of action, sometimes shaped by the participants for the particular co-participants with whom they are engaged – what shall be the balance between those claims on the one hand, and on the other hand those of social structure, with their implication of the constitutive relevance for action and interaction of differentiation, both of participants and of institutional contexts? Clearly there are observations here about the nature of organizations, and perhaps of organizations as participants on one end of the conversation. But how shall we assess their relative claims? When shall we attribute some feature we have noticed about the organization of talk to "internal," conversation structural concerns, and when to "external," social-structural or organizational ones?

Let me introduce here what I will call the "paradox of proximateness," a consideration prompted by various efforts to argue the indispensability of social or legal context for understanding talk.[15] If it is to be argued that some legal, organizational or social environment underlies the participants' organizing some occasion of talk-in-interaction in some particular way, then either one *can* show the *details in the talk* which that argument allows us to notice, and which in return supply the demonstrable warrant for the claim by showing the relevant presence of the sociolegal context in the talk; or one *cannot* point to such detail. If the detail *is* available, then it is the participants' demonstrable orientations *in* the interaction which are the effective agents for the relevant aspects of the interaction (though the parties may also talk in a way which attributes their orientation to some legal constraint, etc.). If the detail *is not* demonstrable, then for the task of explicating the organization and practices of the *talk*, it is not clear what warrant there is for invoking the relevance of the legal and social context or environment which the analyst may want to claim. That is, either there is a proximate, conversationally represented indication of the relevance of context, in which case invocations of more remote context are unnecessary; or there is no conversationally represented indication of the relevance of the aspects of context which have been invoked, in which case the warrant for invoking it has not been established.

An analyst may feel the need to invoke such contexts for the distributional and institutional concerns which animate an inquiry. But if the inquiry is animated by distributional, institutional, or traditional social-structural concerns, why should the character of inquiry into the nature of talk-in-interaction be shaped by considerations extrinsic to *that* enterprise, but felt necessary to another? Indeed, one might argue that the study of talk should be allowed to proceed under its own imperatives, with the hope that its results will provide more effective tools for the analysis of distributional, institutional, and social-structural problems later on than would be the case if the analysis of talk had, from the outset, to be made answerable to problems extrinsic to it.

It may, of course, be the case that talk (or *some* talk) is not analyzable *for its own problematics* without reference to social and institutional contexts of the traditional sort. But that has to be shown. That is, it has to be shown that it is necessary to invoke such contexts in order to understand aspects of the talk itself, rather than aspects of the context in which the talk occurs, or distributional or institutional aspects of that context. (It is, of course, quite a different claim to say that the context is necessary in order to understand the context.) Once it has been shown that some particular spate of talk cannot be adequately analyzed without reference to its "context," it will be necessary to elucidate what in its claimed context is needed to understand the talk, and how to articulate and blend such analysis of context with analysis of the talk. Such a blend will need to adapt, but nonetheless incorporate, such previously discussed constraints on analysis as relevance and procedural consequentiality.

In considering the respective concerns for conversational structure and social structure, then, we must first be clear about the overall commitments and preoccupations of inquiry. It is one thing to be addressed to the understanding of talk-in-interaction as the object of inquiry, and to ask how references to social structure bear on it and might need or permit incorporation in it. It is quite another to be addressed to understanding distributional or institutional or social-structural features of social life, and to ask how talk-in-interaction figures in their social production. I have taken the former of these enterprises as the premise of my discussion. I think the latter enterprise would benefit from analyzing talk by methods appropriate for the analysis of talk in its own right. But the latter enterprise *can* be understood as a development quite independent of the one concerned with the fundamental organization of talk-in-interaction – as a kind of extension of mainstream institutional sociology. In that regard, it could be quite free of the analytic constraints under which conversation analysis has developed. On the other hand, that enterprise, too, might find a quite fresh turning were it to respect the constraints on the study of talk-in-interaction in its own right.

Conclusion

These then are three sorts of issues mobilized, or remobilized, for me when the talk turns to "talk and social structure." However lively our intuitions, in general or with respect to specific details, that it matters that some participants in data we are examining are police, or female, or deciding matters which are specifically constrained by the law or by economic or organizational contingencies, however insistent our sense of the reality and decisive bearing of such features of "social structure" in the traditional sense, the challenge posed is to find a way to show these claims, and show them from the data in three respects:

1   that what is so loomingly relevant for us (as competent members of the society or as professional social scientists) was relevant for the parties to the interaction we are examining, and thereby arguably implicated in their production of the details of that interaction;
2   that what seems inescapably relevant, both to us and to the participants, about the "context" of the interaction is demonstrably consequential for some specifiable aspect of that interaction; and
3   that an adequate account for some specifiable features of the interaction cannot be fashioned from the details of the talk and other conduct of the

participants as the vehicle by which *they* display the relevance of social-structural context for the character of the talk, but rather that this must be otherwise invoked by the analyst, who furthermore has developed defensible arguments for doing so.

In brief, the issue is how to convert insistent intuition, however correct, into empirically detailed analysis.

This is a heavy burden to impose. Meeting it may well lead to exciting new results. But if it is not to be met in one or more respects, arguments will have to be put forward that the concerns I have discussed are no longer in point, are superseded by other considerations, or must yield to the new sorts of findings that are possible if one holds them in abeyance. Simple invocation of the burden of the sociological past will not suffice.

With respect to social structure, then, as with respect to other notions from social science's past such as "intention," the stance we might well consider is treating them as programmatically relevant for the parties, and hence for us. In principle, some one or more aspects of who the parties are and where/when they are talking may be indispensably relevant for producing and grasping the talk, but these are not decisively knowable a priori. It is not for us to *know* what about context is crucial, but to *discover* it, and to discover *new sorts* of such things. Not, then, to privilege sociology's concerns under the rubric "social structure," but to discover them in the members' worlds, if they are there.

Otherwise, we risk volunteering for a path which has led close inquiry into social life astray in the past, but which we now have an opportunity to avoid. In the past, one has needed a special warrant or license to examine closely the details of ordinary life and conduct. Whether it was the "defectiveness" of the people involved as with the mentally ill or retarded or physically handicapped, their moral taint as with criminals, delinquents or other versions of "evil," or the possibilities of enhanced efficacy, as in the improvement of production processes or bureaucratic administration, or enhanced justice or fairness, there was always a "good reason" for looking closely at the details of conduct.

With the license came a shaped focus, either on a target population, a target set of behaviors, or a target aspect of conduct which one examined. What was found was then generally attributed to the license under which one found it. Thus, early investigations into the language of schizophrenics (see Kasanin 1944) came upon the phenomenon of a spate of talk being touched off by the sound of some word in a prior utterance (so-called "clang association"), a phenomenon which students of conversation will recognize as not uncommon in ordinary talk. But having found it through the close examination of schizophrenic talk (talk which could be so closely examined by virtue of its speakers' diagnoses), it was taken as specially characteristic of such talk. So also with children's talk, etc.

If the study of conversation and talk-in-interaction is once again required to be "licensed," whether by practical concerns or by the institutionalized interests of traditional disciplines, then we may well find ourselves attributing – now to "social structure" – what are the indigenous features of talk-in-interaction. Should we not give the latter a chance to be recognized in their own right, especially since they constitute their own sociology in any case?

Notes

These reflections were prepared to serve as the opening presentation of the Talk and Social Structure Conference. In some places they address once again matters taken up in an earlier paper (Schegloff 1987a), but different facets of those matters or in a more detailed fashion. My thanks to Jennifer Mandelbaum for contributions of tact and clarity in the preparation of this written version. I am also indebted to Deirdre Boden, Paul Drew, Douglas Maynard and especially Jack Whalen, whose reactions to an earlier draft, or to the reactions of others to the earlier draft, helped in my efforts to arrive at a text which might be understood as I meant it.

1 Of course, these need not be *competing* claims; the aim must be to make them complementary. For a penetrating treatment of many of the issues taken up here, cf. Heritage 1984a: 280–90.

2 A similar argument is made in Schegloff 1987c for explicating how cultural/linguistic context has the consequences attributed to it. Aspects of prosody may well have consequences for misunderstanding in cross-cultural interaction (e.g., Gumperz 1982), but understanding how they issue in the particular misunderstandings which ensue will require explicating what in the structure of talk-in-interaction converts that prosody into that *type* of misunderstanding.

3 Reasons both of relevance and of procedural consequentiality motivated a decision not to characterize the "Opening up closings" paper (Schegloff and Sacks 1973) as contextually specific to American culture, as had been requested by an anthropologically oriented referee (cf. p. 291, note 4, and also Sacks, Schegloff and Jefferson 1974, p. 700, note 10, on the same issue). That request invoked on behalf of anthropology a cultural sense of "context," parallel to the invocation by sociologists of social-structural senses of "context."

4 A penetrating account along these lines of the constituting of a speech exchange system through practices of talking, in this case of "the job interview," may be found in Button 1987, see also Heritage and Greatbatch, 1991.

5 I leave aside here the exclusion of interactional considerations (Jefferson 1974) which can bear on where and how repair is initiated, an exclusion which allows the depiction of the initiation of repair in strictly grammatical terms.

6 One could harbor a concern that the setting of the Zimmerman/Maynard data *is* procedurally consequential for the organization of topic talk which is their focus, since the participants in their experiment were asked to talk while knowing they were to be interrupted for the start of an experiment in a "few minutes" (Maynard and Zimmerman 1984), a prospect which may well constrain the sort of topic talk participants undertake. There are naturalistic settings which are in many respects similar (such as medical waiting rooms, though there is no injunction to talk there) in which the seriousness of this concern might be assessed.

7 In addition, as several readers of an earlier version of this chapter have pointed out, Zimmerman has in various other writings (both general, as in Wilson and Zimmerman 1980, and other reports of the project on the police, such as Whalen and Zimmerman 1987, 1990) aligned himself with the principles of analysis with which the text here is preoccupied. What is at issue in the ensuing discussion is, then, not a difference over principle, but a concern about how general theoretical and analytic principles are embodied in the *practice* of analysis and its reports. It is a concern with the vulnerability of a newer and technical stance toward the materials of talk-in-interaction in the face of an older stance and idiom, one which furthermore mobilizes our vernacular intuitions despite our contrary resolve.

8   For example, he writes: "Of particular interest here is the fact that making a request engages an organization rather than simply an individual, and thus, varying with the circumstances of the call, encounters contingencies of response which are evident to the organizational personnel receiving the request, but are perhaps unknown or only vaguely perceived by the caller. Thus, a complaint or request routinely involves some processing, that is, some course in which its features – many of which have yet to be made evident – are fit to the requirements of organizational response" (p. 220).

9   One candidate is suggested in another report from the same project (Whalen and Zimmerman 1990). There they suggest that when the call to the police comes from another organization, the police do not undertake to test out the robustness of the report by the caller, as they do when the caller is a "private party," apparently taking it that an "organizational caller" would already have established the actionability of the reported state of affairs. Here the bearing of "organizations" is not the fact that the police *are* an organization, but is rather what they do by virtue of their *interlocutor* being an organization. And what is critical for the way the police complaint-taker proceeds is not just that the complainant actually *is* an organization, but the complaint-takers' *orientation* to its being an organization, and inferences occasioned by that orientation. Still, the argument is that the police conduct themselves differently by virtue of the property of their interlocutor that he speaks for an organization.

10   The key here is the juxtaposition of contextually specialized materials with others of canonical form. This sort of tack is taken in the analysis of conversational openings in calls to the police in another report from the same research project (Whalen and Zimmerman 1987), and on other analytic objects in such recent work as Button 1987, Clayman 1989, and Heritage 1985. Analysis along such lines may prove attractive as well for materials such as those reported on in Maynard's conference paper (1991) which concerned parents of retarded children being informed of the retardation by clinic personnel. Such materials might well invite first an account of the structure of announcement sequences in general, then an account of "bad news" announcement sequences in particular, and then the introduction of the particular setting and task under examination, and the ways in which they informed the enactment or realization or modification of such sequences, insofar as they could be shown to be oriented to by the participants (cf. Schegloff 1988).

     On occasion the literature already provides an account of the non-contextually specialized form of the talk (e.g., for the matters taken up in Whalen and Zimmerman 1987) needed for comparative examination. In most cases, however, the investigator of institutionally specialized forms will need to supply the more generic analysis as well (as in Heritage 1985, for example). In general, the most promising path for research in this area, it seems to me, is for all students of (claimedly) institutionally specialized conduct to work with generic forms as well, if possible.

11   A subsequent paper (Whalen and Zimmerman 1987: 178) describes this position as follows (attributing it to Wilson 1985, but not to Zimmerman 1984):

     When callers report or describe events such as crimes, fires or accidents to a representative of the police, fire department or ambulance service, they engage the occupational responsibilities of such a recipient. The force of a description or event as a request is achieved by the alignment of the identities of teller and recipient in a particular way: as a reporting party or complainant speaking to the agent of an organization officially responsible for dealing with such matters. This is accomplished by the completion of the opening identification sequence (categorical self-identification by dispatcher / acknowledgement by caller) occasioned by the telephone summons. This alignment establishes a sequentially realized institutional context for hearing reports/descriptions as requests.

But Whalen and Zimmerman go on to broaden their account of how the openings of these calls work, and to deepen our understanding of the relevance structure which the police bring to the incoming calls. They show convincingly that even silence or "ambient sounds" on the line (without any confirmation by caller of the relevance of the police institutional self-identification) are treated by the police as possible calls for assistance. (This is to my mind the most cogent basis for arguing that "hearability as a complaint" draws on institutional context.) In developing a basis for this, they drive the account backwards in the structure of the occasion – to the orientations of the police participants in the conversations' "pre-beginnings" (Schegloff 1979a: 27, 34; Whalen and Zimmerman 1987: 180–1) – the moments preceding the first utterance of the conversation itself. What they deepen thereby is our understanding of the orientations which the *police* bring to the talk. What I am concerned with in the text here is, on the other hand, what the *callers* show they bring to the talk, *in* the talk, and after the convergence of identification in the opening.

12   There are other forms of talk in which a caller's first turn displays an orientation to the police, *does* "calling the police," for example, by referring to a car as being "vandalized" (Wilson, 1991), or, more generally, by use of proto-technical terminology of the criminal law or policing. Jack Whalen (personal communication) reports such forms to be "very frequently employed" in complainants' reports to the police. In a later paper from the same research project (Whalen and Zimmerman 1990), complainants' reports to the police are taken up, but their formulations of "the trouble" are left for treatment in a separate paper.

13   Heritage (1984: 280–90) offers a similar treatment of questions and questioning.

14   These two formats could be examined in concert with a third which might prove instructive. It was Alene Terasaki who suggested several years ago (in work which did not come to written fruition) that "announcements" seem to be prepared by their speakers so as to be deliverable in single sentence formats. This is commonly done through one or more pre-expansions or pre-sequences (in addition to the familiar "pre-announcement"). The prospect is, then, to compare (a) a single, multi-unit turn format, with (b) a single-unit turn followed by insertion sequences, with (c) a single-unit turn "prepared" by pre-sequences. It is unlikely, however, that the third of these possibilities will be found in police call data.

15   The point is occasioned most directly by Mehan's conference presentation (1991). Mehan aims to account for the distribution of a school district's disposition of special education cases, in particular the non-allocation of any cases to one program in particular. The account is built from a description of the organization's ways of processing cases, in which a meeting at which disposition is decided and accepted by the parent figures centrally. Mehan argues that various features of the meeting, including the non-mention of certain program possibilities and the order in which the several phases of the discussion are taken up, are centrally conditioned by various features of the legal and economic context in which the school district finds itself (including various provisions of formal law). This claim is not grounded in overt specifiable details of the talk, however.

References

Atkinson, J. M. and Drew, P. 1979: *Order in Court: The Organisation of Verbal Interaction in Judicial Settings*. London: Macmillan.

Atkinson, J. M. and Heritage, J. (eds) 1984: *Structures of Social Action: Studies in Conversation Analysis*, Cambridge: Cambridge University Press.

Blau, P. M. 1977: *Inequality and Heterogeneity: A Primitive Theory of Social Structure*. New York: Free Press/Macmillan.

Boden, D. 1994: *The Business of Talk: Organizations in Action*. Cambridge: Polity Press.

Button, G. 1987: Answers as interactional products: two sequential practices used in interviews. *Social Psychology Quarterly*, 50, 160–71.

Clayman, S. 1989: The production of punctuality: social interaction and temporal organization. *American Journal of Sociology* 95, 659–91.

Goffman, E. 1961: *Encounters*. Indianapolis: Bobbs-Merrill Educational.

—— 1983: The interaction order. *American Sociological Review* 48, 1–17.

Gumperz, J. 1982: *Discourse Strategies*. Cambridge: Cambridge University Press.

Heritage, J. 1984: *Garfinkel and Ethnomethodology*. Cambridge: Polity Press.

—— 1985: Analyzing news interviews: aspects of the production of talk for an "overhearing" audience. In T. van Dijk (ed.), *Handbook of Discourse Analysis*, vol. 3: *Discourse and Dialogue*. London: Academic Press, 95–119.

Heritage, J. and Greatbatch, D. 1991: On the institutional character of institutional talk: the case of news interviews. In Deirdre Boden and Don H. Zimmerman (eds), *Talk & Social Structure: Studies in Ethnomethodology and Conversation Analysis* Berkeley: University of California Press, 93–137.

Jefferson, G. 1974: Error correction as an interactional resource. *Language in Society*, 2, 181–99.

Kasanin, J. S. 1944: *Language and Thought in Schizophrenia*. Berkeley: University of California Press.

Levelt, W. J. M. 1983: Monitoring and self-repair in speech. *Cognition*, 14, 41–104.

Levinson, S. C. 1979: Activity types and language. *Linguistics*, 17, 356–99.

Maynard, D. W. 1991: The perspective-display series and the delivery and receipt of diagnostic news. In Deirdre Boden and Don H. Zimmerman (eds), *Talk & Social Structure: Studies in Ethnomethodology and Conversation Analysis*, Berkeley: University of California Press, 164–91.

Maynard, D. W. and Zimmerman, D. H. 1984: Topical talk, ritual and the social organisation of relationships. *Social Psychology Quarterly*, 47, 301–16.

Mehan, H. 1991: The school's work of sorting students. In Deirdre Boden and Don H. Zimmerman (eds), *Talk & Social Structure: Studies in Ethnomethodology and Conversation Analysis*, Berkeley: University of California Press, 71–89.

Mehan, H., Hertweck, A. and Meihls, J. L. 1986: *Handicapping the Handicapped: Decision Making in Students' Educational Careers*. Stanford: Stanford University Press.

Parsons, T. 1937: *The Structure of Social Action*. New York: McGraw-Hill.

Sacks, H. 1964–5: Harvey Sacks: Lectures 1964–1965, edited by Gail Jefferson, with an introduction/memoir by Emanuel A. Schegloff, *Human Studies* (1989), 12(3–4) 211–393.

—— 1972a: An initial investigation of the usability of conversational data for doing sociology. In D. Sundow (ed.), *Studies in Social Interaction*, New York: Free Press, 31–74.

—— 1972b: On the analyzability of stories by children. In J. J. Gumperz and D. Hymes (eds), *Directions in Sociolinguistics*, New York: Holt, Rinehart and Winston, 325–45.

Sacks, H., Schegloff, E. and Jefferson, G. 1974: A simplest systematics for the organization of turn-taking for conversation. *Language*, 50, 696–735.

Schegloff, E. 1967: The first five seconds: the order of conversational openings. Unpublished Ph.D. dissertation, Department of Sociology, University of California, Berkeley.

—— 1972: Notes on a conversational practice: formulating place. In D. Sudnow (ed.), *Studies in Social Interaction*, New York: Macmillan/Free Press, 75–119.

—— 1979a: Identification and recognition in telephone conversation openings. In G. Psathas (ed.), *Everyday Language: Studies in Ethnomethodology*. New York: Irvington Press, 23–78.

—— 1979b: The relevance of repair to syntax-for-conversation. In T. Givon (ed.), *Syntax and Semantics 12: Discourse and Syntax*, New York: Academic Press, 261–88.

—— 1987a: Between micro and macro: contexts and other connections. In J. Alexander et al. (eds), *The Micro–Macro Link*, Berkeley: University of California Press.

—— 1987b: Analyzing single episodes of interaction: an exercise in conversation analysis. *Social Psychological Quarterly* 50, 101–14.

—— 1987c: Some sources of misunderstanding in talk-in-interaction. *Linguistics*, 25, 201–18.

—— 1988: On an actual virtual servo-mechanism for guessing bad news: a single-case conjecture. *Social Problems* 35, 442–57.

—— 1990: On the organization of sequences as a source of "coherence" in talk-in-interaction. In Bruce Dorval (ed.), *Conversational Organization and its Development*, vol. 38 in the series, Advances in Discourse Processes, Norwood, NJ: Ablex, 51–77.

Schegloff, E. A. and Sacks, H. 1973 (1974): Opening up closings. *Semiotica*, 7, 289–327. Reprinted 1974 in Roy Turner (ed.), *Ethnomethodology*, Harmondsworth: Penguin, 233–64.

Schegloff, E., Jefferson, G. and Sacks, H. 1977: The preference for self-correction in the organization of repair for conversation. *Language*, 53, 361–82.

Sharrock, W. W. and Turner, R. 1978: On a conversational environment for equivocality. In J. Schenkein (ed.), *Studies in the Organization of Conversational Interaction*, New York: Academic Press, 173–98.

West, C. 1979: Against our will: male interruptions of females in cross-sex conversations. *Annals of the New York Academy of Science*, 327, 81–97.

—— 1984: *Routine Complications: Troubles in Talk Between Doctors and Patients*. Bloomington, IN: Indiana University Press.

Whalen, M. R. and Zimmerman, D. H. 1987: Sequential and institutional contexts in calls for help. *Social Psychology Quarterly*, 50, 172–85.

—— 1990: Describing trouble: epistemology in citizen calls to the police. *Language in Society*, 19, 465–92.

Wilson, T. P. 1985: Social structure and social interaction. Unpublished ms., Department of Sociology, University of California, Santa Barbara.

—— 1991: Social structure and the sequential organization of interaction. In Deirdre Boden and Don H. Zimmerman (eds), *Talk & Social Structure: Studies in Ethnomethodology and Conversation Analysis*, Berkeley: University of California Press, 22–43.

Wilson, T. P. and Zimmerman, D. H. 1980: Ethnomethodology, sociology, and theory. *Humboldt Journal of Social Relations*, 7, 52–88.

Zimmerman, D. H. 1984: Talk and its occasion: the case of calling the police. In D. Schiffrin (ed.), *Meaning, Form, and Use in Context: Linguistic Applications*, George-town University Roundtable on Language and Linguistics, Washington, DC: Georgetown University Press, 210–28.

Zimmerman, D. and West, C. 1975: Sex roles, interruptions and silences in conversations. In B. Thorne and N. Henley (eds), *Language and Sex: Difference and Dominance*, Rowley, MA: Newbury House, 105–29.

14 Refusing Invited Applause: Preliminary Observations from a Case Study of Charismatic Oratory

J. Maxwell Atkinson

> The natural leaders in distress have been holders of specific gifts of the body and spirit; and these gifts have been believed to be supernatural, not accessible to everybody. The concept of "charisma" is here used in a completely "value-neutral" sense.
>
> *Max Weber*

A Conversation-Analytic Approach to the Study of Oratory

This chapter reports some observations from a program of research in which the approach and findings of conversation analysis are being applied to the study of courtroom interaction (see Atkinson & Drew, 1979; Drew, 1985; Pomerantz, 1982). One of the interests prompted by such work is public speaking more generally and the ways in which interaction between orators and audiences compares and contrasts with everyday conversational interaction (Atkinson, 1982). This in turn has led to the collection of audio and video recordings of public speaking in a variety of settings other than courtrooms. This chapter is one of a series of reports on the devices used by orators to elicit or invite displays of approval from their audiences (see also Atkinson, 1983, 1984a,b). Taken together, these various investigations represent an attempt to develop the sort of comparative analysis of speech exchange systems that has been recommended by Sacks, Schegloff, and Jefferson (1974).

For present purposes, the phenomenon described here is characterized as the "refusal of invited applause" and is, in a very large corpus of recorded political speeches, an extremely rare occurrence. Almost all the instances so far observed, however, are in the speeches of one politician, the Right Honourable Anthony Wedgewood Benn, M.P., former Labour Cabinet minister and leading spokesman for the left wing of the Labour Party. Not only does he employ the device with extraordinary regularity (sometimes in 100% of all instances where applause occurs in the course of a speech), but he also appears to be the only contemporary British politician who routinely does so. And, from an analytic point of view, it is of particular interest that he is also widely regarded as one of the most charismatic orators currently operating on the British political scene. In addition to describing the device, then, this chapter also suggests how its use by a public speaker may provide audiences and commentators with a basis for arriving at more than usually favorable assessments of his effectiveness as an orator and, by implication, of the popularity of his policies. Before proceeding to report the observations, however, it is necessary first to provide a brief outline of the earlier work from which they have been developed.

Some Interactional Dimensions of Oratory

It has been suggested elsewhere that a central practical problem faced by any public speaker is that of how to hold the attention of his audience and that various rhetorical techniques can be understood as methods or devices for resolving this problem (Atkinson, 1982; Atkinson & Drew, 1979). One reason why the sustained attentiveness of audiences at public settings is so continually problematic is that a major incentive for paying attention to what a current speaker is saying in the course of conversational interaction becomes largely inoperative in multiparty gatherings where one speaker speaks at a time. As Sacks et al. (1974) have pointed out, close and detailed monitoring of what a present speaker is saying is essential if other parties to a conversation are to be in a position to know exactly when they may start a next turn or what may appropriately be said. But public speeches, lectures, sermons, and the like tend to be very much longer than turns at talk in conversation, and audience members can typically relax in (or be frustrated by) the knowledge that they are unlikely to get a chance to speak at all. In other words, they have little opportunity and are under no obligation to produce a display of their understanding or appreciation of what a speaker has just said. What is recurrently relevant as a reason for paying close attention to each current turn in a sequence of conversational interaction may thus become largely irrelevant in interactional environments where one speaker speaks for most or all of the time to recipients who speak for little or none of the time.

The absence of much in the way of an audience response, however, is not merely a potential source of difficulty for orators seeking to attract the attention and approval of their audiences; it also poses problems for analytic observers with an interest in identifying practices that are successfully used to elicit audience attentiveness and affiliation. It means that the researcher is deprived of a resource that has proved crucially important in conversation-analytic inquiries, namely the capacity to inspect a next turn in order to discover how a speaker analyzed and responded to a previous turn. Thus, while various details in the way a public speech is produced may sound intuitively as though they might have been designed to elicit audience attention or approval, the absence of a next turn that can be examined prevents any such claims from being supported or strengthened with reference to what the audience members themselves actually made of some particular sequence of talk.

Viewed in these terms, points where audiences produce collective displays of approval (e.g., by clapping, cheering, laughing) and disapproval (e.g., by booing, jeering, heckling) are particularly promising sequential environments for analytic purposes. They are places where members of an audience take a more than usually active and noticeable part in the interaction. By producing such responses, the audience provides fairly concrete and unambiguous evidence that it had been paying close attention at least to the immediately preceding segment of talk. Observational studies can therefore be directed to an examination of how such segments are designed and delivered, and the present research has so far focused on sequences in response to which audiences produce displays of approval or affiliation.[1]

Several observations can be made about the way in which orators and their audiences coordinate their activities in the course of a speech (Atkinson, forthcoming a). It can be noted that audiences do not produce displays of approval at any moment whatsoever and without regard for where a speaker has got to in what he is saying. Rather they wait until a possible completion point has been (or is about to be) reached before getting a response under way. In other words, response onset occurs either immediately after (i.e., with no gap) or just before an orator completes what he has just been saying. Examples of these two sequential positions can be seen in fragments (1) and (2) respectively:[2]

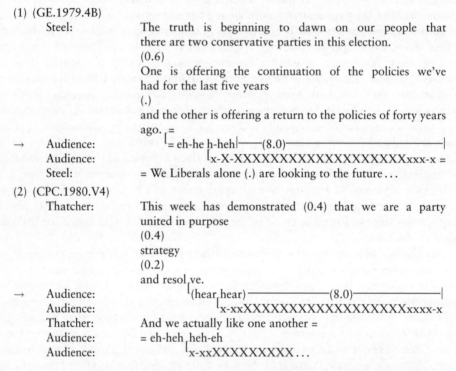

(1) (GE.1979.4B)

    Steel: The truth is beginning to dawn on our people that there are two conservative parties in this election.
(0.6)
One is offering the continuation of the policies we've had for the last five years
(.)
and the other is offering a return to the policies of forty years ago. ⌈=

→   Audience: ⌊= eh-he h-heh⌊——(8.0)————————⌋
    Audience: ⌊x-X-XXXXXXXXXXXXXXXXXXXxxx-x =
    Steel: = We Liberals alone (.) are looking to the future...

(2) (CPC.1980.V4)

    Thatcher: This week has demonstrated (0.4) that we are a party united in purpose
(0.4)
strategy
(0.2)
and resol⌈ve.

→   Audience: ⌊(hear⌈hear) —————————(8.0)————⌋
    Audience: ⌊x-xxXXXXXXXXXXXXXXXXXXxxxx-x
    Thatcher: And we actually like one another =
    Audience: = eh-heh⌈heh-eh
    Audience: ⌊x-xxXXXXXXXXX...

These extracts not only illustrate how audiences typically coordinate their responses to occur close to a possible completion point in the talk but also draw attention to a similarly recurrent feature of the way most orators (with the notable exception discussed below) orient to such responses. Thus it can be seen that Steel and Thatcher both defer continuation until the applause has subsided. By withholding further talk while applause is in progress, orators can thereby be heard to treat it as an appropriate thing for the audience to be doing at that point and as an activity to be accorded priority over that of continuing or attempting to continue with the speech. Insofar as public speakers and their audiences can thus be seen to be collaborating in the production and preservation of one activity at a time (i.e., either talk by the speaker or a response by the audience), it would appear that the turn-taking system operative in these large-scale public gatherings resembles the turn-taking system for conversation more closely than might be thought at first (Sacks et al., 1974).

Two further relevant recurrent features of audience responses are also evident in fragments (1) and (2). First, with extraordinary regularity, bursts of applause have been found to last for around eight ($\pm$ one) seconds. And there is also some evidence that, when the duration is longer than nine seconds or shorter than seven seconds, the response may be hearable as being respectively more or less enthusiastic than usual (Atkinson, 1984a,b). Second, "a burst of applause" is a remarkably accurate way of describing the way in which the intensity of clapping increases after initial onset, as is the use of words like "subside" for referring to the way it terminates. Thus, as can be seen from Figure 14.1, a typical burst of applause reaches maximum intensity within a second or so from its starting point, remains relatively flat for about six seconds, and then falls away somewhat more slowly than it began.

This tendency for applause to reach maximum intensity so soon after onset has an important implication for the way something said by an orator can be heard to receive a more than usually enthusiastic response. There are grounds for supposing that such an impression is more likely when the audience response begins somewhat before the speaker reaches a completion point. This suggestion arises partly from listening to instances where applause onset occurs after a delay and partly from what is known from studies of conversation about the tendency for agreements and other affiliative responses to be produced early in relation to the object with which affiliation is being displayed (Pomerantz, 1975, 1984). If the applause starts early enough, its intensity will rise in such a way that, by the time the speaker stops talking, it will already have reached, or be close to, its maximum. A consequence of this, discussed below, is that an orator who pauses at such a point finds that attempts to continue are drowned out by the just-started ovation.

Given that affiliative responses are so closely coordinated with the immediately preceding talk, audiences must presumably have methods for anticipating that and when they should show approval in advance of a completion point being reached by a speaker. In other words, the precise timing of response onset that is so recurrently exhibited in these sequential environments presumably depends on members of an audience being able to analyze successfully the talk for features that (1) display the point being made as one worthy of being affiliated with, and (2) project an upcoming place where such a response may appropriately begin.

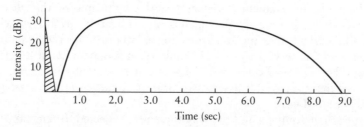

Figure 14.1   Electronic reading of applause intensity. Shaded curve, talk; unshaded curve, applause. (Taken from a PM 200 Pitch and Intensity Analyzer, manufactured by Voice Identification, Inc., Somerville, New Jersey. I am grateful to R. A. W. Bladon, Director of the Oxford University Phonetics Laboratory, for his help in making this and other readings possible.)

Research suggests that a range of devices, methods, or procedures are available to speakers for getting a group of people more or less simultaneously to produce an identical next activity, such as standing up, cheering, or clapping (Atkinson, 1984a,b; Atkinson & Drew, 1979, Chap. 3). It also suggests that, if this is to be successfully accomplished, it may be necessary for a speaker to employ a number of devices in combination with each other. Otherwise, he would have to rely on all the members of his audience being so equally attentive to the ongoing proceedings that each and every one of them would recognize some single device being used on its own and then produce the sequentially relevant next action being projected by it. By employing several devices, all of which project the same action as the relevant thing to be done next, a speaker can substantially reduce the likelihood of audience members failing to notice any of them.

This general claim about the effectiveness of mobilizing a number of devices at once is consistent with some of the findings from the present research. And while it is not possible here to detail all the observations made so far, a necessary preliminary to what follows is summarized enough to give a sense for what is meant by invited applause.

Techniques for Inviting Applause: A Summary

Observably recurrent properties of sequences from public speeches that occasion affiliative responses include certain regularities in the contents or substance of the point being made, the verbal constructions used in making a point, and various intonational, rhythmic, and nonverbal displays. For present purposes, however, attention is confined to matters of substance and verbal construction.

With overwhelming regularity, applause and other displays of approval occur after a speaker has made an assertion that is hearable either as praise for his own side (party's position, activities, policies, proposals, personnel) or as an attack on or criticism of his opponents. It can be noted that extracts (1) and (2) above both involve assertions of this sort. In the former, Mr. Steel (leader of the Liberal Party) attacks the Labour and Conservative Parties in a speech delivered during the general election of 1979. And in the latter, taken from a speech on the final day of the 1980 Annual Conference of the Conservative Party, Mrs. Thatcher can be heard to praise virtues of the party as demonstrated by the week's proceedings.

A feature of such assertions is that they typically start by giving advance notice that a favorable statement about "us" or an unfavorable statement about "them" is about to be made. In fragment (1), Steel does this by proposing that *there are two conservative parties in this election*, which is readily hearable by anyone who knows him to be a Liberal as prefacing and projecting an attack on his two main opponents (the Labour and Conservative parties). Similarly, in fragment (2), it is evident from the moment Thatcher indicates that she is about to describe what *this week has demonstrated* that a favorable assessment of *us as a gathering of the party faithful* will shortly be produced.

In terms of their contents and the way these are projected, fragments (1) and (2) exemplify features that are massively recurrent in the talk that precedes audience displays of approval. In a count run on 100 instances where applause occurred in the course of political speeches, it was found that assertions praising "us" or attacking "them" (or some combination of both) were involved in 95% of the cases.[3]

The verbal constructions used to build the assertions in fragments (1) and (2) are also examples of those most recurrently deployed before affiliative audience responses, namely two-part contrasts at arrows A and B in (1) and three-part lists at arrows a, b, and c, in (2):

(1)   Steel: The truth is beginning to dawn on our people that there are two conservative parties in this election.
                    (0.6)
a →   { One is offering the continuation of the policies we've had for the last five years
                    (.)
b →   { and the other is offering a return to the policies of forty years ago. ⌜=
       Audience: ⌊= eh-he⌜h-heh|——(8.0)———|
       Audience: ⌊x-X-XXXXXXXxxx-x
(2)   Thatcher: This week has demonstrated (0.4) that we are a party united in
a →   purpose
                    (0.4)
b →   strategy
                    (0.2)
c →   and resol⌜ve.
       Audience: ⌊(hear⌜hear)|
       Audience: ⌊x-xxXXXXXXXXXXXXXXXXXxxxx-x

These types of verbal construction appear to be both very adaptable for building assertions involving praise or criticism and extremely effective as methods for projecting a recognizable completion point that can be anticipated by audience members and responded to when it is reached. Thus a hearer who successfully identifies what is currently being said as the first part of a two-part contrast can readily work out what it will take to complete the second part and hence be ready to produce a response when that has been done. And, as Jefferson has noted, three-part lists have a similar potential for projecting utterance completion:

> list completion can constitute utterance completion; i.e. a point at which another can or should start talking. Crucially, *forthcoming completion is projectable from the point at which a list is recognizably under way*; i.e. given two items so far, a recipient can see that a third will occur, and that upon its occurrence utterance completion can have occurred whereupon it will be his turn to talk. (Jefferson, 1980, p. 13; my emphasis)

While these remarks were based on studies of conversational interaction, the present research suggests that it only requires the substitution of *respond collectively* for *talk* to make them equally applicable to turn transitions between an orator and his audience in a large-scale public setting.

A sense for the extent to which these verbal constructions recur in sequences preceding applause can be obtained from the results of a statistical exercise similar to that referred to above. This showed that, in the sample of political speeches examined, 63% of the affiliative responses occurred after a contrast, 17% after a three-part list, and 10% after a contrast and list were deployed in combination with each other. On present evidence, then, these two types of verbal construction appear to be involved in something like 90% of all instances where applause occurs in the course of political speeches.

The general argument emerging from this research is that such sequences of talk are built up over their course in a way that (1) informs the audience that what is in progress is something in response to which a collective display of approval would be a relevant next thing to do and (2) projects a point at which completion can be anticipated in advance of its being reached, enabling the audience to produce an immediate or early response. Where devices that work to accomplish such ends are mobilized by orators, it would appear that the sequence of talk thereby produced is made available to be analyzed and treated by audience members as constituting an invitation to applaud. Moreover, the capacity to analyze and respond to it as such depends on members of an audience paying particularly close attention to what is being said, at least from the first point at which it becomes evident that the forth-coming relevance of a response is in the process of being projected.

With this summary, it is now possible to consider how a public speaker can refuse invited applause and the possible implications this may have for assessments of his skill as an orator.

Refusing Invited Applause

Postresponse Continuation

Marked overlap competition

Observations of sequences where applause occurs during speeches by Mr. Wedge-wood Benn suggest that he makes regular use of all the procedures so far identified in the present research and that a single instance often involves the combined deploy-ment of almost all of them at once. In the light of the above summary, for example, fragment (3) can be viewed as something of a technical masterpiece:[4]

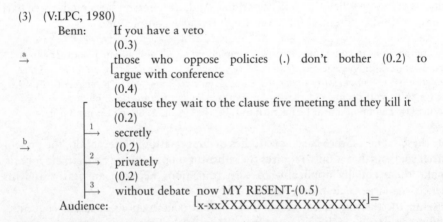

(3)   (V:LPC, 1980)
         Benn: If you have a veto
                     (0.3)
     a   those who oppose policies (.) don't bother (0.2) to
     →   [argue with conference
                     (0.4)
                     because they wait to the clause five meeting and they kill it
                     (0.2)
              1   secretly
     b   →   (0.2)
     →   2   privately
              →   (0.2)
              3   without debate now MY RESENT-(0.5)
         Audience: [x-xxXXXXXXXXXXXXXXXXX]=

In this extract from a speech to the 1980 Labour Party Conference, Benn contrasts what his opponents (identifiable here as his former cabinet colleagues in the Call-aghan government) do not do but ought to do with what they do do but ought not to do. The second part of the contrast is then completed with a three-part list that elaborates and concludes the criticism of "them." To anyone familiar with recent debates within British politics, the sequence is readily recognizable as a strong attack on the then-established leadership of the Labour Party, and as such it projects the relevance of a display of approval by Benn's left-wing allies at the Conference.

Given that the extract can, in terms of the earlier discussion, be viewed as a particularly finely crafted invitation to applaud, it is of some interest to note that Benn does not stop talking when the audience response begins. Without pausing at all, he continues to talk across the transition space to a point just beyond that where the applause reaches maximum intensity and, as he does so, he raises his voice in response to the increasing volume of the applause (indicated in the transcript by capital letters). Furthermore, what he says here is very different from the talk that is more usually found in slight overlap with applause onset. Early audience responses typically overlap with the final syllable(s) involved in completing a previous assertion (see above), whereas in this case Benn continues beyond completion to project a shift into the beginning of a next assertion. A fairly immediate consequence of this is that he has to break off in the middle of a word in response to the level of intensity reached by the applause.

Even at this early stage after response onset it is possible to get a sense for how a proposal to continue can be heard as a refusal to acknowledge that such an audience response is a relevant next action. For, as was noted earlier, the majority of public speakers, by making no attempt to continue beyond a projected completion point until after the applause has subsided, can be heard to acknowledge or accept the appropriateness of applause as a response to what they have just said. A proposal to continue, however, is not only hearable as a refusal to acknowledge the applause but also as an announcement that the speaker had been expecting to proceed without interruption, that the just-started display of affiliation had come as something of a surprise to him, and hence also that it had not been projected, prompted, or invited by what he had said (or how he had said it). And, insofar as it displays that he is intent on carrying on with his speech, it can also be heard to propose that the speaker accords higher priority to the business of developing his argument than to waiting around to accept (or savor) the plaudits of the audience. However, he is then observably prevented from so doing by the intensity of the audience's response to his prior assertion (at *RESENT-*). At a very early point after the proposal to continue, then, it is already possible to see how the unfolding interaction is exhibiting features that can already be interpreted as reflecting favorably on the speaker and the point he has just made.

Against this, it might be argued that too much is being made of so brief an attempt to continue and perhaps even that to overshoot a completion point in this fashion could equally well be seen as evidence of oratorical incompetence as manifested in a failure to notice that a response was now relevant and under way.

In fact, overshooting a completion point is a regular feature in the speeches of less effective orators. However, it differs from what occurs here in that it appears to arise when a speaker is using a text and reads past a completion point without apparently noticing the relevance or occurrence of an audience response (the speaker's eyes being focused on the script rather than the audience). Also, unlike

Benn, less competent orators tend to look embarrassed or surprised on being forced to break off and make no further attempts to continue until the applause has subsided.

But quite apart from the fact that a range of highly effective projection devices have just been deployed, an interpretation of oratorical incompetence receives little support from the video tape. In common with most great orators, Benn is seldom to be seen using a script, and this speech is no exception. Throughout this particular extract, he was continually looking directly at his audience and could therefore hardly have failed to notice the beginnings of a response even before proposing to continue beyond completion. There is also some evidence of a response on his part to applause onset in that, having not blinked his eyes at all while producing the assertion, he does blink just after *debate* (i.e., at the point where the applause starts). Furthermore, had he been somehow out of touch with what his audience was doing, it seems rather unlikely that he would have been able to coordinate the volume of his own delivery with the increasing intensity of the audience response (*now MY RESENT-*). Nor would such an interpretation be consistent with the way this sequence develops subsequently, where there is further evidence of his displaying a continuing sensitivity to the level of applause intensity. For, after two more attempts to continue, each of which progresses a little further than the last, he does not actually proceed with the next point until the applause has begun to subside:

```
(3a)  (Continuation of fragment 3)
      Benn:            without debate ⌈now  MY RESENT- (0.5)                     ⌉=
      Audience:                       ⌊x-xxXXXXXXXXXXXXXXXX⌋=

      Benn:            ⌈my resentment (2.0) my resentment (.) about⌉=
      Audience:      =⌊XXXXXXXXXXXXXXXXXXXXXXXXXXXXXX⌋=

  →   Benn:            ⌈theuh (0.5) my resentment about the exclusion⌉=
      Audience:      =⌊XXXXXXXxxxxxxxxxxxxxxxxxxxxxxxxxxxxxx⌋=

  →   Benn:            ⌈of the House⌉ of Lords and you mustn't . . .
      Audience:      =⌊xxxxxxxx-x-⌋
```

From this it emerges that *now MY RESENT-*is only the first of several occasions where Benn proposes continuation but can then be seen to be prevented from so doing by the intensity of the affiliative response. It thus marks the start of a period of overlap competition between speaker and audience, which has some interesting similarities with what has been reported elsewhere about the way this can operate in the course of conversational interaction (Jefferson & Schegloff, n.d.). For example, Ken's talk in line 3 of the following fragment involves repeated restarts that closely resemble those by Benn in the one above:

```
(4)  (Jefferson & Schegloff, n.d., p. 11)
     Ken:         No, they're women who'v devo ⌈ded their li-        ⌉
     Roger:                                     ⌊They're women ⌋that hadda=

 →   Ken:       =⌈their-    ⌈their life-           ⌈their life, to uh
     Roger:     =⌊bad love  ⌊life'n became nuns.hh ⌊heh hh!
                 (0.6)
     Ken:         the devotion of the church.
```

With respect to this form of overlapping talk, Jefferson and Schegloff have noted that

> it appears that participants routinely distribute their talk into displays of Turn Occupant (with a single coherent continuous utterance) and Turn Claimant (with a repeated recycle of an utterance component). These activities can be examined for their status as Marked or Unmarked competitive forms; i.e., for their explicit attention to, or displayed dismissal of, the fact of overlap and the trouble it might cause for hearing–understanding. (Jefferson & Schegloff, n.d., p. 24)

Viewed in these terms, the overlapping talk by Benn in fragment (3) displays him as a Turn Claimant engaged in Marked overlap competition with a Turn Occupant (the audience) in Unmarked competition.

From the point of view of the present analysis, this has at least two interesting implications. The first is that it is Benn who is initiating the competition from the first restart onwards. The second is that, as far as their relative effectiveness at winning the competition is concerned (i.e., getting to speak in the clear of overlap), recycled restarts appear to be a less effective method than merely continuing to speak, or in the present case to applaud, through and beyond the restarts (Jefferson, 1979; Jefferson & Schegloff, undated). In other words, the technique used by Benn would seem to be one that both brings the problem of overlap into existence in the first place and is at the same time unlikely to bring about an immediate solution to the problem thereby created.

It would therefore appear that, if favorable assessments are likely to be made by observers (whether audience members, party managers, media commentators, or others) when an orator is seen to be having trouble making himself heard above the roars of the crowd, the use of this simple technique can have considerable advantages for a professional politician. Such a "problem," it may be noted, does not arise for the majority of political orators who make no attempt to continue after a response starts and who wait for it to subside before doing so.

Unmarked overlap competition

Making attempts to continue with a further point after applause onset (marked overlap competition) is only one of the ways in which Mr. Benn routinely talks in overlap with the affiliative responses of his audiences. Another involves him in continuing to talk without any restarts and is more like what has been referred to as "unmarked" overlap competition. An example of this is to be found at a crucial point in the speech made to the 1980 Labour Party Conference, which has subsequently become known as his Thousand Peers Speech (a discussion of the press coverage received by this fragment is contained in Atkinson, 1984a).

```
(5)  (V12:LPC, 1980)
     Benn:              ...an immediate bill is to do what the movement
                        has wanted to do (.) for a HUNDRED YEARS (0.7)
                                      [
     Audience:           x-xxxXXXXXXXXXXXXXXXXXXXXX]=
     Benn:              AND TO GET RID OF THE HOUSE OF LORDS (0.5)
                       [
     Audience:        =XXXXXXXXXXXXXXXXXXXXXXXXXXXX...
```

In this extract Benn pauses briefly just after applause onset and then continues, not to produce repeated restarts but to complete the point on which he had already embarked prior to the audience's response. One of the interesting things about the sequence is that the audience begins to applaud very early in relation to projected completion, thereby displaying that it can already anticipate (and approve of) what he is about to say. Under such circumstances, the speaker can safely continue through to completion without worrying about whether or not what he says will be heard, as he now knows that the audience knows what it will be. However, when it comes to developing the point further, and hence in a direction that the audience may not be able to anticipate, he reverts to the use of repeated restarts until the intensity of the applause declines to a level at which he can rely on being heard.

```
(5a)  (Continuation of fragment 5)
  →    Benn:        =...LORDS (0.5) AND IF I MAY SAY SO (2.0)
       Audience:   =[...XXXXXXXXXXXXXXXXXXXXXXXXXXXXX]=
  →    Benn:        WE SHALL HAVE TO DO IT (3.0) WE SHALL
       Audience:   =[XXXXXXXXXXXXXXXXXXXXXXXXXXXXXXX]=
       Benn:        HAVE TO DO IT (0.5) BY UHH BY CREATING
       Audience:   =[XXXXXXXXXXXXXXXXXXXXXXXXXXXXXXXXX]=
       Benn:        A THOUSAND PEERS AND THEN ABOLISHING=
       Audience:   =[XXXXxxxxx-x]
       Benn:        =the peerage as well (.) at the time that the bill goes through-
```

In this sequence, then, the overlapping talk involves unmarked competition with the applause up to the completion point that early response onset could be taken to have anticipated. After half a second, the speaker initiates a phase of marked competition with *AND IF I MAY SAY SO* and by repeating *WE SHALL HAVE TO DO IT*. It was noted earlier that speakers who engage in competitive overlapping talk of this sort can be heard to be having trouble speaking or to be prevented from doing so by the rapturous reception from their audience. This fragment is therefore of some interest in that it provides evidence that the speaker specifically orients to such an interpretation in the design of what he says on continuing beyond the completion point. Thus, insofar as *IF I MAY SAY SO* can be heard to be asking permission to proceed, it can also be heard as responsive to the fact that there is an obstacle in the way of his saying more at that particular point in the interaction (see also *AND MAY I SAY:UH* ... at an almost identical sequential position in fragment [6] below). A continuing orientation to the level of applause intensity is again displayed by the repeated restarts that follow and the way he defers carrying on without further restarts until the audience response has begun to die away.

On present evidence, then, it appears that marked and unmarked competitive talk is finely coordinated both with the current level of applause intensity and with where the speaker has got to in the course of what he is saying. Both have the effect of creating a situation in which the speaker is having to struggle to make himself heard in the face of his audience's enthusiasm, but neither involves any risk that the contents of what he is saying will be lost on them.

Viewed in these terms, the following extract from a *New York Times* article on the different styles of oratory employed by John F. Kennedy and Richard Nixon in the 1960 U.S. presidential election campaign is of some interest. It not only reports that

Kennedy often engaged in competitive overlapping talk with the applause but also interprets it in the favorable way that is made available by such occurrences:

> When the crowds start to applaud, he [Kennedy] is often carried by his own momentum through the first outburst, smothering the roar.
>
> CONVEYS SENSE OF CONVICTION
>
> For all this, his platform style conveys a sense of passion and conviction that seems to reach the crowd, even when his reasoning is lost. (*New York Times*, September 25, 1960)

In the light of the present observations, then, what is reported here was apparently unmarked overlap competition. However, if Kennedy employed this in a manner similar to Benn, it must be doubted how far any of his reasoning was lost.

Repeating Invitation–Refusal Sequences

The availability of techniques for inviting and refusing applause means that it is possible for an orator to use a further invitation to refuse applause that has just been invited. This is what appears to happen on several successive occasions in fragment (6).

(6) (LPSC, 5:1980)

Benn: Comrades when we return to power we shall inherit (0.4) a situation (0.2) as critical (0.2) as the 1945 Labour government (0.8). Then there were three million (0.4) men and women in the services who had to be demobilized and put back into industry Hitler had tried to destroy by bombing. (1.0) We shall find two or three million (0.8) demoralized long-term unemployed (0.8) who have to be put back to work in factories (.)

a →   NOT THAT HITLER HAS BOMBED (.)
b →   BUT THAT THATCHER AND JOSEPH HAVE CLOSED. (0.7) AND IT WILL BE A MAJOR⌐
Audience: x-xx-XXXXXXXXXXXXXXX⌐=
Benn: ⌐TASK (0.4) that we have to undertake
Audience: =[XXXXXXXxxxxxxxxxxxxxxxxxxxxxxxxx⌐=
Benn: ⌐(1.8) AND MAY I SAY:UH- (0.4)SOMETHINGUH⌐
Audience: =[xxxxxxxxxxxxxxxxxxxxxxxxxxxxxxxxxxxxxxxxx⌐=
Benn: ⌐VERY SIMPLE (0.8) ⌐Is it not perhaps time we spoke
Audience: =[xxxxxxxxxxxxxx-x-x⌐
c → d →   in language that extended a bit beyond the economic jargon that has been the curse of so much of the postwar years =
Audience: = x-;x-x-xxxxxxxxxxx-x-x
Benn: ⌐I AM WAITING FOR⌐ US TO SAY MORE
e →   OFTEN (0.8) THAT SOME THINGS ARE RIGHT
f →   AND SOME THINGS ARE WRONG=
Audience: = x-xxXXX⌐ XXXXXXXXXXXXXXXXXXXXXXXX⌐
Benn: ⌐THAT IT IS WRONG (0.8) TO-UH-UH   ⌐=
Audience: ⌐XXXXXXXXX xxxxxxxxxxxxxxxxxxxxxxxxxxx-x-x-x⌐=
g →   =[CUT DOWN ON MONEY FOR KIDNEY MACHINES⌐=
h →   = AND SPEND FIVE BILLION (.) ON A NEW POLARIS SUBMARINE⌐THAT IT IS WRONG⌐=
Audience: ⌐x-x-xxXXXXXXXXX⌐=

Benn: ⌐TO DO (.) MANY OF THE THINGS THAT ARE NOW
              =⌐
Audience: ⌐XXXXXXXXXXXXXXXXXXXXXxxxxxxxxxxxxxxxxx-x⌐
 ↑   ↑
 i   j   DONE in the interests of profit and loss-

The first burst of applause occurs just after Benn has produced a somewhat dramatic
and even poetic (given the way "demoralized" rhymes with "demobilized") contrast.
After a period of overlap competition, during which he defers continuation until he
is in the clear, he produces a rhetorical question that contrasts the language "we"
ought to speak with economic jargon (at arrows c and d). He continues in overlap
with a slight flutter of applause, which fails to reach maximum intensity, to give an
example of what he means, which turns out to involve a further contrast (*RIGHT-
WRONG* at e and f. This is followed immediately by applause and, after half a
second, a further proposal to continue from Benn. As the applause subsides, he goes
on to produce a contrast between money spent on kidney machines and that spent
on submarines armed with nuclear weapons. After yet another immediate response,
he carries on talking to a completion point involving another contrast.

   While it is obviously difficult to get a sense for what this sequence sounds like from
the transcript, no one who has heard the tape recording has sought to disagree with
the suggestion that it is hearable as a tour de force, or as a particularly electrifying or
spellbinding piece of oratory. There are grounds for supposing that such a reading is
made possible by the speaker's repeatedly refusing to acknowledge the relevance of
applause, each time doing so by proceeding to the deployment of yet another applause
elicitation device. Such a strategy would appear to have at least two important
implications for the audience response, over and above those already discussed earlier.

   First, it may be noted that talking in competition with applause can have the effect
of curtailing the duration of a burst once in progress. This is particularly so if the
speaker continues before the audience response has had time to reach maximum
intensity, as occurs just after arrow d in fragment (6). In other words, members of
the audience may respond to the overlapping talk by dropping out of the competition that has been initiated. One consequence of this, which is evident in every
instance where applause occurs in fragment (6), is that the audience produces a
substantially shorter burst of applause than is usual (i.e., less than the eight $\pm$ one
seconds referred to above). Thus, if audience members do orient to applause of
differing durations as being more or less appropriate, as is suggested by the fact that
they recurrently produce seven-, eight-, or nine-second bursts, they may find themselves being repeatedly prevented from displaying an "adequate" response in the
course of a sequence like (6) above. Viewed in these terms, then, it is possible to see
how repeated postresponse continuations by a speaker can work to bottle up his
audience in such a way that, by the time he finally permits it to respond without
further competition, they may be literally bursting to applaud.

   A second and related feature of this process would appear to have the effect of
heightening the attentiveness of the audience to what the speaker is saying, which in
turn is likely to reduce the chances of anyone failing to notice the next applause-
elicitation device. It was noted above that to propose continuation after response onset
involves a proposal that the just-started applause had been neither expected nor
invited. As such, it can also be heard to suggest that the audience had produced its
response in an inappropriate place. If audience members draw such a conclusion, then,

it may provide them with a greater incentive for paying closer attention than usual to what the speaker says next. For, having just responded in a wrong place, they may be prompted to monitor the subsequent talk more carefully in order to respond in a right place the next time, and thereby avoid being seen to make the same mistake again.

Repeated refusals to acknowledge the relevance of applause thus appear to constitute a highly effective method for an orator to hold his audience in rapt attention, such that it is poised in a state of readiness to display approval at the next possible opportunity. Given that Mr. Benn is the only contemporary British politician who routinely and recurrently employs these techniques, it may be no coincidence that his speeches are so regularly reported in the media as having received a "rapturous reception" from the audience. Nor may it be a coincidence that so much of his support within the Labour Party derives from groups who have had the opportunity of hearing him address them in person (notably the local constituency branches, 80% of which voted for him in his unsuccessful attempt to be elected deputy leader of the party at the 1980 Annual Conference).[5]

Concluding Remarks

The present research was initially undertaken in response to difficulties associated with obtaining analytic access to the ways in which audiences analyze and respond to sequences of talk by public speakers in settings like courtrooms, where gross displays of attentiveness and affiliation do not routinely occur. Work done so far suggests that there are a range of identifiable techniques or procedures recurrently used by speakers in the production of sequences that precede audience displays of affiliation. There are also grounds for supposing that it is now possible to begin to describe just what it is about the way some individual orators perform that can result in their being regarded as outstandingly effective or charismatic speakers. Research also suggests that it will be equally possible to do the reverse, namely to identify recurrent features in the production of ineffective or "boring" oratory.

This is not to claim that this chapter has dealt with all or even most of the practices that may be relevant to achieving recognition as a charismatic orator, nor that Mr. Benn is the only politician ever to have deployed those described here as methods for refusing invited applause. They do, however, appear to be strongly implicated in the genesis of such a reputation, not just for the reasons outlined above, but also because the only other orators so far identified as having routinely talked in competition with applause were two of the most unequivocally charismatic leaders of the postwar period, John F. Kennedy and Martin Luther King.

One general conclusion from the present study, then, runs counter to the traditional view of charisma as involving supernatural gifts of the sort referred to in the opening quotation from Max Weber. It raises the possibility that there may be a more systematic technical basis for being regarded as charismatic, at least as far as oratory is concerned. A frequent response to this suggestion after oral presentations of these data and findings has been expressions of concern that the identification of such techniques might lead to their being taught, practiced, and exploited by anyone with political ambitions. However, even if they eventually turn out to be skills of a sort that can be readily learned and mastered by erstwhile mediocre performers, this would not necessarily be grounds for abandoning further inquiries. Indeed, it would arguably make it all the more important that our understanding of such practices and how they work should not only be as thorough as we can make it, but should also be disseminated to as wide an audience as possible.

From a more analytic point of view, several other points can be noted by way of conclusion. One is that the present study suggests that research conducted within the framework of conversation analysis may have progressed to a point where it is possible to address inquiries to issues associated with individual variation in human conduct. Thus, if it is the case that differences between individual public speakers can be understood with reference to their deployment of different practices or devices, a similar approach may also have potential for understanding differences between individual interactants in other settings. This may be particularly so as far as other types of multiparty interaction (e.g., in courtrooms, classrooms, lecture theatres), where the operational dynamics of public speaking are obviously important but are as yet only vaguely understood in their details. With such issues in mind, work is in progress on the way counsel address jurors at the end of court hearings, one interest being in the extent to which they mobilize devices similar to those used in political oratory as they attempt to elicit approval from an audience that listens in silence (Atkinson, 1982a).

Appendix: Summary of Main Transcription Symbols

The transcription conventions used in this paper are based on those developed by Gail Jefferson, with modifications to represent applause.

C: Mister ⟩Hezzletine⟨

Word(s) spoken between the signs ⟩ ⟨ are delivered faster than the surrounding talk.

Audience: XXXXXXXX — Loud applause

Audience: xxxxxxxx — Quiet applause

Audience: -x- — Isolated or single clap

Audience: -x-x-xx- — Spasmodic or hesitant clapping

Audience: xxxXXXXXxxx — Applause amplitude increases or decreases

|————(8.0)————|
Audience: -x-xxXXXXXXxxx-

Duration of applause from onset (or prior object) to nearest tenth of a second. Number of X's does not indicate duration of applause, except where it overlaps with talk (see next example).

Keene: ...for A:lien
Audience: ⌐X-XXXXXXX

Applause onset with continuation through and beyond overlapping talk.

B: it is wr o:ng (0.5) to:uhh
A: XXXXXXXXXXXXXXXXXX-
      XXXXXXX

Applause continues while an overlapping speaker pauses before continuing to talk in overlap.

(0.5) (.)

Numbers indicate pause lengths to nearest tenth of a second. Dot indicates micropause (less than 0.2 seconds).

Acknowledgment

Parts of the argument included here have been presented at meetings of the Sociology of Language Study Group of the British Sociological Association, Cambridge (1980) and Aberystwyth (1981), the U.S. Law and Society Association, Amherst (1981), the Symposium on Connectedness in Sentence, Text and Discourse, Tilburg (1982), and to seminars at the Universities of Aston, Cambridge, London (L.S.E.), Surrey, Oxford, and York, at the University of California, Los Angeles, Columbia University, and Duke University (North Carolina). For their helpful comments at various stages of the research, I am particularly grateful to Paul Drew, John Heritage, Gail Jefferson, and Anita Pomerantz. Needless to say, however, responsibility for the errors that remain is entirely mine.

Further discussion of these and other factors associated with charismatic oratory is contained in Atkinson (1984a).

Notes

1   Points where audiences produce displays of disapproval and disaffiliation suggest themselves as an equally interesting focus for analysis. So far, however, relatively little work has been done in this direction, partly because it seemed less relevant to the original interest in how advocates address jurors, and partly because it seemed less likely that speakers would specifically build their talk with a view to eliciting such responses.

2   The speeches from which extracts are included here were made during the 1979 British General Election (GE, 1979), the 1980 Annual Conference of the Conservative Party (CPC, 1980), the 1980 Annual Conference of the Labour Party (LPC, 1980), and the Labour Party Special Conference held in May 1980 (LPSC, 5:1980). Simplified transcripts are used throughout, mainly in response to complaints from readers of earlier papers that the inclusion of symbols representing intonational and prosodic shifts made them difficult to read. Their omission, however, should not be interpreted as an indication that such matters are unimportant in the process of applause elicitation (see Atkinson, 1984a,b). A key to the main transcription conventions used is provided in the Appendix.

3   This and a further statistical exercise reported below were conducted in order to give a sense for what is implicated by phrases like "overwhelmingly recurrent." It should be stressed, however, that the sample of instances examined for counting purposes, while quite large, was not derived from strict principles of random sampling. Moreover, it would appear that the problem of generating a random sample from materials such as these would be a much more complicated exercise than might be thought at first sight.

4   Though not discussed in the present context, part of the basis for viewing this fragment as a technical masterpiece involves the way Benn's arm and hand movements are finely coordinated with structural and lexical features of the unfolding talk. Additionally, it exhibits some of the prosodic and intonational features that have been found to recur in applause elicitation sequences.

5   Since the defeat of the Labour government at the 1979 general election, Mr. Benn has devoted an extraordinary amount of energy to traveling around Britain to address local political meetings. During 1980, for example, it is reported that he made more than 400 speeches (over and above those made on the floor of the House of Commons), a rate of productivity that exceeds that achieved in a whole lifetime by some of the most celebrated orators of classical Greece.

References

Atkinson, J. M. (1982b). Understanding formality: The categorisation and production of "formal" interaction. *British Journal of Sociology, 33*, 86–117.

Atkinson, J. M. (1982a). *Addressing jurors*. Paper presented at the British Psychological Society (Welsh Branch) International Conference on Law and Psychology, Swansea.

Atkinson, J. M. (1983). Two devices for generating audience approval: A comparative study of public discourse and texts. In K. Ehlich et al. (Eds.), *Connectedness in Sentence, Text and Discourse*, (pp. 199–236) Tilburg: Tilburg Papers in Linguistics.

Atkinson, J. M. (1984a). *Our masters' voices: The language and body language of politics*, London and New York, Metheun.

Atkinson, J. M. (1984b). Public speaking and audience responses: Some techniques for inviting applause. In J. M. Atkinson and J. C. Heritage (Eds.), *Structures of social action: Studies in conversation analysis* (pp. 370–409). Cambridge: Cambridge University Press.

Atkinson, J. M. and Drew, P. (1979). *Order in court: The organisation of verbal interaction in judicial settings*. London: Macmillan; Atlantic Highlands, NJ: Humanities Press.

Drew, P. (1982). *Disputes about "proper descriptions" in cross-examination*. Paper presented at the BSA Sociology of Language Study Group Conference, Oxford.

Drew, P. (1985). Analyzing the use of language in courtroom interaction. In *Handbook of Discourse Analysis, 3*, 133–59.

Jefferson, G. (1979). *Some aspects of overlap competition*. Lecture given at the University of Warwick, Department of Sociology.

Jefferson, G. (1980). *List construction as a task and resource*. Paper presented at the First German–British Colloquium on Ethnomethodology and Conversation Analysis, Konstanz.

Jefferson, G. and Schegloff, E. A. (n.d.). *Sketch: Some orderly aspects of overlap in natural conversation*. Los Angeles: University of California, Department of Sociology.

Pomerantz, A. (1975). *Second assessments*. Unpublished doctoral dissertation, School of Social Sciences, University of California, Irvine.

Pomerantz, A. (1982). *Presenting evidence in arguing over facts*. Paper presented at the Annual Meetings of the American Sociological Association, San Francisco.

Pomerantz, A. (1984). Agreeing and disagreeing with assessments: Some features of preferred/ dispreferred turn shapes. In J. M. Atkinson and J. C. Heritage (Eds.), *Structures of social action: Studies in conversation analysis* (pp. 57–101). Cambridge: Cambridge University Press.

Sacks, H., Schegloff, E. A., and Jefferson, G. (1974). A simplest systematics for the organization of turn-taking for conversation. *Language, 50*, 696–735.

Part V

Research Using Artifacts as Primary Sources

As I indicated in the general introduction, anthropology has for some time been home to both social and natural scientists. However, the analytic relationship between these two approaches to theorizing the human condition has always been uncertain. In place of systematic efforts to rigorously synthesize debates regarding the "social" and "natural" dimensions of human life, there has grown up instead a fairly well honored division of labor wherein scientific disputes very rarely cross the nature/culture border. When social scientists have sought to analyze the material aspects of social life they have therefore tended overwhelmingly to leave aside questions of the *nature* of material objects and confine their attention to the cultural meanings and uses to which such things are put. No doubt, this encapsulation of the social scientific engagement with material objects has been unnecessarily limiting. Contemporary research in science studies has offered new and important insights into the dynamic interface of "social" and "natural" processes that fully deserve to be pursued further. However, before moving into these newer territories it will behoove us to appreciate the very important work that has been, and will continue to be, accomplished by more venerable lights.

In his essay, "The Interpretation of Documents and Material Culture," Ian Hodder provides a far-reaching statement of the distinctive value that documents and material objects possess for social scientists. Compared to other sorts of data, documents and material objects endure. Hence, for those who would study historically distant peoples and events, documents and material objects are often the only types of data available. Moreover, such data may possess a special relevance to those who would hope to study the expressions of people who have historically been muted or denied voice. But just as with other types of data, the analysis of documents and material artifacts must be accomplished with respect to the particular forms of life in which they were produced and/or used. And it is here that most of our methodological puzzles begin to emerge. Exactly how shall these contexts be considered? Just like other elements of culture, documents and material artifacts may be analyzed with respect to both their symbolic and their mundane utility. One major challenge of analysis is thus to infer the extent to which the former or the later should be emphasized in any particular instance. Another distinctive complication arises from the fact that artifacts produced in one context may be put to use in ways that were not originally anticipated. Many objects we have inherited from our forebears are meaningful/useful to us in ways quite different from the ways they were meaningful/useful to them. How, then, might these multiple meanings and uses be properly disentangled from one another? Though the use of artifacts as data undeniably presents unique analytic challenges, Hodder suggests these challenges can generally be handled with techniques familiar to those acquainted with other varieties of comparative social research.

In "Professional Vision," Charles Goodwin moves us from considerations of material artifacts as clues to the workings of absent social worlds, to an analysis of how material artifacts are made to figure in particular varieties of ongoing professional activity. The bearing of his remarks on our own particular brand of professional work is readily apparent. Goodwin's analysis speaks to the details of human interactions with material artifacts by highlighting three pervasive techniques of engagement: coding; highlighting; and graphic representation. Among other things, *coding* schemes are "used to transform the world into the categories and events that are relevant to the work of the profession" (p. 608). One way in which we engage the material world is to classify it into instances of more general categories we consider interesting or useful. Another way we do so is through *highlighting*, or marking elements of the material world as particularly important or relevant to present concerns. Thus, in addition to categorizing things, we also rank them with respect to their practical importance. Finally, we engage the material world by generating *graphic representations* of it. According to Goodwin, graphic representations include such things as diagrams, graphs, photographs, and maps. And he writes,

> A theory of discourse that ignored graphic representations would be missing both a key element of the discourse that professionals engage in and a central locus for the analysis of professional practice. Instead of mirroring spoken language, these external representations complement it, using the distinctive characteristics of the material world to organize phenomena in ways that spoken language cannot – for example, by collecting records of a range of disparate events onto a single visible surface. (p. 611)

Goodwin shows us that our encounters with materiality are socially mediated at the most primordial levels of praxis and perception. In contrast to the Cartesian image of a socially isolated cognizing subject, Goodwin offers us an image of subjective praxis and perception always already shot through with culturally inherited resources. Because both our perceptual and practical engagement with nature are mediated through such culturally inherited devices as coding schemes, highlighting, and graphic representations, they are also mediated through the various communities of people who generate, transmit, and police the use of these devices. Though his examples of professional vision are taken from archeology and courtroom proceedings, Goodwin makes a persuasive case that these arguments are equally applicable to the professions we know as natural sciences. In my view, the methodological value of his analysis in no small part consists in its provision of conceptual resources for comparing scientific and non-scientific encounters with the material world under a single analytic auspices.

The last paper in this section is Chandra Mukerji's "Artwork: Collection and Contemporary Culture." In this paper Mukerji illuminates us as to the processes at work when certain types of objects come to be distinguished as "art." What is it that distinguishes art objects from mere commodities or consumer items? More specifically, how do items once mass produced under the explicit guise of industrial commodities get transformed into art objects? Mukerji analyzes the case of American motion pictures. In the first half of the twentieth century, the American movie studios consistently opposed the view that their products were anything other than simple entertainments – mass-produced for mass consumption in much the same way as are canned foods. In a fascinating analysis, Mukerji argues that American motion pictures should be viewed as prototypical of a more general trend in American culture wherein seemingly scarce industrial commodities are adopted and recommended by aficionados as collectibles. Mukerji traces the historical events surrounding the transformation of American movies into art objects, thereby offering an exciting sociological glimpse into the ever-changing material landscapes of our contemporary culture.

Reference

Goodwin, Charles. 1994. "Professional Vision." *American Anthropologist* 96 (3).

Further Reading on Research Using Artifacts as Primary Sources

Casper, Monica J. 1998. *The Making of the Unborn Patient: A Social Anatomy of Fetal Surgery*. New Brunswick, NJ: Rutgers University Press.

Garfinkel, Harold, Michael Lynch, and Eric Livingston. 1981. "The Work of a Discovering Science Construed with Materials from the Optically Discovered Pulsar." *Philosophy of the Social Sciences* 11: 131–58.

Gottdiener, Mark. 1995. *Postmodern Semiotics: Material Culture and the Forms of Postmodern Life*. Cambridge, MA: Blackwell.

Haraway, Donna J. 1991. *Simians, Cyborgs, and Women: The Reinvention of Nature*. London: Routledge.

Knorr-Cetina, Karin. 1999. *Epistemic Cultures: How the Sciences Make Knowledge*. Cambridge, MA: Harvard University Press.

Latour, Bruno, and Steve Woolgar. 1979. *Laboratory Life: The Social Construction of Scientific Facts*. Beverly Hills: Sage.

Lynch, Michael. 1985. *Art and Artifact in Laboratory Science: A Study of Shop Work and Shop Talk in a Research Laboratory*. London: Routledge.

Miller, Daniel, ed. 1998. *Material Cultures: Why Some Things Matter*. Chicago: University of Chicago Press.

Mukerji, Chandra. 1983. *From Graven Images: Patterns of Modern Materialism*. New York: Columbia University Press.

—— 1997. *Territorial Ambitions and the Gardens of Versailles*. New York: Cambridge University Press.

Pickering, Andrew. 1995. *The Mangle of Practice: Time, Agency, & Science*. Chicago: University of Chicago Press.

Schwartz, Donna. 1989. "Visual Ethnography: Using Photographs in Qualitative Research." *Qualitative Sociology* 12(2): 119–54.

Stocking, George W., ed. 1985. *Objects and Others: Essays on Museums and Material Culture*. Madison, WI: University of Wisconsin Press.

—— 1988. *Bones, Bodies, Behavior: Essays on Biological Anthropology*. Madison, WI: University of Wisconsin Press.

Tilley, Christopher. 1999. *Metaphor and Material Culture*. Malden, MA: Blackwell.

Vera, Hernan. 1989. "On Dutch Windows." *Qualitative Sociology* 12(2): 215–34.

15 The Interpretation of Documents and Material Culture

Ian Hodder

This chapter is concerned with the interpretation of mute evidence – that is, with written texts and artifacts. Such evidence, unlike the spoken word, endures physically and thus can be separated across space and time from its author, producer, or user. Material traces thus often have to be interpreted without the benefit of indigenous commentary. There is often no possibility of interaction with spoken emic "insider" as opposed to etic "outsider" perspectives. Even when such interaction is possible, actors often seem curiously inarticulate about the reasons they dress in particular ways, choose particular pottery designs, or discard dung in particular locations. Material traces and residues thus pose special problems for qualitative research. The main disciplines that have tried to develop appropriate theory and method are history, art history, archaeology, anthropology, sociology, cognitive psychology, technology, and modern material culture studies, and it is from this range of disciplines that my account is drawn.

Written Documents and Records

Lincoln and Guba (1985, p. 277) distinguish documents and records on the basis of whether the text was prepared to attest to some formal transaction. Thus records include marriage certificates, driving licenses, building contracts, and banking statements. Documents; on the other hand, are prepared for personal rather than official reasons and include diaries, memos, letters, field notes, and so on. In fact, the two terms are often used interchangeably, although the distinction is an important one and has some parallels with the distinction between writing and speech, to be discussed below. Documents, closer to speech, require more contextualized interpretation. Records, on the other hand, may have local uses that become very distant from officially sanctioned meanings. Documents involve a personal technology, and records a full state technology of power. The distinction is also relevant for qualitative research, in that researchers may often be able to get access to documents, whereas access to records may be restricted by laws regarding privacy, confidentiality, and anonymity.

Despite the utility of the distinction between documents and records, my concern here is more the problems of interpretation of written texts of all kinds. Such texts are of importance for qualitative research because, in general terms, access can be easy and low cost, because the information provided may differ from and may not be available in spoken form, and because texts endure and thus give historical insight.

It has often been assumed, for example, in the archaeology of historical periods, that written texts provide a "truer" indication of original meanings than do other types of evidence (to be considered below). Indeed, Western social science has long privileged the spoken over the written and the written over the nonverbal (Derrida, 1978). Somehow it is assumed that words get us closer to minds. But as Derrida has shown, meaning does not reside in a text but in the writing and reading of it. As the text is reread in different contexts it is given new meanings, often contradictory and always socially embedded. Thus there is no "original" or "true" meaning of a text outside specific historical contexts. Historical archaeologists have come to accept that historical documents and records give not a better but simply a different picture from that provided by artifacts and architecture. Texts can be used alongside other forms of evidence so that the particular biases of each can be understood and compared.

Equally, different types of text have to be understood in the contexts of their conditions of production and reading. For example, the analyst will be concerned with whether a text was written as result of firsthand experience or from secondary sources, whether it was solicited or unsolicited, edited or unedited, anonymous or signed, and so on (Webb, Campbell, Schwartz, and Sechrest, 1966). As Ricoeur (1971) demonstrates, concrete texts differ from the abstract structures of language in that they are written to do something. They can be understood only as what they are – a form of artifact produced under certain material conditions (not everyone can write, or write in a certain way, or have access to relevant technologies of reproduction) embedded within social and ideological systems.

Words are, of course, spoken to do things as well as to say things – they have practical and social impact as well as communication function. Once transformed into a written text the gap between the "author" and the "reader" widens and the possibility of multiple reinterpretations increases. The text can "say" many different things in different contexts. But also the written text is an artifact, capable of transmission, manipulation, and alteration, used and discarded, reused and recycled – "doing" different things contextually through time. The writing down of words often allows language and meanings to be controlled more effectively, and to be linked to strategies of centralization and codification. The word, concretized or "made flesh" in the artifact, can transcend context and gather through time extended symbolic connotations. The word made enduring in artifacts has an important role to play in both secular and religious processes of the legitimation of power. Yet there is often a tension between the concrete nature of the written word, its enduring nature, and the continuous potential for rereading meanings in new contexts, undermining the authority of the word. Text and context are in a continual state of tension, each defining and redefining the other, saying and doing things differently through time.

In a related way, the written texts of anthropologists and archaeologists are increasingly coming under scrutiny as employing rhetorical strategies in order to establish positions of authority (e.g., Tilley, 1989). Archaeologists are used to the idea that their scientific activities leave traces and transform the worlds they study. Excavations cannot be repeated, and the residues of trenches, spoiltips, and old beer cans remain as specific expressions of a particular way of looking at the world. The past has been transformed into a present product, including the field notes and site reports. Ethnographic field notes (Sanjek, 1990) also transform the object of study into a historically situated product, "capturing" the "other" within a familiar routine. The field text has to be contextualized within specific historical moments.

I shall in this chapter treat written texts as special cases of artifacts, subject to similar interpretive procedures. In both texts and artifacts the problem is one of situating material culture within varying contexts while at the same time entering into a dialectic relationship between those contexts and the context of the analyst. This hermeneutical exercise, in which the lived experience surrounding the material culture is translated into a different context of interpretation, is common for both texts and other forms of material culture. I will note various differences between language and material culture in what follows, but the interpretive parallels have been widely discussed in the consideration of material culture as text (e.g., Hodder, 1991; Moore, 1986; Tilley, 1990).

Artifact Analysis and Its Importance for the Interpretation of Social Experience

Ancient and modern buildings and artifacts, the intended and unintended residues of human activity, give alternative insights into the ways in which people perceived and fashioned their lives. Shortcuts across lawns indicate preferred traffic patterns, foreign-language signs indicate the degree of integration of a neighborhood, the number of cigarettes in an ashtray betrays a nervous tension, and the amount of paperwork in an "in" tray is a measure of workload or of work efficiency and priority (Lincoln and Guba, 1985, p. 280). Despite the inferential problems surrounding such evidence, I wish to establish at the outset that material traces of behavior give an important and different insight from that provided by any number of questionnaires.

"What people say" is often very different from "what people do." This point has perhaps been most successfully established over recent years by research stemming from the work of Bill Rathje (Rathje and Murphy, 1992; Rathje and Thompson, 1981). In studies in Tucson, Arizona, and elsewhere, Rathje and his colleagues collected domestic garbage bags and itemized the contents. It became clear that, for example, people's estimates about the amounts of garbage they produced were wildly incorrect, that discarded beer cans indicated a higher level of alcohol consumption than was admitted to, and that in times of meat shortage people threw away more meat than usual as a result of overhoarding. Thus a full sociological analysis cannot be restricted to interview data. It must also consider the material traces.

In another series of studies, the decoration of rooms as well as pots and other containers has been interpreted as a form of silent discourse conducted by women, whose voice has been silenced by dominant male interests. Decoration may be used to mark out, silently, and to draw attention to, tacitly, areas of female control, such as female areas of houses and the preparation and provision of food in containers. The decoration may at one level provide protection from female pollution, but at another level it expresses female power (Braithwaite, 1982; Donley, 1982; Hodder, 1991).

The study of material culture is thus of importance for qualitative researchers who wish to explore multiple and conflicting voices, differing and interacting interpretations. Many areas of experience are hidden from language, particularly subordinate experience. Ferguson (1991) has shown how study of the material traces of food and pots can provide insight into how slaves on plantations in the American South made sense of and reacted to their domination. The members of this normally silenced group expressed their own perspective in the mundane activities of everyday life.

Analysis of such traces is not a trivial pursuit, as the mundane and the everyday, because unimportant to dominant interests, may be of great importance for the expression of alternative perspectives. The material expression of power (parades, regalia, tombs, and art) can be set against the expression of resistance. The importance of such analysis is increased by the realization that material culture is not simply a passive by-product of other areas of life. Rather, material culture is active (Hodder, 1982). By this I mean that artifacts are produced so as to transform, materially, socially, and ideologically. It is the exchange of artifacts themselves that constructs social relationships; it is the style of spear that creates a feeling of common identity; it is the badge of authority that itself confers authority. Material culture is thus *necessary for* most social constructs. An adequate study of social interaction thus depends on the incorporation of mute material evidence.

Toward a Theory of Material Culture

Having established that the study of material culture can be an important tool for sociological and anthropological analysis, it is necessary to attempt to build a theory on which the interpretation of material culture can be based. A difficulty here has been the diversity of the category "material culture," ranging from written texts to material symbols surrounding death, drama, and ritual, to shopping behavior and to the construction of roads and airplanes. As a result, theoretical directions have often taken rather different paths, as one can see by comparing attempts to build a comprehensive theory for technological behavior (Lemonnier, 1986) and attempts to consider material culture as text (Tilley, 1990).

Ultimately, material culture always has to be interpreted in relation to a situated context of production, use, discard, and reuse. In working toward that contextual interpretation, it may be helpful to distinguish some general characteristics and analogies for the different types of material culture. In this attempt to build a general theory, recent research in a range of disciplines has begun to separate two areas of material meaning.

Some material culture is designed specifically to be communicative and representational. The clearest example is a written text, but this category extends, for example, to the badge and uniform of certain professions, to red and green stop and go traffic lights, to smoke signals, to the images of Christ on the cross. Because this category includes written texts, it is to be expected that meaning in this category might be organized in ways similar to language. Thus, as with words in a language, the material symbols are, outside a historical context, often arbitrary. For example, any design on a flag could be used as long as it differs from the designs on other flags and is recognizable with its own identity. Thus the system of meanings in the case of flags is constructed through similarities and differences in a semiotic code. Miller (1982) has shown how dress is organized both syntagmatically and paradigmatically. The choice of hat, tie, shirt, trousers, shoes, and so on for a particular occasion is informed by a syntax that allows a particular set of clothes to be put together. On the other hand, the distinctions among different types of hats (bowler, straw, cloth, baseball) or jackets constitute paradigmatic choices.

The three broad areas of theory that have been applied to this first type of material meaning derive from information technology, Marxism, and structuralism. In the first, the aim has been to account for the ways in which material symboling can provide adaptive advantage to social groups. Thus the development of complex symboling systems allows more information to be processed more efficiently (e.g., Wobst, 1977). This type of approach is of limited value to qualitative research because it is not concerned with the interpretation and experience of meaningful symbols. In the second, the ideological component of symbols is identified within relations of power and domination (Leone, 1984; Miller and Tilley, 1984) and increasingly power and systems of value and prestige are seen as multiple and dialectical (Miller, Rowlands, and Tilley, 1989; Shanks and Tilley, 1987). The aim of structuralist analysis has been to examine design (e.g., Washburn, 1983) or spatial relationships (e.g., Glassie, 1975; McGhee, 1977) in terms of underlying codes, although here too the tendency has been on emphasizing multiple meanings contested within active social contexts as the various directions of poststructuralist thought have been debated (Tilley, 1990).

In much of this work the metaphor of language has been applied to material culture relatively unproblematically. The pot appears to "mean" in the same way as the word *pot*. Recent work has begun to draw attention to the limitations of this analogy between material culture and language, as will become clear in my consideration of the second type of material culture meaning. One can begin to explore the limitations of the analogy by considering that many examples of material culture are not produced to "mean" at all. In other words, they are not produced with symbolic functions as primary. Thus the madeleine cookie discussed in Proust's *A la recherche du temps perdu* (*Swann's Way*) was produced as an enticing food, made in a shape representing a fluted scallop. But Proust describes its meaning as quite different from this symbolic representation. Rather, the meaning was the evocation of a whole series of childhood memories, sounds, tastes, smells surrounding having tea with his mother in winter.

Many if not most material symbols do not work through rules of representation, using a language-like syntax. Rather, they work through the evocation of sets of practices within individual experience. It would be relatively difficult to construct a grammar or dictionary of material symbols except in the case of deliberately representational or symbolic items, such as flags and road signs. This is because most material symbols do not mean in the same way as language. Rather, they come to have abstract meaning through association and practice. Insofar as members of society experience common practices, material symbols can come to have common evocations and common meanings. Thus, for example, the ways in which certain types of food, drink, music, and sport are experienced are embedded within social convention and thus come to have common meaning. A garlic crusher may not be used overtly in Britain to represent or symbolize class, but through a complex set of practices surrounding food and its preparation the crusher has come to mean class through evocation.

Because objects endure, have their own traces, their own grain, individual objects with unique evocations can be recognized. The specific memory traces associated with any particular object (a particular garlic crusher) will vary from individual to individual. The particularity of material experience and meaning derives not only from the diversity of human life but also from the identifiability of material objects. The identifiable particularity of material experience always has the potential to work against and transform society-wide conventions through practice. Because of this dialectic between structure and practice, and because of the multiple local meanings that can be given to things, it would be difficult to construct dictionaries and grammars for most material culture meanings.

Another reason for the inability to produce dictionaries of material culture returns us to the difficulty with which people give discursive accounts of material symbolism. The meanings often remain tacit and implicit. A smell or taste of a madeleine cookie may awake strong feelings, but it is notoriously difficult to describe a taste or a feel or to pin down the emotions evoked. We may know that in practice this or that item of clothing "looks good," "works well," or "is stylish," but we would be at a loss to say what it "means" because the item does not mean – rather, it is embedded in a set of practices that include class, status, goals, aesthetics. We may not know much about art, but we know what we like. On the basis of a set of practical associations, we build up an implicit knowledge about the associations and evocations of particular artifacts or styles. This type of embedded, practical experience seems to be different from the manipulation of rules of representation and from conscious analytic thought. Material symbolic meanings may get us close to lived experience, but they cannot easily be articulated.

The importance of practice for the social and symbolic meanings of artifacts has been emphasized in recent work on technology (Schlanger, 1990). Each technical operation is linked to others in operational chains (Leroi-Gourhan, 1964) involving materials, energy, and gestures. For example, some clays are better for throwing than others, so that type of clay constrains whether a manufacturer can make thrown pots or hand-built statuettes. Quality of clay is related to types of temper that should be used. All such operational chains are nondeterministic, and some degree of social choice is involved (Lemonnier, 1986; Miller, 1985). All operational chains involve aspects of production, exchange, and consumption, and so are part of a network of relations incorporating the material, the economic, the social, and the conceptual.

The practical operational chains often have implications that extend into not only social but also moral realms. For example, Latour (1988) discusses hydraulic door closers, devices that automatically close a door after someone has opened it. The material door closer thus takes the place of, or delegates, the role of a porter, someone who stands there and makes sure that the door stays shut after people have gone through. But use of this particular delegate has various implications, one of which is that very young or infirm people have difficulty getting through the door. A social distinction is unwittingly implied by this technology. In another example, Latour discusses a key used by some inhabitants of Berlin. This double-ended key forces the user to lock the door in order to get the key out. The key delegates for staff or signs that might order a person to "relock the door behind you." Staff or signs would be unreliable – they could be outwitted or ignored. The key enforces a morality. In the same way "sleeping policemen" (speed bumps) force the driver of a car to be moral and to slow down in front of a school, but this morality is not socially encoded. That would be too unreliable. The morality is embedded within the practical consequences of breaking up one's car by driving too fast over the bumps. The social and moral meanings of the door closer, the Berlin key, or the speed bump are thoroughly embedded in the implications of material practices.

I have suggested that in developing a theory of material culture, the first task is to distinguish at least two different ways in which material culture has abstract meaning beyond primary utilitarian concerns. The first is through rules of representation. The second is through practice and evocation – through the networking, interconnection, and mutual implication of material and nonmaterial. Whereas it may be the case that written language is the prime example of the first category and tools the prime example of the second, language also has to be worked out in practices from which it derives much of its meaning. Equally, we have seen that material items can be placed within language-like codes. But there is some support from cognitive psychology for a general difference between the two types of knowledge. For example, Bechtel (1990, p. 264) argues that rule-based models of cognition are naturally good at quite different types of activity from connectionist models. Where the first is appropriate for problem solving, the second is best at tasks such as pattern recognition and motor control. It seems likely then that the skills involved in material practice and the social, symbolic, and moral meanings that are implicated in such practices might involve different cognitive systems than involved in rules and representations.

Bloch (1991) argues that practical knowledge is fundamentally different from linguistic knowledge in the way it is organized in the mind. Practical knowledge is "chunked" into highly contextualized information about how to "get on" in specific domains of action. Much cultural knowledge is nonlinear and purpose dedicated, formed through the practice of closely related activities. I have argued here that even the practical world involves social and symbolic meanings that are not organized representational codes but that are chunked or contextually organized realms of activity in which emotions, desires, morals, and social relations are involved at the level of implicit taken-for-granted skill or know-how.

It should perhaps be emphasized that the two types of material symbolism – the representational and the evocative or implicative – often work in close relation to each other. Thus a set of practices may associate men and women with different parts of houses or times of day, but in certain social contexts these associations might be built upon to construct symbolic rules of separation and exclusion and to build an abstract representational scheme in which mythology and cosmology play a part (e.g., Yates, 1989). Such schemes also have ideological components that feed back to constrain the practices. Thus practice, evocation, and representation interpenetrate and feed off each other in many if not all areas of life. Structure and practice are recursively related in the "structuration" of material life (Giddens, 1979; see also Bourdieu, 1977).

Material Meanings in Time

It appears that people both experience and "read" material culture meanings. There is much more that could be said about how material culture works in the social context. For instance, some examples work by direct and explicit metaphor, where similarities in form refer to historical antecedents, whereas others work by being ambiguous and abstract, by using spectacle or dramatic effect, by controlling the approach of the onlooker, by controlling perspective. Although there is not space here to explore the full range of material strategies, it is important to establish the temporal dimension of lived experience.

As already noted, material culture is durable and can be given new meanings as it is separated from its primary producer. This temporal variation in meaning is often related to changes in meaning across space and culture. Archaeological or ethnographic artifacts are continually being taken out of their contexts and reinterpreted within museums within different social and cultural contexts. The Elgin Marbles housed in the British Museum take on new meanings that are in turn reinterpreted antagonistically in some circles in Greece. American Indian human and artifact remains may have a scientific meaning for archaeologists and biological anthropologists, but they have important emotive and identity meanings for indigenous peoples.

Material items are continually being reinterpreted in new contexts. Also, material culture can be added to or removed from, leaving the traces of reuses and reinterpretations. In some cases, the sequence of use can give insight into the thought processes of an individual, as when flint flakes that have been struck off a core in early prehistory are refitted by archaeologists today (e.g., Pelegrin, 1990) in order to rebuild the flint core and to follow the decisions made by the original flint knapper in producing flakes and tools. In other cases, longer frames of time are involved, as when a monument such as Stonehenge is adapted, rebuilt, and reused for divergent purposes over millennia up to the present day (Chippindale, 1983). In such an example, the narrative held within traces on the artifact has an overall form that has been produced by multiple individuals and groups, often unaware of earlier intentions and meanings. Few people today, although knowledgeable about Christmas practices, are aware of the historical reasons behind the choice of Christmas tree, Santa Claus, red coats, and flying reindeer.

There are many trajectories that material items can take through shifting meanings. For example, many are made initially to refer to or evoke metaphorically, whereas through time the original meaning becomes lost or the item becomes a cliché, having lost its novelty. An artifact may start as a focus but become simply a frame, part of an appropriate background. In the skeuomorphic process a functional component becomes decorative, as when a gas fire depicts burning wood or coal. In other cases the load of meaning invested in an artifact increases through time, as in the case of a talisman or holy relic. Material items are often central in the backward-looking invention of tradition, as when the Italian fascist movement elevated the Roman symbol of authority – a bundle of rods – to provide authority for a new form of centralized power.

This brief discussion of the temporal dimension emphasizes the contextuality of material culture meaning. As is clear from some of the examples given, changing meanings through time are often involved in antagonistic relations between groups. Past and present meanings are continually being contested and reinterpreted as part of social and political strategies. Such conflict over material meanings is of particular interest to qualitative research in that it expresses and focuses alternative views and interests. The reburial of American Indian and Australian aboriginal remains is an issue that has expressed, but perhaps also helped to construct, a new sense of indigenous rights in North America and Australia. As "ethnic cleansing" reappears in Europe, so too do attempts to reinterpret documents, monuments, and artifacts in ethnic terms. But past artifacts can also be used to help local communities in productive and practical ways. One example of the active use of the past in the present is provided by the work of Erickson (1988) in the area around Lake Titicaca in Peru. Information from the archaeological study of raised fields was used to reconstruct agricultural systems on the ancient model, with the participation and to the benefit of local farmers.

Method

The interpretation of mute material evidence puts the interactionist view under pressure. How can an approach that gives considerable importance to interaction with speaking subjects (e.g., Denzin, 1989) deal with material traces for which informants are long dead or about which informants are not articulate?

I have already noted the importance of material evidence in providing insight into other components of lived experience. The methodological issues that are raised are not, however, unique. In all types of interactive research the analyst has to decide whether or not to take commentary at face value and how to evaluate spoken or unspoken responses. How does what is said fit into more general understanding? Analysts of material culture may not have much spoken commentary to work with, but they do have patterned evidence that has to be evaluated in relation to the full range of available information. They too have to fit different aspects of the evidence into a hermeneutical whole (Hodder, 1992; Shanks and Tilley, 1987). They ask, How does what is done fit into more general understanding?

In general terms, the interpreter of material culture works between past and present or between different examples of material culture, making analogies between them. The material evidence always has the potential to be patterned in unexpected ways. Thus it provides an "other" against which the analyst's own experience of the world has to be evaluated and can be enlarged. Although the evidence cannot "speak back," it can confront the interpreter in ways that enforce self-reappraisal. At least when a researcher is dealing with prehistoric remains, there are no "member checks" because the artifacts are themselves mute. On the other hand, material culture is the product of and is embedded in "internal" experience. Indeed, it could be argued that some material culture, precisely because it is not overt, self-conscious speech, may give deeper insights into the internal meanings according to which people lived their lives. I noted above some examples of material culture being used to express covert meanings. Thus the lack of spoken member checks is counteracted by the checks provided by unspoken material patterning that remain able to confront and undermine interpretation.

An important initial assumption made by those interpreting material culture is that belief, idea, and intention are important to action and practice (see above). It follows that the conceptual has some impact on the patterning of material remains. The ideational component of material patterning is not opposed to but is integrated with its material functioning. It is possible therefore to infer both utilitarian and conceptual meaning from the patterning of material evidence.

The interpreter is faced with material data that are patterned along a number of different dimensions simultaneously. Minimally, archaeologists distinguish technology, function, and style, and they use such attributes to form typologies and to seek spatial and temporal patterning. In practice, however, as the discussion above has shown, it has become increasingly difficult to separate technology from style or to separate types from their spatial and temporal contexts. In other words, the analytic or pattern-recognition stage has itself been identified as interpretive.

Thus at all stages, from the identification of classes and attributes to the under-standing of high-level social processes, the interpreter has to deal simultaneously with three areas of evaluation. First, the interpreter has to identify the contexts within which things had similar meaning. The boundaries of the context are never "given"; they have to be interpreted. Of course, physical traces and separations might assist the definition of contextual boundaries, such as the boundaries around a village or the separation in time between sets of events. Ritual contexts might be more formalized than or may invert mundane contexts. But despite such clues there is an infinity of possible contexts that might have been constructed by indigenous actors. The notion of context is always relevant when different sets of data are being compared and where a primary question is whether the different examples are comparable, whether the apparent similarities are real.

Second, in conjunction with and inseparable from the identification of context is the recognition of similarities and differences. The interpreter argues for a context by showing that things are done similarly, that people respond similarly to similar situations, within its boundaries. The assumption is made that within the context similar events or things had similar meaning. But this is true only if the boundaries of the context have been correctly identified. Many artifacts initially identified as ritual or cultic have later been shown to come from entirely utilitarian contexts. Equally, claimed cross-cultural similarities always have to be evaluated to see if their contexts are comparable. Thus the interpretations of context and of meaningful similarities and differences are mutually dependent.

The identification of contexts, similarities, and differences within patterned mate-rials depends on the application of appropriate social and material culture theories. The third evaluation that has to be made by the interpreter is of the relevance of general or specific historical theories to the data at hand. Observation and inter-pretation are theory laden, although theories can be changed in confrontation with material evidence in a dialectical fashion. Some of the appropriate types of general theory for material culture have been identified above. The more specific theories include the intentions and social goals of participants, or the nature of ritual or cultic as opposed to secular or utilitarian behavior.

In terms of the two types of material meaning identified earlier, rules of represen-tation are built up from patterns of association and exclusion. For example, if a pin type is exclusively associated with women in a wide variety of contexts, then it might be interpreted as representing women in all situations. The aspect of womanhood that is represented by this association with pins is derived from other associations of the pins – perhaps with foreign, nonlocal artifacts (Sorensen, 1987). The more richly networked the associations that can be followed by the interpreter, and the thicker the description (Denzin, 1989) that can be produced, the subtler the interpretations that can be made.

For the other type of material meaning, grounded in practice, the initial task of the interpreter is to understand all the social and material implications of particular practices. This is greatly enhanced by studies of modern material culture, including ethnoarchaeology (Orme, 1981). Experimental archaeologists (Coles, 1979) are now well experienced in reconstructing past practices, from storage of cereals in pits to flaking flint tools. Such reconstructions, always unavoidably artificial to some degree, allow some direct insight into another lived experience. On the basis of such knowledge the implications of material practices, extending into the social and the moral, can be theorized. But again it is detailed thick description of associations and contexts that allows the material practices to be set within specific historical situations and the particular evocations to be understood.

An example of the application of these methods is provided by Merriman's (1987) interpretation of the intentions behind the building of a wall around the elite settlement of Heuneberg, Germany, in the sixth century B.C. (an example similar to that provided by Collingwood, 1956). In cultural terms, the Hallstatt context in central Europe, including Germany, can be separated from other cultural areas such as the Aegean at this time. And yet the walls are made of mud brick and they have bastions, both of which have parallels only in the Aegean. In practice, mud brick would not have been an effective long-term form of defense in the German climate. Thus some purpose other than defense is supposed. The walls are different from other contemporary walls in Germany and yet they are similar to walls found in the Aegean context. Other similarities and differences that seem relevant are the examples of prestige exchange – valuable objects such as wine flagons traded from the Aegean to Germany. This trade seems relevant because of a theory that elites in central Europe based their power on the control of prestige exchange with the Mediterranean. It seems likely, in the context of such prestige exchange, that the walls built in a Mediterranean form were also designed to confer prestige on the elites who organized their construction. In this example the intention of the wall building is interpreted as being for prestige rather than for defense. The interpretation is based on the simultaneous evaluation of similarities and differences, context and theory. Both representational symbolism (conferring prestige) and practical meanings (the building of walls by elites in a non-Mediterranean climate) are considered. For other examples of the method applied to modern material culture, see Hodder (1991) and Moore (1986).

Confirmation

How is it possible to confirm such hypotheses about the meanings of mute material and written culture? Why are some interpretations more plausible than others? The answers to such questions are unlikely to differ radically from the procedures followed in other areas of interpretation, and so I will discuss them relatively briefly here (see Denzin, 1989; Lincoln and Guba, 1985). However, there are some differences in confirming hypotheses regarding material objects. Perhaps the major difficulty is that material culture, by its very nature, straddles the divide between a universal, natural science approach to materials and a historical, interpretive approach to culture. There is thus a particularly marked lack of agreement in the scientific community about the appropriate basis for confirmation procedures. In my view, an interpretive position can and should accommodate scientific information about, for example, natural processes of transformation and decay of artifacts. It is thus an interpretive position that I describe here.

The twin struts of confirmation are coherence and correspondence. Coherence is produced if the parts of the argument do not contradict each other and if the conclusions follow from the premises. There is a partial autonomy of different types of theory, from the observational to the global, and a coherent interpretation is one in which these different levels do not produce contradictory results. The partial autonomy of different types of theory is especially clear in relation to material culture. Because material evidence endures, it can continually be reobserved, reanalyzed, and reinterpreted. The observations made in earlier excavations are continually being reconsidered within new interpretive frameworks. It is clear from these reconsiderations of earlier work that earlier observations can be used to allow different interpretations – the different levels of theory are partially autonomous. The internal coherence between different levels of theory is continually being renegotiated.

As well as internal coherence there is external coherence – the degree to which the interpretation fits theories accepted in and outside the discipline. Of course, the evaluation of a coherent argument itself depends on the application of theoretical criteria, and I have already noted the lack of agreement in studies of material culture about foundational issues such as the importance of a natural science or humanistic approach. But whatever their views on such issues, most of those working with material culture seem to accept implicitly the importance of simplicity and elegance. An argument in which too much special pleading is required in order to claim coherence is less likely to be adopted than is a simple or elegant theory. The notion of coherence could also be extended to social and political issues within and beyond disciplines, but I shall here treat these questions separately.

The notion of correspondence between theory and data does not imply absolute objectivity and independence, but rather embeds the fit of data and theory within coherence. The data are made to cohere by being linked within theoretical arguments. Similarly, the coherence of the arguments is supported by the fit to data. On the other hand, data can confront theory, as already noted. Correspondence with the data is thus an essential part of arguments of coherence. There are many aspects of correspondence arguments that might be used. One is the exactness of fit, perhaps measured in statistical terms, between theoretical expectation and data, and this is a particularly important aspect of arguments exploiting the mute aspects of material culture. Other arguments of correspondence include the number of cases that are accounted for, their range in space and time, and the variety of different classes of data that are explained. However, such numerical indications of correspondence always have to be evaluated against contextual relevance and thick description to determine whether the different examples of fit are relevant to each other. In ethnographic and historical contexts correspondence with indigenous accounts can be part of the argument that supports contextual relevance.

Other criteria that affect the success of theories about material culture meaning include fruitfulness – how many new directions, new lines of inquiry, new perspectives are opened up. Reproducibility concerns whether other people, perhaps with different perspectives, come to similar results. Perhaps different arguments, based on different starting points, produce similar results. I have already noted that one of the advantages of material evidence is that it can continually be returned to, unexcavated parts of sites excavated and old trenches dug out and reexamined.

Intersubjective agreement is of considerable importance although of particular difficulty in an area that so completely bridges the science-humanity divide. The success of interpretations depends on peer review (either informal or formally in journals) and on the number of people who believe, cite, and build on them.

But much depends too on the trustworthiness, professional credentials, and status of the author and supporters of an interpretation. Issues here include how long the interpreter spent in the field and how well she or he knows the data: their biases, problems, and unusual examples. Has the author obtained appropriate degrees and been admitted into professional societies? Is the individual an established and consistent writer, or has he or she yet to prove her- or himself? Does the author keep changing her or his mind?

In fact, the audience does not respond directly to an interpretation but to an interpretation written or staged as an article or presentation. The audience thus responds to and reinterprets a material artifact or event. The persuasiveness of the argument is closely tied to the rhetoric within which it is couched (Gero, 1991; Hodder, 1989; Spector, 1991; Tilley, 1989). The rhetoric determines how the different components of the discipline talk about and define problems and their solutions.

Conclusion

Material culture, including written texts, poses a challenge for interpretive approaches that often stress the importance of dialogue with and spoken critical comment from participants. Material culture evidence, on the other hand, may have no living participants who can respond to its interpretation. Even if such participants do exist, they may often be unable to be articulate about material culture meanings. In any case, material culture endures, and so the original makers and users may be able to give only a partial picture of the full history of meanings given to an object as it is used and reinterpreted through time.

The challenge posed by material culture is important for anthropological and sociological analysis because material culture is often a medium in which alternative and often muted voices can be expressed. But the "reader" of material culture must recognize that only some aspects of material culture meaning are language-like. The meaning of much material culture comes about through use, and material culture knowledge is often highly chunked and contextualized. Technical operations implicate a wide network of material, social, and symbolic resources and the abstract meanings that result are closely tied in with the material.

The methods of interpretation of material culture center on the simultaneous hermeneutical procedures of context definition, the construction of patterned similarities and differences, and the use of relevant social and material culture theory. The material culture may not be able directly to "speak back," but if appropriate procedures are followed there is room for the data and for different levels of theory to confront interpretations. The interpreter learns from the experience of material remains – the data and the interpreter bring each other into existence in dialectical fashion. The interpretations can be confirmed or made more or less plausible than others using a fairly standard range of internal and external (social) criteria.

References

Bechtel, W. (1990). Connectionism and the philosophy of mind: An overview. In W. G. Lycan (ed.), *Mind and cognition: A reader.* Oxford: Basil Blackwell.

Bloch, M. (1991). Language, anthropology and cognitive science. *Man, 26,* 183–98.

Bourdieu, P. (1977). *Outline of a theory of practice.* Cambridge, UK: Cambridge University Press.

Braithwaite, M. (1982). Decoration as ritual symbol. In I. Hodder (ed.), *Symbolic and structural archaeology* (pp. 80–8). Cambridge: Cambridge University Press.

Chippindale, C. (1983). *Stonehenge complete.* London: Thames & Hudson.

Coles, J. M. (1979). *Experimental archaeology.* London: Academic Press.

Collingwood, R. (1956). *The idea of history.* Oxford, UK: Oxford University Press.

Denzin, N. K. (1989). *Interpretive interactionism.* Newbury Park, CA: Sage.

Derrida, J. (1978). *Writing and difference.* London: Routledge & Kegan Paul.

Donley, L. (1982). House power: Swahili space and symbolic markers. In I. Hodder (ed.), *Symbolic and structural archaeology* (pp. 63–73). Cambridge, UK: Cambridge University Press.

Erickson, C. L. (1988). Raised field agriculture in the Lake Titicaca Basin: Putting ancient agriculture back to work. *Expedition, 30*(3), 8–16.

Ferguson, L. (1991). Struggling with pots in Colonial South Carolina. In R. McGuire and R. Paynter (eds.), *The archaeology of inequality* (pp. 28–39). Oxford: Basil Blackwell.

Gero, J. (1991). Who experienced what in prehistory? A narrative explanation from Queyash, Peru. In R. Preucel (Ed.), *Processual and postprocessual archaeologies* (pp. 126–89). Carbondale: Southern Illinois University.

Giddens, A. (1979). *Central problems in social theory.* London: Macmillan.

Glassie, H. (1975). *Folk housing in middle Virginia.* Knoxville: University of Tennessee Press.

Hodder, I. (1982). *Symbols in action.* Cambridge, UK: Cambridge University Press.

Hodder, I. (1989). Writing archaeology: Site reports in context. *Antiquity, 63,* 268–74.

Hodder, I. (1991). *Reading the past.* Cambridge, UK: Cambridge University Press.

Hodder, I. (1992). *Theory and practice in archaeology.* London: Routledge.

Latour, B. (1988). Mixing humans and nonhumans together: The sociology of a door closer. *Social Problems, 35,* 298–310.

Lemonnier, P. (1986). The study of material culture today: Towards an anthropology of technical systems. *Journal of Anthropological Archaeology, 5,* 147–86.

Leone, M. (1984). Interpreting ideology in historical archaeology. In D. Miller and C. Tilley (eds.), *Ideology, power and prehistory* (pp. 25–36). Cambridge, UK: Cambridge University Press.

Leroi-Gourhan, A. (1964). *Le geste et la parole.* Paris: Michel.

Lincoln, Y. S., and Guba, E. G. (1985). *Naturalistic inquiry.* Beverly Hills, CA: Sage.

McGhee, R. (1977). Ivory for the sea woman. *Canadian Journal of Archaeology, 1,* 141–59.

Merriman, N. (1987). Value and motivation in prehistory: The evidence for "Celtic spirit." In I. Hodder (ed.), *The archaeology of contextual meanings* (pp. 111–16). London: Unwin Hyman.

Miller, D. (1982). Artifacts as products of human categorisation processes. In I. Hodder (ed.), *Symbolic and structural archaeology* (pp. 89–98). Cambridge, UK: Cambridge University Press.

Miller, D. (1985). *Artifacts as categories.* Cambridge, UK: Cambridge University Press.

Miller, D., Rowlands, M., and Tilley, C. (1989). *Domination and resistance.* London: Unwin Hyman.

Miller, D., and Tilley, C. (1984). *Ideology, power and prehistory.* Cambridge: Cambridge University Press.

Moore, H. (1986). *Space, text and gender.* Cambridge, UK: Cambridge University Press.

Orme, B. (1981). *Anthropology for archaeologists.* London: Duckworth.

Pelegrin, J. (1990). Prehistoric lithic technology. *Archaeological Review from Cambridge, 9,* 116–25.

Rathje, W., and Murphy, C. (1992). *Rubbish! The archaeology of garbage.* New York: HarperCollins.

Rathje, W., and Thompson, B. (1981). *The Milwaukee Garbage Project.* Washington, DC: American Paper Institute, Solid Waste Council of the Paper Industry.

Ricoeur, P. (1971). The model of the text: Meaningful action considered as text. *Social Research, 38,* 529–62.

Sanjek, R. (ed.). (1990). *Fieldnotes: The makings of anthropology.* Albany: State University of New York Press.

Schlanger, N. (1990). Techniques as human action: Two perspectives. *Archaeological Review from Cambridge, 9,* 18–26.

Shanks, M., and Tilley, C. (1987). *Reconstructing archaeology.* Cambridge: Cambridge University Press.

Sorensen, M.-L. (1987). Material order and cultural classification. In I. Hodder (ed.), *The archaeology of contextual meanings* (pp. 90–101). Cambridge, UK: Cambridge University Press.

Spector, J. (1991). What this awl means: Toward a feminist archaeology. In J. M. Gero and M. W. Conkey (eds.), *Engendering archaeology* (pp. 388–406). Oxford: Basil Blackwell.

Tilley, C. (1989). Discourse and power: The genre of the Cambridge inaugural. In D. Miller, M. Rowlands, and C. Tilley (eds.), *Domination and resistance* (pp. 41–62). London: Unwin Hyman.

Tilley, C. (ed.). (1990). *Reading material culture.* Oxford: Basil Blackwell.

Washburn, D. (1983). *Structure and cognition in art.* Cambridge, UK: Cambridge University Press.

Webb, E. J., Campbell, D. T., Schwartz, R. C., and Sechrest, L. (1966). *Unobtrusive measures: Nonreactive research in the social sciences.* Chicago: University of Chicago Press.

Wobst, M. (1977). Stylistic behavior and information exchange. *University of Michigan Museum of Anthropology, Anthropological Paper, 61,* 317–42.

Yates, T. (1989). Habitus and social space. In I. Hodder (ed.), *The meanings of things* (pp. 248–62). London: Unwin Hyman.

16 Professional Vision

Charles Goodwin

Discursive practices are used by members of a profession to shape events in the domains subject to their professional scrutiny. The shaping process creates the objects of knowledge that become the insignia of a profession's craft: the theories, artifacts, and bodies of expertise that distinguish it from other professions. Analysis of the methods used by members of a community to build and contest the events that structure their lifeworld contributes to the development of a practice-based theory of knowledge and action.[1] In this article, I examine two contexts of professional activity: archaeological field excavation and legal argumentation. In each of these contexts, I investigate three practices: (1) *coding*, which transforms phenomena observed in a specific setting into the objects of knowledge that animate the discourse of a profession; (2) *highlighting*, which makes specific phenomena in a complex perceptual field salient by marking them in some fashion; and (3) *producing and articulating material representations*. By applying such practices to phenomena in the domain of scrutiny, participants build and contest *professional vision*, which consists of socially organized ways of seeing and understanding events that are answerable to the distinctive interests of a particular social group.

In the 1992 trial of four white police officers charged with beating Mr. Rodney King, an African-American motorist who had been stopped for speeding, a videotape of the beating (made without the knowledge of the officers by a man in an apartment across the street) became a politically charged theater for contested vision. Opposing sides in the case used the murky pixels of the same television image to display to the jury incommensurate events: a brutal, savage beating of a man lying helpless on the ground versus careful police response to a dangerous "PCP-crazed giant" who was argued to be in control of the situation. By deploying an array of systematic discursive practices, including talk, ethnography, category systems articulated by expert witnesses, and various ways of highlighting images provided by the videotape, lawyers for both sides were able to structure, in ways that suited their own distinctive agendas, the complex perceptual field visible on the TV screen.

The Rodney King trial provides a vivid example of how the ability to see a meaningful event is not a transparent, psychological process but instead a socially situated activity accomplished through the deployment of a range of historically constituted discursive practices. It would, however, be quite wrong to treat the selective vision that is so salient in the King trial as a special, deviant case, merely a set of lawyers' tricks designed to distort what would otherwise be a clear, neutral vision of objective events unambiguously visible on the tape. All vision is perspectival and lodged within endogenous communities of practice. An archaeologist and a farmer see quite different phenomena in the same patch of dirt (for example, soil that will support particular kinds of crops versus stains, features, and artifacts that provide evidence for earlier human activity at this spot). An event being seen, a relevant *object of knowledge*, emerges through the interplay between a *domain of scrutiny* (a patch of dirt, the images made available by the King videotape, etc.) and a set of *discursive practices* (dividing the domain of scrutiny by highlighting a figure against a ground, applying specific coding schemes for the constitution and interpretation of relevant events, etc.) being deployed within a *specific activity* (arguing a legal case, mapping a site, planting crops, etc.). The object being investigated is thus analogous to what Wittgenstein (1958: 7) called a *language game*, a "whole, consisting of language and the actions into which it is woven."

My Own Practices for Seeing

It is not possible to work in some abstract world where the constitution of knowledge through a politics of representation has been magically overcome. The analysis in this article makes extensive use of the very same practices it is studying. Graphic representations, including transcripts of talk, diagrams, and frame grabs of scenes recorded on videotape, are annotated and highlighted in order to make salient specific events within them. Such highlighting guides the reader to see within a complex perceptual field just those events that I find relevant to the points I am developing. Applying a category such as *highlighting, graphic representation*, or *coding scheme* to diverse practices in different environments is itself an example of how coding schemes are used to organize disparate events into a common analytical framework. It is thus relevant to note briefly why I made the representational choices that I did.

To analyze how practice is organized as a temporally unfolding process encompassing both human interaction and situated tool use, I require as data records that preserve not only sequences of talk but also body movements of the participants and the phenomena to which they are attending as they use relevant representations. I use videotapes as my primary source of data, recognizing that, like transcription, any camera position constitutes a theory about what is relevant within a scene – one that will have enormous consequences for what can be seen in it later – and what forms of subsequent analysis are possible. A tremendous advantage of recorded data is that they permit repeated, detailed examination of actual sequences of talk and embodied work practices in the settings where practitioners actually perform these activities. Moreover, others can look at – and possibly challenge – my understanding of the events being examined.

As part of continuing fieldwork focusing ethnographically on how scientists actually do their work, activities at one archaeological field school in Argentina and two in the United States were videotaped. All the material analyzed in this article is drawn from one of the American field schools. Tapes of the first Rodney King trial were made from broadcasts of Court TV. I was unable to record the entire trial, so my own recordings were supplemented by an edited summary of the trial purchased from Court TV. The second trial was not broadcast on either radio or television. I was able to get into the courtroom only for the prosecution's closing arguments.

Practices of transcription constitute one local site within anthropology where the politics of representation emerge as a practical problem.[2] For a journal article, the rich record of complicated vocal and visual events moving through time provided by a videotape must be transformed into something that can silently inhabit the printed page.

Both linguistic anthropologists and conversation analysts have devoted considerable complementary and overlapping attention to questions of how talk should be transcribed, including the issue of how speakers themselves parse the stream of speech into relevant units. A major analytic focus of conversation analysis is the description of the procedures used by participants in the midst of talk-in-interaction to construct the events that constitute the lived lifeworld within ongoing processes of action.[3] This has required developing methods of transcription that permit detailed analysis of actors' changing orientations as events unfold though time. Linguistic anthropologists, concerned with maintaining the complex structure of oral performance, have argued that the division of talk into lines within a transcript should make visible to the reader how the speaker organized his or her talk into relevant units.[4] I have tried to do that in this article, breaking lines at intonational units and indenting the continuation of units too long to fit within the page margins. Given the rich interplay of different kinds of units in the stream of speech, the divisions I've made should not be treated as anything more than a provisional attempt to deal with a very complicated issue. In all other respects, my transcription uses the system developed by Gail Jefferson[5] for the analysis of conversation. The conventions most relevant to the analysis in this article include the use of *bold italics* to indicate talk spoken with special emphasis, a left bracket ([) to mark the onset of overlapping talk, and numbers in parentheses – for example, (1.2) – to note the length of silence in seconds and tenths of seconds. A dash marks the cut-off of the current sound. A equal sign indicates "latching," signifying that there is no interval between the end of one unit and the beginning of a next. Transcribers' comments are italicized in double parentheses; single parentheses around talk indicate a problematic hearing. Punctuation symbols are used to mark intonation changes rather than as grammatical symbols: a period indicates a falling contour; a question mark, a rising contour; and a comma, a falling-rising contour, as might be found in the midst of a list.

Coding Schemes

Central to the organization of human cognition are processes of classification. *Coding schemes* are one systematic practice used to transform the world into the categories and events that are relevant to the work of the profession (Cicourel 1964, 1968). For example, linguists classify sounds in terms of phonetic distinctions; sociologists classify people according to sex and class.

The pervasive power of coding schemes to organize apprehension of the world is demonstrated in particularly vivid fashion in scientific work. Ethnographic analysis of what is usually considered the epitome of abstract, objective, universal, disembodied cognition – Western science – has revealed it to be a patchwork of situated, disparate, locally organized cultures in which knowledge is constituted through a variety of social and political processes.[6] Central to the cognitive processes that constitute science are both material objects (tools and machines of many different types) and writing practices quite unlike those typically studied by anthropologists investigating literacy. In order to generate a data set, collections of observations that can be compared with each other, scientists use coding schemes to circumscribe and delineate the world they examine. When disparate events are viewed through a single coding scheme, equivalent observations become possible.

Let us briefly investigate this process using the example of a field school for young archaeologists. The medium in which archaeologists work is dirt. Students are given a form that contains an elaborate set of categories for describing the color, consistency, and texture of whatever dirt they encounter. They are even expected to taste a sample of the dirt to determine how sandy it is. Moreover, some of the categories are supported by additional tools of inscription, such as a Munsell color chart, used by archaeologists all over the world as a standard for color descriptions.

The process of filling in the form requires physical, cognitive, and perceptual work. Thus, in order to determine the color of a specimen of dirt, the students must obtain a sample with a trowel, highlight it by squirting it with water, and then hold the sample under the holes in the Munsell color chart (see figure 16.1). The Munsell book encapsulates in a material object the theory and solutions developed by earlier workers faced with this task of classification (Hutchins 1993). The pages juxtapose color patches and viewing holes that allow the dirt to be seen right next to the color sample, providing a historically constituted architecture for perception.

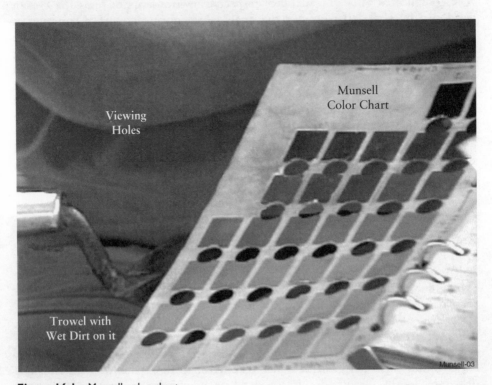

Figure 16.1 Munsell color chart

Though apparently distant from the abstract world of archaeological theory and from the debates that are currently animating the discipline, this encounter between a coding scheme and the world is a key locus for scientific practice, the place where the multifaceted complexity of "nature" is transformed into the phenomenal categories that make up the work environment of a scientific discipline. It is precisely here that nature is transformed into culture.

Despite the rigorous way in which a tool such as this one structures perception of the dirt being scrutinized, finding the correct category is not an automatic or even an easy task (Goodwin 1993). The very way in which the Munsell chart provides a context-free reference standard creates problems of its own. The color patches on the chart are glossy, while the dirt never is, so that the chart color and the sample color never look exactly the same. Moreover, the colors being evaluated frequently fall between the discrete categories provided by the Munsell chart. Two students at the field school looking at exactly the same dirt and reference colors can and do disagree as to how it should be classified. However, the definitiveness provided by a coding scheme typically erases from subsequent documentation the cognitive and perceptual uncertainties that these students are grappling with, as well as the work practices within which they are embedded.

The use of such coding schemes to organize the perception of nature, events, or people within the discourse of a profession carries with it an array of perceptual and cognitive operations that have far-reaching impact. First, by using such a system, a worker views the world from the perspective it establishes. Of all the possible ways that the earth could be looked at, the perceptual work of students using this form is focused on determining the exact color of a minute sample of dirt. They engage in active cognitive work, but the parameters of that work have been established by the system that is organizing their perception. Insofar as the coding scheme establishes an orientation toward the world, it constitutes a structure of intentionality whose proper locus is not an isolated, Cartesian mind but a much larger organizational system, one that is characteristically mediated through mundane bureaucratic documents such as forms. Forms, with their coding schemes, allow a senior investigator to inscribe his or her perceptual distinctions into the work practices of the technicians who code the data. Such systems provide an example of how distributed cognition is organized through the writing practices that coordinate action within an organization (Smith 1990: 121–2).

Highlighting

Human cognitive activity characteristically occurs in environments that provide a complicated perceptual field. A quite general class of cognitive practices consists of methods used to divide a domain of scrutiny into a figure and a ground, so that events relevant to the activity of the moment stand out. For example, forms and other documents packed with different kinds of information are a major textual component of many work environments. Faced with such a dense perceptual field, workers in many settings *highlight* their documents with colored markers, handwritten annotations, and stick-on notes. In so doing they tailor the document so that those parts of it which contain information relevant to their own work are made salient. Psychologists have long talked about figure/ground relations as a basic element of human perception. Situating such processes not only within the mind but as visible operations on external phenomena has a range of significant consequences. As we will see in subsequent examples, through these practices structures of relevance in the material environment can be made prominent, thus becoming ways of shaping not only one's own perception but also that of others.

Highlighting will be examined first in the work practices of archaeologists. In looking at the earth, archaeologists attend to an array of color distinctions in order to discern the traces of past human structures. For example, even though a post that supported a roof of an ancient house has long since decayed, the earth where it stood will have subtle color differences from the dirt around it. Archaeologists attempt to locate *features* such as these post molds[7] by scrutinizing the earth as they dig. Categories of relevance to the profession, such as post molds, are thus used to structure interpretation of the land-scape. When a possible feature is found, the archaeological category and the traces in the dirt that possibly instantiate it are each used to elaborate the other in what has been called the *documentary method of interpretation*.[8] Thus the category "post mold" provides a texture of intelligibility that unifies disparate patches of color into a coherent object. These patches of color in turn provide evidence for the existence in this patch of dirt of an instance of the object proposed by the category.

Features can be difficult to see. In order to make them visible to others, the archaeologist outlines them by drawing a line in the dirt with a trowel (see figure 16.2). By doing this the archaeologist establishes a figure in what is quite literally a

Figure 16.2   Post mold

very amorphous ground. This line in the sand has very powerful persuasive consequences. As a visible annotation of the earth, it becomes a public event that can guide the perception of others while further reifying the object that the archaeologist proposes to be visible in the color patterning in the dirt. The perceptual field provided by the dirt is enhanced in a work-relevant way by human action on it. Through such highlighting and the subsequent digging that it will help to organize, the archaeologist discursively shapes from the materials provided by the earth the phenomenal objects – that is, the archaeological features – that are the concerns of his or her profession.

Graphic Representations as Embodied Practice

Most linguists analyzing literacy have focused on the writing of words, sentences, and other written versions of spoken language. However, graphic representations of many different types constitute central objects in the discourse of various professions. Scientific talks and papers are best seen not as a purely linguistic text but as a reflexive commentary on the diagrams, graphs, and photographs that constitute the heart of a presentation.[9] More generally, since the pioneering work of Latour and Woolgar (1979), the central importance of *inscriptions* in the organization of scientific knowledge has become a major focus of research. A theory of discourse that ignored graphic representations would be missing both a key element of the discourse that professionals engage in and a central locus for the analysis of professional practice. Instead of mirroring spoken language, these external representations complement it, using the distinctive characteristics of the material world to organize phenomena in ways that spoken language cannot – for example, by collecting records of a range of disparate events onto a single visible surface.

To explore such issues and prepare the ground for investigation of how lawyers articulated graphic representations in the Rodney King trial, the practices that archaeologists use to make maps will now be investigated. This will allow us to examine the interface between writing practices, talk, human interaction, and tool use as these professionals build representations central to the work of their discipline. A team of archaeologists is at work producing a map (see figure 16.3). This particular map is of a *profile*, the layers of dirt visible on the side of one of the square holes that are dug to excavate a site. Maps of this sort are one of the distinctive forms of professional literacy that constitute archaeology as a profession.

To demarcate what the archaeologist believes are two different layers of dirt, a line is drawn between them with a trowel. The line and the ground surface above it are then transferred to a piece of graph paper. This is a task that involves two people. One measures the length and depth coordinates of the points to be mapped, using a ruler and a tape measure. He or she reports the measurements as pairs of numbers, such as "At forty, plus eleven point five" (see figure 16.4). A second archaeologist transfers the numbers provided by the measurer to a piece of graph paper. After plotting a set of points, he or she makes the map by drawing lines between them. What we find here is a small activity system that encompasses talk, writing, tools, and distributed cognition as two parties collaborate to inscribe events they see in the earth onto paper.

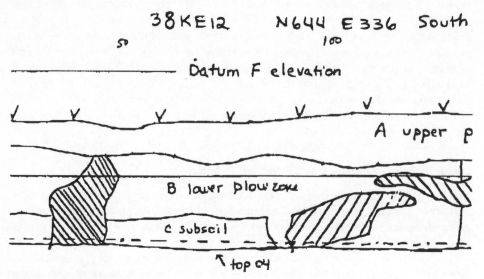

Figure 16.3 Map scan

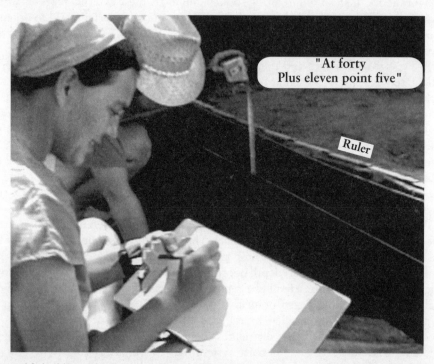

Figure 16.4 Measuring and writing for an archaeological chart

The activity of inscription that we will now examine begins with a request from Ann, the writer, to Sue, the measurer (lines 1–2):

| 1 | Ann: | Give me the ground surface over here |
| 2 | | to about *ninety*. |

3		(1.7)
4	Ann:	No-No-Not *at* ninety. =
5		From you *to* about ninety.

However, before Sue has produced any numbers, indeed before she has said anything whatsoever, Ann, who is her professor, challenges her, telling her that what she is doing is wrong (lines 4–5). How can Ann see that there is something wrong with a response that has not even occurred yet? Crucial to this process is the phenomenon of *conditional relevance* (Schegloff 1968). A first utterance creates an interpretive environment that will be used by participants to analyze whatever occurs after it. Here no subsequent talk has yet been produced. However, providing an answer in this activity system encompasses more than talk: before speaking the set of numbers, Sue must first locate a relevant point in the dirt and measure its coordinates. Both her movement through space and her use of tools such as the tape measure are visible events.[10]

As Ann finishes her directive, Sue is holding the tape measure against the dirt at the left or zero end of the profile. However, just after hearing "ninety," Sue moves both her body and the tape measure to the right, stopping near the 90 mark on the upper ruler. By virtue of the field of interpretation opened up through conditional relevance, Sue's movement and tool use as elements of the activity she has been asked to perform can now be analyzed by Ann and found wanting. Immediately after this Ann produces her correction (lines 4–5).

Additional elements of cognitive operations that Ann expects Sue to perform in order to make her measurements are revealed as the sequence continues to unfold. Making the relevant measurements presupposes the ability to locate where in the dirt measurements should be made. Sue's response to the correction calls this presupposition into question and leads to Ann telling her explicitly, in several different ways, what she should look for in order to determine where to measure. The process begins after Ann tells Sue to measure points between 0 and 90 (line 5). Sue does not immediately move to this region but instead hesitates for a full second (line 6) before replying with a weak "Oh."

1	Ann:		Give me the ground surface over here
2			to about *ninety*.
3			(1.7)
4	Ann:		No-No-Not *at* ninety. =
5			From you *to* about ninety.
6	Sue:		(1.0) Oh.
7	Ann:	→	Wherever there's a change in slope.
8	Sue:		(0.6) Mm kay.

In line 7 Ann moves from request to instruction by telling Sue what she should be looking for in the landscape: "Wherever there's a change in slope." Though most approaches to the study of meaning in language focus on the issue of how concepts can best be defined (for example, componential analysis and other approaches to semantics), Wittgenstein (1958: 242) notes that "If language is to be a means of communication there must be agreement not only in definitions but also (queer as this may sound) in judgments." In the present case, in order to use what Ann has just said to pursue the task they are collaboratively engaged in, Sue must be able to find in the dirt what will count as "a change in slope." As the party who has set her this task, Ann is in a position to evaluate her success. Sue again moves her tape measure far to the right (see figure 16.5, image A). At this point, instead of relying on talk alone to make explicit the phenomena that she wants Sue to locate, Ann moves into the space that Sue is attending to (image B) and points to one place that should be measured while describing in more vernacular language what constitutes "a change in slope": "where it *stops* being flat" (line 11). She then points to additional places for measurement (lines 13–17).

Labeling what Ann does here either deictic gesture or ostensive definition does not do adequate justice to its complexity. Analysis of the gesture cannot focus on the gesture alone or on some possible mental state of the speaker it is externalizing (effectively drawing an analytic bubble at the skin of the actor); it requires simultaneous attention to the environment that the hand is highlighting, the talk that sets the coding problem for the addressee, and the activity that these participants are working to accomplish. Talk and gesture mutually elaborate on each other within a framework of action that includes at least three components: (1) a semantic description, such as "a change in slope"; (2) a complex perceptual field where an instantiation of that category is to be located; and (3) the hand of an actor moving within that perceptual field. The activity in progress, including the sequence of talk within which these ostensive demonstrations emerge, provides a relevant language game that can be used to make inferences about precisely which features of the complex perceptual field being pointed at should be attended to. What Sue is being taught is not something that falls within the scope of language as an isolated system – not a definition (she already knows what a "change in slope" is in the abstract) – but a mode of practice, how to code a relevant perceptual field in terms of categories that are consequential for her work. In turn this process is embedded within the larger activity of doing archaeological fieldwork, as well as a local interactive field that structures participants' mutual access to both each other and the domain of scrutiny where relevant work is being done. Within such an interactive field, the actions that Sue is expected to perform enable Ann to evaluate her comprehension and, where relevant, to take remedial action in subsequent moves. The cognitive activities occurring here are situated, distributed, and interactively organized. In this process coding tasks (Sue is set the problem of finding an example of a particular category in the materials she is looking at) and highlighting (the movement of Ann's hand that displays where a solution to Ann's problem is to be found) function together in the production of a relevant graphic representation (the map).

One of the things that is occurring within this sequence is a progressive expansion of Sue's understanding as the distinctions she must make to carry out the task assigned to her are explicated and elaborated. In this process of socialization through language,[11] growth in intersubjectivity occurs as domains of ignorance that prevent the successful accomplishment of collaborative action are revealed

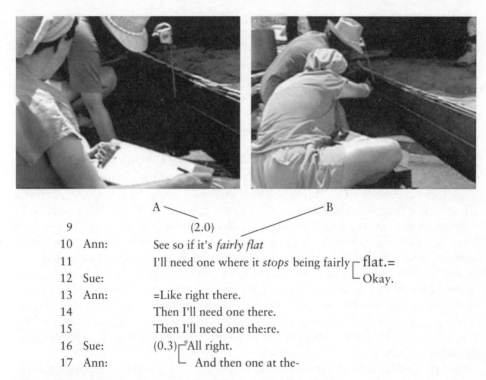

```
                          A ⟍                    B
    9                         (2.0)
   10   Ann:        See so if it's fairly flat
   11                I'll need one where it stops being fairly ⌐ flat.=
   12   Sue:                                                   ⌐ Okay.
   13   Ann:        =Like right there.
   14               Then I'll need one there.
   15               Then I'll need one the:re.
   16   Sue:        (0.3)⌐°All right.
   17   Ann:             ⌐ And then one at the-
```

Figure 16.5 Talk and gesture mutually elaborate on each other

and transformed into practical knowledge – a way of seeing that is sufficient to complete the job at hand – in a way that allows Sue to understand what Ann is asking her to do and make an appropriate, competent response to her request.

It would, however, be quite wrong to see the unit within which this intersubjectivity is lodged as being simply two minds coming together to do the work at hand. Instead, the distinctions being explicated, the ability to see in the very complex perceptual field provided by the landscape to which they are attending those few events that count as points to be transferred to the map, are central to what it means to see the world as an archaeologist and to use that seeing to build the artifacts, such as this map, that are constitutive of archaeology as a profession. All competent archaeologists are expected to be able to do this; it is an essential part of what it means to *be* an archaeologist,[12] and it is to these professional perceptual standards that Sue is being held accountable. The relevant unit for the analysis of the intersubjectivity at issue here is thus not these individuals as isolated entities but archaeology as a profession, a community of competent practitioners, most of whom have never met each other but nonetheless expect each other to be able to see and categorize the world in ways that are relevant to the work, tools, and artifacts that constitute their profession.

This sequence brings together an important range of cognitive phenomena relevant to the organization of human action, including interaction with both other human beings and the world itself, talk as a form of social action, writing practices, and the construction of cognitive artifacts that provide relevant representations of the world. These inscription practices are accomplished through the appropriate use of artifacts such as graph paper, rulers, and tape measures. Supporting such tool use are sets of perceptual structures, the ability to see what and where to measure. Moreover, we are able to glimpse how these structures are passed on from one generation to the next through apprenticeship.

Contested Vision

The use of coding schemes, highlighting practices, and the articulation of graphic representations to organize perception will now be examined in another professional setting: the courtroom. On March 3, 1991, an amateur video photographer taped a group of Los Angeles police officers administering a very violent beating with metal clubs to an African-American motorist, Mr. Rodney King, who had been stopped for a traffic violation. When the tape was broadcast on television, there was public outrage, and four police officers involved in the beating were put on trial for excessive use of force. The principal piece of evidence against them was the tape of the beating. The violence it showed was so graphic that many people assumed that a conviction was almost automatic. However, the jury found the police officers innocent, a verdict that triggered the Los Angeles uprising. At a second federal trial a year later, two of the four officers were convicted of violating King's civil rights and two were acquitted.

Perhaps surprisingly, the main evidence used in the defense of the police officers was the tape showing them beating King. Indeed, one of the officers convicted in the second trial, Sergeant Stacy Koon, spent much of his time between the two trials watching and rewatching the tape, seeing how it looked when projected on different walls in his house. Rather than wanting to minimize the events on the tape, he told a reporter that

> if we had our way, we'd go down to Dodger Stadium and rip off that big-screen Mitsubishi and bring it into the courtroom and say, "Hey, folks, you're in for the show of your life because when this tape gets blown up it's awesome." (Mydans 1993d: A10)

For Rodney King the experience of looking at the tape was quite different: "It's sickening to see it. It makes me sick to my stomach to watch it" (Newton 1993a: A16).

At the first trial the prosecution presented the tape of the beating as a self-explicating, objective record. Thus the chief prosecutor said,

> What more could you ask for? You have the videotape that shows objectively, without bias, impartially, what happened that night. The videotape shows conclusively what happened that night. It can't be rebutted. (Mydans 1993b: A7)

But the lawyers defending the police officers did not treat the tape as a record that spoke for itself. Instead they argued that it could be understood only by embedding the events visible on it within the work life of a profession. The defense proposed that the beating constituted an example of careful police work, a form of professional discourse with the victim in which he was a very active coparticipant – indeed, the party who controlled the interaction.

To successfully make this claim, the defense provided the jury with ethnography about police practices and with a coding scheme to be used to analyze the events on the tape. The power of coding schemes to control perception in this fashion was central to the defense strategy. The defense contended that if the police officers could legitimately see King's actions as aggressive and a threat to them, then the police were entitled to use force to protect themselves and take him into custody. The central point debated within the trial was what the police officers who beat King perceived him to be doing. These perceptions were treated not as idiosyncratic phenomena lodged within the minds of individual police officers but as socially organized perceptual frameworks shared within the police profession.

These assumptions about the conventions maintained by the police had two consequences for the organization of discourse within the courtroom: (1) police perceptions, as a domain of professional competence, can be described and analyzed through use of highlighting, coding schemes, and graphic representations; (2) in that these perceptions are not idiosyncratic phenomena restricted to individuals but frameworks shared by a profession, *expert testimony* is possible. An expert who was not present at the scene can describe authoritatively what police officers could legitimately see as they looked at the man they were beating.

Expert testimony is given a very distinctive shape within the adversarial system of the American courtroom.[13] Each side hires its own experts and attacks the credibility of its opponents' experts. Moreover, the use of expert witnesses intersects with rules establishing what counts as adequate proof. Reasonable doubt can be created by muddying the water with a plausible alternative. In the words of the lawyer for Officer Theodore Briseno, one of the defendants:

> Your experts really don't have to be better than their [the prosecution's] experts. All you've got to have are experts on both sides. I think [jurors] wonder: "How could we as lay people know beyond a reasonable doubt, when the experts can't decide?" (Lieberman 1993b: A32)

Such a strategy can be quite successful. One of the jurors who acquitted the police officers in the first King trial said, "Our instructions of how we could consider evidence stated ... if there are two reasonable explanations for an event, we had to pick the one that points to innocence, not the one that points to guilt" (Lieberman 1993b: A32).

Coding Aggression as Professional Practice

Allowing expert testimony on the use of force by the police had the effect of filtering the events visible on the tape through a police coding scheme, as articulated by an expert who instructed the jury how to see the body movements of the victim in terms of that system. What one finds in the trial is a dialogic framework encompassing the work of two different professions, as the discourse of the police with one of their suspects is embedded within the discourse of the courtroom.

In order to measure police perception, a coding scheme for the escalation of force was applied to the tape: (1) if a suspect is aggressive, the proper police response is escalation of force in order to subdue him; (2) when the suspect cooperates, then force is de-escalated. When an expert applies this coding scheme to the tape, a new set of finely differentiated events is produced, described through appropriate language drawn from the social sciences. In the words of one expert:

> Expert: There were,
>   ten distinct (1.0) uses of force.
>   rather than one single use of force.
>
>   ...
>
>   In each of those, uses of force
>   there was an escalation and a de escalation, (0.8)
>   an assessment period, (1.5)
>   and then an escalation and a de-escalation again. (0.7)
>   And another assessment period.

The massive beating is now transformed into ten separate events, each with its own sequence of stages.

The use of this category system radically transforms the images visible on the tape by placing them within an expert frame of reference. Thus when King is hit yet another blow, this is transformed from a moment of visible violence – what the prosecution in the second trial will instruct the jury to see as "beating a suspect into submission" – into a demonstration that the "period of de-escalation has ceased":

> Defense: Four oh five, oh one.
> | We see a blow being delivered. | =
>   = Is that correct.
> Expert: That's correct.
> | The-force has been again escalated (0.3)
>   to the level it had been previously, (0.4)
>   and the de-escalation has ceased. |
>
>   ...
>
> Defense: And at-
>   At this point which is,
>   for the record four thirteen twenty nine, (0.4)
> | We see a blow being struck
>   and thus the end of the period of, de-escalation? |
>   Is that correct Captain.
> Expert: | That's correct.
>   Force has now been elevated to the previous level, (0.6)
>   after this period of de-escalation. |

A reader looking at this sequence might argue that what the expert is saying is a mere tautology: if someone is being hit again, then – almost by definition – any period of de-escalation of force (the moments when the suspect is not being hit) has ceased. However, much more than tautology is involved. By deploying the escalation/de-escalation framework, the expert has provided a coding scheme that transforms the actions being coded into displays of careful, systematic police work. One of the defense lawyers said that what he wanted to show the jury was that "what looks like uncontrolled uh brutality and random violence is indeed a very disciplined and controlled effort to take King into custody" (interview with Court TV, CRT 018:03:30). A major resource for affecting such a perceptual transformation is the use of coding schemes such as the one articulated above by the defense's expert witness. Such schemes provide the jury with far from neutral templates for viewing and understanding in a particular way the events visible on the tape.

These structures also define the instruments of violence visible on the tape. Earlier it was noted how the conditional relevance of an utterance creates a context that shapes interpretation of the events it points to. When the escalation framework was first introduced, the defense attorney showed the jury a chart of *tools* used by the police that included not only the batons with which they were beating him but also the kicks that they administered:

Defense: And this chart will show you the *tools*
                that Sergeant Koon had available to him on March third.
                . . .
                The next tool up, (1.9)
                Is: (0.3) a side handle baton. (0.8)
                a metal (0.3) baton. (1.0)
                is: a tool (0.8)
                to protect yourself (0.9)
                and to take people into custody. (1.0)
                And in addition to that (0.3)
                on the same level with this (0.5)
                the experts will tell you as well as Sergeant Koon, (0.4)
                that there are *kicks*,

A coding scheme, classifying phenomena visible on the tape as tools required for the work of a particular occupation, is deployed to move what the prosecution described as brutal "cowardly stomps" inflicted on a prone, beaten man into a domain of professional police work.

The escalation/de-escalation framework was taught in the police academy as a guide for appropriate action when applying force. It generated a second coding scheme focused on the suspect's body. Central to the case made by the defense was the proposal that the police officers themselves were required to evaluate King's actions as either *aggressive* or *cooperative* in order to decide whether to escalate or de-escalate force – that is, whether they should hit him again. The key perceptual decision posed in the analysis of the tape thus becomes whether the police officers can legitimately see the suspect as aggressive, in which case, it is argued, they are justified in applying further force. The following is from the cross-examination of defendant Laurence Powell, the officer who landed the most blows on King:

Prosecutor: You can't look at that video and say
                that every one of those blows
                is reasonable can you.
                (1.0)
Powell: Oh I *can* if I put my perceptions in.

Crucially, the defense argues that an interpretive framework focused on the suspect's actions vests control of the situation in the victim, since his actions control the response of the police:

> *Defense:*   Rodney **King**
> and Rodney King alone
> was in control of the situation.

The net effect of buying into this category system as a framework for the interpretation of the tape is a most consequential structuring of the dense and complicated perceptual field provided by the tape, with the suspect/victim King becoming the figure, the focus of minute scrutiny, while the officers performing the beating recede into the background.

Expert Testimony: An Ethnography of Seeing

To analyze the tape in these terms, the defense calls Sergeant Charles Duke from the Los Angeles Police Department as an expert on the use of force by the police (see figure 16.6). Commentators on the first trial considered Duke to be the most important and persuasive witness in the case.

At the point where we enter the following sequence, the prosecutor has noted that King appears to be moving into a position appropriate for handcuffing him and that one officer is in fact reaching for his handcuffs – the suspect is being cooperative.

1	Prosecutor:	So uh would you,
2		again consider this to be:
3		a nonagressive, movement by Mr. King?
4	Sgt. Duke:	At this time no I wouldn't. (1.1)
5	Prosecutor:	It is aggressive.
6	Sgt. Duke:	Yes. It's starting to be. (0.9)
7		This foot, is laying flat, (0.8)
8		There's starting to be a *bend.* in uh (0.6)
9		this leg (0.4)
10		in his butt (0.4)
11		The buttocks area has started to rise. (0.7)
12		which would put us,
13		at the beginning of our *spec*trum again.

Here the process of coding events within a relevant perceptual field becomes an open contest as prosecution and defense use a range of discursive practices to debate whether body movements of King visible on the videotape should be coded as cooperative or aggressive. By noting both the submissive elements in King's posture and the fact that one of the officers is reaching for his handcuffs, the prosecutor has tried to make the case that the tape demonstrates that at this point the officers perceive King as cooperative. If he can establish this point, hitting King again would be unjustified and the officers should be found guilty of the crimes they are charged with. The contested vision being debated here has very high stakes.

To rebut the vision proposed by the prosecutor, Duke uses the semantic resources provided by language to code as aggressive extremely subtle body movements of a

Figure 16.6   Sergeant Duke analyzes the Rodney King video tape. Historical still of the Rodney King Beating courtesy of George Holliday © 1991 George Holliday. All rights reserved. NO REPRODUCTION OF THIS STILL MAY BE MADE WITHOUT THE PRIOR WRITTEN CONSENT OF GEORGE HOLLIDAY

man lying facedown beneath the officers (lines 7–11). Note, for example, not only his explicit placement of King at the very edge, the beginning, of the aggressive spectrum (line 13) but also how very small movements are made much larger by situating them within a prospective horizon through repeated use of "starting to" (line 6, 18, 11), for example, "The buttocks area has started to rise." The events visible on the tape are enhanced and amplified by the language used to describe them.

This focusing of attention organizes the perceptual field provided by the videotape into a salient figure, the aggressive suspect, who is highlighted against an amorphous background containing nonfocal participants, the officers doing the beating. This structuring of the materials provided by the image is accomplished not only through talk but also through gesture. As Duke speaks, he brings his hand to the screen and points to the parts of King's body that, he is arguing, display aggression (see figure 16.7). In looking at how the senior archaeologist pointed to where examples of the categories her student was searching for could be found, it was noted how a category, a gesture, and the perceptual field that it was articulating mutually elaborated on each other. Here the touchable events on the television screen provide visible *evidence* for the description constructed through talk. What emerges from Duke's testimony is not just a *statement*, a static category, but a *demonstration* built through the active interplay between the coding scheme and the domain of scrutiny to which it is being applied. As talk and image mutually enhance each other, a demonstration that is greater than the sum of its parts emerges. Simultaneously,

TCR 00:04·03:02

Figure 16.7 Sergeant Duke shows display of aggression by Rodney King. Historical still of the Rodney King Beating courtesy of George Holliday © 1991 George Holliday. All rights reserved. NO REPRODUCTION OF THIS STILL MAY BE MADE WITHOUT THE PRIOR WRITTEN CONSENT OF GEORGE HOLLIDAY

King, rather than the officers, becomes the focus of attention as the expert's finger, articulating the image, delineates what is relevant within it.

By virtue of the category systems erected by the defense, the minute rise in King's buttocks noted on the tape unleashes a cascade of perceptual inferences that have the effect of exonerating the officers. A rise in King's body is interpreted as aggression, which in turn justifies an escalation of force. Like other parties faced with a coding task, the jury members were led to engage in intense, minute cognitive scrutiny as they looked at the tape of the beating to decide the issues at stake in the case. However, once the defense's coding scheme is accepted as a relevant framework for looking at the tape, the operative perspective for viewing it is no longer a layperson's reaction to a man lying on the ground being beaten but instead a microanalysis of the movements being made by that man's body to see if it is exhibiting aggression.

The expert witnesses for the defense simultaneously construct actions as both rational and without moral responsibility, in the case of the police, and as mindlessly mechanical and morally responsible, in the case of Rodney King.[14] Thus references to phenomena such as "an assessment period" imply rational deliberation on the part of the police without individual moral responsibility in terms other than the correctness of assessment – for example, the agentless passive voice of "We see a blow being delivered," "The force has again been escalated," and "kicks" as tools of the trade. On the other hand, King is characterized both as an almost mindless, moving force – for example, "The buttocks area has started to rise" – and as being "in control of the situation." This is accomplished in part by the disassembly of King's body from a responsible agent into a bunch of moving parts that become the triggering mechanism for a typified process to which, it is argued, the police are required to respond in a disciplined, dispassionate way. Discourses of rationality, of mechanism, and of moral responsibility are simultaneously, but strategically and selectively, deployed.

In the first trial, though the prosecution disputed the analysis of specific body movements as displays of aggression, the relevance of looking at the tape in terms of such a category system was not challenged. Observers considered this to be a very serious mistake (Lieberman 1993a: A26). A key difference in the second trial, which led to the conviction of two of the officers, was that there the prosecution gave the jury alternative frameworks for interpreting the events on the tape. These included both an alternative motive for the beating, namely that the police officers were teaching a lesson to a man who had been disrespectful to them (Mydans 1993c), and an alternative interpretation of the movements of King's body that Sergeant Duke highlighted, namely as normal reactions of a man to a beating rather than as displays of incipient aggression. In the prosecution's argument, King "cocks his leg" not in preparation for a charge but because his muscles naturally jerk after being hit with a metal club. The prosecution's alternative interpretive template also instructed the jury to look at the physical behavior of the police officers who were not hitting King, portraying them as nonchalantly watching a beating rather than poised to subdue a still dangerous suspect. Instead of restricting focus to the body of King, the prosecution drew the jury's attention to the slender stature of Officer Briseno, the officer sent in alone at the end of the beating to handcuff the man that the defense was portraying as a dangerous giant. The prosecutor in the second trial also emphasized to the jury inherent contradictions in the arguments being made by the defense. The defense had portrayed King as both a cunning martial arts expert, scanning the scene to plot his next move, and as a man crazed by drugs. Instead, the prosecution argued, he was simply a beaten man who fell helplessly to the ground.[15] Though most of the evidence used in the two trials was the same (most crucially the tape), the prosecutors in the second trial were able to build discursively their own interpretive frameworks to counter those that had been so effectively deployed by the defense, and thus provide their jury with ways of looking at the tape that had not been available to the first jury.

The perspectival framework provided by a professional coding scheme constitutes the objects in the domain of scrutiny that are the focus of attention. By using the coding scheme to animate the events being studied, the expert teaches the jury how to look at the tape and how to see relevant events within it (Shuy 1982: 125). He provides them with an ethnography of seeing that situates the events visible on the tape within the worklife and phenomenal world of a particular work community. Here this ethnographer is not an outside anthropologist but an actual member of the community whose work is being explicated. Expert testimony in court forces members of a discourse community to become metapragmatically aware of the communication practices that organize their work, including, in this case, violence as a systematic mode of discourse capable of being described scientifically as professional practice in minute detail.

Insofar as the courtroom provides a dialogic framework encompassing the discourse of two different professions, scrutiny is occurring on a number of distinct levels: first, police scrutiny of the suspect's body as a guide for whether to beat him; second, scrutiny by those in court, including the jury and expert witnesses, as they assess the scrutiny of the police;[16] and third, within the framework of this article, our scrutiny of how those in the courtroom scrutinize the police scrutinizing their victim.

Graphic Demonstrations and Material Artifacts: The Birth of Rodney King as a Visible Actor

The perceptual field provided by the tape was manipulated and enhanced in other ways as well. At the very beginning of the tape, while the camera was still slightly out of focus, King ran toward the officers. On the tape itself, this event is hard to see: it happens very quickly and is difficult to discern in the midst of a dark but very complex perceptual field filled with other events, including numerous police officers, a police car, and King's own car, which, because of its light color and lack of movement, is the most salient object in the frame – indeed, the only item that can be easily recognized. The images visible on the tape are made even more difficult to see by the movement of the zooming camera and its lack of focus.

One of the defense attorneys in the first trial had photographs made from individual tape frames. The photos were cropped, enlarged, and pasted in sequence to form a display over a meter long that was placed in front of the jury on an easel. The salience of King in these images was amplified through use of *highlighting*. As the defense attorney unveiled his display, he placed clear overlays with large white lines outlining King's body on top of the photos (see figure 16.8). Earlier we saw an archaeologist weave a post mold into existence by drawing a line through subtle patches of color differences in a bit of dirt. Here the defense attorney uses similar-procedures for enhancing objects in the domain of scrutiny to call forth from the murky pixels on the video screen the discursive object that is the point of his argument, a large, violent, charging African-American man who was so dangerous that hitting him 47 times with metal clubs was reasonable and justified. By virtue of the figure/ground relationship established through such highlighting, the police officers, all situated beyond the boundaries of the lines drawn by the lawyer, recede into the background.

When videotape is used as the medium for displaying King's movements, a sense of what is happening as events unfold rapidly through time can be obtained only by replaying the tape repeatedly while trying to select from the confusing images on the screen that subset of visible events on which one is trying to concentrate. The work of the viewer is radically changed when these scenes are transformed into the photographic array. Movement through time becomes movement through space, that is, the left-to-right progression of the cropped frames. Each image remains available to the viewer instead of disappearing when its successor arrives, so that both the sequence as a whole and each event within it can be contemplated and rescanned at leisure. Much of the visual clutter[17] in the original images is eliminated by cropping the photos.

Figure 16.8 Use of white lines to highlight King's body. Historical still of the Rodney King Beating courtesy of George Holliday © 1991 George Holliday. All rights reserved. NO REPRODUCTION OF THIS STILL MAY BE MADE WITHOUT THE PRIOR WRITTEN CONSENT OF GEORGE HOLLIDAY

In his analysis of similar representational practices in scientific discourse, Lynch (1988) wrote about them providing an *externalized retina*. The defense lawyer makes precisely the same argument, stating that by enhancing the image in this way, he is able to structure the world being scrutinized so that it reveals what his client perceived (lines 5–8):

```
 1   Defense:     Rodney King, (0.4) in the very beginning, (1.0)
 2                in the first six frames, (2.2)
 3                of this incident, (2.4)
 4                Went (4.7) from the grou:nd, (0.4) to a charge. (1.2)
 5                And what Sergeant Koon will tell you=
 6                =this is his rendi:tion, (0.4) of what he sa:w. (0.7)
 7                ((Laying White Line Overlays on Top of Photos))
 8                This is how he perceived it. (3.6)
 9                But once he saw Rodney King,
10                ri:se to his feet, (1.2) and attack at Powell, (1.4)
11                That in Koon's mind, (0.9) in charge of his officers (1.2)
12                that Rodney King has set the tone. (1.6)
13                Rodney King, (1.1) was trying to get in that position.
```

Once again talk and visual representation mutually amplify each other. Descriptors such as "a charge" (line 4) provide instructions for how to see the highlighted sequence on the easel, while that very same sequence provides seeable proof for

Figure 16.9   Sergeant Duke discusses officer stepping on King's neck. Historical still of the Rodney King Beating courtesy of George Holliday © 1991 George Holliday. All rights reserved. NO REPRODUCTION OF THIS STILL MAY BE MADE WITHOUT THE PRIOR WRITTEN CONSENT OF GEORGE HOLLIDAY

the argument being made in the defense attorney's talk. (At the second trial, King testified that he ran after one of the officers said, "We're going to kill you nigger. Run.") At line 13 the defense attorney points with his finger toward the last photo in the series, the one where King is actually making contact with Officer Powell. This deictic gesture establishes that image as the referent for "that position" at the end of line 13 – the attacking position that the defense is arguing Rodney King was repeatedly trying to gain. Traditional work on gesture in interaction (and deixis in linguistics) has drawn a bubble around the perimeters of the participants' bodies. The body of the actor has not been connected to the built world within which it is situated. In these data the graphic display that receives the point is as much a constructed discursive object as the pointing finger or the spoken words; all three mutually elaborate on each other. Theoretical frameworks that partition the components of this process into separate fields of study cannot do justice to the reflexive relationship that exists between the talk, the gesture, and the artifacts that have been built and put in place precisely to receive that pointing. It is necessary to view all these phenomena as integrated components of a common activity.

The Power to Speak as a Professional

I will now briefly investigate the phenomenal structure and social organization that provide the ground from which the power to speak as a professional emerges.

Expert witnesses, such as Sergeant Duke, are entitled to speak about events in the courtroom because of their membership in a relevant community of practitioners. Duke's voice can be heard because he is a police officer, an expert on police use of force, and thus someone who can speak about what the police officers on the tape are perceiving as they look at King writhing on the ground. The structure of Duke's expertise, which gives him his right to speak authoritatively, creates a situated perspective from which events on the tape are viewed.

		After demonstrating by playing the videotape that Mr. King appears to be moving his right hand behind his back with the palm up.
1	Prosecutor:	That would be the position you'd want him in. =
2		= Is that correct. (0.6)
3	Sgt. Duke:	Not, (0.2) Not with uh:, (0.2) the way he is. (0.6)
4		His uh:, (0.4) His leg is uh
5		Is bent in this area. (0.6)
6		Uh:, (0.2) Had he moved in this hand here being uh:
7		(0.4) straight up and down.
8		That causes me concern (0.7)
9	Prosecutor:	Uh does it also cause you concern that
10		someone's *step*ped on the back of his neck.
11	Sgt. Duke:	(0.6) No it does not.

Here, as in the data examined earlier, Duke displays intense concern about very small movements of King's leg and hand (lines 4–8). However, when asked about the fact that an officer has stepped on the back of King's neck (see figure 16.9), Duke states in effect that violent actions performed by police officers against their suspect cause him no concern at all (lines 9–11). The events on the tape are being viewed and articulated by Duke from a local, situated perspective – that of the police who are beating King – which is precisely his domain of expertise.

Insofar as the perceptual structures that organize interpretation of the tape are lodged within a profession and not an isolated individual, there is a tremendous asymmetry about who can speak as an expert about the events on the tape and thus structure interpretation of it. Here Duke states that his training makes it possible for him to "perceive the perceptions" of the police officers, but that he has no access to the perceptions of the man they are beating, since Duke himself has "never been a suspect":

1	Sgt. Duke	They're taught to evaluate.
2		And that's what they were doing in the last two
3		frames.
4		Or three frames.
5	Prosecutor:	Can you read their mind uh, (1.4) Sergeant Duke.

6		(1.3)
7	Sgt. Duke:	I can, (0.4) form an opinion based on my training.
8		and having trained people,
9		what I can perceive that their perceptions are.
10		(0.6)
11	Prosecutor:	Well what's Mr. King's perceptions at this time.
12		(0.6)
13	Sgt. Duke:	I've never been a suspect.
14		I don't know.

While administering a beating like this is recognized within the courtroom as part of the work of the police profession, no equivalent social group exists for the suspect. Victims do not constitute a profession. Thus no expert witnesses are available to interpret these events and animate the images on the tape from King's perspective. In the second trial, King was called as a witness, but he could not testify about whether the police officers beating him were using unreasonable force since he lacked "expertise on the constitution or the use of force" (Newton 1993a: A16).

The effect of all this is the production of a set of contradictory asymmetries. Within the domain of discourse recorded on the videotape, it is argued that King is in control of the interaction, and that is what the first jury found. But within the discourse of the courtroom, no one can speak for the suspect. His perception is not lodged within a profession and thus publicly available to others as a set of official discursive procedures. Within the discourse of the trial, he is an object to be scrutinized, not an actor with a voice of his own. However, within the discourse made visible on the tape, he is constituted as the controlling actor.

The way in which professional coding schemes for constituting control and asymmetry in interaction are used by the police to justify the way that they beat someone alerts us to ethical problems that can arise when we put our professional skills as social scientists at the service of another profession, thereby amplifying its voice and the power it can exert on those who become the objects of its scrutiny.

Conclusion

Central to the social and cognitive organization of a profession is its ability to shape events in the domain of its scrutiny into the phenomenal objects around which the discourse of the profession is organized: to find archaeologically relevant events such as post holes in the color stains visible in a patch of a dirt and map them or to locate legally consequential instances of aggression or cooperation in the visible movements of a man's body. This article has investigated three practices used to accomplish such professional vision – coding schemes, highlighting, and the production and articulation of graphic representations – in the work settings of two professions: an archaeological field excavation and a courtroom.

Such work contributes to efforts by linguistic anthropologists, practice theorists, and conversation analysts to develop anthropologically informed analyses of human action and cognition as socially situated phenomena, activities accomplished through ongoing, contingent work within the historically shaped settings of the lived social world. In this process some traditional dichotomies that have isolated subfields from each other, such as the assignment of language and the material world to separate domains of inquiry, disappear. The ability to build and interpret a material cognitive artifact, such as an archaeological map, is embedded within a web of socially articulated discourse. Talk between coworkers, the lines they are drawing, measurement tools, and the ability to see relevant events in the dirt all mutually inform each other within a single coherent activity. Simultaneously, the practices clustered around the production, distribution, and interpretation of such representations provide the material and cognitive infrastructure that make archaeological theory possible.

Within such a framework, the ability to see relevant entities is lodged not in the individual mind but instead within a community of competent practitioners. This has a range of consequences. First, the power to authoritatively see and produce the range of phenomena that are consequential for the organization of a society is not homogeneously distributed. Different professions – medicine, law, the police, specific sciences such as archaeology – have the power to legitimately see, constitute, and articulate alternative kinds of events. Professional vision is perspectival, lodged within specific social entities, and unevenly allocated. The consequences that this had for who was entitled to instruct the jury about what was happening on the Rodney King videotape support Foucault's (1981) analysis of how the discursive procedures of a society structure what kinds of talk can and cannot be heard, who is qualified to speak the truth, and the conditions that establish the rationality of statements.

Second, such vision is not a purely mental process but instead is accomplished through the competent deployment of a complex of situated practices in a relevant setting. An earlier generation of anthropologists, influenced by Saussure's notion of *langue*, brought precision and clarity to their analytic projects by focusing on the grammars of cultural phenomena such as category systems and myths while ignoring the courses of practical action within which categories and stories were articulated in the endogenous scenes of a society's everyday activities. The procedures investigated in this article move beyond the mind of the actor to encompass features of the setting where action is occurring. Through practices such as highlighting, coding, and articulating graphic representations, categories (post molds, aggression) are linked to specific phenomena in a relevant domain of scrutiny, creating a whole that is greater than the sum of its parts – for example, an actual instantiation of a post mold or a visible demonstration of aggression. As argued by Wittgenstein (1958), a category or rule cannot determine its own application; seeing what can count as a "change of slope" or "aggression" in a relevant domain of scrutiny is both a contingent accomplishment and a locus for contestation – even a central site for legal argument. Categories and the phenomena to which they are being applied mutually elaborate each other.[18] This process is central among those providing for ongoing change in legal and other category systems.

Third, insofar as these practices are lodged within specific communities, they must be learned (Chaiklin and Lave 1993; Lave and Wenger 1991). Learning was a central activity in both of the settings examined in this article, but the organization of that learning was quite different in each. Like students in an anthropology class being lectured about events in another culture, the jury at the Rodney King trial was instructed by an expert about what a police officer (someone who they would never be) could see in the events visible on the tape (see Figure 16.10). On the other

Figure 16.10 Instruction by experts: Sergeant Duke showing police officer perspective; archaeologist showing measurement technique. Historical still of the Rodney King Beating courtesy of George Holliday © 1991 George Holliday. All rights reserved.

hand, the young archaeologist, crouching in the dirt and struggling to determine where in it to properly position one of the tools of her profession, was learning to be a competent practitioner. The dirt in front of her was a locus for embodied practice, not an object of contemplation.

Consistent with recent research in conversation analysis on the interactive organization of work settings (Drew and Heritage 1992), different ways of learning and their associated modes of access to the phenomena being scrutinized were constituted in each setting through the alternative ways that human interaction was organized. Though ultimately the jury decided the case, throughout the trial its members never had the chance to question the expert witnesses who were lecturing them, but instead sat week after week as a silent audience. They had the opportunity to use the tools relevant to the analysis that they were charged with performing – that is, the opportunity to play the tape themselves – only when they were alone in the jury room. By way of contrast, Ann, the senior archaeologist, was positioned to monitor not only the dirt her student was studying but also embodied actions of that student within a field of relevant action.[19] Instead of being positioned as an expert lecturing to an audience, Ann's own ability to perform a relevant next action was contingent on the competent performance of her student; Ann could not mark her map until Sue had produced a necessary measurement. Each was dependent on the other for the moment-by-moment accomplishment of a common course of action. To make that happen, Ann first provided Sue with successive descriptions of what to look for and then got down in the dirt to point to relevant phenomena, thus adjusting in detail to the problems her student was visibly facing. The necessity of collaborative action not only posed tasks of common understanding as practical problems but also exposed relevant domains of ignorance, a process crucial to their remedy. In brief, though instruction was central to what both the archaeologists and the expert witnesses in the courtroom were doing, within each setting learning processes, encompassing participation frameworks, and modes of access to relevant phenomena were shaped into quite different kinds of events by the alternative ways that interaction was structured.

Despite very marked differences in how each setting was organized, common discursive practices were deployed in both. There seem to be good reasons why the configuration of practices investigated in this article are generic, pervasive, and consequential in human activity. First, processes of classification are central to human cognition, at times forming the basic subject matter of entire fields such as cognitive anthropology. Through the construction and use of coding schemes, relevant classification systems are socially organized as professional and bureaucratic knowledge structures, entraining in fine detail the cognitive activity of those who administer them, producing some of the objects of knowledge around which the discourse in a profession is organized, and frequently constituting accountable loci of power for those whose actions are surveyed and coded. Second, though most theorizing about human cognition in the 20th century has focused on mental events – for example, internal representations – a number of activity theorists, students of scientific and everyday practice, ethnomethodologists, and cognitive anthropologists have insisted that the ability of human beings to modify the world around them, to structure settings for the activities that habitually occur within them, and to build tools, maps, slide rules, and other representational artifacts is as central to human cognition as processes hidden inside the brain. The ability to build structures in the world that organize knowledge, shape perception, and structure future action is one way that human cognition is shaped through ongoing historical practices. Graphic representations constitute a prototypical example of how human beings build external cognitive artifacts for the organization and persuasive display of relevant knowledge. This article has investigated some of the ways in which relevant communities organize the production and understanding of such representations through the deployment of situated practices articulated within ongoing processes of human interaction.[20] Human activity characteristically occurs in environments that provide a very complicated perceptual field. A quite general class of cognitive practices consists of methods for highlighting this perceptual field so that relevant phenomena are made salient. This process simultaneously helps classify those phenomena, for example, as an archaeological feature rather than an irrelevant patch of color in the dirt, or as an aggressive movement. Practices such as highlighting link relevant features of a setting to the activity being performed in that setting.

In view of the generic character of the issues that these practices address, it is not surprising that they frequently work in concert with each other, as when Sergeant Duke's pointing finger linked a category in a coding scheme to specific phenomena visible in a graphic representation. The way in which such highlighting structures the perception of others by reshaping a domain of scrutiny so that some phenomena are made salient, while others fade into the background, has strong rhetorical and political consequences. By looking at how these practices work together within situated courses of action, it becomes possible to investigate quite diverse phenomena within a single analytical framework. As these practices are used within sequences of talk-in-interaction, members of a profession hold each other accountable for – and contest – the proper perception and constitution of the objects of knowledge around which their discourse is organized.[21]

Notes

I am very deeply indebted to Gail Wagner and the students at her archaeological field school for allowing me to investigate the activities in which they were engaged. Without their openness and support, the analysis being reported here would not be possible. I owe a tremendous debt to Lucy Suchman for demonstrating to me how important the way in which participants tailor and reshape objects in work settings in order to accomplish local tasks is to any understanding of human cognition and action (see, for example, Suchman 1987). I wish to thank Christopher Borstel, Lisa Capps, Aaron Cicourel, Janet Keller, John Heritage, Bernard Hibbits, Cathryn Houghton, Hugh Mehan, Curtis Renoe, Lucy Suchman, Patty Jo Watson, and most especially Candy Goodwin for helpful and insightful comments on an earlier version of this analysis.

An earlier version of this article was presented as a plenary lecture at the International Conference on Discourse and the Professions, Uppsala, Sweden, August 28, 1992, and in colloquia at UCLA, the University of California at Santa Barbara, the University of California at San Diego, and the University of South Carolina.

1   See Bourdieu 1977, Chaiklin and Lave 1993, Hanks 1987, and Lave and Wenger 1991 for contemporary work on practice theory. Analyses of how cognition makes use of phenomena distributed in everyday settings can be found in Lave 1988, Rogoff 1990, Rogoff and Lave 1984, and Suchman 1987. Hutchins (1993) provides a very clear demonstration of how cognition is not located in the mind of a single individual but is instead embedded within distributed systems, including socially differentiated actors and external representations embodied in tools. Dougherty and Keller (1985) demonstrate how cognitive frameworks and material features of a setting mutually constitute each other. Recent work by linguistic anthropologists on the discursive constitution of context can be found in Duranti and Goodwin 1992. Work on activity theory (Engeström 1987; Wertsch 1985) growing out of the pioneering work of Vygotsky (1978) has long stressed the mediated, historically shaped character of both cognition and social organization. Though focused on the organization of sequences of talk rather than tool-mediated cognition, the field of conversation analysis (Atkinson and Heritage 1984; Drew and Heritage 1992; Sacks 1992; Sacks et al. 1974) has developed the most powerful resources currently available for the analysis of the interactive organization of emerging action with actual settings (Goodwin 1990), including the way in which each next action relies on prior action for its proper interpretation while simultaneously reshaping the context that will provide the ground for subsequent action.
2   For example, see Ochs 1979 and Scheiffelin and Doucet 1994.
3   See Heritage 1984 and Sacks et al. 1974.
4   For further discussion, see Du Bois et al. 1993, Gumperz 1982, Sherzer and Woodbury 1987, and Tedlock 1987.
5   An elaboration of this system can be found in Sacks et al. 1974 on pp. 731–3.
6   See Haraway 1989, Latour 1987, Latour and Woolgar 1979, Lynch 1985, Lynch and Woolgar 1988, and Pickering 1992.
7   Archaeologists distinguish between post molds and post holes. In order to place a post that will support a roof or other structure, people frequently dig a pit substantially larger than the post itself. After the post is in place, dirt is packed around it to support it. The larger pit is called a post hole, while the hole created by the post itself is called a post mold.
8   See Garfinkel 1967, Goodwin 1992, and Heritage 1984.
9   For analysis of how graphic representations are articulated in the mist of scientific practice, see Goodwin 1990 and Ochs et al. 1994. The more general issue of graphic representations in the discourse of science has been an important topic in the sociology of scientific knowledge (for example, Lynch 1988 and Lynch and Woolgar 1988).
10 For analysis of how participants read the movement of another's body through socially defined space, see Duranti 1992.

11 For extensive analysis of the reflexive relationship between socialization and language, see the work of Ochs and Schieffelin (for example, Ochs 1988; Ochs and Schieffelin 1986; Schieffelin 1990; Schieffelin and Ochs 1986).

12 The practices at issue here have consequences for not only the production of such maps but also their reading. Competent archaeologists know that the dots on a map, the only points in the landscape that have actually been measured, have a different status than the lines connecting the dots. Thus they will sometimes discard the lines and rely only on the dots for subsequent analysis.

13 See Drew 1992, pp. 472–4, and Shuy 1982.

14 I am deeply indebted to Lucy Suchman for bringing the phenomena discussed in this paragraph to my attention.

15 The prosecution arguments at the second trial noted here are drawn from my notes made at the closing argument and from newspaper reports.

16 The ability to record events on videotape and replay them in the court created baroque possibilities for layering and framing the perception of events. At the second trial, one of the defendants, Officer Briseno, chose not to testify. However, the prosecution received permission to play for the jury videotape of his testimony at the first trial in which he criticized the actions of the other defendants. "That placed jurors in the federal trial in the unusual position of watching a defendant on one videotape describe yet another videotape" (Newton 1993b: A25). The jury was able to watch "as the taped Officer Briseno spoke from the monitor accompanied by the word *Live*, while the real Officer Briseno sat passively with the other defendants, following his own year-old words on a transcript" (Mydans 1993a: A14).

17 The notion of what events constitute "clutter" to be eliminated is of course an important political decision being made by the party who reshapes the image for presentation to the jury.

18 See Goodwin 1992, Heritage 1984, and Keller and Keller 1993.

19 The most thorough analysis of how archaeology is learned as a mode of embodied practice can be found in Edgeworth 1991.

20 See also Goodwin 1990.

21 Professional settings provide a perspicuous site for the investigation of how objects of knowledge, controlled by and relevant to the defining work of a specific community, are socially constructed from within the settings that make up the lifeworld of that community – that is, endogenously, through systematic discursive procedures. This should not, however, be taken to imply that such processes are limited to professional discourse. The way in which we reify our realities through practices such as highlighting and coding are pervasive features of human social and cognitive life.

References

Atkinson, J. Maxwell, and John Heritage, eds. 1984. *Structures of Social Action*. Cambridge: Cambridge University Press.

Bourdieu, Pierre. 1977. *Outline of a Theory of Practice*. Richard Nice, trans. Cambridge: Cambridge University Press.

Chaiklin, Seth, and Jean Lave, eds. 1993. *Understanding Practice: Perspectives on Activity and Context*. Cambridge: Cambridge University Press.

Cicourel, Aaron V. 1964. *Method and Measurement in Sociology*. New York: Free Press.

—— 1968. *The Social Organization of Juvenile Justice*. New York: Wiley.

Dougherty, Janet W. D., and Charles Keller 1985. "Taskonomy: A Practical Approach to Knowledge Structures." In *Directions in Cognitive Anthropology*. J. W. D. Dougherty, ed. pp. 161–74. Urbana: University of Illinois Press.

Drew, Paul 1992. "Contested Evidence in Courtroom Examination: The Case of a Trial for Rape." In *Talk at Work: Interaction in Institutional Settings*. P. Drew and J. Heritage, eds. Pp. 470–520. Cambridge: Cambridge University Press.

Drew, Paul, and John Heritage, eds. 1992. *Talk at Work: Interaction in Institutional Settings* Cambridge: Cambridge University Press.

Du Bois, John, Stephen Schuetze-Coburn, Danae Paolino, and Susanna Cumming. 1993. "Outline of Discourse Transcription." In *Talking Data: Transcription and Coding Methods for Language Research*. J. A. Edwards and M. D. Lampert, eds. Hillsdale, NJ: Lawrence Erlbaum.

Duranti, Alessandro. 1992. "Language and Bodies in Social Space: Samoan Ceremonial Greetings." *American Anthropologist* 94(3): 657–91.

Duranti, Alessandro, and Charles Goodwin, eds. 1992. *Rethinking Context: Language as an Interactive Phenomenon*. Cambridge: Cambridge University Press.

Edgeworth, Matthew. 1991. The Act of Discovery: An Ethnography of the Subject-Object Relation in Archaeological Practice. Doctoral thesis, Program in Anthropology and Archaeology, University of Durham.

Engeström, Yrjö. 1987. *Learning by Expanding: An Activity-Theoretical Approach to Developmental Research*. Helsinki: Orienta-Konsultit Oy.

Foucault, Michel. 1981. "The Order of Discourse." In *Untying the Text: A Post-Structuralist Reader*. R. Young, ed. Pp. 48–78. Boston: Routledge, Kegan, Paul.

Garfinkel, Harold. 1967. *Studies in Ethnomethodology*. Englewood Cliffs, NJ: Prentice-Hall.

Goodwin, Charles. 1990. Perception, Technology and Interaction on a Scientific Research Vessel. Paper presented at the Annual Meeting of the American Anthropological Association, New Orleans.

—— 1992 Transparent Vision. Paper presented at the Workshop on Interaction and Grammar, Department of Applied Linguistics, UCLA, May 1, 1992. (Subsequently reprinted in *Interaction and Grammar*, Elinor Ochs, Emanuael Schegloff, and Sandra Thompson, eds. Cambridge: Cambridge University Press, 1996.)

—— 1993. "The Blackness of Black: Color Categories as Situated Practice." In Proceedings from the Conference on Discourse, Tools and Reasoning: Situated Cognition and Technologically Supported Environments, Lucca, Italy, November 2–7. Lauren Resnick, Clotilde Pontecarvo, and Roger Saljo, eds.

Goodwin, Marjorie Harness. 1990. *He-Said-She-Said: Talk as Social Organization among Black Children*. Bloomington: Indiana University Press.

Gumperz, John J. 1982. *Discourse Strategies*. Cambridge: Cambridge University Press.

Hanks, William. 1987. "Discourse Genres in a Theory of Practice." *American Ethnologist* 14(4): 668–92.

Haraway, Donna. 1989. *Primate Visions: Gender, Race, and Nature in the World of Modern Science*. New York: Routledge.

Heritage, John. 1984. *Garfinkel and Ethnomethodology*. Cambridge: Polity Press.

Hutchins, Edwin. 1993. "Learning to Navigate." In *Understanding Practice: Perspectives on Activity and Context*. S. Chaiklin and J. Lave, eds. Pp. 35–63. Cambridge: Cambridge University Press.

Keller, Charles, and Janet Dixon Keller. 1993. "Thinking and Acting with Iron." In *Understanding Practice: Perspectives on Activity and Context*. S. Chaiklin and J. Lave, eds. Pp. 125–43. Cambridge: Cambridge University Press.

Latour, Bruno. 1987. *Science in Action: How to Follow Scientists and Engineers through Society*. Cambridge, MA: Harvard University Press.

Latour, Bruno, and Steve Woolgar. 1979. *Laboratory Life: The Social Construction of Scientific Facts*. London: Sage.

Lave, Jean. 1988. *Cognition in Practice*. Cambridge: Cambridge University Press.

Lave, Jean, and Etienne Wenger. 1991. *Situated Learning: Legitimate Peripheral Participation*. Cambridge: Cambridge University Press.

Lieberman, Paul. 1993a. "King Case Prosecutors Must Scale Hurdles of History." The *Los Angeles Times*, February 7, pp. A1, A26.

—— 1993b. "King Trial May Come Down to a Case of Expert vs. Expert." The *Los Angeles Times*, April 4, pp. A1, A32.

Lynch, Michael. 1985. *Art and Artefact in Laboratory Science*. London: Routledge and Kegan Paul.

—— 1988. "The Externalized Retina: Selection and Mathematization in the Visual Documentation of Objects in the Life Sciences." *Human Studies* 11: 201–34.

Lynch, Michael, and Steve Woolgar, eds. 1988. *Representation in Scientific Practice*. Cambridge, MA: MIT Press.

Mydans, Seth. 1993a. "Defendant on Videotape Gives Trial an Odd Air." The *New York Times*, April 7, p. A14.

—— 1993b. "Prosecutor in Beating Case Urges Jury to Rely on Tape." The *New York Times*, April 21, p. A7.

—— 1993c. "Prosecutor in Officers' Case Ends with Focus on Beating." The *New York Times*, April 9, p. A8.

—— 1993d. "Their Lives Consumed, Los Angeles Officers Await Trial." The *New York Times*, February 2, p. A10.

Newton, Jim. 1993a. "'I Was Just Trying to Stay Alive,' King Tells Federal Jury." The *Los Angeles Times*, March 10, pp. A1, A16.

—— 1993b. "King Jury Sees Key Videotape; Prosecutors Rest." The *Los Angeles Times*, April 7, pp. A1, A25.

Ochs, Elinor. 1979. "Transcription as Theory." In *Developmental Pragmatics*. E. Ochs and B. B. Schieffelin, eds. Pp. 43–72. New York: Academic Press.

—— 1988. *Culture and Language Development: Language Acquisition and Language Socialization in a Samoan Village*. Cambridge: Cambridge University Press.

Ochs, Elinor, Patrick Gonzales, and Sally Jacoby. 1996. "'When I Come Down, I'm in a Domain State': Grammar and Graphic Representation in the Interpretive Activity of Physicists." In *Interaction and Grammar*. E. Ochs, E. A. Schegloff, and S. Thompson, eds. Cambridge: Cambridge University Press.

Ochs, Elinor, and Bambi B. Schieffelin. 1986. *Language Socialization across Cultures*. New York: Cambridge University Press.

Pickering, Andrew, ed. 1992. *Science as Practice and Culture*. Chicago: The University of Chicago Press.

Rogoff, Barbara. 1990. *Apprenticeship in Thinking*. New York: Oxford University Press.

Rogoff, Barbara, and Jean Lave. 1984. *Everyday Cognition: Its Development in Social Context*. Cambridge, MA: Harvard University Press.

Sacks, Harvey. 1992. *Lectures on Conversation*. 2 vols. Gail Jefferson, ed. Oxford: Basil Blackwell.

Sacks, Harvey, Emanuel A. Schegloff, and Gail Jefferson. 1974. "A Simplest Systematics for the Organization of Turn-Taking for Conversation." *Language* 50: 696–735.

Schegloff, Emanuel A. 1968. "Sequencing in Conversational Openings." *American Anthropologist* 70: 1075–95.

Schieffelin, Bambi B. 1990. *The Give and Take of Everyday Life: Language Socialization of Kaluli Children*. Cambridge: Cambridge University Press.

Schieffelin, Bambi B., and Rachelle Charlier Doucet. 1994. "The 'Real' Haitian Creole: Metalinguistics and Orthographic Choice." *American Ethnologist* 21(1): 176–200.

Schieffelin, Bambi B., and Elinor Ochs. 1986. "Language Socialization." In *Annual Review of Anthropology*. B. J. Siegel, A. R. Beals, and S. A. Tyler, eds. Pp. 163–246. Palo Alto: Annual Reviews, Inc.

Sherzer, Joel, and Anthony C. Woodbury, eds. 1987. *Native American Discourse: Poetics and Rhetoric*. Cambridge: Cambridge University Press.

Shuy, Roger. 1982. "The Unit of Analysis in a Criminal Law Case." In *Analyzing Discourse: Text and Talk*. D. Tannen, ed. Washington, DC: Georgetown University Press.

Smith, Dorothy E. 1990. *Texts, Facts and Femininity*. London: Routledge.

Suchman, Lucy A. 1987. *Plans and Situated Actions: The Problem of Human Machine Communication*. Cambridge: Cambridge University Press.

Tedlock, Dennis. 1987. "Hearing a Voice in an Ancient Text: Quiché Maya Poetics in Performance." In *Native American Discourse: Poetics and Rhetoric*. J. Sherzer and A. C. Woodbury, eds. Pp. 140–75. Cambridge: Cambridge University Press.

Vygotsky, L. S. 1978. *Mind in Society: The Development of Higher Psychological Processes*. Cambridge: Harvard University Press.

Wertsch, James. 1985. *Culture, Communication, and Cognition: Vygotskian Perspectives*. Cambridge: Cambridge University Press.

Wittgenstein, Ludwig. 1958. *Philosophical Investigations*. G. E. M. Anscombe and R. Rhees, eds. G. E. M. Anscombe, trans. 2nd edition. Oxford: Blackwell.

17 Artwork: Collection and Contemporary Culture

Chandra Mukerji

During the 1950s critics in the United States began to write about film as an art form. Their ideas were not particularly new since intellectuals in Eastern Europe, France, Italy, and Japan had written in a similar vein around the turn of the century (Liehm and Liehm 1977; Robinson 1973; Leprohon [1966] 1972; Richie 1971) and such notions had been widely accepted throughout Western Europe since the 1920s (Robinson 1973; Lawder 1975). What is interesting is that Americans had been particularly resistant to this kind of thinking until the post-World War II era (Hampton [1931] 1970; Crowther 1957; Jowett 1976); yet by the 1960s a majority of U.S. cognoscenti found themselves embarrassed by those who continued to think of film as an exclusively popular entertainment.

One could argue that American anti-intellecutualism (Hofstader 1963) had once more desensitized Americans to the obvious artistic value of a medium and that the redefinition of film as an art form was rectification of an error. But that would be misleading. The literature on film as art that grew out of the 1950s certainly made this kind of argument, but it was a literature of aesthetic advocacy, not social science. In many countries, including India and Egypt as well as the United States, people simply did not consider film to be an art form (Barnouw and Krishnaswamy 1963; Tunstall 1977; Sadoul 1966). Early elite audiences regarded film as a threat to traditional art and so dismissed it as commercial culture created by upwardly mobile and ambitious people with no training or interest in art traditions. Films were seen (as they sometimes are today) as pap fed to the masses, industrial commodities produced to make industrialists rich by exploiting people's desires for both entertainment and escape from the burden of their daily lives (Indian Cinematograph Committee 1928; Schiller 1976; Jowett 1976).

The definitional transformation of film from industrial commodity to art form should be of particular interest to sociologists, who rarely associate art with products of industrial manufacture. According to stereotype and social theory, industrial goods are considered important for shaping the contemporary economy and social relations of production (see, for instance, Baran and Sweezy 1966; Blauner 1964; Feuer 1959; Smelser 1959; Rostow 1963; Heilbroner 1962; Thompson 1963). Few sociologists attribute any significance to the cultural meaning or design of industrial commodities, two notable exceptions being Veblen ([1899] 1953) and Braverman (1974). Art, on the other hand, is significant to scholars because it embodies cultural symbolism and allows those with imaginative gifts to find lasting meaning in transient events (see, for example, Dewey 1934; D. Bell 1976; Rosenberg and Fliegal 1965; Lukács 1964; Solomon 1974). This view of art discourages sociologists from discussing "commercial" culture (popular culture, mass culture) in the same context as artworks (for exceptions, see Gans 1975; Becker 1978). Most consider the aesthetic differences between artworks and other objects more important than any similarities there might be between them (see, for example, Grana [1962] 1964; D. Bell 1976).

In this paper I hope to demonstrate some virtues in studying the continuities between fine art and commercial culture. Right now our understanding of the arts tends to be limited to what can be learned by comparing one medium to another (for instance, how films are like novels or how paintings are like prints). The result is that we know relatively little about how the products of the film industry, for example, are like the products of other industries. The tendency to conceive of plastic combs in people's pockets and paintings in museums as completely unrelated kinds of objects obscures an important connection between the two: both are designed to have cultural meanings and social uses. By recognizing and clarifying this and other shared characteristics of artworks, craft goods, and industrial commodities, sociologists can begin to use concepts and models from the sociology of art to analyze broader patterns of material culture, and vice versa.

The redefinition of U.S. films provides an opportunity to take a fresh look at this continuity between industrial commodities and art. The case of film appears to be one of many where an industrial commodity has become "worth saving" just as it was threatened with extinction. In the 1950s, when the definition of film as art gained currency, U.S. filmmakers faced enormous economic difficulties, and it seemed the industry itself might collapse.

Since that time diverse industrial commodities have increasingly been collected by museums as art (for example, posters, furniture, and other objects whose aesthetic qualities are particularly apparent) and by the general public as collectibles or "nostalgia pieces" (mostly everyday practical goods like Depression glassware and old Coke bottles, which have both sentimental and documentary value).[1] If, as seems likely, this revaluation of old industrial goods constitutes a pattern that may be generalized to describe other commodities, then it seems important to understand this process. It may be that people are finding lasting value in the transient processes and commonplace objects that characterized the early industrial era.

To explore this possibility a few important topics have to be discussed. First, it is necessary to understand something about the design of commodities, including how they are designed for market. Second, it is important to study patterns of everyday collection, what makes objects worth preserving, and how people go about saving them from neglect. One can then examine art to see how it acts as the major and prototypical collection system for preserving cultural objects. With this background both the problems faced by film-as-art advocates and the bases for their success appear part of a larger pattern of revaluating industrial goods.

Design in Production

Workers who make objects of any sort do not randomly design and produce works; they carry with them cultural assumptions about how chairs, cars, paintings, or TV ads should look and function (Becker 1974, 1978). Although it may seem odd to think of plumbers and electricians as culture producers, they act like artists when they organize their work around conventional conceptions of how plumbing and wiring should be done (based in part on building code regulations but also on occupational norms). Landscape architects planting trees around a new house, people producing wallpaper and fabric designs, and storeowners displaying their wares in shop windows all share one common design problem: how to work from precedent to design an object that is similar enough to objects that are already legitimated as gardens, wallpaper, or window displays to suggest what kind of object it is supposed to be.

The human habit of transforming raw materials into objects is possible because people can imagine a product from their labors that is "worth making" and strive to achieve that goal. The cognitive skill behind production has been called many names. Braverman (1974) talks about the "power of conceptual thought"; others speak of the human capacity to design (Papanek 1972) or previsualization (Mukerji 1977; White 1968). The terms are less important than the capacity they describe; people can design objects they want to make because they can preconceive them.

Most of the time people use this skill not to introduce radical kinds of goods to the world but to make new versions of familiar objects. To do this they base some of their designs on precedents or design features of previously produced work essential to their identification and use.

Design precedents may last so long that even those who produce goods can be quite unaware of their designs' historical roots. Objects such as chairs have had consistent design features over such a long period of history that many modern U.S. chairs resemble European medieval ones. Some designs even remain relatively stable through changes in modes of production. People in the United States going to discount stores can buy mass-produced reproductions of Victorian chairs which were originally designed to be handmade. Artifacts of the cultural past are brought into the present through the use of design precedents, not necessarily because designers revere the past in some abstract way, but because they find some historical design features useful for their own contemporary purposes. Moreover, this is as true of those who design industrial commodities as of those who make craft goods or who attempt to produce art.

Commodity Design for Market

Part of any design conception includes anticipating the work's economic value. Just as people use precedents to determine what features make objects recognizable, they consider how to design objects to give them economic value. They do this by examining how similar objects have done on the market before. Goods made by both artisans and industry are produced to please large numbers of people.[2] People producing these commodities compare the costs of making objects to their anticipated returns from sales.

This economic logic is both a rough description of a more complex process and an incomplete picture of commodity design. To make a salable coffee cup, potters or industrial designers must make one that feels good in the hand, holds a hot liquid without disintegrating, does not fall over when set on a table, and looks nice to people. The economic value of goods depends on their design, and there is some evidence of this in the early industrial revolution. "The great revolution of capital importance was that of printed calico. The combined effort of science and art was needed to force a difficult and unpromising material, cotton, to bear every day so many brilliant transformations and then, when it was thus transformed, to distribute it everywhere and to put it within range of the poor" (Cipolla 1973, pp. 63–64). Veblen presents a less glowing report of the tastes of these times and how objects had to be designed to be salable: "It is notorious that in their selection of serviceable goods in the retail market, purchasers are guided more by the finish and workmanship of the goods than by any marks of substantial serviceability. Goods, in order to sell, must have some appreciable amount of labor spent in giving them the marks of decent expensiveness, in addition to what goes to give them efficiency for the material use which they are to serve" (Veblen [1899] 1953, p. 113). It may be of crucial importance to commodity designers to consider how goods made from their preconceptions will be produced and marketed, but it is also important to them to design objects consumers will find both recognizable and appealing.

Collection

People not only make things, they look at them, talk about them, develop opinions about them, buy them, sell them, use them, throw them away, break them, or put them away in the attic, museum, garage, or basement. In other words, people live with what they (or others) produce.

There are probably a limited number of things that people do with objects. Among them, collecting goods may have the greatest consequences for material culture. Not only are "saved" works kept in the cultural environment for a longer period of time than those that are broken and/or thrown away, but they are also made available for future generations to use as design precedents. Grandma's hat in the attic may not seem like much until a similar hat appears in the fashion section of a newspaper as the latest design from Paris being picked up by U.S. designers. This is not to say that all the things people save will become important to future designs, only that objects not collected will not be available for future use.[3]

Commodity design (as described in the previous section) does not concern itself with collection. The greatest economic value of commodities is supposed to be their initial sale, not their future resale value. Most commodities are expected to depreciate in value over time.[4] That is why it may be surprising to find so many Americans now collecting nostalgia pieces and other industrially produced collectibles. These objects, which once would have been thrown away, have developed new value (and markets) as collectors' items because so many of their counterparts have disappeared, making them relatively scarce. Collectibles seem to be commodities on the brink of extinction, saved by people who saw in them some lasting importance.

Lasting Design Values

The process of collecting goods is filled with value judgements. It is quite obvious that people decide whether or not they like an object before deciding to keep it.

What is less obvious is the complexity of this process. What makes an object worth making is not necessarily what makes it worth saving; as a result, collecting often involves a reassessment of the object to identify those features that might make it worth having in the future.

There are many examples of collectors' items that have been given new significance in being redefined for collection. For instance, lots of people save old tire innertubes to use as water toys, investing these objects with a practical value that was not envisioned by their designers. Similarly, parents often save their children's drawings for sentimental reasons that were not of concern to the children at the time the drawings were made. Anthropologists collect potsherds as evidence for their research, giving these scraps of clay academic significance. Finally, collectors of primitive art make gallery shows out of works produced for practical or sacred purposes. I use all these examples to suggest that the redefinition of objects that accompanies their collection is a widespread pattern that may depend on practical, sentimental, and documentary values as well as aesthetic ones.

Not only do people quite literally save objects in collections, they also save some design features of old versions of goods by adapting them in their designs for new ones. Based on notions about the practical value of traditional tool design, contemporary mass-produced hammers, saws, and screwdrivers look very much like their handmade turn-of-the-century ancestors. Based on the notion that family relationships can give objects lasting sentimental value, the people who make Hallmark cards produce "keepsakes" for relatives to give one another for important family occasions such as Christmas, birthdays, graduation, anniversaries, and weddings. Finally, people use ideas about aesthetics and the history of art to produce contemporary works with identifiable relationships to meritorious precedents.

Whether people save whole objects or only aspects of their designs, and whether they save them for sentimental, documentary, practical, or aesthetic reasons, they render these design features available to future designers. Where objects or design features are valued for reasons not anticipated by their producers, two sets of precedents may be drawn from the same work. Some features of pot fragments in museums may interest potters, and others may interest anthropologists. The way in which an object is redefined when it is collected, then, may influence the ways in which future generations will attend to its design. All collected designs may go through a special evaluation procedure before collection, and the "lasting value" of a given design may vary according to the nature of this evaluation.

Artwork

The work of art seems to be a prototypical collectors' item[5] in that artwork, as a class of objects, developed with the emergence of collectors in Renaissance Italy.

> The collector and the artist working independently of the customer are historically correlative; in the course of the Renaissance they appear simultaneously and side by side. The change does not, however, occur all at once; it represents a long process. The art of the early Renaissance still bears an, on the whole, workmanlike character, varying

according to the nature of the commission, so that the starting-point of production is to be found mostly not in the creative urge, the subjective self-expression and spontaneous inspiration of the artist, but in the task set by the customer. The market is, therefore, not yet determined by the supply but by the demand...[Artists] tried to emancipate themselves from these restraints upon their freedom as soon as conditions in the art market allowed. This occurred when the place of the mere consumer of art was taken by the amateur, the connoisseur, and the collector – that is, by that modern type of consumer who no longer orders what he needs but buys what is offered. (Hauser 1951, pp. 40–41)

If we believe Hauser's (1951) argument,[6] a fruitful way to understand art would be to examine art collection.

Contemporary art markets still depend on collectors. But there are two major changes in collection patterns from the ones Hauser (1951) describes. Today, institutions (primarily museums, but also some foundations and businesses) have become more important to the art market than individual collectors, and most collectors invest in art when they collect it.

In the present system, artists seem to have lost many of the advantages they gained in the Renaissance by developing a distinctive role; most of them cannot make a living from the sale of their work (see Christopherson 1977; Adler 1975; Becker 1974, 1976), and many have lost much of their autonomy by taking jobs in universities or other bureaucracies (see Adler 1975; Rosenblum 1973; Mukerji 1977). Again, in the present system, artworks tend to have relatively little market value when artists first sell them, but they can gain tremendous value through collection and resale.

The work of art gains much of its prestige and economic meaning because elites invest in it when they collect it and have the power to manipulate the value of their collections by making the identification of art problematic and limiting membership in that category of objects (see Zolberg 1974; Christopherson 1977; Sears 1941).

It is in the interest of those who profit from art investments to encourage the use of esoteric aesthetic systems in evaluating art. Such criteria help to legitimate a scarcity of "great art," while technical evaluations help to protect the autonomy of the art world. If people with fewer stakes in maintaining the scarcity of good art could make judgements about the quality of art, the economy of the art would could be upset. For example, a group of museum goers might consider a modern, abstract painting to be a piece of garbage, but the economic value of the work would not be affected since these judgements would not have the weight of those made with technical language by "insiders."

The autonomy of the art world in some ways parallels the autonomy of the professions (see Freidson 1974). Just as professionals gain much of their prestige because they are able to judge their professional performance and control recruitment of new members to the professions, major art collectors gain prestige for their collections by choosing the reigning aesthetic theories and helping to control the kinds of work that gain institutional legitimacy.

Art maintains its distinctiveness through the efforts of collectors to protect their investments. They support a distinctive market for artworks by singling out some goods as collectors' investments based on intense scrutiny of their aesthetic merit.

Collecting Commodities as Art

Given the previous descriptions of the art world and the character of commodity design, it seems quite unreasonable to imagine commodities not designed for collection, ever acceding to the status of art. Artworks are valued for their scarcity, and commodities (particularly industrial commodities) are valued for their mass reproducibility. Walter Benjamin explores this problem in the following way:

> That which withers in the age of mechanical reproduction is the aura of the work of art. This is a symptomatic process whose significance points beyond the realm of art. One might generalize by saying: the technique of reproduction detaches the reproduced object from the domain of tradition. By making many reproductions it substitutes a plurality of copies for a unique existence ... The uniqueness of a work of art is inseparable from its being imbedded in the fabric of tradition. This tradition itself is thoroughly alive and extremely changeable. An ancient statue of Venus, for example, stood in a different tradition context with the Greeks, who made it an object of veneration, than with the clerics of the Middle Ages, who viewed it as an ominous idol. Both of them, however, were equally confronted with its uniqueness, that is, its aura.... The work of art reproduced becomes the work of art designed for reproducibility. From a photographic negative, for example, one can make any number of prints; to ask for the "authentic" print makes no sense. But the instant the criterion of authenticity ceases to be applicable to artistic production, the total function of art is reversed. (Benjamin 1969, pp. 555–6)

The traditional ways of locating artworks, based on their uniqueness and authenticity, cannot be used to locate mass-produced works of art. Industrial commodities, designed for mass production and sale, simply do not pretend to be unique and are not valued for their "authenticity" (in the literal sense of having a known origin and/ or author). Since access to the marketplace and the success of goods on the mass market are major systems for evaluating industrial designs, and since market success is in part measured by the quantity of objects mass produced and marketed from each design prototype, industrial production tends to discourage the creation of unique objects with independently valuable designs.

In contrast, craft commodities may have an "author" and be unique, but they are not usually made to develop lasting value, independent of the value for which they were produced. Today plumbing or other craft traditions are protected and innovations in plumbing techniques limited by building codes which are meant to distinguish between good and bad work but also to allow for a large amount of good work to be both created and legitimated. Codes are strict enough to discourage massive amounts of amateur work, making the work of professional plumbers more valuable, but they are not detailed enough to distinguish outstanding from adequate work. In this system almost everyone can have good plumbing (or plumbing that is recognizable within the traditional value systems), but probably little rare and independently valuable plumbing is identifiable.

Particularly industrial commodities but also craft goods are designed to reach a mass audience. Good plumbers and talented industrial designers are recognized for their ability to make work at relatively low cost and high mass appeal for quick sale rather than lasting significance.

The differences among art, craft, and industrial goods have been enhanced by the social norms that make artists critical of "commercial" work, craftspeople critical of the poor quality of industrial goods, and business-people critical of artists and craftspeople because they are not "progressive" and cling to "old ways" in the face of change. But what allows people to identify lasting value in commodities, belying Benjamin's (1969) argument, is that art, craft, and commodities can be and frequently are carriers of the same design traditions. In spite of the structured hostilities among artists, craftspeople, and industrial designers, all have been known to look to the others' work for precedents (or ideas) for their own work (see Becker 1978; Bluestone 1957; Papanek 1972; Newhall 1964). As a result, it is possible to find in pottery, as well as film, the use of aesthetics that would appear sophisticated even to some of the more conservative members of the art world.

The U.S. Film Business

The founders of America's film studios were not in film to explore aesthetic values but to make money. They were not from elite backgrounds, had no training in high culture, and apparently were not self-trained in it, either. They were close to the stereotype of ambitious and upwardly mobile people that elites disliked and imagined were using film to make a sleazy business rather than a fine art (see Jowett 1976; Sklar 1975; Hampton [1931] 1970).

For their part, the businessmen who ran the studios were convinced that thinking about film as an art form was a business mistake, one the Europeans had made which destroyed their supremacy in international filmmaking (Hampton [1931] 1970). They were not against improving film quality, but, according to Hampton ([1931] 1970), they wanted improvements to appeal to their audiences, not to improve their reputations as culture producers.

> Something unforeseen was happening to the mind of the mob. In some mysterious manner, millions of human beings were refuting the dogma that mass mentality could not, or would not, move ahead.... There was merely a ceaseless, irresistible drift of millions of plain people to little ticket-windows to buy amusement – cheap, flimsy amusement that aroused the disgust and scorn of the intelligentsia. But all the time the demand was for better pictures, and they had to be devised and manufactured, not by intellectuals, but by mere business men whose only purpose was to make money by selling better shows to their customers. (Hampton (1931) 1970, pp. 121–2)[7]

The "mere business men" that Hampton describes did not make all the improvements in film quality on their own. They hired people to work for them and frequently they recruited people who had fine arts backgrounds, the most notable of them being D. W. Griffith.

Griffith came from a "genteel" family, wanted to be a writer, tried to become a stage actor and failed, and turned to the film business for work (see Sklar 1975). One does not need to elaborate in this paper the scope of his contribution to U.S. filmmaking. What is important here is that he was one of a long line of people with an elite background and/or training in fine art who brought elements of high culture into this entertainment business.

By the 1920s large numbers of people with literary and theatrical backgrounds entered Hollywood. This huge influx was stimulated by the growing legitimacy of the film business and the need for writers and trained actors and actresses to handle the dialogue on sound films (see Carey 1975; Robinson 1973; Crowther 1957).

This pattern of recruitment created a longstanding conflict between "money people" and "talent," where the money people generally won (Powdermaker 1950). The studio moguls might need "talent" to make their business run, but they jealously guarded their control over film production. Films were the commodity they traded and around which they had built huge business organizations. They were the ones with the connections to banks and other sources of capital; they had created the vertical monopolies that made the studio system so strong; they had the international distribution circuits; and they had the "talent" on contract (see Jowett 1976; Sklar 1975; Balio 1976a; Crowther 1957).[8]

This model of the U.S. studio system reached its apex in the 1940s (Tunstall 1977), when it also began to receive the major blows which were to hurt it even more noticeably in the 1950s. The House Un-American Activities Committee was beginning its investigations (Jowett 1976; Hellman 1976); television was becoming a true mass medium (Jowett 1976; Tunstall 1977); and the studios were forced to divest themselves of their theaters in the antitrust decision known as the Paramount Decision (Jowett 1976; Tunstall 1977). The loss of control over distribution at home was matched by growing distribution problems in Europe, where countries put up trade restrictions to reduce U.S. dominance in their home markets (Jowett 1976; Robinson 1973; Tunstall 1977).

The wisdom of hindsight suggests that the response of U.S. filmmakers to these problems was sometimes as destructive to the business as the problems themselves. The HUAC hearings stimulated mass blackballing which depleted Hollywood of some of its great talents; the film studios used their contracts and longstanding association with the remaining talent to keep them from working in television; and U.S. companies began to make films in cooperation with European film companies to get around their distribution problems, sometimes further weakening European competition and sometimes simply making film production more difficult (see Tunstall 1977; Jowett 1976; Guback 1969; Balio 1976b; Hellman 1976; Sklar 1975).

By the mid-1950s the studio system, which had made filmmaking in the United States such good business, appeared to be in serious financial difficulty. The businessmen who had held such a tight rein over the studios seemed to be losing control over their organizations, their audiences, and their ability to define filmmaking.

U.S. Film as Art

While the U.S. studio system was faltering, a new type of movie theater was developing: the "art house."

One post-war phenomenon which did much to influence both the production and distribution of American films was the growth and success of specialized movie theaters which exhibited "art" films. It was especially heartening to see this development at precisely the time that television was wreaking havoc in Hollywood, for it indicated the existence of a hard core of serious motion picture patrons who were prepared to pay to see films of good quality, or with provocative themes. By 1956, there were over 220 such specialized movie theaters in the United States, devoting their exhibition time to films from other countries, reissues of old-time Hollywood "classics," documentaries and independently made American films with off-beat themes.... There were another 400 movie houses which exhibited specialty films on a part-time basis. Almost all of these art houses were located in the large metropolitan areas, and in college and university communities. (Jowett 1976, pp. 377–8)

These art houses were not big business[9] since they appealed to such a small segment of the U.S. movie-going population, but they did provide a new market for films with aesthetic merit, providing a new legitimacy for films that was welcomed by filmmakers during this period of financial crisis.

U.S. filmmakers could have gained a sense of aesthetic legitimacy for their work much earlier than they were willing to do so. As early as 1915 some American writers had described the "art" in film (Lindsay [1915] 1970; Ramsaye [1926] 1964), but their ideas seem to have had little impact on either audiences or U.S. filmmakers. In the 1930s the Museum of Modern Art opened its film library and asked for cooperation from the studios in developing their collection; the studios were reluctant to help (Jowett 1976). Cine clubs had developed in the 1930s to show "specialty" films, particularly documentaries, but these groups were resisted rather than encouraged by Hollywood (Jowett 1976). It seems to have taken the crises of the 1940s–1950s to have brought the film-as-art notion into fashion.

The economic problems U.S. studios faced at home during the late forties and early fifties encouraged them to increase their international distribution (Guback 1969). To do this U.S. companies increased their European coproductions (Tunstall 1977) and began importing more European art films (Jowett 1976). Through this expanded trade, art house audiences in the United States may have acquired a new perspective on their domestic product, coming to see U.S. films as art.

In 1957 Arthur Knight published a book that was to become the prototypical American film-as-art history.[10] His work is an international film history that attempts to describe the aesthetic development of the medium. He does not try to account for the growth of filmmaking in all the countries of the world, but rather focuses on periods of filmmaking in various (primarily European) countries when a large number of films produced were acclaimed on aesthetic grounds. "In the arts, one discovers in various countries and at different times that happy combination of social, cultural and economic forces which provides creative artists with just the right stimulus to produce their best work.... The same process can also be discerned in the motion picture, with the sole difference that the creative history of this art has been crammed into little more than fifty years" (Knight 1957, p. 6).

Knight's (1957) analysis takes stock of the film industry's economic problem: he suggests that the threat posed to the film industry by television is at least in part created by filmmakers' misunderstanding of the aesthetic potential of their medium.

He is less harsh than compassionate with the U.S. film studios, showing concern for their future and the fate of U.S. films.

In this work Knight (1957) assumes a role likely to appeal to elites. He acts as a critic-advocate (Wolfe 1975) trying to bring to the attention of art connoisseurs works whose aesthetic value is deserving of their attention. Many critics of traditional art media were adopting a similar stance to make their reputations as champions of new schools of artists, so Knight's tone in this work sounded a familiar note in the art world (Wolfe 1975).

By 1957 there was probably a large audience in the United States ready to hear what Knight had to say. Many people had been going to art houses, seeing European films, hearing that Europeans thought of film as art, and learning that many U.S. films were revered in Europe. These audiences were probably quite prepared to accept Knight's ideas about the aesthetic importance of the medium and eager to understand the artistic value in film.

The Artistic Value of Film

Anyone who has faced Benjamin's (1969) work or considered independently the logical problems involved in viewing mass-produced films as art may be surprised by the lack of concern for this issue in film-as-art books. Most authors of film books use a stroke of definitional magic to avoid this problem; they write as though films were handcrafted objects lovingly created by the artist-director. Their rhetoric rarely suggests that businessmen have kept a close eye on film production and used films for mass distribution to gain tremendous profits. By discreetly shunning film's business significance, writers can provide films with the bases for the "aura" that Benjamin (1969) expects in art; they treat films as though they had authenticity (or auteurs) and uniqueness (handcrafted production).

This style of analysis stands out in studies of film because it is so obviously a restricted and one-sided way of regarding film production. Films are necessarily made by groups of people. There is even some evidence that decisions about film content are often made by many different members of film crews (see Mukerji 1976). It is probably also erroneous to assume that film directors always take charge of the same set of decisions for any film. To think that one person, the director, is selected as the "creator" of a film is either a self-serving move for people who want to claim film as an art form or another expression of the Western capitalist cult of individuality (Lomax 1968).

The extensive film-as-art literature that has developed in the United States explores three major themes to show the reader the artistic value in film: the aesthetic heritage (particularly literature and drama) that has helped shape the use of the film medium, the aesthetic possibilities designed into the film medium, and the genius of great directors in exploring the expressive possibilities of film.

These books are written in a variety of forms, but they all "make" film an art by analyzing films and patterns of filmmaking that fit the rhetoric of art history/criticism. Some histories use Knight's (1957) style of analysis to study international filmmaking or filmmaking in a given country (see, for instance, Robinson 1973; Richie 1971; Leprohon [1966] 1972). Others present directors' lives and their ideas about film (cf. Seton, 1960; Sarris 1967; Renan 1967), and still others analyze conventions of film production (see Stephenson and Debrix 1965; Bluestone 1957). Taken as a body of literature these books do not so much argue that film is an art form as assume that its status as art is unquestionable.

Benesch ([1945] 1965) describes the purpose of art history as the identification of aesthetic problems and their resolution by artists. Gans (1975) describes the central characteristic of the high-taste group as a "creator-orientation." By both these measures, the film books written in the United States since the fifties use the style of art history/criticism to analyze films.

Authors of this film literature present the public with methods for making aesthetic evaluations of films, methods for understanding the lasting value of "classics" and recognizing what distinguishes them from lesser films. Readers can learn from them, as they learn from most art history/criticism literature, what great works have been made, who made them, and what technical examinations of these works reveal. Defining films as an art is one way to make films meaningful after their initial market value no longer applies.

While histories of film based on the definition of film as business are likely to discuss films such as *Ben Hur* and *Cleopatra*, which were either big money-makers or terribly expensive to produce, film-as-art histories tend to include films by people like Melies whose business sense was not great but whose films were technically innovative. Depending on how the object category, film, is defined, what is deemed important in films can vary tremendously.

From Commodity to Collectible

Just as art is the prototypical collection system, the redefinition of film from commodity to art may be prototypical of the growing redefinition of U.S. industrial commodities as collectibles. In the film case, this redefinition was accomplished through exposure of Europeans to American films and exposure of Americans to both European art films and European definitions of U.S. films as art just at the time when the U.S. film business was having trouble making films valuable commodities.

European ideas about the aesthetic value of American films had little effect in the United States until the film business faced possible financial failure. Until that time American film moguls had marketed U.S. films in part on the "glamour" of the film business made possible by the financial success of film studios. European film critics might never have shown great interest in the aesthetics of U.S. films if this U.S. definition of films as commodities had not been so dominant in the United States. If American critics had developed elaborate aesthetic critiques of U.S. films, European critics might have decried the lack of aesthetic quality in U.S. films just as they had previously derided the low quality of U.S. paintings and writing. In lauding U.S. films European critics could give Americans the kind of backhanded compliment they have often used in describing American culture; they could laud U.S. films while muttering about the insensitivity of Americans which blinded them to aesthetic merits of their own art form.[11] But the economic crises of the studios in the fifties encouraged Americans to embrace the notion of film as art and use it to attract new audiences to movie theaters.

This pattern for the redefinition of U.S. films suggests some general dimensions which could explain other forms of contemporary collection. The most important factor seems to be potential scarcity. Once it appears that a given kind of object is on the verge of extinction (in the sense that it may not be manufactured for much longer), then loyal consumers may try to develop reasons for sustaining its production by searching for and identifying design features which make that kind of object particularly valuable. In modern industrial societies manufacturers routinely phase out old products that are not selling well and introduce new ones in the hopes of improving their sales. Through a combination of planned and unplanned obsolescence, many mass-produced objects become scarce just a few years after their original manufacture. When consumers find themselves continuously asked to change their buying habits to adjust to manufacturers' production decisions, some conflicts of interest are likely to arise where consumers find worth keeping objects that producers no longer find worth making. This situation may stimulate collection.

As I mentioned earlier, people can collect objects for sentimental, documentary, and practical reasons as well as for aesthetic ones. When objects are on the verge of extinction people may search for some combination of these reasons to maintain the manufacture of or at least the secondhand trade in those objects. The film case suggests some sources for redefining these goods as "worth keeping." Where products have been distributed to a range of different social groups, consumers may already have a rich mine of different reasons for valuing these goods. Where unprofitable goods are distributed to new social groups in an effort to extend their market value (the case with films), the new consumers may add even more ideas about the value of these goods which can be used to point out the significance of their designs. These definitions can be used to give objects new market value, either as commodities with new uses and potential for initial sales or as collectibles with lasting or resale value.

Artwork seems to be the prototypical collectible because its major value lies in its resale trade rather than in its initial sales. The way goods become defined as art, including film's redefinition as art, represents one of many ways in which people define pieces of material culture as "worth keeping" or collectible, making them available as design precedents for future generations to use in shaping their contemporary culture.

Notes

The author would like to thank Bennett Berger, Cesar Grana, Joseph Gusfield, and David Phillips for their criticism of and support for this work.

1   The growing public interest in collectibles is reflected in a *New Yorker* (July 4, 1977) piece that describes a meeting of advisors to the *American Heritage Dictionary* where the proper spelling of collectibles/collectables was debated.
2   Artisans such as carpenters, masons, and plumbers, who contract jobs, apparently only have to please individual clients. More realistically, each job is a public showpiece because it may be used as evidence of the artisan's work, either attracting or repelling customers.
3   For a discussion of this problem in research on fashion, see Q. Bell (1976).
4   It was suggested to me that houses were an exception to this rule. I doubt that is the case. When houses appreciate in value, it is usually the result of rising property values. On the other hand, there are some commonly collected items which do appreciate in value over time – stamps and coins, for example.

5 This notion of art as collector's item may appear to be undermined by conceptual art, but it also characterizes this objectless art form when documentation of the conceptual piece becomes a collector's item.

6 Gombrich (1963) has written a strong piece of criticism on Hauser's work that questions, among other things, Hauser's accuracy in describing the financial transactions of artists in the Renaissance. While he identifies inaccuracies, he does not refute the argument that Hauser advances. He appears simply offended by the assumptions behind social histories of art, feeling that institutional patterns are not as uniform as Hauser might suggest and that these patterns could never account for what is interesting about art – aesthetics.

7 The populist rhetoric Hampton uses contains a strong antielite, antiintellectual component that Gans (1975) finds characteristic of the low-taste group.

8 The longstanding conflict between stars and studio heads was in large part responsible for the growth of United Artists (see Balio 1976a).

9 These art houses provided film studios with some relief for their distribution problems. By showing European films in theaters that had previously block-booked films from only one of the major studios, they killed two birds with one stone: they developed reciprocal trade agreements with European countries, and they could claim to have divested themselves of control over theaters without allowing theaters to book films from a competing U.S. studio.

10 The significance of Knight's book as precedent for future film books is described in Thompson's (1975) review of film textbooks.

11 The contrariness of European film critics vis-à-vis American critics has been borne out by recent events, where Europeans are praising American action films just as U.S. critics are decrying film violence (see Drew 1978).

References

Adler, J. 1975. "Innovative Art and Obsolescent Artists." *Social Research* (Summer): 360–78.

Balio, T. 1976a. *United Artists*. Madison: University of Wisconsin Press.

—— 1976b. *The American Film Industry*. Madison: University of Wisconsin Press.

Baran, P., and P. Sweezy. 1966. *Monopoly Capital*. New York: Modern Reader.

Barnouw, E., and S. Krishnaswamy. 1963. *Indian Film*. New York: Columbia University Press.

Becker, H. S. 1974. "Art as Collective Action." *American Sociological Review* 39 (December): 767–76.

—— 1976. "Art Worlds and Social Types." *American Behavioral Scientist* 19 (July): 703–18.

—— 1978. "Arts and Crafts." *American Journal of Sociology* 83 (January): 862–89.

Bell, D. 1976. *Cultural Contradictions of Capitalism*. New York: Basic Books.

Bell, Q. 1976. *On Human Finery*. New York: Schocken.

Benesch, O. (1945) 1965. *The Art of the Renaissance in Northern Europe*. Greenwich, Conn.: Phaidon.

Benjamin, W. 1969. "The Work of Art in the Age of Mechanical Reproduction." In *Illuminations*, edited by H. Arendt. Translated by H. Zohn. New York: Schocken.

Blauner, R. 1964. *Alienation and Freedom*. Chicago: University of Chicago Press.

Bluestone, G. 1957. *Novels into Film*. Berkeley and Los Angeles: University of California Press.

Braverman, H. 1974. *Labor and Monopoly Capital*. New York: Monthly Review Press.

Carey, D. 1975. *The Hollywood Posse*. New York: Houghton Mifflin.

Christopherson, R. 1977. "Work and Honor." Ph.D. dissertation, University of California, Davis.

Cipolla, C. 1973. *The Fontana Economic History of Europe*. Vol. 4, no. 1. London: Collins/ Fontana.

Crowther, B. 1957. *The Lion's Share*. New York: Dutton.

Dewey, J. 1934. *Art as Experience*. New York: Capricorn.

Drew, B. 1978. "The Man Who Paid His Dues." *American Film* 3, no. 3 (December-January): 22–27.

Feuer, L., ed. 1959. *Marx and Engels: Basic Writing on Politics and Philosophy*. Garden City, N.Y.: Doubleday.

Freidson, E. 1974. *Profession of Medicine*. New York: Dodd & Mead.

Gans, H. 1975. *Popular Culture and High Culture*. New York: Basic.

Gombrich, E. H. 1963. *Mediations on a Hobby Horse*. London: Phaidon.

Grana, C. (1962) 1964. "John Dewey's Social Art and the Sociology of Art." In *The Arts in Society*, edited by R. Wilson. Englewood Cliffs, N.J.: Prentice-Hall.

Guback, T. 1969. *The International Film Industry*. Bloomington: Indiana University Press.

Hampton, B. (1931) 1970. *The History of the American Film Industry from Its Beginnings to 1931*. New York: Dover.

Hauser, A. 1951. *The Social History of Art*. Vols. 2 and 4. New York: Vintage.

Heilbroner, J. 1962. *The Making of Economic Society*. Englewood Cliffs, N.J.: Prentice-Hall.

Hellman, L. 1976. *Scoundrel Time*. Boston: Little, Brown.

Hofstader, R. 1963. *Anti-Intellectualism in American Life*. New York: Knopf.

Indian Cinematograph Committee. 1928. *Report of the Indian Cinematograph Committee, 1927–28*. Madras: Government of India Press.

Jowett, G. 1976. *Film: The Democratic Art*. Boston: Little, Brown.

Knight, A. 1957. *The Liveliest Art*. New York: Mentor.

Lawder, S. 1975. *The Cubist Cinema*. New York: New York University Press.

Leprohon, P. (1966) 1972. *The Italian Cinema*. New York: Praeger.

Liehm, M., and A. Liehm. 1977. *The Most Important Art*. Berkeley and Los Angeles: University of California Press.

Lindsay, V. (1915) 1970. *The Art of the Moving Picture*. New York: Liveright.

Lomax, A. 1968. *Folk Song Style and Culture*. Washington, D.C.: American Academy for the Advancement of Science.

Lukács, G. 1964. *Realism in Our Time*. New York: Harper.

Mukerji, C. 1976. "Having the Authority to Know." *Sociology of Work and Occupations* 3 (February): 63–87.

—— 1977. "Film Games." *Symbolic Interaction* 1 (December): 20–31.

Newhall, B. 1964. *The History of Photography*. Garden City, N.Y.: Doubleday.

Papanek, V. 1972. *Design for the Real World*. New York: Bantam.

Powdermaker, H. 1950. *Hollywood: The Dream Factory*. Boston: Little, Brown.

Ramsaye, T. (1926) 1964. *A Million and One Nights*. London: Cass.

Renan, S. 1967. *An Introduction to the American Underground Film*. New York: Dutton.

Richie, D. 1971. *Japanese Cinema*. Garden City, N.Y.: Doubleday.

Robinson, D. 1973. *The History of World Cinema*. New York: Stein & Day.

Rosenberg, B., and N. Fliegal. 1965. *The Vanguard Artist*. Chicago: Quadrangle.

Rosenblum, B. 1973. "Photographers and Their Photographs." Ph.D. dissertation, Northwestern University.

Rostow, W. 1963. *The Economics of Take-Off into Sustained Growth*. New York: St. Martin's.

Sadoul, G. 1966. *The Cinema in Arab Countries*. Paris: UNESCO.

Sarris, A. 1967. *Interviews with Film Directors*. New York: Avon.

Schiller, H. 1976. *Communications and Cultural Domination*. New York: International Arts and Sciences.

Sears, C. 1941. *Some American Primitives*. Boston: Houghton-Mifflin.

Seton, M. 1960. *Sergei M. Eisenstein*. New York: Grove.

Sklar, R. 1975. *Movie-made America*. New York: Vintage.

Smelser, N. 1959. *Social Change in the Industrial Revolution*. Chicago: University of Chicago Press.

Solomon, M. 1974. *Marxism and Art*. New York: Vintage.

Stephenson, R., and J. R. Debrix. 1965. *The Cinema as Art*. Baltimore: Penguin.

Thompson, E. P. 1963. *Making of the English Working Class*. New York: Vintage.

Thompson, R. 1975. "The Deadliest Art." *American Film* 1 (December): 70, 71, 78.

Tunstall, J. 1977. *The Media Are American*. New York: Columbia University Press.

Veblen, T. (1899) 1953. *The Theory of the Leisure Class*. New York: New American Library.

White, M. 1968. *The Zone System Manual*. Hastings-on-Hudson: Morgan & Morgan.

Wolfe, T. 1975. *The Painted Word*. New York: Farrar, Straus & Giroux.

Zolberg, V. 1974. "The Art Institute of Chicago." Ph.D. dissertation, University of Chicago.

Index

Ablon, J., 67n
aboriginal remains, 273
acculturation, 41
activity theory, 308n
activity types *see* speech activities
Adam, 37
Adams, R. N., 65n
address forms, 195
Adler, J., 318
Aida (Spanish Harlem resident), 174
Alasuutari, P., 113
Alexander, Jeffrey C., 16
Alger, Horatio, 181
Alinsky, Saul, 66n
American Anthropological Association,
    41
American Indian remains, 273
American Journal of Sociology, 61
Anderson, Elijah, 182
Anderson, Nels, 64n, 65n, 66n, 81
Angell, Robert, 82
animism, 39, 42
announcements, 241n
Anthropological Institute, 39
anthropology
    American cultural, 40–1
    Anglo-American tradition, 40
    biblical tradition, 26, 36–7
    British social, 41–3
    colonial context, 11
    crisis/reinvention of, 45–6
    critique of evolutionism, 27, 40–1, 42–3
    and Darwinism, 27, 38–9
    definition of domain of, 35–6
    differentiation of national traditions,
        38–40
    Graeco-Roman tradition, 26, 37
    history of, 26–7, 35–47
    internal disputes, 14–15
    international, 44
    otherness, 26, 36, 46
    polygenetic tradition, 26, 37–8
    racism, 14, 27, 45
    reflexivity, 46
    scientific authority, 11–12

applause
    audiences, 191, 244–59
    length of, 247
    post-response continuation, 250–5
    refusal of, 250–7
    repeating invitation–refusal sequences,
        255–7
    techniques for inviting, 244–50
archaeology, 267
    coding schemes, 284–5
    graphic representations, 287–92
    highlighting, 286–7
    learning practices, 305–6
Ardener, Edwin, 90
Ardener, Shirley, 90
Arensberg, Conrad, 54
Argentina, 178
argument, presentation of, 206
Aronsson, K., 129
art houses, 321–2, 326n
artifacts *see* artwork; material culture
Artificial Intelligence, 199, 215
artwork
    collection/collectibles, 314, 316–20,
        324–5, 325n
    commodity design for market, 315–16
    design in production, 314–15
    lasting design values, 316–17
    mass-produced commodities as, 264–5,
        313–25
    motion pictures as art, 264–5, 313–14,
        320–5
    and women, 92, 103–4
Arunta peoples, 41, 42
Asad, Talal, 11
assault, 92
Association of Social Anthropologists, 43
assumptions, 6–7, 8–10, 82–3, 199
Atkinson, J. Maxwell, 308n
    charismatic oratory, 191, 244–59
    courtroom interaction, 222, 228, 244, 258
    devices to produce applause, 248
    duration of applause, 247
    holding audience attention, 245
    structures of social action, 223

Atkinson, J. Maxwell (*cont.*)
  talk as grounding of social interaction, 102
  unmarked overlap competition, 253
Atkinson, Paul, 12
Atlas, Jay, 217*n*, 218*n*
audience segregation, 154
audiences, applause, 191, 244–59
Austin, John, 190, 202–3, 213
autobiography, 79

Bacon, Francis, 3
Bakhtin, Mikhail, 11, 18*n*
Balio, T., 321, 326*n*
Bannister, Robert C., 15
Baran, P., 313
Barnes, J. A., 154
Barnouw, E., 313
Barthes, Roland, 189
Barton, A. H., 54–5
Bauman, R., 196
Bayesian probability theory, 18*n*
Bechtel, W., 272
Becker, Howard S.
  artworks, 314, 318, 320
  design, 315
  development of fieldwork in sociology, 52, 58, 63*n*, 64*n*, 65*n*, 66*n*
  deviance, 67*n*
  interviews, 101
  life histories, 75–6, 79–87, 136
  phenomenology, 61
Bell, D., 313
Bell, Q., 325*n*
Belnap, N. D., 203
Ben Hur, 324
Benedict, Ruth, 41
Benesch, O., 324
Benjamin, Walter, 319, 320, 323
Benn, Anthony Wedgewood, 244–5, 250–7, 259*n*
Bennie (Spanish Harlem resident), 171–2, 176
Bensman, J., 65*n*, 168*n*
Berger, P. L., 113
Bergson, H., 131
Berlin, B., 195
Bielby, Denise D., 93
Big Pete (Spanish Harlem resident), 173, 178
Bittner, E., 61, 66*n*, 160, 166

Bladon, R. A. W., 247
blame-the-victim theory, 174–5
Blau, Peter, 221
Blauner, Bob, 100–1, 107*n*
Blauner, R., 313
Bloch, M., 272
Bloor, M. J., 155, 168–9*n*
Blount, B., 196
Bluestone, G., 320, 324
Blumenbach, Johann, 37
Blumer, H., 113
Blumer, Herbert, 14, 15
  attitudes, 9
  checking out ethnographic observations, 168*n*
  development of fieldwork in sociology, 27, 50, 51, 52, 54–5, 56, 60, 63*n*, 66*n*
  sensitizing concepts, 60
  symbolic interactionism, 51
Boas, Franz, 13, 14, 27, 46, 47
  critique of evolutionism, 40–1
  definition of anthropology, 35, 36
  otherness, 36
Boden, Deirdre, 93, 104, 222
body language, 102
Bogdan, Robert, 99–100
Bogen, David, 11
Booth, Charles, 63*n*, 136, 141, 142
Bosanquet, Helen D., 142
Bourdieu, Pierre, 2, 12, 16, 272, 308*n*
Bourgois, Phillipe, 137, 171–85
Bowles, Samuel, 176
Braithwaite, M., 268
Braverman, H., 313, 315
Brazil, D., 217*n*
Briggs, C., 112, 113
Briseno, Theodore, 293, 299, 309*n*
British Association for the Advancement of Science, 40
Broca, Paul, 38, 40
Brown, P., 199, 217*n*
Brown, Richard H., 104
Bruner, J., 131
Bruyn, S. T., 61
Bulkin, Elly, 90
Bulmer, Martin, 14, 15, 64*n*
Bunzl, Matti, 13
Burawoy, Michael, 16
Bureau of Ethnology, 39–40
Burgess, Ernest. W., 51, 52, 53, 64*n*, 80
Button, G., 239*n*, 240*n*

Calhoun, Craig, 16, 17*n*
Cambridge School, 42
Camic, Charles, 14
Campbell, D. T., 267
Capps, Lisa, 77, 127–31
Caputi, Jane, 107*n*
caregiving, 121–3
Carey, D., 321
Carey, J. T., 53, 64*n*
Carnap, Rudolf, 2
case studies, 15, 53
Cassel, J., 67*n*
Cavan, R., 64*n*
Cavan, Sherri, 148
Cederborg, A.-C., 129
cephalic index, 40
certainty displays, 129–31
Chafe, W., 127
Chaiklin, Seth, 305, 308*n*
Chalmers, A. F., 5, 12
Chapoulie, Jean-Michel, 13, 14, 25, 27–8,
    49–67
charismatic oratory, 191, 244–59
    interactional dimensions of, 245–8
    marked overlap competition, 250–3
    refusal of invited applause, 250–7
    repeating invitation–refusal sequences,
        255–7
    techniques for inviting applause, 248–50
    unmarked overlap competition, 253–5
Charniak, E., 199
Chicago tradition, 51–7, 80–1
child care, 105
Chino (Spanish Harlem resident), 172–3,
    174, 176–7, 179, 181
Chippindale, C., 273
Chodorow, Nancy J., 14, 15
Chomsky, Noam, 189
Christopherson, R., 318
Cicourel, Aaron V., 61, 67*n*, 112, 113,
    283
Cipolla, C., 316
clang association, 238
classical evolutionism, 39
Clayman, S., 240*n*
Cleopatra, 324
Clifford, James, 11, 12, 18*n*, 104
coding schemes, 264, 281, 282, 283–5,
    293–300, 307
Cohen, Colleen Ballerino, 104
Cole, P., 217*n*

Coles, J. M., 276
Coles, Robert, 101
collection/collectibles, of art, 314, 316–20,
    324–5, 325*n*
collective action, 83–4
Collingwood, R., 276
Collins, Patricia Hill, 16, 90
Collins, Randall, 16
colonialism, 11
commodity design, 315–16
communicative competence, 215
community studies, 80–1
comparative method, 27–8, 39, 53, 58–60
complaint sequences, 233–4, 241*n*
conditional relevance, 289
conflict, 52
conjugated oppression, 183–4
consciousness raising, 90, 93
constructionism, 113
controlled experiments, 86
conversation *see* interviews
conversation analysis, 93, 102–4, 283,
    308*n*
    context of talk, 189–90
    inter-disciplinary nature, 222–3
    and social action, 223
    see also charismatic oratory; speech
        activities; talk-in-interaction
Converse, Jean, 116–17, 118, 120
Conwell, C., 53
Copans, Jean, 62*n*
Coulter, Jeff, 7
Coulthard, Malcolm, 217*n*
courtroom-in-session, as a context, 228–9
crack economy, 137, 171–85
Crane, L. E., 155
cranial topology, 40
creative interviewing, 117–18
credibility, narratives, 127
Cressey, Paul G., 50, 55, 64*n*, 65*n*, 66*n*
Crowther, B., 313, 321
Csordas, Thomas J., 15
cultural anthropology, 41, 56
cultural determinism, 47
cultural reproduction theory, 176–7
culture, 40–1, 46–7, 56
culture of resistance, 176
culture of terror, 177–81
culture-of-poverty theory, 174–5, 181
Current Anthropology, 44
Cushman, R., 154

Dahrendorf, Ralf, 14
Dalton, M., 58, 65*n*, 66*n*
Daly, Mary, 107*n*
Daniels, Arlene Kaplan, 60, 66*n*, 89
Darroch, Vivian, 89
Darwinism, 27, 38–9
data collection/analysis, 12
Davis, F., 58, 61, 66*n*, 148
Davis, Mike, 175, 177
De Gerando, J.-M., 49, 50, 62*n*
Debrix, J. R., 324
Debro, J., 65*n*, 66*n*
decorations, 268
defensive maneuvers, 92
degradation, 82–3
deixis, 202
delinquency, 81–5
Denzin, N. K., 274, 275, 276
Derrida, J., 267
design, 314–16
determinism, cultural, 47
Deutscher, Irwin, 9, 61, 65*n*
DeVault, Marjorie L.
    data collection/analysis, 12
    feminist interview strategies, 76, 88–107,
        113, 121, 124
Dewey, J., 313
dialects, 189
dialogue, 165–7, 168
diglossia, 195
dignity, search for, 182–3
Dilthey, Wilhelm, 13
Diner, S. J., 53
disciplinary development, 35–6
discourse analysis, 102–4
    see also charismatic oratory; speech
        activities; talk-in-interaction
discovery, acts of, 1–2
dispute domains, 2–3, 7, 9, 10–13, 16, 17*n*
divination, 204
documents
    communicative and representational
        design, 269
    and context, 267
    distinction from records, 266
    interpretation of, 263, 266–8
    see also ethnographic texts
Dollard, John, 82
Domhoff, G. William, 176
Donley, L., 268
Doucet, Rachelle Charlier, 308*n*

Dougherty, Janet W. D., 308*n*
Douglas, Jack D., 57, 61, 116, 117–18, 120,
    155
Drew, B., 326*n*
Drew, Paul, 16, 308*n*, 309*n*
    conversation analysis in work settings, 306
    courtroom interaction, 222, 228, 244
    devices to produce applause, 248
    holding audience attention, 245
drug economy, 137, 171–85
Du Bois, John, 308*n*
Dubin, S. C., 66*n*
Duke, Charles, 296–8, 302, 303–4, 306, 307
Duranti, Alessandro, 308*n*
Durkheim, Emile, 40, 43, 50, 52, 60, 62
Duster, Troy, 67*n*

Eames, Edwin, 174
École d'Anthropologie, 40
Edgeworth, Matthew, 309*n*
Elgin Marbles, 273
emancipation, 58, 66*n*
Emerson, Robert M., 10, 65*n*
    data collection/analysis, 12
    ethnographic texts, 137, 154–69
    formal rules in organizations, 61
Engeström, Yrjö, 308*n*
Enlightenment, 3
episodes, 195
Erickson, C. L., 274
ethnicity, 273–4
ethnographic fieldwork, 27–8, 44, 49–67
    see also interviews; observational
        fieldwork
ethnographic texts
    dialogue, 165–7, 168
    inaccuracy/unfairness of, 160–2
    neutrality, 164, 166
    organizational and political audiences,
        162–4
    as outside point of view, 158–60, 166
    participants' response, 137, 154–69
    structure of relevancies, 166
    subjectivism, 166
    transformation of study object, 267
ethnology, 26–7, 35, 41, 43
ethnomethodology, 113
Evans-Pritchard, E. E., 62*n*
Eve, 37
evolutionism, 27, 38–9, 40–1, 42–3
experiment as context, 229–30

experimentation, 3–4, 86
expert testimony, 293–4, 296–300, 303–4
eyewitness testimonies, 130

facts, discovery of, 1–2
falsification, 5, 7–9
family discourse, 124
family therapies, 129–30
Faris, Ellsworth, 52
Faris, Robert, 64n
Faught, J., 64n
feeding, 91–2, 95–7
feminism, 113
    interviews, 76, 88–107
Ferguson, C., 195
Ferguson, L., 268–9
Feuer, L., 313
Feyerabend, Paul K., 2, 12
fiction, 79
fieldwork, 27–8, 44, 49–67
    see also interviews; observational
        fieldwork
Fillmore, C., 202
film, as an art form, 264–5, 313–14, 320–5
Firth, Raymond William, 14
Fisher, B. M., 51
Fisher, Sue, 102
Fishman, C. H., 129
Fishman, Pamela M., 102
Fison, Lorimer, 42
flags, system of meanings, 269
Fliegal, N., 313
Foley, Doug, 176
Fordham, Signithia, 176
formal logic, 2
formality, activities, 195
Foucault, Michel, 16, 305
Fowler, F. J., 114
Fraser, B., 199
Frazer, James G., 42
freedom, 31–2
Freese, Jeremy, 15
Freidson, E., 52, 60, 318
Fretz, Rachel I., 12
Freudian psychoanalysis, 42
Frye, Marilyn, 95, 105
functionalism, 43–4

Gadamer, Hans-Georg, 13
Galenic traditions, 36
Galileo Galilei, 3

Galtung, Johan, 84
Gans, H., 314, 324, 326n
Garfinkel, Harold, 11, 89, 308n
    collaborative nature of meaning
        construction, 124
    formulations, 157, 159
    intrinsic "artfulness" of social life, 15
    knowledge construction, 112
    meaning-making, 119
    phenomenology, 61
    practical reasoning, 119
    process of meaning production, 113
Gato (Spanish Harlem resident), 171–3, 176,
    178
Gazdar, G., 214
Geer, B., 63n, 64n, 65n
Geertz, Clifford, 14, 189
generative grammar theory, 189
Gergen, Kenneth J., 16
Gero, J., 278
gesture, 102
Gibson, James J., 9
Giddens, Anthony, 16, 272
Gillen, Frank, 41, 42
Gilligan, Carol, 107n
Gintis, Herbert, 176
Giroux, Henry, 176
Glaser, B. G., 60
Glassie, H., 270
Goffman, Erving
    fieldwork, 49, 52, 65n, 67n, 136–7,
        148–53
    social structure and interaction, 224, 235
Gohre, Paul, 63n
Gold, R. L., 65n, 66n
Gold, Ray, 140
Gombrich, E. H., 326n
Gonja people, 203–4, 207, 214
Goode, Judith, 174
Goodwin, Charles, 15
    color categories, 285
    gesture and body language, 102
    material artifacts in professional work,
        263–4, 281–309
Goodwin, Marjorie H., 102
Goody, E., 203, 204, 207
Gorden, R. L., 112
Gordon, D., 199, 214
Gould, L., 155
Gouldner, A. W., 65n
Grana, C., 314

graphic representations, 264, 281, 282, 287–92, 300–2, 307
Greatbach, D., 239n
greetings, questions in, 203, 213–14
Grice, Paul, 190, 214, 215, 216n
  maxims of conversation, 199, 200, 201, 202
Griffith, Alison, 98–9
Griffith, D. W., 320–1
Guba, E. G., 155, 266, 268, 276
Guback, T., 321, 322
Gubrium, Jaber F., 16, 17n
  active interview data analysis, 124
  active interviewing, 76–7, 112–25
  data collection/analysis, 12
  family discourse, 124
  interpretive practice, 119
  interview respondents, 115
  meaning-making process, 113
  sensitivity to representational matters, 112
Gumperz, John, 189, 195, 308n
  classroom interaction, 208
  misunderstandings due to cultural origins, 215, 217n, 239n
Gusfield, J. R., 65n

Habermas, Jürgen, 16, 18n
Haddon, A. C., 41
Haldeman, H. R., 200
Hall, O., 66n
Halliday, Terence C., 11
Ham, 37
Hamblin, C. L., 217n
Hampton, B., 313, 320
Handler, R., 168
Hanks, William, 308n
Hanson, Norwood R., 9
Haraway, Donna, 2, 308n
Harding, Sandra, 12, 16, 113
Harrah, D., 203
Harre, Rom, 2, 12, 16
Harrison, Faye, 174
Hartsock, Nancy M., 89
Hauser, A., 318, 326n
Havel, V., 131
Hayner, N., 64n
Hazelrigg, Lawrence E., 16
Heilbroner, J., 313
Hellman, L., 321
Hempel, Carl G., 2, 5, 6
Henley, Nancy, 89

Herasimchuk, E., 208
Heringer, J. T., 199
Heritage, John, 16, 89, 239n, 240n, 308n, 309n
  conversation analysis in work settings, 306
  mass media news, 222
  notion of context, 162
  process of meaning production, 113
  questions and questioning, 241n
  speech exchange system, 239n
  structures of social action, 223
  talk as grounding of social interaction, 102
Hertweck, A., 222
heteroglossia, 11, 18n
highlighting, 264, 281, 282, 285–7, 296–300, 307
Hintikka, J., 217n
Hippocratic traditions, 36
historians, 145–6
historical reconstruction, 41
Hodder, Ian
  activity of material culture, 269
  decoration of rooms, 268
  interpretation of documents and material culture, 263, 266–78
  use of rhetoric, 278
Hofstader, R., 313
Holliday, George, 297, 298, 301, 302, 306
Hollis, Martin, 13
Holstein, James A., 16, 17n
  active interview data analysis, 124
  active interviewing, 76–7, 112–25
  collaborative nature of interview data, 113
  data collection/analysis, 12
  family discourse, 124
  interpretive practice, 119
  interview respondents, 115
  meaning-making process, 113
  sensitivity to representational matters, 112
hooks, bell, 90, 107
Horn, L., 202
hospitalization decisions, 160–1
household routines, 91–2, 95–7, 105–6
Howitt, A. W., 42
Howson, Colin, 18n
Hughes, Everett
  observational fieldwork, 27–8, 49, 50–3, 63n, 135–6, 139–47
  theory of social disorganization, 51, 64n

Hughes, H. M., 63n, 64n
Hull, R. D., 203
human practice, 13–16
Humphreys, L., 66n
Hunt, James, 38
Hunter, Albert, 104
Hutchins, Edwin, 284, 308n
Hyman, H. H., 112, 114
Hymes, Dell, 189, 195–6, 215

illocutionary force, 202–3, 214–15
Indian Cinematograph Committee, 313
Indio (Spanish Harlem resident), 181
individual action, 83–4
inductive inference, 5, 7
industrialization, 52
inference, in discourse, 197–202, 215
information technology, 270
inscription practices, 287–92
insertion sequences, 232–3, 235
Institut d'Ethnologie, 44
institutional processes, 82–3
insults, 196–7
interactionism, 51–62
   questions, 202–15, 217n
   see also charismatic oratory; interviews;
      talk-in-interaction
international anthropology, 44
interpretive anthropology, 47
interrogation, 200
interrogative series, 232, 235
interviews, 135
   active interview data analysis, 124
   active nature of, 76–7, 112–25
   active subject, 119–20
   bias, 123–4
   constructing topics, 91–3
   creativity, 117–18
   editing/transcribing, 99–104
   feminist strategies, 76, 88–107
   interpretive practice, 119
   listening, 94–9
   meaning-making process, 113–14, 119,
      123–5
   narrative incitement, 120–3
   recording of, 99–100
   subject behind the respondent, 115–16
   survey interviews, 116–17
   traditional images of, 114–18
   writing, 104–6, 125
Irvine, J., 195, 203

Jackie (Spanish Harlem resident), 173–4, 178
James, William, 42
Janowitz, Morris, 11
Japhet, 37
Java Man, 40
jealousy, 33
Jefferson, Gail, 189, 195, 199, 202, 239n
   context in talk-in-interaction, 228
   list completion leading to utterance
      completion, 249
   multiple utterance format, 235
   overlapping talk, 252–3
   repairs in speech, 229, 230
   speech exchange systems, 228, 229, 244
   transcription conventions, 102, 258, 283
Jewish community, 31, 33
Johns, C., 217n
joking relationships, 204
Jones, D. J., 67n
Joseph, Gloria I., 90
Jowett, G., 313, 320, 321, 322
Julio (Spanish Harlem resident), 172–3, 174,
   177, 178–9
Junker, Buford H., 59, 65n, 135, 139, 140, 141

Karttunen, L., 217n
Kasanin, J. S., 238
Katz, J., 214
Katz, Jack, 12, 15
Kay, P., 195
Keenan, E. O., 195, 203
Keller, Charles, 308n, 309n
Keller, Janet Dixon, 309n
Kellogg, Paul, 141
Kennedy, John F., 254–5, 257
Kenny, A., 193
Ketcham, K., 130
King, Martin Luther, 257
King, Rodney, 281–2, 292–304, 305–6
kinship, 42
Kirk, J., 116
Kitsuse, John, 67n
Kittel, Dorothy, 140
Kluckhohn, Clyde, 82
Kluckhohn, F. R., 64n
Knight, Arthur, 322–3
Knorr-Cetina, Karin, 2, 10, 15
knowledge construction, active interviewing,
   112–13
Koon, Stacy, 292
Kornblum, William, 177

Kramarae, Cheris, 89, 107*n*
Krishnaswamy, S., 313
Kroeber, A. L., 40
Kuhn, Manfred, 51
Kuhn, Thomas S., 2, 10
Kuklick, Henrika, 14
Kundera, M., 130, 131

labor, division of, 59
labor migration, 175
laboratory as context, 229–30
Labov, William, 127, 189, 196–7
Lakoff, G., 193, 199, 214
Lakoff, Robin, 89
land ownership, 31
Landesco, J., 64*n*
Langlois, C., 63*n*
language
    biblical anthropological tradition,
        37
    definitive importance of, 189
    interactive organization of, 189–90
    and material culture, 270, 272
    second language teaching, 196
    as social action, 190
    and socialization, 290–1
    and speech activities, 190, 193–218
    structuralist accounts, 189
    and women, 76, 88–107
language games, 193–4, 196, 207–12,
    215–16, 282
Lanterman–Petris–Short (LPS) Act,
    160
LaPiere, Richard, 55, 65*n*
Latour, Bruno, 271, 287, 308*n*
Lave, Jean, 305, 308*n*
Lawder, S., 313
Lazarsfeld, Paul F., 50, 54–5
Leacock, Eleanor Burke, 174
legal texts, 50
leisure, as language term, 89
Lemert, Edwin, 67*n*
Lemonnier, P., 269, 271
Lengermann, Patricia Madoo, 15
Leone, M., 270
LePlay, F., 50, 63*n*, 64*n*, 141
Leprohon, P., 313, 323
Leroi-Gourhan, A., 271
Levelt, Willem, 229, 230
Lévi-Strauss, Claude, 44, 189
Levine, Alan, 4

Levine, Donald N., 11
Levinson, Stephen
    activity types and language, 190, 193–218,
        232
    address forms, 195
Lewis, D., 193, 200
Lewis, Jill, 90
Lewis, Oscar, 174
Lidz, C. W., 155
Lieberman, Paul, 293, 299
Liebow, E., 66*n*
Liehm, A., 313
Liehm, M., 313
life histories, 75–6, 79–87
lifeworld, and ethnography, 154
Lincoln, Y. S., 155, 266, 268, 276
Lindesmith, Alfred R., 15
Lindsay, V., 322
linearization problem, 229
linguistics, 189
Linnaeus, 37
listening, 94–9
Livingston, Eric, 11
local ethnography, 80–1
Lofland, John, 148, 149
Lofland, L., 51, 64*n*
Loftus, E. F., 130
logic, 2
Lohman, J. D., 64*n*
Lomax, A., 323
Luce, R. D., 200
Luckmann, T., 113
Lucretius, 37
Lugones, Maria C., 90
Lukács, G., 313
Lukes, Steven, 13
Lynch, Michael, 2, 10, 11, 301, 308*n*

McCall, G. J., 51
Maccoby, E. E., 114
Maccoby, N., 114
McGhee, R., 270
McKay, Henry D., 53, 64*n*, 81
MacKenzie, John, 51
MacKinnon, Catharine, 90
McLennan, John, 39, 42
Macleod, Jay, 176
Madge, John, 114
Malinowski, Bronislaw
    criticism of methods, 14
    functionalism, 43

observational fieldwork, 13, 42, 50, 62–3*n*, 64*n*, 141
  rituals, 195
mana, 42
Mangione, T. W., 114
Manning, P. K., 61, 62, 66*n*
Manning, P. L., 113
map-making, 287–92
Marco (Spanish Harlem resident), 178
Marcus, George E., 12, 104, 154
Marett, R. R., 42
marriage, evolution of, 39
Marx, Karl, 62
Marxism, 270
Mascia-Lees, Frances E., 104
material culture
  artifact analysis, 268–9
  coding schemes, 264, 281, 282, 283–5, 293–300, 307
  confirmation of hypotheses, 276–8
  graphic representations, 264, 281, 282, 287–92, 300–2, 307
  highlighting, 264, 281, 282, 285–7, 296–300, 307
  identification of context, 275
  interpretation of, 263, 266–78
  and language, 270, 272
  meanings in time, 272–4
  methodological issues, 274–6
  notion of coherence, 277
  notion of correspondence, 277
  practice and evocation, 271–2
  in professional work, 263–4, 281–309
  recognition of similarities and differences, 275
  relevance of historical theories, 275
  rules of representation, 269–70, 272
  theory of, 269–72
  see also artwork
Matthews, F. H., 64*n*
Matza, David, 67*n*
Mauss, Marcel, 44
Maxwell, Andrew, 174
Maynard, Douglas W., 93, 222, 230, 239*n*, 240*n*
Mead, George Herbert, 51, 61, 63*n*, 80, 83, 141
Mead, Margaret, 47, 141
meal preparation, 91–2, 95–7

meaning, 13–16, 27
  active interviewing, 113–14, 119, 123–5
  material culture, 269–74
Mehan, H., 222, 241*n*
Meihls, J. L., 222
Melies, George, 324
memory, 77, 127–31
memory culture, 41
Merriman, N., 276
Merritt, M., 203
Merton, R. K., 50, 53, 54, 59, 64*n*
Methodenstreit, 13
middle class, 50
Mies, Maria, 88
Miller, Casey, 89
Miller, D., 269, 270, 271
Miller, Gale, 11, 17*n*
Miller, Jean Baker, 94
Miller, M. L., 116
Miller, S. M., 65*n*
Minsky, Marvin, 199
Minuchin, S., 129
Mishler, Elliot G., 89, 98, 104, 107*n*, 113
misinformation experiments, 130
mobility, strangers, 26, 31
Moerman, Michael, 104
Moore, F. C. T., 62*n*
Moore, H., 268, 276
Morgan, J., 217*n*
Morgan, Lewis Henry, 39, 42–3
Morton, Samuel G., 38
mothering, 98–9
motherwork, 105
motion pictures, as an art form, 264–5, 313–14, 320–5
Mukerji, Chandra
  artist's autonomy, 318
  decision-making in films, 323
  mass-produced commodities as artwork, 264–5, 313–25
  previsualization, 315
Mulkay, Michael, 10
Munby, J., 196
Munsell color chart, 284–5
Murphy, C., 268
mutedness, 90
Mydans, Seth, 292, 299, 309*n*

narrative authenticity, 77, 127–31
Nash, D., 154
Nash-Webber, B. L., 199

nature
  unity and constancy of, 4
  universal laws of, 5
New York Times, 200, 254–5
New Yorker, 325*n*
Newhall, B., 320
Newton, Sir Isaac, 3
Newton, Jim, 292, 304, 309*n*
Nichols, J., 127
Niebrugge-Brantley, Jill, 15
Nixon, Richard, 254
Notes and Queries in Anthropology, 39, 42
nursing home residents, 119–20

Oakley, Ann, 88, 94
Obershall, A. R., 63*n*
objective probability theory, 5–7
objectivity, strangers, 25–6, 31–2
observation language, 9
observational fieldwork, 41–2, 44, 135–7
  Chicago tradition, 51–7, 80–1
  culture and ideology in the crack economy,
    137, 171–85
  development in sociology, 49–67
  emphasis on bodies, 136–7, 149
  exploiting place, 151–3
  getting into place, 150–1
  Goffman on, 49, 52, 65*n*, 67*n*, 136–7,
    148–53
  Hughes on, 27–8, 49, 50–3, 63*n*, 135–6,
    139–47
  Malinowski on, 13, 42, 50, 62–3*n*, 64*n*,
    141
  note taking, 137, 152–3
  Park on, 27, 51, 52, 53, 135, 141, 142
  participants' reading of texts, 137, 154–69
  place in social science, 139–47
  self-discipline, 150–1
  sociology of work studies, 50, 57–60
  in United States post-1960, 60–2
occupational studies, 50, 57–60
Ochs, Elinor, 77, 104, 127–31, 308*n*, 309*n*
official statistics, 50
ontological anguish, 92
oppression, 183–4
oratory *see* charismatic oratory
organizational contexts, 10–12
Orme, B., 276
others
  history of anthropology, 26, 36, 46
  strangers, 25–6, 30–4, 50, 143–4

Outhwaite, William, 13
overlap competition, 250–5

Paget, Marianne A.
  editing and feminist discourse, 106
  interviews, 89, 93, 94, 107*n*
  women artists, 92, 103–4
paleoanthropology, 46
Palmer, V., 65*n*, 142
Papanek, V., 315, 320
Papito (Spanish Harlem resident), 173
paradox of proximateness, 236
Paramount Decision, 321
Parent-Duchâtelet, 50
Park, Robert E., 14, 60, 64*n*
  conflict, 52
  interaction, 52
  life histories, 80
  observational fieldwork, 27, 51, 52, 53,
    135, 141, 142
  social disorganization, 51
  urban development, 51
Parsons, Talcott, 14, 50, 59, 64*n*, 189, 223
Pelegrin, J., 273
Perls, F., 201
Perry, William, 43
personal relations, 32–3
Pestello, Fred P., 9
Pestello, H. Francis, 9
Peters, Suzanne, 105
Peyrère, Isaac de la, 37
phenomenology, 61
phonemics, 189
phonetics, 189
physical anthropology, 26–7, 35, 40, 44
Pickering, Andrew, 10, 308*n*
Pirsig, Robert M., 1
Platt, Jennifer, 11, 14, 15, 53, 64*n*, 66*n*
Platt, M., 203
police, calls to, 231–5, 240–1*n*
Pollner, Melvin
  data collection/analysis, 12
  ethnographic texts, 137, 154–69
  process of meaning production, 113
Polsky, N., 65*n*, 66*n*
Pomerantz, A., 244, 247
Pool, Ithiel de Sola, 118–19, 121
Pope, E., 203
Popper, Karl R., 2, 7
Porter, Theodore M., 14
positivism, 15–16

post molds, 286, 308*n*
postmodernism, 113
poststructuralism, 113
poverty, 174–5, 181
Powdermaker, H., 321
Powell, Brian, 15
Powell, J. W., 39, 40
Powell, Laurence, 295
practical knowledge, 272
practice theory, 281, 308*n*
Pratt, Minnie Bruce, 90
Preiss, J. J., 65*n*
prestige exchange, 276
Prichard, James Cowles, 38
primitive mentality, 27, 40
private, as language term, 89
probability theory, 5–7, 18*n*
process, notion of, 83–4
professional vision, 263–4, 281–309
Propp, V. I., 124
Proust, Marcel, 270
Psathas, George, 89
psychiatric emergency teams, 155–64
psychic unity, 39
public, as language term, 89
public speaking, 191, 244–59
Putnam, Hilary, 4, 7, 9, 13, 16
Putnam, Theodore M., 2
Putumayo massacres, 178

questionnaire research, 54–5, 142–3
questions, in speech activities, 202–15, 217*n*
Quine, W. V. O., 13

Rabinow, Paul, 4, 11, 13
racism, 14, 27, 45, 175, 176
Radcliffe-Brown, A. R., 14, 27, 43
Raiffa, H., 200
Ramsaye, T., 322
Rassenkunde, 44
Rathje, Bill, 268
rationalizations, 149
Raushenbush, W., 64*n*
records, distinction from documents, 266
Redfield, Robert, 53, 54, 63*n*
reflexivity, 46
Reinharz, Shulamit, 88, 94, 106, 113
Reissman, C. K., 124
religion, evolution of, 39, 42
religious cults, 184
remembering, 77, 127–31

Renan, S., 323
request sequences, 231–3
respect, 182–3
Retzius, Anders, 40
Richardson, Laurel, 98, 104
Richie, D., 313, 323
Ricoeur, P., 131, 267
Riesman, David, 63*n*, 65*n*, 84
ritual insults, 196–7
rituals, 42, 195
Rivers, W. H. R., 42, 43
Robinson, D., 313, 321, 323
Rock, P., 57
Rogers, C. R., 114
Rogoff, Barbara, 308*n*
Rose (Spanish Harlem resident), 173–4
Rose, A. M., 51
Rosenberg, B., 313
Rosenblum, B., 318
Ross, J., 214
Rostow, W., 313
Roth, J. A., 66*n*, 67*n*
Rothman, Barbara Katz, 99
Rousseau, J., 38
routines, 91–2, 95–7
Rowlands, M., 270
Roy, D., 58, 66*n*
Rubin, Lillian, 100
Ryan, William, 174

Sacks, Harvey, 189, 195, 199, 201, 202, 221, 308*n*
  attentiveness to speakers, 245
  characterization of participants in talk-in-interaction, 224–5, 226, 227
  collaborative nature of meaning construction, 124
  context in talk-in-interaction, 228, 239*n*
  formulations, 157, 159
  multiple utterance format, 235
  question–answer pair, 203
  repairs in speech, 229, 230
  speech exchange systems, 228, 229, 244
  turn-taking system, 245, 247
Sadock, J., 193, 213, 214
Sadoul, G., 313
Sanches, M., 196
sandwich generation, 121
Sanjek, R., 267
Sankoff, Gillian, 148
Sapir, Edward, 41

Saraceno, Chiaro, 89
Sarbin, T., 130
Sarris, A., 323
Sassen-Koob, Saskia, 175
Saussure, Ferdinand de, 189, 305
Sawers, Larry, 175
Schank, R., 199
Schatzman, L., 65n, 155
Schegloff, Emanuel, 16, 96, 189, 195, 199, 202
  conditional relevance, 289
  context in talk-in-interaction, 227–31, 239n
  cultural/linguistic context, 239n
  insertion sequence, 232
  multiple utterance format, 235
  overlapping talk, 252–3
  repairs in speech, 229, 230
  request sequences, 232
  social structure and conversational structure, 231–7
  speech exchange systems, 228, 229, 244
  talk and social structure, 190–1, 221–41
Schenkein, Jim, 102
Schieffelin, Bambi B., 203, 308n, 309n
Schiller, H., 313
schizophrenia, 238
Schlanger, N., 271
schooling, 98
Schuman, Howard, 116–17, 118, 120
Schutz, A., 51, 61, 121, 155, 165
Schwartz, C. G., 65n
Schwartz, M. S., 65n
Schwartz, R. C., 267
science
  coding schemes, 283–4
  as competition, 2
scientific methodologies, 2–10
Searle, John, 190, 199, 204, 216n
  questions, 213
  speech acts, 193, 213, 214
Sears, C., 318
Sechrest, L., 267
Seignobos, C., 63n
self-reflection, 131
Seligman, Charles, 42
Sem, 37
Seton, M., 323
Shanks, M., 270, 274
Shapin, Steven, 2, 10
Sharpe, Patricia, 104

Sharrock, W. W., 233, 235
Shaw, Clifford, 53, 64n, 75, 79n, 81
Shaw, Linda L., 12
Sherzer, Joel, 196, 308n
Shibutani, T., 63n
Shils, Edward, 54, 64n
shit work, 156
Shuy, Roger, 299, 309n
sign systems, linguistics, 189
Silverman, D., 112, 113, 124
Silvers, Ronald J., 89
Simmel, Georg, 53, 60
  as figurehead of social science, 13
  intersecting social circles, 221
  stranger, 25–6, 30–4, 50
Simmons, J. L., 51
single studies, 85–6
Skepticism, 4
Sklar, R., 320, 321
slavery, 268–9
Small, Albion W., 142
Smelser, N., 313
Smith, Barbara, 90
Smith, Carlotta, 217n
Smith, Dorothy E., 88, 106, 113
  coding schemes, 285
  data collection/analysis, 12
  feminist writing, 104
  household activities, 89
  interviews, 93, 98–9
  mothering, 98–9
  positivism, 16
  women's standpoint, 89
Smith, Grafton Elliot, 43
Smith, William Robertson, 42
Snodgrass, J., 64n
social action, 223
social disorganization theory, 51, 64n
social distance, 195
social organization, 10–12, 42
social process, 83–4
social psychology, 85
social reproduction theories, 176
social structure
  definition, 221–2
  and talk, 190–1, 221–41
social surveys, 15, 81, 116–17, 135–6, 141–3
social work, 53, 142
socialization, 82–3
  and language, 290–1
Société d'Anthropologie Française, 44

socio-biology, 47
Solomon, M., 313
Sorensen, M.-L., 275
sounding, 196–7
Spanish Harlem, 137, 171–85
Spector, J., 278
speech
    Ethnography of Speaking, 195–6
    gender differences in, 90
speech activities
    definition, 190, 195
    and inference, 197–202, 215
    and language, 190, 193–218
    role of questions, 202–15, 217n
    structural elements, 196–7, 202
speech acts, 190, 193, 213, 214
speech events, 195
speech exchange systems, 228–30, 244
Speed, John, 37
Spelman, Elizabeth V., 90
Spencer, Baldwin, 41, 42
Spender, Dale, 89, 90, 94, 107
Spradley, J. P., 56
Stacey, Judith, 88
Stack, Carol, 174
Stanko, Elizabeth, 92
Stanley, Liz, 94
Staples, W. G., 113
Star, Susan Leigh, 10
statistical studies, 50, 53
Steel, David, 246, 248, 249
Stein, M. R., 65n
Steinberg, Stephen, 174, 175
Stennius, E., 193, 214
Stephenson, R., 324
Stocking, George W., Jr., 13, 14, 26–7, 35–47
Stoddart, K., 154
Stouffer, Samuel A., 54, 86
strangers, 25–6, 30–4, 50, 143–4
    mobility, 26, 31
    objectivity of, 25–6, 31–2
    as specific form of interaction, 30
Strauss, Anselm L., 51, 52, 57, 60, 65n, 67n, 155
structural semiology, 189
structuralism, 270
subjective probability theory, 18n
Suchman, Lucy A., 16, 308n, 309n
Sudnow, D., 61
survey interviews, 116–17
survey research, 15, 81, 135–6, 141–3

survival concept, 43
Sutherland, E. H., 53, 79n
Sweezy, P., 313
Swift, Kate, 89
symbolic anthropology, 47
symbolic interactionism, 51–62
symboling systems, material culture, 269–72
synchronic functionalism, 43–4
syntactic questions, 217–18n

Tabb, William, 175
talk-in-interaction
    and conversational structure, 191, 231–7
    problem of relevance, 191, 224–7, 234–5, 237
    procedural consequentiality, 191, 227–31, 234–5, 237
    and social structure, 190–1, 221–41
Tannen, D., 217n
Taussig, Michael, 177–8
Tax, Sol, 44
Taylor, C. E., 127
Taylor, Steven J., 99–100
teaching process, 207–12
Tedlock, Dennis, 168, 308n
telling practices, 150
Terasaki, Alene, 241n
Terkel, Studs, 114, 118
Terr, L., 130
texts see documents; ethnographic texts
Thatcher, Margaret, 246, 248, 249
Thomas, W. I., 27, 51, 79n, 142
Thompson, B., 268
Thompson, E. P., 313
Thompson, R., 326n
Thorne, Barrie, 88, 89
Thrasher, F. M., 52, 53, 55, 64n, 65n, 81
Tilley, C., 267, 268, 269, 270, 274, 278
Todd, Alexandra Dundas, 102
Toner, B., 204, 206
Torres Straits Expedition, 41–2
totemism, 42
trader, image of, 26, 30–1
Treichler, Paula A., 107n
tribes, 46
Trobriand Islanders, 42
Tunstall, J., 313, 321, 322
Turner, Bryan S., 15, 16
Turner, Jonathan H., 11

Turner, R., 197–8, 199, 233, 235
Turner, Stephen P., 11, 15
Tyler, S. A., 165
Tylor, E. B., 39, 40, 42

underclass, 175
underground economy, 137, 171–85
unemployed, 175
universal laws, 5
"ur" discourses, 35–6
Urbach, Peter, 18n
urban development theory, 51
urban inner-city society, 137, 171–85
Urban Life, 64n
Urry, James, 13, 14

Valentine, Bettylou, 174
Valentine, Charles, 174
Van Maanen, John, 10, 12, 104
Veblen, T., 313, 316
Vidich, A. J., 65n, 168n
Vigil, James Diego, 185n
Villermé, 50
violence, 177–81
Vygotsky, L. S., 308n

Walker, A. L., 155
wanderers, 30
Warner, Lloyd, 54, 66n
Washburn, D., 270
Wax, M., 63n
Wax, Rosalie, 15, 51, 56, 63n, 65n
Waxman, Chaim, 174
Webb, E. J., 267
Weber, Max, 52, 60
    charisma, 244, 257
    failure at field research, 50
    as figurehead of social science, 13
    research on agricultural workers, 63n
Weinberger, Jerry, 3
Weintraub, R., 154
Weiss, R. S., 57, 63n, 65n
Wenger, Etienne, 305, 308n
Wertsch, James, 308n
West, Candace, 90, 102, 104, 222, 230
Westermarck, Edward, 42
Westley, W. A., 66n
Whalen, M. R., 222, 234, 239n, 240–1n

White, M., 315
Whyte, W. F., 55, 64n, 65n, 155
Williams, Terry, 177
Willis, Paul, 176
Wilson, Edward O., 4
Wilson, T. P., 239n, 240n, 241n
Wilson, William J., 174, 175
Wirth, Louis, 51, 52, 53, 63n, 64n,
    66n
Wise, Sue, 94
Wiseman, Jacqueline, 148, 149, 150, 152,
    155
Wittgenstein, Ludwig, 211, 290, 305
    language games, 196, 215–16, 282
    meaning of utterances, 190, 193
Wobst, M., 270
Wolfe, T., 323
Wolff, Kurt H., 154
women
    artists, 92, 103–4
    decoration of rooms, 268
    defensive maneuvers, 92
    household routines, 91–2, 95–7
    interviews, 76, 88–107
    labeling of experiences, 104–6
    and language, 76, 88–107
    speech, 90
Woodbury, Anthony C., 308n
Woolgar, Steve, 12, 287, 308n
work
    as language term, 89
    sociology of, 50, 57–60
writing
    interviews, 104–6, 125
    observational fieldwork, 137, 152–3
written texts see documents; ethnographic
    texts

Yates, T., 272

Zimmerman, Don H., 93, 102, 104, 222,
    230, 239n
    social structure and conversational
        structure, 231–4, 235, 240–1n
Znaniecki, Florian, 51, 79n, 142
Zolberg, V., 318
Zorbaugh, H. H., 64n
Zweigenhaft, Richard L., 176